Lecture Notes in Computer Science   10605

Commenced Publication in 1973
Founding and Former Series Editors:
Gerhard Goos, Juris Hartmanis, and Jan van Leeuwen

More information about this series at http://www.springer.com/series/7409

Marinos Ioannides (Ed.)

Digital Cultural Heritage

Final Conference
of the Marie Skłodowska-Curie Initial Training Network
for Digital Cultural Heritage, ITN-DCH 2017
Olimje, Slovenia, May 23–25, 2017
Revised Selected Papers

 Springer

Editor
Marinos Ioannides
Cyprus University of Technology
Limassol
Cyprus

ISSN 0302-9743   ISSN 1611-3349 (electronic)
Lecture Notes in Computer Science
ISBN 978-3-319-75825-1   ISBN 978-3-319-75826-8   (eBook)
https://doi.org/10.1007/978-3-319-75826-8

Library of Congress Control Number: 2018934337

LNCS Sublibrary: SL3 – Information Systems and Applications, incl. Internet/Web, and HCI

Cover illustration: The images on the cover are taken from the paper "Rapid Reconstruction and Simulation of Real Characters in Mixed Reality Environments" by M. Papaefthimiou et al. on page 275. They represent the reconstructed monument of ASINOU, which belongs to the UNESCO WHL (http://whc.unesco.org/en/list/351). The upper image illustrates the monument and the lower one the virtual reality representation of the Priest and the frescos of the monument. The church is located on the southern part of Nikitari village on the foothills of the Troodos Mountains in Cyprus (https://www.byzantinecyprus.com/).
The ASINOU monument has been used as the first case study during the research training activities of all the ITN-DCH fellows (http://www.itn-dch.eu/index.php/case-studies/asinou/).

Printed on acid-free paper

This Springer imprint is published by the registered company Springer International Publishing AG
part of Springer Nature
The registered company address is: Gewerbestrasse 11, 6330 Cham, Switzerland

Preface

The Marie Skłodowska-Curie Initial Training Network for Digital Cultural Heritage: Projecting Our Past to the Future (acronym, ITN-DCH) was the first and one of the largest fellowship projects in the area of the e-documentation/e-preservation and CH protection funded by the European Union under the EU FP7 PEOPLE research framework (www.itn-dch.eu). The project started on October 1, 2013, and its consortium comprises 14 full partners and 10 associate members covering the entire spectrum of European CH actors, ranging from academia, research institutions, industry, museums, archives, and libraries. The project aimed to train 20 fellows (16 ESRs and 4 ERs – 500 person months) in the area of CH digital documentation, preservation, and protection in order to provide them with a strong academic profile and market-oriented skills, which will significantly contribute to their career prospects. The consortium and the fellows training program were supported by a prestigious advisory board.

ITN-DCH aimed—for the first time worldwide—to analyze, design, research, develop, and validate an innovative multidisciplinary and intersectorial research training framework that covers the entire lifecycle of digital CH (DCH) research for a cost-effective preservation, documentation, protection, and presentation of cultural heritage. CH is an integral element of Europe and vital for the creation of a common European identity and one of the greatest assets for steering Europe's social and economic development as well as job creation. However, the current research training activities in CH are fragmented and mostly designed to be of a single discipline, failing to cover the whole lifecycle of DCH research, which is by nature multidisciplinary and intersectorial. The training targeted all aspects of CH ranging from tangible (books, newspapers, images, drawings, manuscripts, uniforms, maps, artifacts, archaeological sites, monuments) to intangible content (e.g., music, performing arts, folklore, theatrical performances) and their inter-relationships. The project aimed to boost the added value of CH assets by re-using them in real application environments (protection of CH, education, tourism industry, advertising, fashion, films, music, publishing, video games, and TV) through research on (a) new personalized, interactive, mixed, and augmented reality-enabled e-services, (b) new recommendations in data acquisition, (c) new forms of representations (3D/4D) of both tangible/intangible assets, and (d) interoperable metadata forms that allow for easy data exchange and archiving.

The project was structured in training modules and had as a milestone event a public final conference open to the public. The ITN-DCH fellows as well as other researchers from outside our project had to present their latest research results. The ITN-DCH fellows were responsible for the planning and organization of this unique event, which took place at Olimje in Slovenia in May 2017.

The presented papers were reviewed by the majority of the fellows and their supervisors and illustrate the state of the art in research and development in the area of DCH.

Here, we present 29 papers, selected from more than 100 submissions, which focus on interdisciplinary and multidisciplinary research concerning cutting-edge CH informatics, physics, chemistry, and engineering and the use of technology for the representation, documentation, archiving, protection, preservation, and communication of CH knowledge.

Our keynote speakers Eleanor E. Fink, Alex Yen, and Pavlos Chatzigrigoriou are not only experts in their fields but also visionaries for the future of CH protection and preservation. They promote the e-documentation and protection of the past in such a way for its preservation for the generations to come.

We extend our thanks to all authors, speakers, and everyone whose labor and encouragement made the ITN-DCH final event possible. The Organizing Committee, whose members represent a cross-section of archaeology, physics, chemistry, civil engineering, computer science, graphics and design, library, archive, and information science, architecture, surveying, history and museology, worked tenaciously and finished their work on time.

We express our thanks and appreciation to all the project advisors for their enthusiasm, commitment, free-of-charge work and support for the success of this project and the event. Most of all we would like to thank all the ITN-DCH fellows and the European Commission, CIPA, ISPRS and ICOMOS that entrusted us with the task of organizing and undertaking this unique event.

December 2017   Marinos Ioannides

Organization

General Chair

Marinos Ioannides — Cyprus University of Technology, Cyprus

Scientific Committee

Anais Guillem	University of Ljubljana, Slovenia
Chance Michael Coughenour	University of Stuttgart, Germany
Diego Bellido Castaneda	Arctron3D, Germany
Eirini Papageorgiou	Cyprus University of Technology, Cyprus
Elisavet Konstantina Stathopoulou	National University of Athens, Greece
Emmanouil Alexakis	National University of Athens, Greece
George Bruseker	FORTH, Greece
Georgios Leventis	Cyprus University of Technology, Cyprus
Gina Stavropoulou	KU Leuven, Belgium
Louis Cuel	MiraLab, University of Geneva, Switzerland
Magdalena Ramos Calles	FBK, Italy
Margarita Papaefthymiou	FORTH, Greece
Marleen de Kramer	7 Reasons Medien GmbH, Austria
Matevz Domajnko	Fraunhofer IGD, Germany
Matthew Luke Vincent	University of Murcia, Spain
Nicola Carboni	Centre Nationale de la Recherche Scientifique (CNRS), France
Nikoletta Skordaki	University of Ljubljana, Slovenia
Rossella Suma	University of Warrick, UK
Simon Senecal	MiraLab, University of Geneva, Switzerland
Vasiliki Nikolakopoulou	Cyprus University of Technology, Cyprus

Organizing Committee

Nicola Carboni	Centre Nationale de la Recherche Scientifique (CNRS), France
Margarita Papaefthymiou	FORTH, Greece
Vasiliki Nikolakopoulou	Cyprus University of Technology, Cyprus
Georgios Leventis	Cyprus University of Technology, Cyprus
Pavlos Chatzigrigoriou	Cyprus University of Technology, Cyprus
Matevz Domajnko	Fraunhofer IGD, Germany

Local Committee

Roko Zarnic	President of SAEE, Slovenia
Meta Kržan	Secretary General of SAEE, Slovenia

Acknowledgment and Disclaimer

The Marie Skłodowska-Curie Initial Training Network for Digital Cultural Heritage (ITN-DCH) final conference has been part of the training activity of all the project's fellows, supported by the EU FP7-PEOPLE 2012/3 Programme.

However, the content of this publication reflects only the authors' views and the European Commission, the CIPA, ICOMOS, Cyprus University of Technology, all the ITN-DCH partners/institutions, supervisors and associated partners/institutions, the Slovenian Association for Earthquake Engineering (SAEE) and the EU projects FP7 PEOPLE ITN2013 ITN-DCH and IAPP2012 4D-CH-WORLD, the DARIAH-EU ERIC, the EU DARIAH-CY, the EU H2020 INCEPTION, the EU H2020 CSA ViMM, the CIP ICT-PSP Europeana-Space, the CIP ICT-PSP LoCloud and the EU COST Action TD1406 projects are not liable for any use that may be made of the information contained herein.

Contents

3D Data Acquisition and Modelling of Complex Heritage Buildings

Federica Maietti$^{(\boxtimes)}$ ⓘ, Roberto Di Giulio ⓘ, Marcello Balzani ⓘ, Emanuele Piaia ⓘ,
Marco Medici ⓘ, and Federico Ferrari ⓘ

Department of Architecture, University of Ferrara, via Ghiara 36, 44121 Ferrara, Italy
{federica.maietti,roberto.digiulio,marcello.balzani,
emanuele.piaia,marco.medici,federico.ferrari}@unife.it

Abstract. The ongoing EU funded project "INCEPTION – Inclusive Cultural Heritage in Europe through 3D semantic modelling" proposes a workflow aimed at the achievements of efficient 3D digitization methods, post-processing tools for an enriched semantic modelling, web-based solutions and applications to ensure a wide access to experts and non-experts. Nevertheless, the generation of high quality 3D models can still be very time-consuming and expensive, and the outcome of digital reconstructions is frequently provided in formats that are not interoperable, and therefore cannot be easily accessed. This challenge is even more crucial for complex architectures and large heritage sites, which involve a large amount of data to be acquired, managed and enriched by metadata. In order to face these challenges and to start solving the issues of the large amount of captured data and time-consuming processes in the production of 3D digital models, an Optimized Data Acquisition Protocol (DAP) has been set up. The purpose is to guide the processes of digitization of Cultural Heritage, respecting needs, requirements and specificities of cultural assets, by dealing with issues such as time-consuming processes and limited budget available for 3D documentation, accuracy of 3D models, integration of metadata and semantics into the 3D model and links with multimedia information. The DAP can be followed during the planning and performing of a 3D laser scanner survey of Cultural Heritage, and it is referred to architectural, archaeological, urban and site scales.

Keywords: 3D data acquisition · Semantic modelling · Digital heritage
Optimized data capturing · Heritage documentation

1 Introduction

The integration of digital data and the possibilities of reusing digital resources is an important challenge for protection and conservation of the historic buildings as well as for efficient management in the long term [1]. The need of a future reusable broad and descriptive source of measurement data demands new applications to facilitate information accessing, collected in three-dimensional databases without compromising the quality and amount of information captured in the survey.

© Springer International Publishing AG, part of Springer Nature 2018
M. Ioannides (Ed.): ITN-DCH 2017, LNCS 10605, pp. 1–13, 2018.
https://doi.org/10.1007/978-3-319-75826-8_1

The identification of the multi-function and multi-scale role of the model allows the exploitation of uneasy and complex resources (obtained by the collection of geometric shape and not just of the architectural and urban context) at different levels, over time and by different actors. Here it is the value of accessibility/affordability of the process that until now has been barely allowed spatial scale but through a mere visual navigation often uninterpreted, an approach very far from the knowledge, understanding and conservative needs. The combination of innovative methodologies and protocols, processes, and devices, enhances the understanding of European Cultural Heritage by means of 3D models bringing new knowledge, collaboration across disciplines, time and cost savings in the development and use of 3D digital models [2] (Fig. 1).

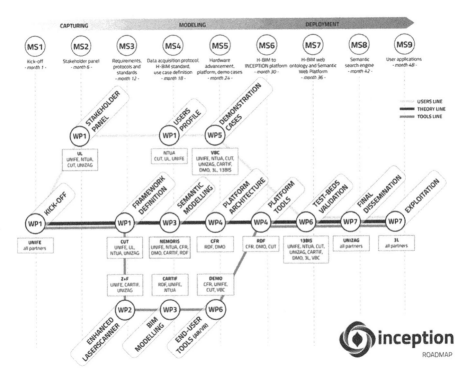

Fig. 1. The INCEPTION roadmap, showing the main project steps under "Capturing", "Modeling" and "Deployment" phases.

In this framework, the project INCEPTION "Inclusive Cultural Heritage in Europe through 3D semantic modelling" [3] is dealing with several challenges related to the 3D documentation and modelling of heritage assets. Starting from the setting up of a common framework for knowledge management, advancement into the integrated 3D data capturing methodology has been accomplished, in order to face the semantic modelling for Cultural Heritage buildings in a H-BIM environment. The main outcome will be the INCEPTION platform, an open-standard web semantic platform for accessing, processing and sharing interoperable digital models. On-site and off-site applications will be developed for a wide range of users.

The project, lasting four years, started in June 2015 and it is now approaching the third year of development. The first stage related to the enhancement in 3D acquisition processes, has been accomplished by improving first of all the integrated data capturing and digital documentation methodologies.

2 3D Survey of Complex Heritage "Spaces": The Geometric Dimension

Within INCEPTION, the architectural space becomes the foundations, the common core and the "connection" for the creation of a protocol for optimizing the 3D documentation of Cultural Heritage. The methodology set as a priority the unconventional features/geometries, unique and complex within heritage, avoiding the "segmentation" of data acquired and facilitating data access and use through an inclusive approach.

Nowadays, the methodologies mainly used, face the problem of the complexity of current tools and the processing of results obtained by using new technologies in representation over the 2D and 3D conventions. These outcomes are very often surprising but sometimes impoverished in the expressive vocabulary of the representation of a proper reference model, which allows investigating the tangible material as well as the intangible intentions.

Architectural space geometry is an essential tool to handle the spatial expression of a drawing useful to accomplish knowledge and conservative process; survey and representation of heritage architectural spaces, gives the opportunity to explore the form from the two-dimensionality to the three-dimensionality of reality and vice versa.

INCEPTION innovation [4] is related to the focus on the heritage spaces (at architectural and urban scale), one of the most important "containers" of cultural expressions identified in the evolution of the concept of European identity. The project develops an integrated approach, it is able to investigate the potential of spaces in order to create new cultural connections and awareness; the architecture is an outstanding example of the multi-layered conceptual dimension of European heritage.

The 3D survey of heritage architectural space needs a common protocol for data capturing and related enhancement of functionalities, capabilities and cost-effectiveness of technologies and documentation instruments. The protocol considers the uniqueness of each site, quality indicators, time-consumption, cost-effectiveness, data accuracy and reliability, additional data and semantic proprieties to be recorded for heritage applications and adaptability to different sites with different historical phases.

The integration of digital data and the possibilities of reusable digital resources is an important challenge for protection and conservation of historical buildings as well as for efficient management in the long term. The need for a future reusable broad and descriptive source of measurement data demands new applications to facilitate information accessing collected in three-dimensional databases without compromising the quality and amount of information captured in the survey (Fig. 2).

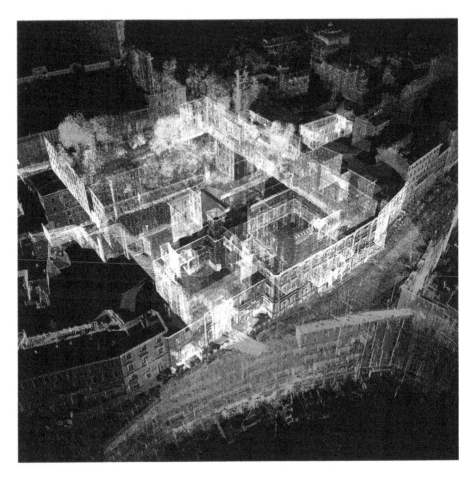

Fig. 2. Example of 3D survey of a complex heritage site, Palazzo Arese Litta in Milan, Italy; visualization of the 3D point cloud of the overall building and the surrounding (DIAPReM).

The 3D survey of heritage "spaces" means:

- to understand how the space (defined by its geometric morphometric characteristics) can be the interface/connection with time dimension; the space/time relation can be an easy, (and affordable) understandable (and therefore inclusive) metaphor of memory (collective and European);
- to understand how space (architectural, urban and environmental) has its own dynamic characteristics that not only gives the chance of an understandable navigation and discovery but also identifies the option of choosing which is the basis of the definition of culture: what to choose and to store in a certain time and why;
- to understand that only through space (and its complexity) it is possible to collect a high level of multi-functional knowledge strongly linked to the multi-scale representational process.

Working at heritage architecture and site scale will allow the identification of the Cultural Heritage buildings semantic ontology and data structure for information catalogue. Current project activities are addressed to a modelling approach within the 3D semantic Heritage-BIM: the integration of semantic attributes with hierarchically and mutually aggregated 3D geometric models is indispensable for management of heritage information. 3D parametric and semantic modelling will lead to the development of semantic 3D re-constructions of heritage building and sites, integrated with additional documents (i.e. pictures, maps, literature) and intangible information (Fig. 3).

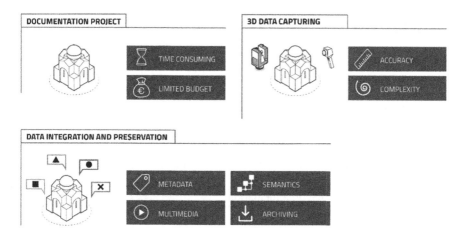

Fig. 3. Main challenges in 3D documentation and conservation for Cultural Heritage related to the main workflow steps.

2.1 Main Challenges in Digital Documentation

The work on 3D data acquisition and modelling of complex heritage buildings has been developed starting from a broader methodological framework. Beyond technical definitions and in-depth specifications regarding measuring instruments and data capturing devices, it is essential to frame the 3D data capturing within the specific field of Cultural Heritage and within the overall concept of heritage documentation [5].

Heritage documentation is basic for understanding our legacy and our cultural identity. Documentation processes are becoming more and more relevant and effective in order to collect data and information allowing knowledge, understanding, assessment, preservation and management intervention on Cultural Heritage.

New technologies and instruments now available, allow us to create integrated digital databases able to collect dimensional data, information related to structures and materials, state of conservation, diagnostic analysis and historical data, making the data capturing an overall integrated process in supporting sustainable decision strategies for conservation, restoration and enhancement of Cultural Heritage.

In this framework, digital technologies are very relevant because they are able to survey very rapidly heritage buildings and sites by collecting millions of spatial coordinates. This 3D acquired data can be used not only for documentation and monitoring purposes but also for digital application (such as virtual tours, virtual tourism, digital reconstructions, etc.) and to create integrated 3D databases for preservation, diagnostics, restoration, and management procedures.

Methods and processes for data collection are continuously developing and today are characterized by effective interdisciplinary. Skills on 3D laser scanner survey, diagnostic procedures and historical researches, as well as about environmental condition assessment or management of metric and dimensional data support the INCEPTION vision of integrated digital documentation for Cultural Heritage assessment.

3   The INCEPTION Optimized Data Acquisition Protocol

In order to face the main challenges related to 3D surveys of complex architectures and to start solving the issue of the large amount of captured data and time-consuming processes in the production of 3D digital models, an Optimized Data Acquisition Protocol (DAP) has been set up [6]. The purpose is to guide the processes of digitization of Cultural Heritage, respecting needs, requirements and specificities of cultural assets, by dealing with the following issues:

- time consuming processes and limited budget available for 3D documentation,
- accuracy of 3D models,
- complexity of the heritage documentation,
- integration of metadata and semantics into the 3D model [7],
- link the 3D object with other multimedia information such as images, structural analysis data, materials, preservation records, etc.,
- archiving of 3D digital records using widely accepted standards.

The assessment and optimization of 3D data acquisition tools allow the improvement of methodological and technological advancement for 3D data acquisition and development of procedural standards [8]. The output is a methodological report for documenting Cultural Heritage by means of 3D data capturing, within a more general methodological procedure of heritage documentation. Since every cultural asset is unique and requires investigations "case by case", according to many different characteristics and to the main purposes of survey and documentation procedures, the protocol is set as flexible guidelines considering different kinds of instruments and devices, different accuracies and levels of detail, etc., in addition to site specifications and the uniqueness of Cultural Heritage.

The DAP can be followed during the planning and performing of a 3D laser scanner survey of Cultural Heritage, and it is referred to as an architectural, archaeological, urban and site scale. It is also referred to as data management (scan registration, data verification) data storage and archive. It is both a methodological procedure and an optimized workflow specification.

The main aims of the INCEPTION DAP are:

- to set up an optimized procedure, based on principles of simplicity and efficiency, for surveying heritage buildings and sites by using different 3D data capturing instruments;

- to provide a workflow for a consistent development of survey procedures for tangible Cultural Heritage and a set of instructions and guidelines for collecting, presenting and storing data;
- to provide a tool able to guide a 3D data capturing procedure able to generate 3D models accessible for a wide range of users;
- to enhance the accuracy and efficiency of 3D data capturing by documentation and instruments integration;
- to support a cost effective and time saving procedure;
- to serve as the basis for the enhancement of functionalities of data capturing technologies and documentation instruments;
- to close the gaps between technical fieldwork and modelling in 3D data capturing.

3.1 Data Acquisition Protocol

The DAP provides a workflow for a consistent development of survey procedures for tangible Cultural Heritage and defines a common background for the use of H-BIM across multiple building types and for a wide range of technical users. Furthermore, this protocol will be useful for any agency, organization or other institution that may be interested in utilizing survey procedures aimed at 3D H-BIM semantic models creation and their implementation for the INCEPTION platform. This protocol is under application and tested on project demonstrations cases, and it will be further improved according to the specific test-bed procedures scheduled in the INCEPTION research project [9].

The DAP is intended to ensure uniformity in 3D digital surveying for all the buildings that will be part of the INCEPTION platform [10]. This protocol considers a wide range of 3D data capturing instruments because of multiple users and different techniques related to specific disciplines. Furthermore, 3D survey instruments and techniques continue to evolve, and this protocol will continue to be reviewed and updated to reflect advances in industry technology, methodology and trends; in every case, the protocol application will ensure data homogenization between surveys tailored to different requirements.

The survey workflow is split into eight main steps that define specific requirements and their related activity indicators:

1. Scan plan
2. Health and safety
3. Resolution requirements
4. Registration mode
5. Control network
6. Quality control
7. Data control and verification
8. Data storage and archive (Fig. 4).

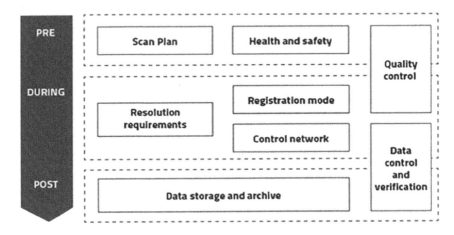

Fig. 4. Workflow steps and activity indicators.

Each step of the workflow is intended as a set of "questions" that become a measuring system to verify the requirements of the survey, and the ability of finding the right answer to define the level quality. On this assumption, every single question becomes an activity indicator [11] that contributes to get a specific evaluation ranking. Not every activity indicator is always compulsory: if in the survey campaign only the minimum number of questions find an answer, the capturing procedure will be classified in the lower ranking. Conversely, if each element is taken into account, the ranking will be the highest.

In the case of direct measurable procedures, the specific activity indicator defines a range of accepted values. Instead, when alternative procedures are available, the protocol specifies their compliance with evaluation categories. For this purpose, there are four incremental categories defined as following:

B: This is the minimum evaluation category to be compliant with the INCEPTION platform. It is intended to be used for very simple buildings or for the creation of low-detailed BIM model for digital reconstruction aimed at VR, AR and visualization purposes. In this case, the metric value of the model is less important than the morphological value.

A: This evaluation category is suitable for documentation purposes where the metric and morphological values are equivalent in terms of impact on the survey that needs to be preliminary scheduled and designed. The registration process of 3D captured data cannot be based only on morphological method but it should be improved by a topographic control network or GPS data (Fig. 5).

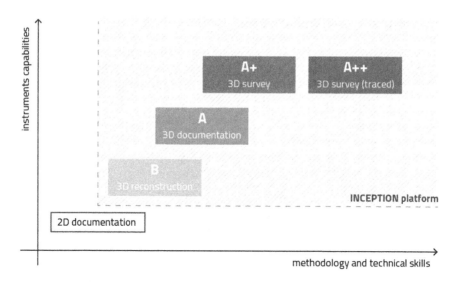

Fig. 5. Evaluation categories.

A+: This evaluation category is most suitable for preservation purposes because only the surveys compliant with this category can be a useful tool for restoration projects that need extremely correct metric data. From this survey, BIM models as well as 2D CAD drawings with 1:20 scale are available. The project phase is more important than previous categories in order to schedule and manage the survey campaign and choose the right technical instruments to perform the data capturing. The management and the correction of metric errors are based on topographic techniques, in particular for what could concern the registration of a different scan. The documentation phase will be developed organizing the information into metadata and paradata [12]. Elements of quality control are integrated into the process.

A++: This evaluation category is suitable for very complex buildings where the capturing process needs to be documented and traced in order to get the maximum control on data or when monitoring processes are developed in a non-continuous time span. The A++ category could be useful even if different teams of technicians work together, simultaneously or in sequence, with different capturing instruments and different accuracies. The A++ category allows the analysis of how a survey has been performed in every single phase: moreover, this capability allows integrating a survey in different times.

A direct correlation between evaluation category and type of building or deployment purposes can be identified. Indeed, complex buildings or advanced deployment purposes need a higher ranked capturing procedure. At the same time, it is necessary to point out that a further standardization should be avoided because every building or site is different from another and there is an increasing number of digital data deployment.

4 Assessment and Added Values by DAP

In order to understand the impact of the INCEPTION DAP, a specific evaluation grid has been set up, starting from the three standard features of quality, time and cost. Each key feature for the evaluation of benefits and added values is specifically addressed looking at the main aims of the INCEPTION project. Since the evaluation process considers the points of view of the end users, who could be either technician or not, features have been developed as below:

- quality can be evaluated as the reliability of the survey;
- time can be evaluated as the usability of the survey;
- cost can be evaluated as the effectiveness of the survey.

Even if the accuracy and the precision are key factors for technicians that are performing the survey, they are strictly connected with the purpose of the survey and for this reason using them for the evaluation of survey quality becomes impossible, in particular from the point of view of an end user. The quality of a survey could be better described as the capability to be compliant with standards and ensure long term support. For this reason, key features of a reliable survey are:

- survey maintenance: possibility to constantly update a survey database during daily use for ordinary purposes, enriching it with new information of minor changes;
- survey integration: possibility to perform major updates and upgrades of a survey, adding a new part of a building or a site previously not included, or performing a more accurate survey of already existing parts;
- tech obsolescence: because the hardware and the data management software are evolving faster and faster, applying strategies to avoid technical obsolescence becomes a key feature to ensure the survey reliability.

The measurement of benefits in terms of time consumption could be performed taking into consideration the usability of the survey. The more usable a delivered survey is, the more time could be saved by the end users that will deal with it. One of the main aims of the procedure is the ability of saving time in the processing phase. The Data Acquisition Protocol and the adoption of a shared standard between suppliers and end users can bring a strong added value in terms of easy usability. For this reason, key features of a usable survey are:

- common procedure: in order to ensure the full understanding of the output;
- collaboration tools: in order for possible data creation by different teams at different times.

The cost of a survey is always dependent on the final quality and time spent to perform the survey. For this reason, the measurement of the effectiveness could be a better parameter to consider in order to evaluate the added value. For this reason, key features of an effective survey are:

- on field flexibility: possibility to use different kinds of instruments on field in order to produce the right amount of qualitative data, without the use of too expensive and unnecessary ones;
- easy deployment: ability to easily use the same delivered survey data for different kinds of deployment and direct application for multiple purposes;
- easy understanding: ability to easily read and understand data delivered with the survey from a low-skilled non-technician end user.

In order to measure benefits and added values by INCEPTION DAP, typical survey and documentation processes in the Cultural Heritage field have been categorized in order to mainly perform a grouping of an infinite number of different, single and specific cases. The main connections between survey categories and DAP evaluation categories have been identified, and the DAP is split in three on the basis of requirements that are needed to reach a better evolution category according to reliability, usability and effectiveness (Fig. 6).

Fig. 6. Data aggregation for the assessment of evaluation categories.

5 Conclusions

The definition of a common framework for documentation and survey of European tangible cultural asset can take advantage by the assessment of the Data Acquisition Protocol. By applying this methodology, it is possible to understand which the main inputs to standardization in 3D data acquisition are. Indeed, it is easy to understand in which direction it is possible to address the standardization process compared to the required benefits.

Thanks to the comprehension of advancement made possible by the protocol adoption, it will be possible, in future developments of this and other research, to focus on the integration of low-end data capturing instruments.

The INCEPTION project shows how the DAP allows us to use the 3D data over time, with different skills, as well as a useful 3D digital data management towards H-BIM [13]. Nevertheless, INCEPTION focuses on open standards like E57 for point clouds and open standard IFC for semantic BIM data managed by Semantic Web-based technology to enable a long-term open access and interrelation of all available data.

INCEPTION innovation in 3D modelling applied to Cultural Heritage starts from the generation of high quality models [14], and therefore from an effective data capturing procedure. The DAP has been developed within a more general methodological procedure of heritage documentation. These guidelines will be gradually developed and updated during the project progress and within future 3D survey application in the field of Cultural Heritage.

Moreover, focusing on needs and requirements of technicians and non-technical users of heritage documentation, DAP assessment increases the benefits to the application of standard procedures in the Cultural Heritage field, starting from the assessment of different types of 3D survey and documentation (features, precision, speed, safety, area or range, environment), results, post processing and usage.

Acknowledgements. The project is under development by a consortium of fourteen partners from ten European countries led by the Department of Architecture of the University of Ferrara. Academic partners of the consortium, in addition to the Department of Architecture of the University of Ferrara, include the University of Ljubljana (Slovenia), the National Technical University of Athens (Greece), the Cyprus University of Technology (Cyprus), the University of Zagreb (Croatia), the research centers Consorzio Futuro in Ricerca (Italy) and Cartif (Spain). The clustering of small medium enterprises includes: DEMO Consultants BV (The Netherlands), 3L Architects (Germany), Nemoris (Italy), RDF (Bulgaria), 13BIS Consulting (France), Z + F (Germany), Vision and Business Consultants (Greece).

The INCEPTION project has been applied under the Work Programme Europe in a changing world – inclusive, innovative and reflective Societies (Call - Reflective Societies: Cultural Heritage and European Identities, Reflective-7-2014, Advanced 3D modelling for accessing and understanding European cultural assets).

This research project has received funding from the European Union's H2020 Framework Programme for research and innovation under Grant agreement no 665220.

References

1. Stylianidis, E., Remondino, F.: 3D Recording, Documentation and Management of Cultural Heritage. Whittles Publishing, Dunbeath (2016)
2. Ioannides, M., Fink, E., Moropoulou, A., Hagedorn-Saupe, M., Fresa, A., Liestøl, G., Rajcic, V., Grussenmeyer, P. (eds.): EuroMed 2016. LNCS, vol. 10059. Springer, Cham (2016). https://doi.org/10.1007/978-3-319-48974-2
3. INCEPTION Homepage. http://www.inception-project.eu/. Accessed 11 Sept 2017
4. Di Giulio, R., Maietti, F., Piaia, E.: 3D documentation and semantic aware representation of Cultural Heritage: the INCEPTION project. In: Proceedings of the 14th Eurographic Workshop on Graphics and Cultural Heritage, pp. 195–198. Eurographic Association (2016)
5. Maietti, F., Ferrari, F., Medici, M., Balzani, M.: 3D integrated laser scanner survey and modelling for accessing and understanding European cultural assets. In: Borg, R.P., Gauci, P., Staines, C.S. (eds.) Proceedings of the International Conference "SBE Malta 2016. Europe and the Mediterranean: Towards a Sustainable Built Environment", pp. 317–324. Gutenberg Press, Malta (2016)
6. Di Giulio, R., Maietti, F., Piaia, E., Medici, M., Ferrari, F., Turillazzi, B.: Integrated data capturing requirements for 3D semantic modelling of Cultural Heritage: the INCEPTION protocol. ISPRS Int. Arch. Photogr. Remote Sens. Spat. Inf. Sci. **XLII-2/W3**, 251–257 (2017)
7. Apollonio, F.I., Giovannini, E.C.: A paradata documentation methodology for the Uncertainty Visualization in digital reconstruction of CH artifacts. SCIRES-IT SCI. Res. Inf. Technol. **5**, 1–24 (2015)

8. Bryan, P., Barber, D., Mills, J.: Towards a standard specification for terrestrial laser scanning in Cultural Heritage–one year on. Int. Arch. Photogr. Remote Sens. Spat. Inf. Sci. **35**(B7), 966–971 (2004)
9. Maietti, F., Di Giulio, R., Balzani, M., Piaia, E., Medici, M., Ferrari, F.: Digital memory and integrated data capturing: innovations for an inclusive Cultural Heritage in Europe through 3D semantic modelling. In: Ioannides, M., Magnenat-Thalman, N., Papagiannakis, G. (eds.) Mixed Reality and Gamification for Cultural Heritage, pp. 225–244. Springer, Cham (2017). https://doi.org/10.1007/978-3-319-49607-8_8
10. De Luca, L., Busayarat, C., Stefani, C., Véron, P., Florenzano, M.: A semantic-based platform for the digital analysis of architectural heritage. Comput. Graph. **35**(2), 227–241 (2011)
11. Eppich, R., Garcia Grinda, J.L.: Management documentation indicators & good practices at Cultural Heritage palces. Int. Arch. Photogr. Remote Sens. Spat. Inf. Sci. **XL-5/W7**, 133–140 (2015)
12. Maravelakis, E., Konstantaras, A., Kritsotaki, A., Angelakis, D., Xinogalos, M.: Analysing user needs for a unified 3D metadata recording and exploitation of Cultural Heritage monuments system. In: Bebis, G., et al. (eds.) ISVC 2013. LNCS, vol. 8034, pp. 138–147. Springer, Heidelberg (2013). https://doi.org/10.1007/978-3-642-41939-3_14
13. Arayici, Y., Counsell, J., Mahdjoubi, L. (eds.): Heritage Building Information Modelling. Taylor & Francis, Oxford (2017)
14. Münster, S., Pfarr-Harfst, M., Kuroczyński, P., Ioannides, M. (eds.): 3D Research Challenges in Cultural Heritage II: How to Manage Data and Knowledge Related to Interpretative Digital 3D Reconstructions of Cultural Heritage. LNCS, vol. 10025. Springer, Cham (2016). https://doi.org/10.1007/978-3-319-47647-6

Low Cost 3D Surveying Methodologies: Colors and Dimensional Accuracy in the Case Study of the Island of Procida, Italy

Maria Chiara Pugliese$^{(\boxtimes)}$ and Cristiana Bartolomei$^{(\boxtimes)}$ (iD)

Bologna University, Bologna, Italy
mariachiarapugliese@libero.it,
cristiana.bartolomei@unibo.it

Abstract. The research has started from the cataloguing of the main low cost photomodeling softwares and technologies that can be found on the Internet. After having selected some programs, the research has been held trying to obtain - using the same set of photos each time - the urban survey of a representative architecture of the island of Procida, which is a little Mediterranean oasis. We have included in our research softwares such as Photoscan, ReMake, ReCap, VisualSFM, and Python.

These programs work starting from an input, which consists in a certain number of photos, to create the output, which is the 3D model of what the photos describe. Having obtained the same model from each program, we will then proceed to analyse each one, in order to find the slightest differences: the main purpose is to understand which low cost programme will give out the best model. The criteria will be mainly based on the colour and dimensional yield that each program will give out.

In conclusion, the main aim of this research is to find the best technologies available, among low cost or licensed programs, which may allow us to get the best survey in the shortest time, in view of further applications in several fields.

Keywords: Photomodeling · 3D models · Urban survey
Low cost technologies

1 Introduction

The last few years have witnessed the development of countless new methodologies and technological innovations in the field of architectural surveying and cataloguing [4]. These methodologies often represent the starting point for subsequent operations, which may eventually lead to structured project work. This might be the case in our investigation.

In the Mediterranean island of Procida, which is perhaps best known for its cultural heritage, due to its being the setting of outstanding literary works, such as "Graziella" by Alphonse De La Martine, and "The island of Arturo" by E. Morante, not to mention several blockbusters, like "Il Postino" or "The English patient", surveying methodologies have been used to produce a catalogue of all the colours used in the facades of the architectures in the island [10]. The main characteristic of this little Mediterranean

© Springer International Publishing AG, part of Springer Nature 2018
M. Ioannides (Ed.): ITN-DCH 2017, LNCS 10605, pp. 14–30, 2018.
https://doi.org/10.1007/978-3-319-75826-8_2

oasis, which has captivated many, is the use of several different colours to decorate the architectural facades that run along the coasts, within the background of a luxuriant vegetation. The result is a colourful and powerful image, which has attracted an ever-increasing number of tourists in the last few years (Fig. 1).

However, some of the characteristic colours of the facades have been changed in time, in consequence of some inappropriate maintenance work done by their owners, who are often unaware of the importance and of the cultural and architectural value of preserving the original image of the place they live in [11]. To make up for their non-compliance with this need, the municipality has recently come to the decision to take action, to prevent the situation from worsening.

Fig. 1. A view of the main Procida's harbour

Thanks to the hard work of many, on 5th February of 2015 the "Colour Plan of Procida" was finally approved. The Colour Plan takes its roots from the analysis of Procida's archives, concerning facade colour history up until recent years. According to the plan, we have two main "colour folders" to which we have to refer when working on the colour of Procida's facades. These two folders refer to the nature of the architecture: one is for the original architecture - the one that was built by the fishermen - and the other one is for the "enriched" architecture.

The writing of the Plan, and the analysis of Procida's facades, which has been held in the seven different boroughs the island is divided in, has been possible thanks to an accurate surveying analysis. It is in this context that we can investigate which methodologies are the best in order to accelerate this process. That implies knowing, among all the possibilities, which way is the best to obtain 3D accurate models as fast as possible and using the fewest sources.

So the aim of our work is to understand which programs are the most suitable to obtain the best 3D survey, with the smallest amount of data to process. The research has started from the cataloguing of the main low cost photomodeling programs and technologies that can be found on the Internet. After having selected the main programs, the research has been held trying to obtain the urban survey of a portion of the island using the same photos each time. These programs work starting from an input, which consists in a certain number of photos, to create the output, which is the 3D model of what the photos describe [7]. Of course the photos will have to accomplish some criteria in order to get the best result [1]. Having obtained the same model from each program, we have then proceeded to analyse each one, in order to find the slightest differences: the main purpose is to understand which low cost programme gives out the best model. The criteria will be mainly based on the colour and dimensional yield that each program will give out.

In conclusion, the main aim of this research was to find the best low cost technologies available, which may allow us to get the best survey in the shortest time, in view of further applications in several fields.

2   The Research: The Best Types of Software

2.1   Software and Workflows

As anticipated, the aim of the research was to analyse the models produced by different photogrammetry programs.

So, the first step of our analysis consisted in identifying the main features of existing software.

Apart from the well known Photoscan by Agisoft, and ReMake, by Autodesk, which is a new version of the widely used 123DCatch, there is a number of open source programmes which can be downloaded on line.

The main open source programmes we have identified are the following: VisualSFM, Python and ReCap.

It must be noted that the data produced by most of the above mentioned programmes, such as for example VisualSFM and Python, need further elaboration of meshes and point cloud, by means of further programmes. Mesh Lab is an open source programme, which is explicitly recommended on the websites of the two programmes to this purpose.

On top of that, there are more types of software, as for example Blender, which allow further mesh elaboration.

Then, we also had to include MeshLab in our research to post-produce and analyse the 3D models obtained from the other programs.

Of course there are many other programs, such as Insight3D, Arc3D, MicMac. Originally we tried to include them in our analysis, but due to various reasons we decided to discard them in a second moment.

This is why, even if this analysis is not exhaustive, we believe that it is complete, because among all the free and open source programs we could find on the internet, the ones we selected were the most complete and promising ones, in our opinion.

After having selected the programs, we tried to analyse their workflow [2].

The canonical workflow, which leads to produce a 3D model, consists in five steps:

(1) Uploading the photos
(2) Aligning Photos
(3) Generating Point cloud
(4) Generating Mesh plus texture
(5) Data processing

We have found out that there's only one program which allows us to follow and control each one of these steps, and that is Photoscan (Fig. 2).

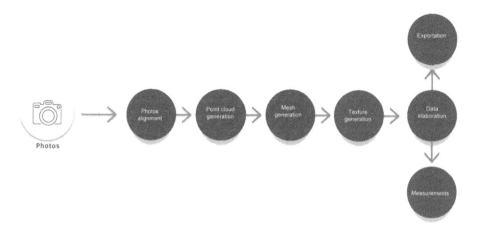

Fig. 2. The canonic workflow

The other programs can be divided in two categories of workflow: one which only leads to point cloud generation, and one which jumps directly to mesh creation, without allowing the user to get the data of the point cloud. To sum up:

Fist type workflow:

(1) Uploading the photos
(2) Aligning Photos
(3) Generating Point cloud

This workflow is described by VisualSFM and Python. We had to use MeshLab to complete this workflow and get the possibility to process the data and analyse the point cloud generated.

Second type workflow:

(1) Uploading the photos
(2) Generating Mesh

This workflow is described by ReMake and ReCap, which are both Autodesk products.

As we can see, among the programs we selected we already have three different possibilities to choose from. We will select the most suitable program according to our final aim [5].

2.2 Our Case Study

To conduct this research we used an average level processor: a notebook with Intel core i5, 8 GB RAM, Radeon Graphics 568 GB available over 916 GB. The camera we used is a Nikon D5100, DSLR type, 18–55 mm focal length, CMOS sensor, 16,2 megapixel resolution.

Fig. 3. Our case study: a single house in Terra Murata, Procida, Italy

The case study we have selected consists in a typical house located in Terra Murata, in Procida, which has been recently renovated (Fig. 3). In this phase of our analysis we didn't need to analyse the colours of the model, so we decided to use this quite isolated building, to proceed with the analysis, as it stands apart from the others, making tri–dimensional measurements easier, compared to terraced houses elsewhere on the island.

In our research we considered the general characteristics of the selected types of software, and their dimensional accuracy performance. We have taken a standard length of 1,04 m, taken on field, as a reference point in comparing the 3D model dimensions.

Here's what we found out.

2.2.1 Photoscan

Photoscan is an Agisoft software which, as anticipated, is the only one which allows the user to follow and control all the steps of the workflow. That is why we can say that it is the most complete (Fig. 4).

Fig. 4. Photoscan dense point cloud

But, even if this is a big pro, it also has some cons: the program requires hardware endowed with high level standards to work at its best and to be able to perform the alignment of many photos. In particular, it is very hard to produce a textured mesh: in our experiments we couldn't get it, using an average standard computer. Moreover, it also takes a very long time to process the data. Among all the selected programs, Photoscan is surely the slowest. On the other hand, we have to say that this problem can be partially solved keeping a very low quality standard (which by the way leads to a very high level mesh) (Fig. 5).

Fig. 5. Photoscan dense point cloud

To sum up:

Supported workflow: complete
Elaboration time: slow
Processor needed: high level
Free: no
User friendly: yes
Number of uploadable photos: no limits
Number of photos: 100
Points of the point cloud: 2090247
Mesh vertices: 395148
Mesh Faces: 489753
Dimensional accuracy: 95,5%; it registered a 1,01 m against 1,04 m of the real dimension.

2.2.2   VisualSFM+Cmvs/Pmvs

VisualSFM is a freeware, which allows us to get a first type workflow. As we can read on the website from which we can download it, "VisualSFM is free for personal, non-profit or academic use". The main freeware is VisualSFM, created by Changchang Wu, but in order to get high level standard information and a dense point cloud we also have to download CMVS/PMVS, by Yasutaka Furukawa. We have to say that this is not a very user friendly program for what concerns the installation, but in order to go through the workflow, the program is quite easy to use.

During the experiment, we noticed that the program had some difficulties in recognizing that all the photos we uploaded belonged to the same architecture. We had to erase a small sub set, in order to prevent it from creating a conflict. We also had to process only 49 photos instead of 100, because the program required an amount of memory that our notebook couldn't handle.

A pro of this programme is that it is undoubtedly very fast in producing the cloud, and its accuracy is high.

For what concerns the generation of a mesh with MeshLab, we had a very disappointing result, as it would predictably need a lot of post production work. Despite that, we will include it in the confrontation of the programs (Fig. 6).

Supported workflow: fist type
Elaboration time: fast
Processor needed: average level
Free: yes
User friendly: yes
Number of photos uploadable: no limits
Number of photos: 49
Points of the point cloud: 1262694
Mesh vertices: 32634
Mesh Faces: 65136
Dimensional accuracy: 99%; it registered 1,03 m against 1,04 m of the real dimension.

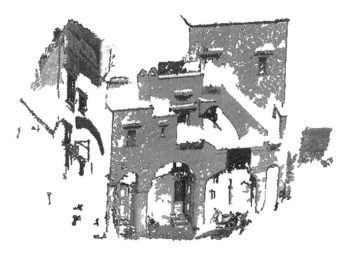

Fig. 6. VisualSFM+Cmvs/Pmvs dense point cloud

2.2.3 Python

This program's interface would consist just in a log window, if we didn't have the possibility to get a more user friendly interface, thanks to an application downloadable for free from the internet. The supported workflow is the same as in VisualSFM, the fist type we analysed. We were quite disappointed with the result we got from this program, arguably because it is a program designed to work at its best in a Gnu/Linux environment, whereas we used a Windows. Another reason why it has produced a bad result may be linked to the fact that this program works best with photos which have been taken with a camera endowed with CCD sensor.

Supported workflow: fist type
Elaboration time: fast
Processor needed: average level
Free: yes
User friendly: no
Number of photos uploadable: no limits
Number of photos: 100
Points of the point cloud: 21564
Mesh vertices: 24372
Mesh Faces: 4592
Dimensional accuracy: %; Both the mesh and the point cloud are very low quality, and we decided not to go further in this analysis.

2.2.4 ReCap

This program allows the user to upload the photo set in order to get a textured mesh back. So it is a second type workflow. The whole process is developed online, and this gives a great advantage: a very low quality processor can be used, giving out the same result as when using a high performance one, since the whole process is developed on

Autodesk online servers. Of course one should remember that since photos are uploaded online, Autodesk may dispose of them as they please. Up to 250 photos can be uploaded to the purpose. In order to analyse the mesh we got, we had to use MeshLab and ReMake (Fig. 7).

Fig. 7. The mesh model

Supported workflow: second type
Elaboration time: slow
Processor needed: low level
Free: yes
User friendly: yes
Number of photos uploadable: up to 250
Number of photos: 100
Points of the point cloud: 1763825; we were able to get these data importing the model in xyz format, thanks to ReMake, and analysing it in MeshLab. But the point cloud is not a product we can directly dispose of using only ReCap.
Mesh vertices: 215592
Mesh Faces: 367266
Dimensional accuracy: 99%; it measured 1,05 instead of 1,04 m.

2.2.5   ReMake

Like ReCap, this software can work both online and offline. However, in order to use it offline you need a high performance processor. The on cloud process allows us to use a very low quality processor, still getting the same results as a high performance processor, as it happens with ReCap. We can use ReMake also to do some postproduction work: measurements, filling mesh holes etc. It is a quite complete program, with a user friendly interface. The only limit is that this program does not allow the user to work on the point cloud (Fig. 8).

Supported workflow: second type
Elaboration time: fast

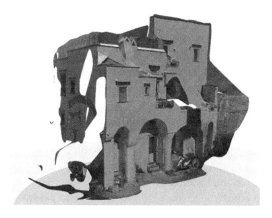

Fig. 8. The mesh model

Processor needed: low level
Free: no
User friendly: yes
Number of photos uploadable: up to 250
Number of photos: 100
Points of the point cloud: 340573; we were able to get these data importing the model in xyz format, and analysing it in MeshLab.
Mesh vertices: 160314
Mesh Faces: 280329
Dimensional accuracy: 93%; it measured 0,97 m instead of 1,04 m.

2.3   Conclusions

We can sum up the main data produced by our analysis:

Table 1. Conclusions

	Photoscan	ReMake	ReCap	VisualSFM	Python
Number of photos	100	100	100	49	100
Calculation time	Slow	Fast	Average	Fast	Fast
External software used[a]	–	MeshLab	ReMake, MeshLab	MeshLab	MeshLab
Points of the dense cloud	2090247	340573	1763825	1262694	21564
Mesh vertices	395148	160314	215592	32634	24372
Mesh faces	489753	280329	367266	65136	48592
Dimensional accuracy[b]	95%	93%	99%	99%	–

[a]Used either to postpone or to analyse the point cloud; for what concerns VisualSFM and Python we used an external software in order to get a mesh too.
[b]Compared to a standard length of 1,04 m.

Best low cost software:

Our first step is to exclude Python from our analysis, despite the fact we realise the poor results we obtained using this programme might basically be due to the fact that data elaboration was not effected in GNU/Linux setting (Table 1).

We will therefore base our analysis on the two remaining valid softwares: VisualSFM and ReCap

VisualSFM, which is freeware, gives out a great quality point cloud. If what we need is a textured mesh, the best one is ReCap, which is free and produces the entire workflow online, even if it doesn't allow any postproduction of the mesh gained, unlike ReMake. Our final evaluation is that the two types of software are on the same level, as they are substantially complementary: ReCap produces a mesh, and Visual SFM produces a cloud. To complete VisualSFM workflow or to postprocess ReCap meshes, we can use the free software MeshLab, which has high potential, even if in our analysis it didn't gave back the results we hoped for.

We can conclude that, depending on the type of result we need, which may be either focused on the cloud or on the mesh, we may choose between these two kinds of software.

Best-licensed software:

As we can see, Photoscan is the only software which can go through the whole workflow, with very high quality results.

If we had to decide which licenced software to buy, our choice would certainly fall on Photoscan. User-friendliness, high precision and completeness in workflow are definitely among its best qualities. As we noted before, this programme needs a high precision calculator in order to show its best potential. Texture generation phase, in particular, seems to be crucial [6]. Besides it tends to overload the computer, and processing times are definitely too long.

Fairly good results can also be observed when using Re Make, as, unlike Photoscan, it shows really fast processing times.

Also in this case our choice will depend on the type of expected results and data.

3   The Research: Colour Accuracy

3.1   Colour Accuracy

The second part of our analysis consisted in studying which programs, among the ones that can produce a textured mesh, will give back the best colour results. We proceeded confronting the mesh colours with the colours registered in the photos we used to produce the mesh itself.

This analysis is only referred to the colours registered on our photographs, which does not necessarily correspond to the real colour of the architectures we used as a case study [12].

The aim of the following analysis is, first of all, accuracy in the identification of colour both in the photographs and in the models obtained using the software we have been analysing in this study.

As a consequence our analysis will basically deal with the following programs: Photoscan, ReCap, ReMake.

Several options have been considered before starting our analysis, in order to compare colour samples in the best possible way. In particular, we investigated the NCS field, we then considered the Sikkens inventory, which was easily accessible for us, and took Pantone colour classification as a reference point.

In the end we decided to adopt more traditional colour classification criteria, to proceed in our analysis, in order to get results which could not be referenced to specific palettes.

CMYK is the short form for Cyan Magenta Yellow Key black. It is a colour model also called tetrachromacy. The letter K in the acronym refers to Key, as the printing systems that use this model use CTP (Computer to plate) technology, in which, by means of a key plate the other three plates of colour (Cyan, Magenta and Yellow) are correctly lined up. The colours that can be obtained with tetrachromacy (Subtractive Synthesis) are a sub-system of the visible variety, so not all of the visible colours can be realised with tetrachromacy. Similarly, not all the colours that can be realised with the sub-system RGB (Red green Blue), - that is, the ones that we can see on our screens (Additive Synthesis) - have correspondence in the CMYK system.

RGB is a colour model of additive type, whose name derives from the three colours it is based on, namely Red Green and Blue. By joining the three colours in their strongest shade, all the light will be reflected to form the colour white.

The choice of colours is related to the physiology of the human eye, as standard photoreceptor cells (called cone cells), which are sensitive to light, respond most to the colours red, green and blue, respectively giving out long, medium and short wave lengths. This is the way the computer perceives, and actually "sees" colours. It is as if every pixel on the screen could be lit by means of a "ray of light" produced by an electronic cannon, which is inside the screen. This ray may be in either a shade of red, or in a shade of green, or blue. The RGB model implies that each shade of each of the three colours is represented by a number ranging between 0 and 255. For example colour black is represented through the RGB value "000" (R = 0 G = 0 B = 0), whereas colour white is represented through the RGB value "255 255 255" (R = 255 G = 255 B = 255). RGB model can therefore represent more than 16 million colours. RGB is an additive model because red green and blue are additive colours. In other words, when mixing Red Green and Blue the white colour is created.

Hue Saturation Brightness (HSB) indicates both an additive method of composition of colours and a way to represent them in a digital system. It is also called Hue saturation method or Hue saturation intensity, and it is a variety of the Hue saturation lightness model. According to this model, any colour is represented through three numbers. The first one represents Hue (ranging from 0 to 360°). Each degree value represents a different colour. From 0° onwards (which represents colour red) increasing degrees stand for different colours in their varying iris shades, and, for example yellow is to be found at 120°, green at 180° and blue at 240, up until colour violet. The second number stands for Saturation, and indicates the quantity or percentage of colour. Its value ranges between 0 and 100, where 0 represents absence of colour and 100 stands for full colour. The third number is Brightness, which can be increased by adding some white or decreased by adding the colour black. In this case 0 stands for colour white and 100 for colour black. As the number progresses towards 0 the colour will be brighter, and it will be darker as the number gets closer to 100.

3.2   The Case Study

We picked two colourful spots in the Corricella waterfront. We got the models of these facades with ReMake, ReCap and Photoscan, and then we analysed their pixels using Photoshop. We decided that the best way to make this analysis was to use as a reference the RGB and HUE values of each pixel, but thanks to Colour HEX we might get further information if needed (Fig. 9).

Fig. 9. Case study

We conducted this analysis picking different pixels located in seven different spots (Fig. 10).

If we compare the photograph used, taken at Corricella, with the pictures obtained using the models we have studied, we will notice that the colours vary slightly.

First of all it must be noted that the colours in the photographs are not necessarily representative of the real colour of the building. Correction of colour distortion in the photographs must be effected even before processing them to create models. To do so we can use a spectrophotometer or compare the real colour of the building with a palette of colours to establish its exact shade of colour. The colour in the photographs will be corrected consequently, and only at this stage the model can be created.

This part of the work will be excluded from our analysis, and given for granted as a pre-requisite. The object of our study, instead, is colour distortion in the act of processing photographs by creating a cloud and finally a mesh.

The comparison we will effect is based on systems HUE and RGB, which are easily accessible for any shade of colour thanks to Photoshop.

In each case study we will identify one or more areas from which we will take samples of colour, and we will try to assess whether the results given out by the programme are constant or inconstant.

Fig. 10. Case study

We will also try to analyse distortion of colour and establish if it is relatively constant in the act of processing photographs, or if it takes place randomly. We will also indicate colour HEX code, which gives extra information for each colour.

3.3 The Analysis

These are the steps we took to conduct this phase of research (Fig. 11):

Fig. 11. Spot selection for colour accuracy analysis

(0) We produced the textured model with each one of the selected software.
(1) We selected the spots we intended to pick the pixels from.

(2) We picked a representative pixel for each spot of the model.
(3) We analysed them in Photoshop, which can easily tell the RGB, HUE and Colour HEX values.
(4) We confronted these values, in particular the RGB, with the values registered by our photographs.

Here below, we will show an example:

(A) Spot selection
(B) Pixel Analysis

We repeated the analysis for each spot, trying to understand which one among the selected types of software gives out the most accurate result. In the end we found out that the programs which give out the best results are the Autodesk ones - in particular ReMake is the best - whereas the one which gives out the worst result is Photoscan (Table 2).

3.4   Conclusions

In the light of the analysis we have carried out the results seem to be fairly consistent in the seven areas of sample study we have chosen. Some imperfections can be due to the poor quality of the models, as it is easily understandable. However, results are overall constant.

It must be remembered that the aim of this study is to identify the programme giving out the best colour performance compared to the original photographs used as starting material, and not compared to the effective colours of the buildings. As we said before, the real colour of the building must be determined through an accurate survey, using adequate tools, and only after that the photographs can be corrected, by modifying the RGB values. There is, of course, a certain error rate determined by the fact that in all cases each pixel is slightly different from adjacent pixels. However we have made sure that the pixels we have used as samples were representative of the area analysed.

Worst result:

Among the programs taken into account (ReCap, ReMake and Photoscan) the worst colour rendering, comparing the set of photographs taken with the final textured model, is obtained using Photoscan. As a matter of fact this programme tends to lower RGB values by 5–10.

Best result:

The programme giving out results which were closer to the original colour in the photographs is ReMake. However also ReCap obtained good results: since both programmes are Autodesk, they probably share some algorithms regulating them, and so their model rendering is similar.

It must be pointed out that all of them gave out a very accurate result. However, for each case we analysed, we always had slightly different results; so it is hard to find a general rule. In the end, each case study could give out different results, and the result we got can probably only be referred to our case study.

Table 2. Pixel Analysis

Photography:

	H 203° S 21% B 68%	R 136 G 159 B 173	#889FAD

ReMake:

	H 202° S 24% B 69%	R 134 G 161 B 177	#86A1B1

ReCap:

	H 203° S 18% B 62%	R 128 G 146 B 157	#80929D

PhotoScan:

	H 206° S 19% B 61%	R 125 G 142 B 155	#7D8E9B

It must be noticed that some slightly contrasting results have been obtained in the two case studies. In the first case study we got the best results with ReMake, whereas in the second study ReCap was more accurate in most cases.

As usual, each case must be considered by itself.

References

1. Apollonio, F.I., et al.: I portici di Bologna. Architettura, Modelli 3D e ricerche tecnologiche. Bononia University Press, Bologna (2015)
2. Guidi, G., Remondino, F.: 3D Modeling from real data. In: Modeling ans Simulation in Engineering. InTech Publisher (2012)
3. Barazzetti, L., Remondino, F., Scaioni, M.: Automated and accurate orientation of complex image sequences. In: International Archives of the Photogrammetry, Remote Sensing and Spatial Information Sciences, vol. XXXVIII-5/W16, pp. 277–284. Coperincus Publications (2011)
4. Remondino, F.: Rilievo e modellazione 3D di siti e architetture complesse. Disegnarecon Ed. (2011)
5. Remondino, F., Gaiani, M., Benedetti, B.: Modelli Digitali 3D in Archeologia: il caso di Pompei. Edizioni della Normale (2010)
6. De Luca, L.: La Fotomodellazione Architettonica. Dario Flaccovio Editore (2011)
7. Guidi, G., Russo, M., Beraldin, J.A.: Acquisizione 3D e modellazione poligonale. Mcgraw Hill Ed. (2010)
8. Tomasi, C., Kanade, T.: Shape and Motion from image streams under ortography-a factorization method. Int. J. Comp. Vis. **9**, 137–154 (1992). vol. 33. Springer Ed.
9. Bethmann, F., Luhmann, T.: Object-based semi-global multi-image matching. In: PFG – Journal of Photogrammetry, Remote Sensing and Geoinformation Science. Springer Ed. (2017)
10. Di Liello, S., Rossi, P.: Procida, Architettura e Paesaggio. Nutrimenti Editore (2017)
11. Cosenza, G., Jodice, M.: Procida, un'Architettura del Mediterraneo. Clean Edizioni (2016)
12. Albissinni, P.: Il waterfront della città-porto di Bisceglie. Modelli digitali 3D per la lettura, interpretazione e rappresentazione dell'immagine urbana. Mario Adda Editore (2008)

3D Digitization of Selected Collection Items Using Photometric Stereo

Jaroslav Valach[1(✉)], Jan Bryscejn[1], Tomáš Fíla[1], Daniel Vavřík[1], and Petra Štefcová[2]

[1] Institute of Theoretical and Applied Mechanics (ITAM),
Academy of Sciences of the Czech Republic, Prosecká 76, 19000 Prague 9, Czech Republic
`valach@itam.cas.cz`
[2] National Museum, Václavské n. 68, 115 79 Prague 1, Czech Republic

Abstract. Digitization of exhibits and the creation of virtual exhibitions is undergoing a period of stormy development and is a dynamic area of care for museum collections. The availability of digital models has a major share in the growing trend of on-line access to collections. At the same time, digitization can improve the protection of items and increase their availability for the public as well as for professionals. It can be performed using procedures based on different physical principles and their technical implementation, with different requirements for the captured objects and different quality levels of the achieved outputs. This paper introduces a technique of 3D digitization based on the principle of photometric stereo. First, it describes typical objects, followed by the physical fundamentals of the method and the selected technical solution. A section on the examples of results introduces the application of this method for creating digital models of various objects and, finally, the conclusion contains contemplations on further development of this method in the future.

Keywords: Digitization · Museum collections · 3D models
Photometric stereo

1 Introduction

Ideal digitization of collections involves a degree of precision that allows future researchers to find answers in the created digital model that were not known and asked at the time of digitization, so that any new research would not have to go "back to the object". Unfortunately, this requirement is in conflict with the capabilities of the current technology as well as ordinary work budgets, and it is therefore necessary to maximize the current options based on an understanding of the goals of documentation and the studied phenomena.

However, the goal is not just to select the right method for the object in question; it has been shown that the problems of commercial digitization solutions used for the purposes of technical documentation of objects consists in unknown parameters determining the capture conditions, which are not controlled by the user and which may vary from case to case according to the undocumented decision-making logic of the application. Compliance with the requirement for full control over the conditions of digitization is another reason why it is worth it to continue developing customized methods.

© Springer International Publishing AG, part of Springer Nature 2018
M. Ioannides (Ed.): ITN-DCH 2017, LNCS 10605, pp. 31–36, 2018.
https://doi.org/10.1007/978-3-319-75826-8_3

The ITAM develops the optical photometric stereo method (hereinafter PS). PS currently lies outside the main stream of 3D scanning, which brings some limitations, but at the same time some benefits and new horizons [1, 3]. Just like other technologies, PS can also provide useful services only if used in compliance with its principles and for the study of suitable object types. Such objects can be characterized as relief-based, i.e. with one embossed side of an exclusive significance and special importance for documenting its shape and condition.

Examples of objects and applications suitable for PS include the digitization of seals, coins, plaques and medals, punches, petroglyphs, but also the shallow reliefs of carved stones, engraved wood or linoleum, and jewels such as cameos and ivory carvings, documentation of carpentry and stone marks, trasology of tool marks. Artefacts from bone products to a detailed study of brush strokes in paintings can also be included. An important area of application of PS is the documentation of degradation of objects and their surfaces, whether they are processes accompanied by material loss or, conversely, by the emergence of an extraneous layer. The possibility to increase the method's sensitivity by changing the conditions of illumination of the studied surface can be employed in this case; such surfaces may include paper fibres or other similarly smooth textured surfaces, which may be indicative for example of the presence of degradation processes, such as corrosion of metals or decay of polymer materials due to solar radiation. These studied signs of damage can cover a large range of dimensions - from single centimetres to meters, for example to detect subsurface defects of plaster, wall paintings and frescoes of historical buildings. The common thing about the aforementioned examples is that they are mostly 2.5D and conventional photographic documentation is unsuitable for them because their appearance may vary significantly depending on the lighting used. Sometimes even the changing appearance resulting from changes in shadows as the object is rotated in light is key for the user to understand the stored information. This claim applies for example to cuneiform tablets, but also to the trasology of marks left by tools used by medieval craftsmen working on beams. Another interesting result of the robustness of the method is the possibility to use even images not created by standard optical systems - but for example by outputs from thermal imaging cameras or a scanning electron microscope - as the input images to be processed by the procedure. Other notable application of digital three-dimensional models of object consists in reverse engineering, which can involve, in case of heritage preservation, speculative filling-in of missing parts of statues (usually noses and limbs) to precisely match the fracture surfaces of the original digitized by photometric stereo.

2   Description of the Method and Technical Resources

PS historically originated in astronomy, where it was used to study the shapes of crater walls on the surfaces of planets. Stereoscopic methods for digitizing remote surfaces would not yield the desired results since the height of the relief is negligible compared with the distance between the Earth and the investigated body. For photometric stereo, the distance (or, more precisely, the ratio of distance and height of surface features) is not a problem: the structure and contrast of the surface in incident light is decisive [2, 4]. PS is able to detect any microscopic surface irregularities, which remain hidden in the margins of error of measurement using other optical methods. The flexibility of the method consists in the fact that the results are independent of the distance from the studied surface and in the scalability of sensitivity by choosing lamp elevation.

The reflected light carries information on the colour of the object's surface (determined by different albedo for different colours), but also on the roughness and granularity of the surface. The human eye has been shaped by evolution to look for shapes and rhythmic regularities in images, based on relative differences in space or in time, but it does not excel in performing measurements through vision. That is any area where digital equipment is used as it has the ability to determine the required quantity accurately.

The technical execution of surface illumination is the core of the PS technical design (Fig. 1). The camera and the studied subject are held in a fixed relative position and the only thing that changes is the illumination of the object; one image is attributable to each change of illumination. The set of surface images constitutes input data that are further processed. To determine the shade and surface inclinations at every point, at least three images of the object are necessary in different lighting conditions, but in an automatic digitization system acquires typically set of fifteen images at minimum. At some

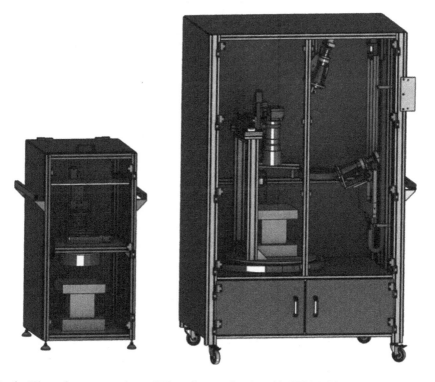

Fig. 1. View of two generations of PS equipment developed in ITAM. The height of the bigger one is approximately 170 cm. The object is placed on a table, where it is illuminated from different directions and inclinations by means of telecentric lamps (i.e. lamps whose beams do not broaden with distance, do not create a cone) and individual scenes are captured by a digital SLR camera.

workplaces, the requirement for varying object illumination is met by switching between many fixed lamps; our solution is based on mechanical movements of lamps with respect to the fixed camera-object pair. The next step in the processing of input data ensures additional calculation of the surface topography using the inclinations of such surfaces.

PS equipment is able to carry out 3D digitization of object surfaces in a fully automated mode, where the position of lamps with respect to the object is changed by means of computer-controlled motorized drives and the camera is operated. Currently, development work focuses on fine-tuning the third-generation system, especially by implementing additional features and improving technical parameters.

The output format is a matrix of heights, wrapped with a texture image. This format is suitable for further calculations and handling operations performed in the Matlab environment. However, to create digital replicas it is useful to be able to convert the data to the STL (stereolitography) format, which is a common input dataset for 3D printers that can change a digital replica into a physical replica. The importance of this step is evident for example in experimental archaeology, where it is important to determine, through physical handling of the object, what it was used for or how it was created, but it cannot be touched because of the uniqueness of the original, while there are no such restrictions for a replica. Another option of using 3D replicas consists in ensuring access to collection items to visually impaired people who can use the sense of touch to get to know the objects. Unlike casts which reproduce the object on the same scale, digital replicas can be scaled – enlarge a small animal to fit in the hand or change an ancient amphitheatre to fit in a shoe box...

3   Reconstruction

It is not possible to present all the results of PS implementation for documenting object surfaces, and attention will be therefore paid to examples depicted in Figs. 2, 3 and 4, which demonstrate some interesting or typical applications. Comments are given

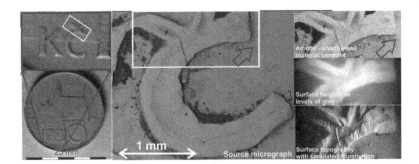

Fig. 2. Example of reconstruction of the surface of a contemporary coin using photometric stereo, carried out based on images from a scanning electron microscope (SEM), demonstrating various scales with which the method can work as well as the initial set of images not formed optically. The selected detail, highlighted with a yellow box, shows the original image as well as a height map and a view of the 3D reconstruction with simulated lighting. (Color figure online)

directly in the captions. The selected examples demonstrate the range of situations in which the PS method can be applied and bring results not achievable by simple photographic documentation and even some 3D digitization methods. Although the class of objects suitable for this technique is limited, it is still a major subset of objects typical to museum collections.

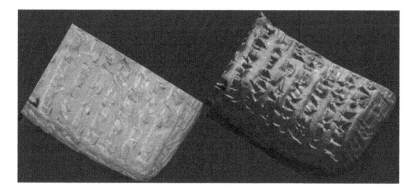

Fig. 3. For experts studying cuneiform tablets, it is essential to be able to rotate the tablets and have the symbols visible in side lighting to deepen the shadows within them. In case of conventional photography or when using a scanner, the legibility remains limited, unlike 3D reconstruction based on PS and enhanced with simulated shadows. (The longer edge is approx. 5 cm long)

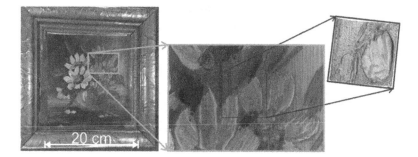

Fig. 4. The 3D details of brush strokes revealing the painter's working method can be separated from their colours to highlight the expressive execution of the work. The 3D dimension can be "amplified" as needed. (Color figure online)

4 Conclusion

This paper describes the photometric stereo method and its technical implementation, including some of its results. The technique offers the possibility to obtain visually compelling digital models of three-dimensional surfaces across a wide range of scales and sources of input images. Taking into account its physical conditions, this method is particularly suitable for "relief" surfaces; its application for objects with complex 3D shapes, for example objects with multiple topologies (such as a cup with a handle), is problematic. Further development will aim to create an easily transportable version of the device because it is easier in terms of organization for institutions, such as museums, to permit the digitization of collection items directly in their premises rather than to negotiate their loan outside the institution, which also requires extra costs of insurance.

Acknowledgements. The paper has been written within the NAKI project "Analysis, Description and Archiving of Collected Information on the Properties of Objects of Cultural Heritage and Application of Such Information in Restoration, Preservation and Research Practice" DG16P02M022.

References

1. Fíla, T., Vavřík, D., Valach, J., Vrba, D., Zlámal, P., Bryscejn, J.: Integrální zařízení pro tvorbu digitalizovaných 3D modelů objektů pomocí metody fotometrického sterea (Integral equipment for the production of digitized 3D models of objects using the photometric stereo method). Institute of Theoretical and Applied Mechanics, Academy of Sciences of the Czech Republic. 2015. Patent file No.: 305606. Patent granted on: 25 November 2015
2. Horn, B.K.P.: The Psychology of Computer Vision. McGraw Hill, New York, pp. 115–155 (1975)
3. Valach, J., Bryscejn, J.: Improved precision of stereometric measurement of relief's surface by means of structured light enhanced photometric stereo method. In: Návrat, T., Fuis, V., Houfek, L., Vlk, M. (eds.) Experimentální analýza napětí 2011 (Experimental stress analysis 2011), pp. 411–415. Czech Society for Mechanics, Brno (2011)
4. Woodham, R.J.: Photometric method for determining surface orientation from multiple images. Opt. Eng. **19**(1), 139–144 (1980)

A DICOM-Inspired Metadata Architecture for Managing Multimodal Acquisitions in Cultural Heritage

Irina-Mihaela Ciortan[1]([✉]), Ruggero Pintus[2], Giacomo Marchioro[1],
Claudia Daffara[1], Enrico Gobbetti[2], and Andrea Giachetti[1]

[1] Department of Computer Science, University of Verona, Verona, Italy
{irinamihaela.ciortan,giacomo.marchioro,
claudia.daffara,andrea.giachetti}@univr.it
[2] Visual Computing Group, CRS4, Pula, Italy
{ruggero,gobbetti}@crs4.it

Abstract. Quantitative and qualitative analyses of cultural heritage (CH) assets need to interconnect individual pieces of information, including a variety of multimodal acquisitions, to form a holistic compounded view of studied objects. The need for joint acquisition brings with it the requirement for defining a protocol to store, structure and support the interoperability of the multisource data. In our work, we are performing multiple imaging studies in order to analyze the material, to monitor the behavior and to diagnose the status of CH objects. In particular, we employ, in addition to coarse 3D scanning, two high-resolution surface data capture techniques: reflectance transformation imaging and micro-profilometry. Given this multivariate input, we have defined a hierarchical data organization, similar to the one used in the medical field by the Digital Imaging and Communications in Medicine (DICOM) protocol, that supports pre-alignment of local patches with respect to a global model. Furthermore, we have developed two supporting tools for multimodal data handling: one for metadata annotation and another one for image registration. In this work, we illustrate our approach and discuss its practical application in a case study on a real CH object – a bronze bas-relief.

Keywords: Metadata · Annotation tools · 3D scanning
Microprofilometry · Reflectance transformation imaging

1 Introduction

The importance of exploiting multimodal 3D capture techniques for artwork documentation is widely recognized [1,2]. Since multiple measurements, often taken with different instruments or at different times, need to be studied together, there is a need for managing all measurements and annotations in a clear and organized

© Springer International Publishing AG, part of Springer Nature 2018
M. Ioannides (Ed.): ITN-DCH 2017, LNCS 10605, pp. 37–49, 2018.
https://doi.org/10.1007/978-3-319-75826-8_4

structure that could ideally converge to a common standard [3]. This need is fulfilled by specific protocols and associated metadata, which allow one to "describe, identify, facilitate the access, usage and management of (digital) resources" [4]. Metadata are essential to record the full life-cycle of a CH asset [5], as well as any intermediary activities involved in generating a digital model from a physical object. In other words, metadata open the gate to interpretation, providing extra-meaning and a legend on how to read and connect raw scientific datasets. The need for order has convinced end-users and stakeholders of CH to add metadata systems to their projects. This resulted in an inflation of project-tailored metadata schemes [5–7], that achieve the ad-hoc purpose for which they were created, but make difficult the task of standardization. The basic idea behind our proposed data organization protocol is to follow the same approach used in DICOM (Digital Imaging and COmmunications in Medicine) [9], the standard used to manage medical imaging studies in hospitals. Our proposal only covers the model of the Information Object definitions used in DICOM and the data acquisition management, though the protocol defines all the aspects related to data communication and device interoperability, that is a really crucial aspect in the development of 3D model archives [8].

However, we believe that the development of a complete standard defining all these aspects could be extremely useful also in the CH domain. An attempt to adapt the complete DICOM standard to other domains has been done, for example, in the field of industrial material analysis with the proposal of DICONDE (Digital Imaging and Communication in Nondestructive Evaluation) [10], a standard for handling, sharing, storing and transmitting information between compliant systems.

This paper is structured as follows: in the upcoming section we describe how we adapted some ideas of the DICOM standard for the needs of the Cultural Heritage domain and how we partially included the Aging and Study levels – which are very appropriate to the rapidly changing nature of CH objects and their complexity in need of the multivariate analysis. Afterwards, we describe two of our tools developed to facilitate and catalyze two important steps in handling CH metadata and data: annotation and registration. Then, we go through our protocol step by step to examine a Case Study on a real CH object – a bronze bas-relief, copy of an Italian Renaissance work of art. It is noteworthy for the wide applicability of our proposed method to mention that we put it in practice within an European Horizon 2020 project, Scan4Reco [11], where we deal with a plethora of CH objects, including samples created in laboratory. Finally, our paper concludes with a discussion and ideas for potential future developments.

2   The Proposed Protocol for Data Annotation

Starting from the DICOM protocol, in our proposed metadata architecture, each object of study (artwork or material sample) is treated as a "patient" and when it undergoes a study, it must be annotated registering its basic information analogously to real patients who get recorded in Radiology Information Systems

(RIS). After each object (artwork or sample) is annotated, it is acquired by several imaging studies and relevant metadata is stored. The metadata are stored at the study level of our hierarchical organization and can be retrieved using the standard information model for Query/Retrieve that in DICOM is based on Patient (object), Study and Series – as shown in Fig. 1. In this hierarchy, we inserted an aging level in order to keep track of possibly different natural or artificial aging procedures performed on the objects. Moreover, for each acquisition technique, we have defined a set of specific metadata fields based on tag-value pairs for each of these three acquisition methods: RTI, Microprofilometer and Low-resolution 3D scanning. End-level data stored in our archives are then not necessarily standard images, but typically data (surfaces, clouds, grids) spatially referenced in a global coordinate system.

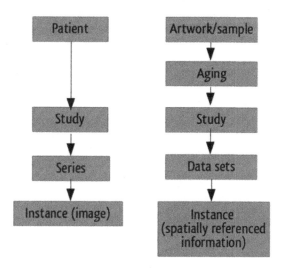

Fig. 1. Query/retrieve Information models for DICOM archives (left) and for our archive (right).

2.1   Object Level

The Object metadata file comprises fields that uniquely identify and describe the origin of the CH asset, together with its physical characteristics, as well as the treatments applied (for example protective coatings) and the aging condition of the object at the time of its recording. The full fields and their corresponding descriptions are enumerated in Table 1.

Table 1. Metadata fields for Cultural Heritage object

Field	Description
UID	Represents a unique combination of alphanumeric characters that references to a sample or an artwork in the project's database
TYPE	The type of artifact: to be chosen between artwork or lab simulated mock-ups (samples)
LOCATION	Geographical place where the object was created
NAME	The text that describes the name of the sample. It also identifies the sample/artwork, but not necessarily unique
AUTHOR	The person who created the sample or the artwork
SOURCE	Where the object comes from: museum collection, research laboratory, cultural institution, etc.
DATE_CREATION	The date when the physical object (sample or artwork) was completed. Format: DD/MM/YY
DETAILS_CREATION	This might refer on how the sample was created, the history, chronology or steps of creation
EXTENT	Refers to the physical dimensions of the sample or artwork (height, width, thickness)
SEMANTICS_DESCRIPTION	The description of semantics has to briefly guide through the content of the sample or artwork. Example 1: the artwork is an Icon depicting Virgin Mary
MATERIALS	The constitutive elements that make up the sample/artwork and their type: metals, pigments, support, etc.
CONDITION	The status of the sample/artwork that might regard the following characteristics: novelty, previous restoration, visible aging effects. Example 1: new, out of the laboratory sample, with no aging effect. Example 2: painting was partially restored, but there is still visible a red pigment discoloration
TREATMENT	Restoration method that an artwork has undergone or the chemical treatment (such as protective coating) applied to a sample at the moment of creation

2.2 Aging Level

The purpose of the Aging metadata file is to monitor any aging process that reacted on the object. Therefore, it is of interest to record the type of aging (natural or artificial), the major factors and agents that lead to the aging effects and the attributes of the object that were mainly affected as a result of the aging process, as listed in Table 2.

Table 2. Metadata fields for the aging process

Field	Description
UID	Unique identifier of the aging process, that can be made up of a unique combination of alphanumeric characters, which ought to be representative of the aging method applied and the time frame. Example 1: UV Exposure t1
TYPE	The category of aging process: artificial (human-provoked) or naturally (due to the passing of time, without human intervention)
DATE	The date when the aging treatment was applied. Format: DD/MM/YY
LOCATION	Geographical place where the aging process has taken place
METHOD_NAME	The name of the aging mechanism involved
SCIENTIST_IN_CHARGE	The person in charge of the conducting or supervising the aging process
DESCRIPTION	Description of the aging method
AGENTS	The bio-chemical agents responsible for the aging
EXPECTED_EFFECTS	The theoretical expected change in the appearance, structure and geometry of the physical object onto which the aging effect was applied
ATTRIBUTES_AFFECTED	The intrinsic properties of the object that were affected by the aging process

2.3 Study Level

Whereas the aging level offers a preliminary versioning of the Cultural Heritage object, the Study level represents the supporting data for each point on the time axis that the object is passing through. The study level can be split into as many acquisition techniques as are implemented (in our case, we used three techniques). Even though each acquisition has its characteristic method, we created groups of metadata fields as a way of coping with the immediate divergence of the techniques. Therefore, the Acquisition metadata fields in our model are further grouped into several wrappers: Study identification, Setup specifications, Hardware specifications, Software specifications, Output files and Spatial reference.

For brevity, in this text we only include the full set of metadata fields for the 3D low resolution imaging system (Table 3). The tables corresponding to the other two techniques (RTI and Microprofilometry) can be fully viewed online on our project's website, Scan4Reco [11], in the document on the Metadata and Joint acquisition protocol published as a deliverable of the project [12].

Similarly to the 3D low-resolution study described in Table 3, RTI groups are populated by Identification (Acquisition ID, Date, Type, Location Name,

Operator Name), Setup specifications (Type, Description), Hardware specifications (the optical characterization of the Digital Camera and other optical accessories: lens, filter, lights, etc.), Software specifications (Camera settings for capture: ISO, aperture, focus, the use of tethering tools), Output files (raw data, derived data and corresponding formats) and Spatial referencing (Camera axis direction and center position; intrinsic parameters). We have defined fields for the microprofilometric acquisition analogously [12].

Therefore, the metadata files for all the acquisition methods manage to both preserve the specificity of each technique and, at the same time, to maintain inter-connectivity between the various methods by exploring a standardized, grouped way to cover all the essential information in similar groups.

Table 3. Metadata fields for Low-resolution 3D scanning

Field	Description
ACQUISITION_ID	Unique ID of the acquisition
ACQUISITION_DATE	Date and time when the acquisition was performed
ACQUISITION_TYPE	The type of study applied to the object, such as: RTI, Microprofilometry, Low-res scanning
LOCATION_NAME	Geographical location of where the acquisition was performed. Example: Verona, Sardinia
OPERATOR_ID	The unique identifier of the operator who performed the acquisition
OPERATOR_NAME	The name of the person who conducted the acquisition
SETUP_DESCRIPTION	Description of the particularities of the setup
SCANNING_DEVICE	The scanning device used for capturing the object and the cloud of points corresponding to the object's geometry
RESOLUTION	The resolution of the scanning device
ACCURACY_VALUE	A numeric value that indicates the accuracy of the 3D scanning procedure
TOOL_VERSION	A numeric value that represents the tool's version used for scanning
OUTPUT_FILE	3D scan file name
OUTPUT_FILE_FORMAT	Mesh/Point cloud format
ORIGIN	XYZ coordinates of the origin in the reference space
ORIENTATION	Unit vectors of the acquisition space in the reference space

3   Metadata Recording Tools

When storing the metadata and using the actual data, there are two main challenges to address. In the first case, the metadata fields need to be annotated in an error-proof manner; in the latter, the multimodal data need to be fetched into the same coordinate system. We are addressing these challenges by implementing helper tools for both annotation and registration processes.

3.1   Metadata Annotation Interface

In order to facilitate the annotation of the metadata fields, a form-based GUI for the generation of the metadata files has been developed using the Qt framework (Fig. 2). The tool lists the fields that need to be filled-in by the data operator. Moreover, to reduce the possibility of error, where possible we are including predefined answers into drop-down boxes, check boxes or radio buttons. Further, the fields include tooltips that provide additional clarification on their meaning. In addition, in case the mandatory fields are not filled-in, the metadata files cannot be saved and the mandatory fields are flagged with a change in the background color. The tool generates the metadata as simple text files and allows both export and import (in case the user wants to verify or modify an existing metadata file). Although new tabs dedicated to generate the metadata of the acquisition level can be added to the graphical user interface in a similar fashion, this tool has been developed for the specific purpose of annotating the Artifact and Aging metadata, following that the Study level can be supported by the acquisition software.

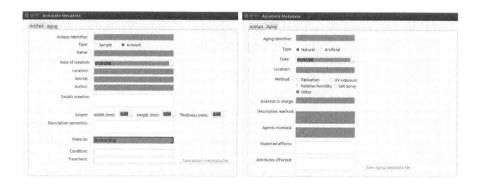

Fig. 2. The interface of the metadata annotation tool. The tool has two tabs: Artifact and Aging. The mandatory fields are emphasized with a cyan background and the save buttons are inactive, since the mandatory fields are not yet inserted.

3.2   Multimodal Data Registration Tool

The RTI and the micro-profilometry data are acquired separately and in distinct times. RTI outputs an image stack, where each 2D image corresponds to a different light position, captured with a fixed camera viewpoint and fixed object scene. On the other hand, the microprofilometer provides 3D information in the form of a height map, by measuring the distance from the probe to the studied surface across an XY grid. So, we need to fuse those multi-modal signals into one common reference frame and keep the fusion information as manageable metadata for further processing. In this way, we can embed together not only geometry data from optical high-res profilometry, but also other geometric information (e.g., normal map) and appearance data (e.g., albedo) from the RTI image stack.

To exploit the fused signals, they need first to be registered. The goal of the procedure that registers the RTI and micro-profilometry data is to compute the mapping (position and orientation) between the 2D domain of the RTI camera sensor and the 3D surface (reference depth map) from the micro-profilometer. The input information for the registration is the micro-profilometry depth map and some data/metadata from RTI – e.g., intrinsic parameters of the camera sensor and/or only one image with the same view point as the RTI data. Since the RTI image stack is captured from a fixed viewpoint and varying lighting conditions, it is sufficient to align just one image to the 3D geometry in order to register all the information in the stack onto the 3D geometry. The image used for the registration could be one of the images in the stack, or, more likely, an image computed by an image stack processing routine (e.g., the normal map field).

A graphical user interface has been developed to help the user with the registration (see Sect. 4 and Fig. 5). It shows the user with two images: one from the RTI (Fig. 5, normal map on the right) and the other from micro-profilometry data (Fig. 5, geometry on the left). Since the intrinsic camera parameters have been already computed for the RTI data in a previous calibration step, the user only needs to select a small set of 2D-3D correspondences (at least three, but likely more for a better, more robust first estimation). Although out of the scope of this paper, an automatic refinement step could be added at the end of the registration pipeline, which might be based on an ICP-like (Iterative Closest Point) optimization or on the possibly available signals that allow for Mutual Information computation.

Finally, the exported registration metadata includes the list of correspondences (i.e., pairs of 2D and 3D positions), the pointers to the geometry and RTI files (i.e., local or remote location of the files), the extrinsic camera parameters (i.e., the view matrix), and the intrinsic camera parameters (i.e., the projective matrix, the distortion coefficients, and the image resolution).

Of course, if the sampling resolution is similar to that of the RTI, the same procedure and metadata can be used to perform and document the registration between RTI data and the geometry acquired with a low resolution 3D scanner.

This example shows how, in addition to providing ways to record registered study information, our proposed metadata architecture is flexible enough to also store information related to the registration process. For instance, our approach allows one to track errors or to improve registration starting from the same data by repeating processing steps using improved/alternative software on the same registration information.

4   Case Study: Bronze Bas Relief

To better illustrate our proposed protocol and the supporting tools, we have chosen a real Cultural Heritage example as a case study. The object consists of a bronze (Cu90-Sn10 alloy) bas-relief, created in 2004 for educational purposes and that was loaned for educational purposes by the Opificio delle Pietre Dure in Florence, Italy. The bas-relief – shown in Fig. 3 – is a copy of one of the bronze panels of the Paradise Door made by Lorenzo Ghiberti for the Baptistery of Florence. The dimensions of the bas-relief are $39 \times 12 \times 2$ cm (width × height × thickness). The surface underwent an artificial patination through the application of iron(III) chloride, giving the surface a brownish appearance. In 2007 it was coated with a protective product and exposed outdoors in an urban environment (central Florence) until 2016. In the following subsections, we will show how we generate the metadata files from this object and how we obtain images referenced in the same coordinate system from multimodal image data.

Fig. 3. The CH object used for our case study: a bronze bas-relief depicting a female figure.

4.1   Filling in the Metadata Fields

To generate the metadata files corresponding to the bas-relief and the details on its aging we used the metadata annotation tool presented in Sect. 3. The user-friendly interface of the tool after correct data entry is shown in Fig. 4.

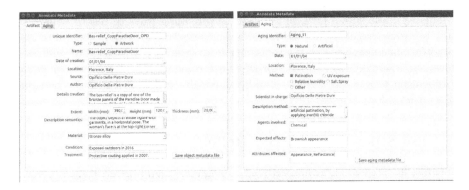

Fig. 4. The interface of the metadata annotation tool, with all the (mandatory) fields filled in. The save buttons are now active.

4.2 Demonstration of Multimodal Data Registration

Another type of metadata are those related to multi-modal registration, which are automatically computed and exported by an alignment routine provided with minimal user input. Figure 5(a) shows an example of how to use the registration tool to select correspondences between the 2D domain of the high resolution normal map, computed from the RTI image stack, and the 3D geometry. In this case, the user has selected 19 pairs and, although the intrinsic camera parameters are typically available from a pre-calibration step, here we show how the tool can calibrate both the camera matrix and the distortion coefficients together with the extrinsic parameters. Figure 5(c) and (b) respectively show the final registered geometry from micro-profilometer and the normal map from RTI. The user performed a similar procedure to register the low resolution geometry from the 3D scanner (Fig. 5(d)) to the high resolution micro-profilometry data; in this case an open source software (Meshlab [13]) was used to register the two surfaces. These three figures demonstrate how the three multi-modal signals perfectly overlap.

5   Discussion

In this paper, we have proposed a DICOM-inspired metadata protocol designed for Cultural Heritage objects. This protocol features inclusion of aging processes and is suitable for annotating multi-modal data. We showed how metadata annotation is crucial for further data reaching a meaningful and holistic analysis of distinct studies that are performed on a CH object. The peculiar aspect of the CH acquisitions is that they are typically done both in 2D and 3D on complete objects or small regions. It is therefore mandatory to record all the information required to align the captured information with a reference 3D frame in order to allow for jointly processing the data. Acquisition devices should store all the metadata useful for the alignment and specific tools for information mapping should be coupled with the them. We implemented this approach in the

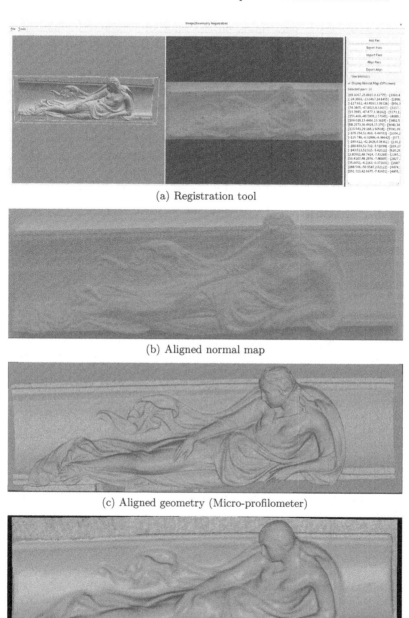

(a) Registration tool

(b) Aligned normal map

(c) Aligned geometry (Micro-profilometer)

(d) Aligned geometry (Low-res Scanner)

Fig. 5. Image-to-geometry registration tool. The registration between 2D images and 3D geometries is assisted by a GUI (a) where the user can select correspondences between points in space and pixels in the image. In this case we use this tool to register the RTI image stack, by using the resulting normal map (b), and the geometry from the micro-profilometer (c); in addition we use Meshlab [13] to align high resolution data (c) with the surface acquired by the low resolution 3D scanner (d).

Scan4Reco project [11] performing on the same objects and at different aging stages the acquisition of high resolution 3D scans, low resolution 3D scans and multi-light image acquisition using custom setups and processing tools.

The case study shown in this paper – the analysis of a bronze bas-relief – recreated the complete path of our pipeline from object annotation to multimodal annotation and, finally, end-data registration.

Our current work can be further improved by adding support for other acquisition methods, integrating them in our protocol and the supporting tools. Another useful future development, that would however require a richer database of studied CH objects, would consist in creating an ontology that would simplify and allow the partial automation of the metadata annotation process.

Acknowledgments. This work was partially supported by the Scan4Reco project funded by European Union's Horizon 2020 Framework Programme for Research and Innovation under grant agreement no 665091.

References

1. Remondino, F.: Heritage recording and 3D modeling with photogrammetry and 3D scanning. Remote Sens. **3**(6), 1104–1138 (2011)
2. Pamart, A., Guillon, O., Vallet, J.-M., De Luca, L.: Toward a multimodal photogrammetric acquisition and processing methodology for monitoring conservation and restoration studies. In: Proceedings of the 14th Eurographics Workshop on Graphics and Cultural Heritage, pp. 207-210. Eurographics Association (2016)
3. Ronzino, P., Hermon, S., Niccolucci, F.: A metadata schema for cultural heritage documentation. In: Capellini, V. (ed.) Electronic Imaging & the Visual Arts: EVA, pp. 36–41 (2012)
4. Stasinopoulou, T., Bountouri, L., Kakali, C., Lourdi, I., Papatheodorou, C., Doerr, M., Gergatsoulis, M.: Ontology-based metadata integration in the cultural heritage domain. In: ICADL, pp. 165–175 (2007)
5. D'Andrea, A., Fernie, K.: CARARE 2.0: a metadata schema for 3D Cultural Objects. In: Digital Heritage International Congress (DigitalHeritage), vol. 2, pp. 137–143. IEEE (2013)
6. Doerr, M., Theodoridou, M.: CRMdig: a generic digital provenance model for scientific observation. In: TaPP (2011)
7. Doerr, M., Gradmann, S., Hennicke, S., Isaac, A., Meghini, C., van de Sompel, H.: The Europeana data model (edm). In: World Library and Information Congress: 76th IFLA General Conference and Assembly, pp. 10–15 (2010)
8. Koller, D., Frischer, B., Humphreys, G.: Research challenges for digital archives of 3D cultural heritage models. J. Comput. Cult. Herit. (JOCCH) **2**(3), 1–7 (2009)
9. Digital Imaging and Communication in Medicine. http://dicom.nema.org/. Accessed 10 Mar 2017
10. ASTM E2339–15, Standard Practice for Digital Imaging and Communication in Nondestructive Evaluation (DICONDE). https://www.astm.org/Standards/E2339.htm. Accessed 10 Sep 2017
11. Scan4Reco project - Multimodal Scanning of Cultural Heritage Assets for their multilayered digitization and preventive conservation via spatiotemporal 4D Reconstruction and 3D Printing. http://scan4reco.eu/scan4reco/. Accessed 12 Sep 2017

12. Scan4Reco project deliverable on metadata: Protocol for joint acquisition of Low-res 3D, Microprofilometry and RTI. http://scan4reco.eu/scan4reco/sites/default/files/documents/scan4reco_d5.2_final.pdf. Accessed 12 Sep 2017

13. Cignoni, P., Callieri, M., Corsini, M., Dellepiane, M., Ganovelli, F., Ranzuglia, G.: Meshlab: an open-source mesh processing tool. In: Eurographics Italian Chapter Conference 2008, pp. 129–136 (2008)

Knowledge Management Using Ontology on the Domain of Artworks Conservation

Efthymia Moraitou[(✉)] and Evangelia Kavakli

Department of Cultural Technology and Communication,
School of Social Sciences, University of the Aegean, Mytilene, Greece
e.moraitou@aegean.gr, kavakli@ct.aegean.gr

Abstract. Conservation is an integral process of collections management aiming to preserve cultural heritage objects in the best possible condition. Object conservation procedures require detailed and accurate documentation in textual or visual records which provide valuable information for the future researcher, curator or conservator. Furthermore, conservation requires the awareness of cultural, historical and scientific information from sources both internal and external which in turn influence the ways in which conservators must approach their work. This integration of different information forms the body of knowledge, relevant to thoughtful decisions on treatment and care of cultural heritage objects. Taking into consideration the diversity of conservation information and associated information sources, the integration cannot be regarded as a trivial task. Therefore, knowledge organization, especially in a concepts level, is necessary. To this end this work presents a domain ontology known as the Conservation Reasoning (CORE) ontology aiming to address the specific requirements of the conservation sector.

Keywords: Knowledge management · Ontology · Semantics
Artworks conservation

1 Introduction

Museums are committed to the conservation of the tangible and intangible heritage of humanity and its environment. As such they acquire, preserve, study, communicate and exhibit artifacts and other objects of artistic, cultural, historical, or scientific importance. In doing so they generate, share and therefore must organize and manage a vast amount of information and sources corresponding to the entire lifetime of each object; from the very moment of its creation to its acquisition from the museum, and from that point of time to the present day [1, 2]. This dynamic condition entails perpetual production of different information categories, associated to the different functions of objects within the museum, as part of a collection, as autonomous objects that can be potentially studied, conserved, exhibited and loaned, as well as part of an institution responsible for their housing and administration [3].

The storage and organization of museum information becomes more demanding considering online availability through internet and data integration or linking. In this case the need of unified information management, and therefore structural or technical,

© Springer International Publishing AG, part of Springer Nature 2018
M. Ioannides (Ed.): ITN-DCH 2017, LNCS 10605, pp. 50–62, 2018.
https://doi.org/10.1007/978-3-319-75826-8_5

syntactical and semantic interoperability, is introduced. Soft information organization, search and retrieval are facilitated by the use -or even the mapping between different-metadata standards and schemes [4]. However, the semantic aspect of knowledge management which includes the definition of concepts' exact meaning requires a different approach. Knowledge representation using ontology creates a context of information intelligent management, allowing the commitment definition of particular concepts/entities and their relations, as well as their use in the semantic web [5, 6].

Artworks conservation, a domain included in the wider museum sector, could benefit greatly from the above mentioned intelligent knowledge management. That becomes better understood considering that object conservation requires the documentation and, most importantly, the awareness of cultural, historical and scientific information from sources both internal and external, which in turn influence the ways in which conservators must approach their work. This integration of different information forms the body of knowledge, relevant to thoughtful decisions on treatment and care of cultural heritage objects.

It is widely recognized that the use of ontologies in the context of the design or integration of information systems, as well as for semantic querying can improve information organization and the quality of the results produced, respectively. Therefore, the development and use of an ontology for artworks conservation, a domain where the information generation and reuse is an integral part of work, was considered beneficial. In the remainder of this paper we first describe the information management requirements pertaining to artworks conservation and provide an overview of related work in the area of conservation knowledge management (Sect. 2). An analysis of artworks conservation concepts is subsequently presented (Sect. 3), which leading to the development of the CORE ontology (Sect. 4). Finally, we conclude with a brief discussion of future trends regarding to the application of ontologies in conservation domain (Sect. 5).

2 Motivation and Related Work

2.1 Conservation Procedures Documentation

Conservation is an integral process of collections management aiming to preserve cultural heritage objects in the best possible condition for future generations. An important part of everyday routine for professional artworks conservators, alongside the treatment and care of the objects, is the collection and production of diverse information. Each artwork presents some particular features inseparable to its creation, use and history, which are neither always known nor stable. The changes that an artwork undergoes may be (a) physical, triggered by an event or its exposure environment, or (b) intentional as a result of its administration, study and treatment. All the evidences and changes are researched and documented by the conservator during conservation procedures. The detailed and accurate documentation, in textual (reports), or visual (photographs, diagrams, designs etc.) records, captures the full story of an object and provides valuable information to future researchers, curators or conservators [7, 8].

A prominent aspect of conservation documentation is that different conservation procedures require different level of detail and focus on different fields of interest. Data capture ensues either from direct examination or analysis processes and diagnosis. Additionally, documentation comprises the record or report of observations, conclusions and activities, during the investigation of artwork condition or environment, as well as during its passive or active conservation. According to different circumstances and different applied methods, the requirement for the way (analytically or briefly) and the modals of information recording (textual with description or checklist, visual with photograph, model, drawing, diagram) may differ [9]. Generally, the material that conservators collect and produce may refer to an object condition –before or after conservation treatment– and pathology, production materials and techniques, applied conservation materials and methods, analysis methods, as well as some administrative information [9–11].

Conservators are interested on what, when, why and how, consequently they often complete their work by searching information repositories. The awareness of existing cultural, historical and scientific information from sources both internal, such as the museum collections management system, or external such as online databases of information on cultural heritage and preservation, influences the conclusions and decisions that conservators make [8]. Each artwork is unique, thus it is treated and studied as a unique case. However, the awareness of similar cases and the processing of relevant information is the key to better inferring, condition state assessment, future management and treatment planning. The conservator's information search and retrieval is often based on report type (condition or conservation), object ID, production materials and techniques, instance of a feature appearance, type of damages, mechanisms and causes of damages.

The above outline the methodology of artworks examination and conservation and confirm the importance of information documentation and search/retrieval throughout the procedure. Considering the diversity of conservation information and associated sources, the management of conservation information cannot be regarded as a trivial task. Therefore, knowledge organization, especially in a concept level, is necessary and an ontology approach could be applied in this direction. Such domain ontology could be useful for information systems design, information integration, development of internet services and semantic querying/search, supporting conservators work.

2.2 Management of Conservation Information

Existing approaches to knowledge management of conservation information are mainly based on the Conceptual Reference Model developed by the ICOM/CIDOC Documentation Standards Group (CIDOC CRM). This formal ontology facilitates the integration and exchange of heterogeneous cultural heritage information, providing semantic definitions and clarifications based on popular metadata standards and schemes on Cultural Heritage domain and museums [12]. In the case of conservation domain CIDOC CRM has been useful, though not always effective. As noticed in the publication about the ARIADNE Conservation Documentation System project [13], sometimes it is almost impossible to fit the phenomenology of damage into one CIDOC CRM class, because the alteration and damage mechanism must be already known in order to classify its evidences. This means that often the known information, in a particular point of time during conservation documentation, cannot be expressed by a CIDOC CRM entity.

On the other hand, OreChem is a data model developed in the context of OreChem project regarding the development of new models for research and dissemination of scientific material in the chemistry community based on the Open Archives Initiative Reuse and Object Exchange (OAI-ORE) model. OreChem has particularly focused on chemistry domain concepts, chemical properties, polymers and measurement techniques [14]. An ontology like this, pertaining to the chemistry domain, is useful for the capturing and management of material analysis results on conservation sector. In particular, the study and analysis of artworks production materials and their chemical changes are often part of the conservation procedures, although constitutes only a subset of the conservators' work which is not always necessary. In the same context the CRM sci (Scientific Chemical Model), is a formal ontology for integrating data about scientific observation, measurements and processed data which could be very useful for the knowledge representation of some aspects of conservation procedures which are included in analysis and examination [15].

Finally, the Ontology of Paintings and Preservation of Art (OPPRA) draws existing ontologies such as CIDOC CRM, OreChem and OIA-ORE. OPPRA focuses on paintings conservation and aims at the description of chemical analysis/characterization data, which can potentially be uploaded into databases and be reused by conservators. Also it facilitates the extraction of structured data from relevant published articles, as well as the integration of conservation data and the unified knowledge management from external and internal databases [16]. It is an interesting approach specific to the conservation domain, though it reflects mainly the concepts, methodology and requirements of experimental procedures and materials analysis.

In conclusion, existing ontologies are either too general and do not cover the different levels of detail and types of conservation information, or focus only on a subset of conservation procedures. This work proposes Conservation Reasoning (CORE), a domain ontology aiming to address the information needs pertaining to each step of the conservation process discusses in Sect. 2.1. To this end, it incorporates a set of interrelated concepts for describing complementary perspectives of the conservation domain described in the following section (Sect. 3).

3   Conceptual Perception of Artworks Conservation

Knowledge representation of artworks conservation requires the determination of general or more specific concepts of the domain. The information material that conservators produce and research could be classified in four main categories: production materials and techniques, pathology, analysis methods, conservation materials and methods. Below a brief analysis of each category is presented.

1. **Production Materials and Techniques:** The artworks often present a complex composition of materials, which can be applied in different ways, forming a final structure and reflecting the artist's technique. The observation and documentation of this composition is approached and analyzed based in two aspects; the structural layers and the particular components. This means that conservators focus both on chemical substances, structures and compounds as well as on the layers that their combination and consecutive application form [10, 11]. Accordingly, conservation reports may document the stratigraphy, referring to the existence of the support, ground, painting, coating etc. layer, with some general material characterization, such as wooden or textile support, aqueous or oily ground, oil paint or tempera, resin coating and so on. Additionally, at the same point in time or after a complementary examination the conservators can be more specific for the exact materials of each layer, reporting for example that a tempera painting layer is composed by egg yolk as binder.

2. **Pathology:** The changes and damages of artworks may be the result of mechanical, physicochemical or biochemical processes caused by environmental factors, human intervention, biological activity and natural aging. Artworks deterioration is perceived as the change of their condition state or even the degradation of their benefits for the society. It is important to notice that the description of artwork pathology includes the research of the cause, the mechanism and the result of the deterioration, as well as the correlation between damages of different layers or materials of the same object. The result of the cause and the triggered mechanism effects the physicochemical, mechanical or visual deterioration of the original materials and layers, appearance of deposits on artworks surfaces and the radical removal or posterior addition of materials and structural layers. A common phenomenon is that only a part of this information can be documented during an examination and that the complete verification of the pathology requires additional research and analysis [13].

3. **Analysis Methods:** Commonly, the physicochemical methods of analysis complement the conservation procedures. The selection of the most appropriate method or the combined application of different methods depends on the purpose of the analysis (e.g. material identification, condition state research, material dating or originality verification, the extend of a damage or a modification study, the stratigraphy study etc.), the kind of material or structural layer, the condition state of the artwork, the available means and the ability to move safely the object. The analysis methods are distinguished in two major categories, the non-destructive and destructive respectively. The destructive methods require the sampling of the artwork materials in order to study the structure or chemical composition. On the other hand, non-destructive methods, based on the use of electromagnetic radiation of the visible and not-visible range of the spectrum, collect valuable information avoiding a potential risk of artwork integrity. Moreover, destructive methods provide a chemical analysis of a particular sample, while non-destructive methods give the opportunity of a whole surface examination [17].

4. **Conservation Materials and Methods:** Conservation methods are applied on the artworks in order to inhibit deterioration, stabilize their condition state, improve their aesthetic or, in some cases, reveal information. Passive or preventive conservation methods aim to deterioration restriction and damage avoiding, therefore the exposure environment and conditions are monitored and controlled. Similarly, active or invasive conservation methods aim to the long-term preservation of the artwork; however they include direct intervention, by the addition or removal of materials and layers. In any case, active conservation treatments are as limited as possible and follow the principle of minimum intervention and irreversibility [18]. Because of the nature and flow of conservation treatments, the documentation and awareness of the removal or addition of original or conservation materials is highly important, though not always easy to achieve.

4 The CORE Approach

4.1 Development Methodology and Tools

The CORE ontology builds upon and extends the CIDOC CRM ontology, thus taking advantage of its basic concepts and relations and ensuring interoperability with compatible cultural data and applications. The extensions are derived in a bottom-up manner based on empirical analysis, scientific knowledge and existing vocabularies of the conservation domain, such as the Art & Architecture Thesaurus (AAT) of Getty Institute [19], the Conservation & Art Materials Encyclopedia Online (CAMEO) of Museum of Fine Arts Boston [20] and the American Institute for Conservation of Art & Historic Works (AIC) wiki [7]. The ultimate goal was the inclusion and organization of entities which could be potentially extended for each type of artwork. However, it should be noted that at this point the development of the ontology is not exhaustive since only byzantine icon conservation has been particularly studied.

The concepts and relations aim to model more accurately the knowledge relating to artworks' conservation concepts, as described in Sect. 3. The initial design of the ontology included a series of conceptual graphs, depicting hierarchical and other entity relationships. The concept-maps were designed with the Cmap Tools tool of version 6.01.01, software developed by the Florida Institute for Human and Machine Cognition (IHMC) [21]. In the same context, an indicative list of competency questions relevant to artwork conservation information search and retrieval requirements was created.

CORE was developed using the free open source software Protégé 2000 (Protégé Desktop version 5.0.0) of Stanford University [22]. Entities attributes and inference rules were also included to support a finer level of granularity for the domain. The achieved organization contributed to the specification of rules/equivalences and restrictions, which are useful for reasoning and semantic querying. The functionality of the ontology was tested by reasoner HermiT 1.3.8.413. In addition, competency questions were expressed as SPARQL and SPARQL DL queries, through SPARQL Query plug-in and Snap-SPARQL view, in order to search/retrieve ontology instances and test the ontology organization and usability. The Snap-SPARQL querying required the activation of the reasoner and retrieved both semantic and inferring information.

4.2   Ontology Entities and Relations

The CORE ontology consists of a base of 11 classes, each of which branch into sub-classes with semantic consistency. As a result, a total of 395 classes is formed. CIDOC CRM top-level classes capture the provenance information about an artwork while the extensions capture the domain related knowledge. The main classes and some sub-classes are as follows:

- **Actor** includes concepts about humans and groups related to activities about artworks.
- **Condition State** includes concepts about the condition characterization of an artwork based on visual examination.
- **Date** refers to a date related to an event and the creation of an information object or some other entity.
- **Dimension** includes concepts about measurable sizes related to an object or its environment.
- **Equipment** includes concepts about objects, instruments or tools related to an activity.
- **Event** includes concepts about processes or activities which an artwork or its environment undergoes.
- **Information Object** includes concepts about inscriptions, publications and documents which report/record or organize/manage data related to artworks, as a result of some condition assessment or measurement activity.
- **Man-Made Object** includes concepts about artworks types, storage/exhibition objects, structural layer types, materials types.
- **Physical Feature** includes concepts about Man-Made Object individual features, which have been observed or assigned.
- **Place** includes concepts about internal/external space and environment.
- **Timespan** includes concepts about time duration.

An interesting field that CORE concepts focus on is the triptych damage cause-mechanism-result that facilitates a clearer definition of what is observed and what is concluded. Particularly the subclass of 'E26 Physical Feature', 'Deterioration' (Fig. 1), and its subclasses, combined with subclasses of 'E5 Event', 'Process' and 'E7 Activity' (Fig. 2), and their subclasses, can potentially capture the reasoning of a conservator and ensure the flexibility to add each time the exact known information. For example, the fact that an environmental change, such as radiation exposure,

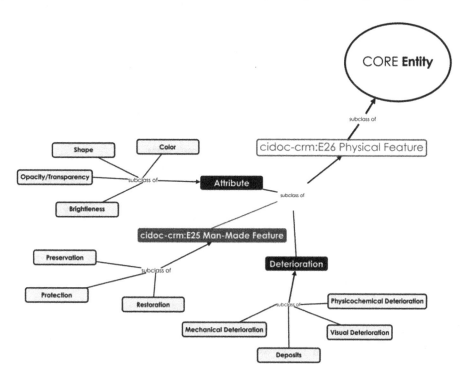

Fig. 1. CORE subclasses of physical feature CIDOC CRM entities

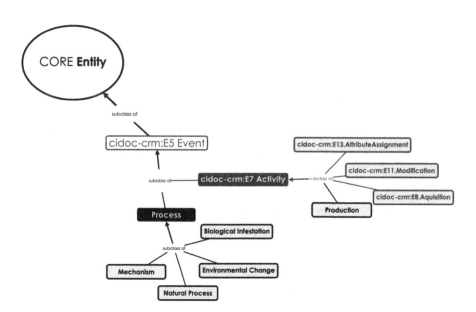

Fig. 2. CORE subclasses of event CIDOC-CRM entity

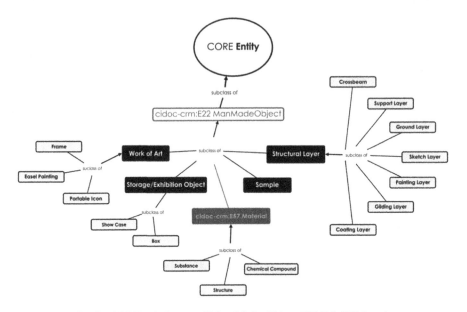

Fig. 3. CORE subclasses of Man-Made Object CIDOC CRM entity

triggers a mechanism, such as an oxidative reaction or particularly photoxidation, which in turn effects the peeling of a painting layer, can be potentially documented.

In a similar manner, the subclasses of 'E22 Man-MadeObject', 'E57 Material' and CORE 'Structural Layer' (Fig. 3) facilitate the association of documented features and activities to a particular material or/and structural layer. For example, the fact that a painting layer consists of pigment and protein binder, in particular egg, can be captured, as well as that a coating layer has been removed using solvent cleaning method. An interesting aspect in this context is that conservation assumptions -and thus knowledge- can be captured as inference rules and restrictions, included in the ontology.

The logical association between CORE classes is expressed as relations (see Table 1). Firstly, the 'is structural layer/has structural layer' relations constitute the connection between the layers and the documented object. Secondly the position determination relations 'overlies/underlies' can describe the layering of the artwork, stating the order of the layers. In addition, the time relations 'before/after' can chronically define the appearance/disappearance of a feature according to another action or event (e.g. before/after conservation). Finally, relations such as 'effects/ effected by', 'has tendency to/is tendency to', 'triggers/triggered by' and 'undergoes/ relates to' express semantic connections between pathology entities.

Table 1. Subset of CORE relations (object properties)

Object property	Domain	Range	SubClassOf	InverseOf
after	Physical Feature	Modification	-	-
before	Physical Feature	Modification	-	-
effected by	Physical Feature	Mechanism or Modification	-	effects
effects	Mechanism or Modification	Physical Feature	-	effected by
has structural layer	Work of Art	Structural Layer	consists of	is structural layer
has tendency to	Man-Made Object	Deterioration	-	is tendency of
is structural layer	Structural Layer	Work of Art	forms part of	has structural layer
is tendency of	Deterioration	Man-Made Object	-	has tendency to
overlies	Structural Layer	Structural Layer	-	underlies
relates to	Event	Man-Made Object or Place	-	undergoes
triggered by	Process	Process or Material	-	triggers
triggers	Process or Material	Process	-	triggered by
undergoes	Man-Made Object or Place	Event	-	relates to
underlies	Structural Layer	Structural Layer	-	overlies

4.3   Competency Questions and Reasoning

Following the development of the CORE ontology, and in order to test its scope and completeness, we investigated its applicability for supporting semantic querying and referring information. To this end information of conservation reports was inserted as individuals of ontology entities and relations, while competency questions were formed as SPARQL and SPARQL DL queries. The questions reflected conservators' requirements on searching, based on relevant studies [16] and the experience of professional conservators.[1]

As found, the semantic organization of concepts, and the corresponding data, can extend conservators questions using subclasses or subproperties which belong in the same semantic class or property respectively. Additionally, classes relations can potentially be used in order to express object features or even correlate them with activities and processes of different time points. Thereby this possibility facilitates the formulation of some interesting questions such as *"Which are the structural layers that*

---

[1] The formulation of competency questions was discussed with conservators from Wooden Artifacts and Byzantine Icons Laboratory of Byzantine and Christian Museum of Athens, Greece.

have ever been recorded about an object" and *"Which are the structural layers of an object since the last conservation treatment".*

Furthermore, inferring information can be generated based on the relations and their inverse or transitive association with others, as well as on the rules and restrictions which can be expressed as equivalences formed using ontology classes and relations. For example, having defined an individual as tempera layer it is inferred that it consists of protein binder, an information that can be used during querying and expand the possibilities of retrieval. Therefore, the existing data of a system could potentially be enriched by subject knowledge.

5 Conclusions

The development and the tests' results indicate that the CORE ontology addresses the requirements related to the conservation processes. Alongside, CORE fulfills desirable criteria of ontology design such as clarity and coherence between the concepts and their relations, extensibility of basic classes to more specific ones and coverage of the domain conceptualization about the information production and reuse. However further work is necessary towards the validation of the ontology, such as testing the ontology in a real setting of a conservation information system which could further evolve it. Also, the study of different artwork types could lead to the inclusion of more specific concepts and the expansion and enrichment of the ontology. Finally, an interesting idea is the addition of entities about different data types, in terms of the multimedia which are used for the documentation of a particular information (e.g. the image representation of a damage), and the possibility of their semantic annotation or correlation with conservation concepts.

The work presented in this paper supports that a domain ontology for artworks conservation could be the base of a semantic search tool development, extending queries and making the information source research faster and more efficient as was studied in [16]. Additional technological applications of ontologies in the conservation field have been reported in the literature. For example, in [23] a global ontology has been proposed towards the semantic integration of information from different data sources. Furthermore, the use of ontologies could contribute to the visualization of semantic information annotating visual and textual data of the same information and presenting them on intelligent interfaces as it is proposed in [24]. Such applications could further facilitate the process of artworks examination, as well as the exchange between Cultural Heritage Institutions.

Acknowledgments. This work was performed and partially supported in the context of the MSc in Cultural Informatics and Communication of the Department of Cultural Technology and Communication of University of the Aegean.

References

1. Jeeser, K., Konsa, K.: Workflow and data exchange between museums: documenting of exhibitions in the Estonian museum information system. Paper presented at the 2014 annual conference of CIDOC, ICOM, access and understanding – networking in the digital era, Dresden, Germany, 6–11 September 2014
2. Marty, P.F., Jones, K.B.: Museum Informatics - People, Information, and Technology in Museums. Routledge, New York, London (2012)
3. Kavakli, E., Bakogianni, S.: Building museum information systems - a knowledge management approach. In: Lipitakis, E.A. (ed.) Proceedings of the Sixth Hellenic-European Conference on Computer Mathematics and its Applications (HERCMA 2003), 25–27 September 2003, vol. 2, pp. 850–857. LEA Publishers, Athens (2003)
4. Chan, L.M., Zeng, M.L.: Metadata interoperability and standardization - a study of methodology, part I: achieving interoperability at the schema level. D-Lib Mag. 12(6), 1–19 (2006)
5. Gómez-Pérez, A., Fernández-López, M., Corcho, O.: Ontological Engineering With Examples from the Areas of Knowledge Management, e-Commerce and the Semantic Web, 1st edn. Springer, London (2005). https://doi.org/10.1007/b97353
6. Sharman, R., Kishore, R., Ramesh, R.: Ontologies: a Handbook of Principles, Concepts and Applications in Information Systems. Springer, New York (2007). https://doi.org/10.1007/978-0-387-37022-4
7. AIC Wiki: Written Documentation (PPC) (2017). http://www.conservation-wiki.com/wiki/Written_Documentation_(PCC). Accessed 20 Aug 2017
8. Letellier, R., Schmid, W., LeBlanc, F.: Recording, Documentation, and Information Management for the Conservation of Heritage Places: Guiding Principles. Getty Conservation Institute, Los Angeles (2007). http://hdl.handle.net/10020/gci_pubs/recordim. Accessed 20 Feb 2017
9. Museum Textile Services, Collection Surveys and Condition Reporting. http://www.museumtextiles.com/uploads/7/8/9/0/7890082/condition_reporting.pdf. Accessed 20 Feb 2017
10. Moore, M.: Conservation documentation and the implications of digitization. J. Conserv. Mus. Stud. 7, 6–10 (2011). https://doi.org/10.5334/jcms.7012
11. Radin, M., Živković, V.: Information management for cultural heritage conservation. Преглед НЦД 23, 22–32 (2013)
12. LeBoeuf, P., Doerr, M., Ore, C.E., Stead, S.: Definition of the CIDOC Conceptual Reference Model, Version 6.2.1 (2015). http://cidoc-crm.org/docs/cidoc_crm_version_6.2.1.pdf. Accessed 20 Feb 2017
13. Naoumidou, N., Chatzidaki, M., Alexopoulou, A.: ARIADNE conservation documentation system: conceptual design and projection on the CIDOC CRM framework and limits. Paper presented at the 2008 annual conference of CIDOC, Athens, Greece, 15–18 September 2008 (2008)
14. Open Archives: OreChem-Cyberinfrastructure for Chemistry. http://www.openarchives.org/oreChem/. Accessed 20 Feb 2017
15. Doerr, M., Kritsotaki, A., Rousakis, Y., Hiebel, G., Theodoridou, M.: Definition of the CRMsci An extension of CIDOC-CRM to Support Scientific Observation, Version 1.2.3 (Draft) (2015). http://www.ics.forth.gr/isl/CRMext/CRMsci/docs/CRMsci1.2.3.pdf. Accessed 20 Feb 2017

16. Hunter, J., Odat, S.: Building a semantic knowledge-base for painting conservators. In: IEEE Seventh International Conference on e-Science Workshops (eScienceW), Stockholm, Sweden, 5–8 December 2011, pp. 173–180 (2011)

17. Kouis, D., Kyriaki-Manesi, D., Zervos, S., Giannakopoulos, G., Cheilakou, E., Koui, M.: Intergrading non destructive testing techniques data for cultural heritage monuments to CIDOC CRM. In: The 9th International Symposium on Conservation of Monuments in the Mediterranean Basin (MONUBASIN), Ankara, Turkey, 3–5 June 2014 (2014)

18. Muñoz-Viñas, S.: Contemporary Theory of Conservation. Butterworth-Heinemann, Oxford (2004)

19. The Getty Research Institute. www.getty.edu/research/tools/. Accessed 20 Feb 2017

20. MFA Cameo: Conservation and Art Materials Encyclopaedia (2017). http://cameo.mfa.org/wiki/Main_Page. Accessed 20 Feb 2017

21. Cmap Tools (2006). http://cmap.ihmc.us/. Accessed 20 Feb 2017

22. Protégé 2000 Wiki. http://protegewiki.stanford.edu/wiki/Main_Page. Accessed 20 Feb 2017

23. Niang, C., Marinica, C., Markhoff, B., Leboucher, E., Malavergne, O., Bouiller, L., Darrieumerlou, C., Laissus, F.: Supporting semantic interoperability in conservation-restoration domain: the PARCOURS project. ACM J. Comput. Cult. Herit. (JOCCH) **10**(16), 1–20 (2017)

24. Messaoudi, T., De Luca, O., Véron, P.: Towards an ontology for annotating degradation phenomena. In: Proceedings of Digital Heritage International Congress DH 2015, Espagne, September 2015 (2015)

Ontology-Based Data Collection
for Heritage Buildings

Andrej Tibaut[1](✉) ⓘ, Branko Kaučič[2] ⓘ, and Daniela Dvornik Perhavec[1] ⓘ

[1] Faculty of Civil Engineering, Transportation Engineering and Architecture,
University of Maribor, Maribor, Slovenia
`andrej.tibaut@um.si`
[2] Initut, Institute of Information Technology Ltd., Ljubljana, Slovenia

Abstract. Innovative application and use of a knowledge-based system may support an HB expert to aggregate data into meaningful information that support any of the HB lifecycle activities: initial analysis from experts, documentation, preventive conservation, restoration, reconstruction, economic aspects of HB, its use and management.

This paper first investigates ontology-based knowledge based systems for HB. Secondly, the need for comprehensive ontology-based data collection for HB suitable for trans-disciplinary domain experts and stakeholders is highlighted based on real HB use case requirements. Finally, conceptual knowledge-based framework in development that includes both an ontology for a HB domain and a knowledge base is briefly presented. It is expected that the presented framework could enable proactive reduction of time for searching solutions for HB, reduction of risks involved, reduction of unplanned events related to costs, time, materials and human resources.

1   Introduction

In heritage building (HB, or CH as a cultural heritage) domain, reconstruction, restoration and thematic change (e.g. tourist attraction, museum) occur frequently. Reconstruction and restoration are one of primary processes to preserve the essence of heritage. Thematic change usually reimburses the stakeholder's investments or provide necessary funds for preserving the heritage. These actions are embodied in complex processes for which (a) experts are usually specialized in specific subareas of heritage buildings and (b) their work significantly relies on work and research of others. Therefore, due to huge and complex pool of information about heritage buildings, experts need appropriate knowledge-based system (KBS) to help them. Specific to the nature of experts' work and need for reuse of others work, appropriate organization of information is needed. Appropriate data collection with all needed facts and relationships is needed. The collected data must be analysed and then an appropriate form for conceptualization, structure, organization and management of the collected data must be developed.

© Springer International Publishing AG, part of Springer Nature 2018
M. Ioannides (Ed.): ITN-DCH 2017, LNCS 10605, pp. 63–78, 2018.
https://doi.org/10.1007/978-3-319-75826-8_6

Innovative application and use of a KBS may support an HB expert to aggregate data into meaningful information that support any of the HB life-cycle activities: first expertise analysis, documentation, preventive conservation, restoration, economic aspects of HB, use and management.

For example, an HB expert specialized in bio-deterioration wants to evaluate the state of conservation of a HB and therefore asks whether the KBS "knows" about abiotic and biotic factors, which determine physical and chemical deterioration of stone materials. The expert may also ask if the KBS "knows" how do biotic factors affect durability of stone. Answers to these questions are needed to properly address preventive conservation and restoration strategies. Or, similarly, owner is preparing an elaborate of investments into HB and is considering different scenarios of HB's usage and how intertwining of works will guarantee enough funds for completing all planned tasks. In such case, stakeholder is deeply interested in knowing different approaches and scenarios of other HBs, correlation with those HBs with its own HB. It is researcher's task to investigate how the use of KBS can provide important answers or directions towards optimized solutions.

KBS needs to integrate heterogeneous information sources and domain ontologies to organize information and direct the search processes. To serve the expert's needs existing knowledge must be captured. In a knowledge capturing process an application would typically try to collect data and then identify categories, subcategories and relations to structure and organize the data set. The knowledge capturing process is part of knowledge engineering research where the task of identifying categories, subcategories and their relations is often referred to as constructing an ontology. As defined in literature, an ontology represents knowledge as a set of concepts within a domain, and the relationships between those concepts, which enables the user to make a meaningful search without in-depth knowledge on a specific domain area. Many general-purpose ontologies exist for general search, data collection, knowledge capture and extraction tasks. Such general-purpose ontologies are FOAF ontology, location ontology, person ontology, etc. There is indeed lack of comprehensively constructed ontologies for HB, although some ontologies that consider parts of HB exist (e.g. European project ARIADNE with its CIDOC CRM Reference Model, region-related cultural heritage ontology, building-shape ontology, etc.). Also, ontologies coming from construction domain (e.g. construction defect ontology, e-COGNOS project, etc.) can be considered as related to HB.

1.1 Motivation

In reality, documentation for AECOO projects (i.e. Technical Data Book) is often incomplete, not available or non-existent. Also, information that is exchanged between stakeholders throughout the lifecycle of a construction project does not necessarily have an understood meaning [19]. In such situations, additional steps are needed outside the project's information system to search for specific technical information. But, such additional searches are costly. There is also a cost for not finding information. Although it's impossible to measure the exact cost of employees not finding information on a company's intranet, the Intranet Cost Analyzer [4] gives a ballpark figure of over 17.000 EUR for a company with 50 employees (50 page visits per day per employee, 20 confusion seconds and average employee annual salary of 50.000 EUR). This is huge cost for not finding information.

Early knowledge management (KM) research in construction industry [21] reports about challenges in transition from information to knowledge management such as (a) construction knowledge resides in the minds of the individuals working within the domain, (b) project-related information is relatively dispersed resource (messages, phone calls, memos, etc.) and KM must optimise its use, (c) knowledge recording process must understand what information must be recorded for later project phases, (d) project data must be managed since its creation, (e) lessons learned throughout the project duration must be recorded in details, (f) interpretation of archived projects depends too much on the people involved in the project, (g) many construction organisations have invested heavily in knowledge management [1], but new approaches to knowledge management must not generate new inefficiency because of technology push within and between organisations, (h) users cannot easily find project-related knowledge or do not know what accumulated knowledge is available [14].

Further, knowledge in the AECOO was classified [21] according to the needs of the lifecycle of buildings and infrastructures: domain knowledge, organisational knowledge and project knowledge.

There have been many attempts to create specific ontologies for AECOO domains, such as overall construction ontology [9,19], construction safety [20], or detection of railway objects [11].

The purpose of domain ontology is to support knowledge reuse and sustainability and therefore it is particularly appropriate to implement for HB domain because HBs are much closer to maintenance [12], reuse [3] and sustainability [13,15] than new buildings and infrastructure. There has been attempts to formulate the ontological status [18] of HBs related to conservation practice, which concludes that more heterogeneous understanding (knowledge) of HB objects is required. De Luca et al. [5] proposed a semantic-based platform for multi-field analysis of architectural heritage buildings. Catalogues for HBs as online knowledge bases with semantic representation can be ontology driven websites [2]. Also ontologies for specific HBs have been developed gathering all information in one site by combining different information sources in standardized (i.e. Semantic Wikipedia) but also proprietary form [10].

This paper first investigates ontology-based knowledge based systems for HB. Secondly, the need for comprehensive ontology-based data collection for HB suitable for trans-disciplinary domain experts and stakeholders is highlighted based on real HB use case requirements. Finally, conceptual knowledge-based framework in development that includes both an ontology for a HB domain and a knowledge base is briefly presented. It is expected that the presented framework could enable proactive reduction of time for searching solutions for HB, reduction of risks involved, reduction of unplanned events related to costs, time, materials and human resources.

2   Data Collection for Heritage Buildings Projects

HB reconstruction, renovation and conservation projects (also RRC projects) are different than new buildings projects also because they combine different scientific disciplines. They are generally based on knowledge from historical, cultural, architectural and engineering domains attributed to the historical building. HB demonstrate the original use of old materials, technologies, and contain many information and knowledge.

Generally, a construction project can be described as a determined system, but previous phases affect the next and thus redirect the determined system towards the stochastic one [7]. In every case of stochastic behaviour uncertainties appear, which generally mean that there is no enough previous knowledge available to conclude the task.

2.1   Collecting Data for Heritage Buildings

At the beginning of each RRC project, HB data must be collected to minimise the consequences of uncertainties, which arise during the project. This includes descriptive data about HB, construction materials, techniques and methods of construction. The data can be collected in several ways [6]:

- non-destructive (or destructive) inspection of HB,
- analysis of archived HB projects from historical records,
- digitalization of data from historical records, and
- analysis of legislation (regulations, standards, rules for construction and building materials).

As part of our research following national sources (databases) of HB data were assessed:

- Building Cadastre,
- SIRAnet browser, and
- Web portal eHeritage.si.

The most complete database for buildings and parts of buildings in Slovenia represents the Building Cadastre maintained by the Survey and Mapping Authority of the Republic of Slovenia. From the database following data can be collected: location coordinates, cadastral municipality, description of construction, construction year, reconstruction year, corresponding infrastructure and other facilities (elevator, etc.).

In Slovenia, data about HB are managed by the Ministry of Culture of the Republic of Slovenia. The cadastre contains 28048 units (cities, villages, squares, centres, settlements, etc.).

The SIRAnet browser is maintained by The Regional Archives Maribor. Using the SIRAnet it is possible to search for historical records data from all regional archives in Slovenia. Result sets include building plans and other descriptive data.

A web-based database eHeritage.si contains digital cultural heritage from Slovenia including maps, pictures and descriptions. Figure 1 shows the use case for the Baroness House [8] from the database.

Fig. 1. Baroness' House archived in the eHeritage.si

2.2 Use Case: Baroness' House

For the purpose of our research a HB named Baroness' [16] House located in the Maribor city center was chosen (Fig. 2).

The Baroness' House is one of the most beautiful and best preserved Secession buildings in Maribor. It is one of the over seventy buildings in Maribor built by Architect Fritz Friedriger who graduated from the Vienna Academy of Architecture. In Maribor, he settled in around 1894. First, he collaborated with architect Robert Schmidt. In 1910, he founded a new company in partnership with his younger colleague, Max Czeike. After the First World War, he decided to move to Graz (Austria) in 1920, where he soon died. His clients were middle class citizens, for example, F. Havliček, S. Gruber, A. Sedlatchek, A. Badl and Baroness Mixich Rast.

The House is declared (the Decree on Cultural and Historic Monuments in the Municipality of Maribor (MUV, No.5/1992)), as an important artistic and architectural monument. It was entered in the Registry of Slovenian Cultural Heritage under the number 6174.

The Baroness' House, with its southern façade, provides direct support for the G2 building of the University of Maribor Faculty of Electrical Engineering and Computer Science built in 2004 and as such demonstrates coexistence of heritage and modern architecture. In the past, the house has been deteriorating since the seventies, the plaster gradually came off, and the ornaments and builders' carpentry and joinery deteriorated due to a lack of maintenance but the most of architectural elements are original (floor mosaics, facades elements, flowers, masks, stairs, etc.).

Fig. 2. Baroness' House: after reconstruction in 2015, front view (Photo courtesy of Bogdan Dugonik)

Residents of the house made arbitrary and unsuitable alterations - almost all original windows on the front façade were replaced, and some of the openings that were intended for windows were transformed into doors (Fig. 3).

Conservation Project. The Baroness' House was poorly maintained. Conservation project started in 2006 and finished with Baroness' House revitalization in 2015. Conservation strategy was to preserve the building and establish the monument's primary visual and material manifestation - elements of the exterior and interior.

It was necessary to asses, restore and maintain the following attributes of the building:

- dimensions (size),
- roof inclination,
- type of roofing - brick covering,
- all profiling and decorations on façade, which is a combination of ceramic renders and bands,
- original building furniture - windows and doors in the interior and exterior (including hooks) - primarily, new should be a precise copy of the existing ones (both in material, division, profiling, design, and colour); secondarily, replaced by appropriate and in accordance with the models of existing ones,
- basic ground plan (restoring of the original state, demolition of unsuitable and secondary walls),

Fig. 3. Alterations made by residents (Photos courtesy of Bogdan Dugonik)

- all elements with more complex forged details (fences, grids) and other original forged details, and
- the original flooring (parquet, natural stone, etc.) - in the case of new paving it was necessary to use natural materials.

Time from 2006 (start the project) to 2011 (start to prepare reconstruction design planes) was intended for analysis of the building and preparation of reports.

Following the requirements, most of the original material were used. The brick elements were cleaned under high-pressure air and used to replace original design (Fig. 4).

Fig. 4. Baroness' House: reconstruction of brick elements (Photos courtesy of Daniela Dvornik Perhavec)

The stairs made of grey stony concrete were well preserved. They were only cleaned, and remediated in certain places. The staircase fence was metallic, with a typical secessionist lining, which was preserved in the original form where possible, the rest was restored, cleaned and protected (metal parts and wooden holders), and the missing parts were replaced by appropriate copies (castings).

The floor in the lid was covered with terrazzo, trimmed with dark grey and thin red stripes. Terrazzo floor in the entire building was preserved, except where the damage was substantial. All damaged sculptural details were replaced. Missing façade ceramics was supplemented by the original model (Fig. 5).

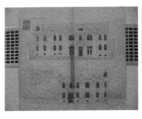

Fig. 5. Original façade plan (left), original picture from 1966 (middle) and façade before reconstruction (right) (Provincial Archive Maribor)

The wooden roofing was replaced by a steel construction covered by bricks. The plastering on all facades was removed, and builder's was replaced.

All works were carried out with the constant supervision of the construction engineer, geomechanics engineer, humidity technologist and other experts.

The main goal of the reconstruction project in 2015 was to preserve the building and establish the monument's primary visual and material manifestation - both partially (elements of the exterior and interior) and in its entirety. The reconstruction works precisely replicated the floor plan of the former bourgeois building with large adjoining rooms and anterooms bordering a shared hallway on the courtyard side. One of the most important goals was also to modernize the building in accordance with current standards and its new purpose: the facilitation of scientific research and educational activities of the Faculty of Electrical Engineering and Computer Science. The house has turned into a public building, which means that seismic safety is one of the most important aspect of reconstruction. In this aim the reinforced concrete slabs had been laid at the floor level and connected with the façade and internal load-bearing walls via anchorages (Fig. 6). New elements required for new purpose have been added, especially the glass atrium with the gallery in the courtyard area. Due to the new intended purpose, the load-bearing capacity increased by $100 \, \text{kg/m}^2$.

Reconstruction Project. Galleries and terraces above the open courtyard constitute new construction elements in the Baroness' House. Steel construction replaced the wooden roofing, the plastering on all façades removed, and builders' carpentry and joinery replaced. In the interior, all deteriorated ceiling parts replaced with reinforced concrete form. Despite these alterations, all important elements of the monument were preserved and some of them were even highlighted.

The entire façade profile and ornaments were restored and builder's carpentry and joinery replicated except for the portal on the western façade. The original

Fig. 6. Baroness' House: construction site (Photo courtesy of by Bogdan Dugonik)

window and door openings were restored, and the roof was covered with tiles and tin. In the interior, the stairs railings and the terrazzo tiled hallways and staircase were restored. All interior doors were preserved, restored or replicated (Fig. 7).

The reconstruction required the close cooperation of the owner, the architect, contractor as well as conservation and restoration experts.

During the reconstruction new steel constructions were built-in:

- steel roof construction,
- construction of the glazing of the terrace,
- construction of platform and bridge - rafts in the ground level,
- construction of platform and bridge - stairs in the level of the floor (connected with the structure of the glazing of the terrace), and
- sub-construction of elevator and glazing of elevator shaft.

3 Knowledge Based Systems for Collecting Data About HB

New and innovative semantic applications (i.e. Semantic MediaWiki) can utilize knowledge-bases with the advanced searching and querying mechanisms provided by SPARQL. One such SPARQL example is to query knowledge-base for historical buildings where specific type and dimension of brick was used for walls. Since masonry brick is found on nearly every continental historic building, the query

Fig. 7. Baroness' House, 2015: night view after reconstruction (Photos courtesy of Bogdan Dugonik)

results can be used during a restoration project to learn from another previously completed restoration projects.

In addition to that, semantic applications can also employ reasoning mechanisms to infer logical consequences from asserted facts in knowledge-base. Semantic reasoning is an advancement to what was previously referred to as case-based reasoning approach. For semantic reasoning a knowledge base composed of ontology (or many interlinked ontologies) and semantic rules is needed.

In consequence, proper knowledge engineering in construction projects related to HB results in KBS acting as a consultation system, which supports more effective management of HB projects.

3.1 Conceptual Knowledge Base Framework

Conceptual knowledge-based framework (KBF) consists of two parts, a process "HB data capturing" and an architecture "Knowledge based system" which are interconnected with the ontology (Fig. 8). Main objective of iterative "HB data capturing" process is to produce "final" ontology representing HBs and HB related processes and activities. As presented in Sect. 2, "HB documentation" exist in various formats and levels of digitalization, e.g. paper documents, voice recordings, video materials, images, database records, etc. forming data collections. HBs as main objects of interest are not necessarily entirely treated in sense of documentation and still represent valuable source of new information that can be organized and documented. The HB documentation is usually prepared and/or used by various HB experts (e.g. from fields of reconstruction, renovation, conservations, bio-deterioration, etc.) and stakeholders. In general stakeholders have some influence or relation toward HB and vice-versa (individuals, groups and organizations, e.g. owners of heritage buildings or lands, private funders, finance institutions, legislation institutions, data providers, HB service providers, and other various HB related stakeholders).

In process of producing "final" ontology, not all the work need to be done from the scratch. Usually ontology experts search for related ontologies and include them into final result "HB ontology+". Some ontologies can be directly connected to HB, some can be indirectly (e.g. ontology about building materials, which is useful for all types of buildings and therefore also HBs), and some serve as supporting or core ontologies for representation of core elements (e.g. time, location, person, etc.). In addition, some ontologies are appropriate entirely, some only partly, some need some changes or improvements, or some are inappropriate. All participating ontologies contribute to "final" ontology.

When a version of "final" ontology is produced in current process iteration, that ontology is usually revised by experts and interested stakeholders. Based on the review feedback a new iteration of the process might start. For example, experts may identify missing chunk of information, some HB related service provider will provide that information (e.g. by analyzing HB and preparing documentation) and new information and knowledge will result in new "final" ontology. Several methodologies for preparation of ontologies exist to produce best possible ontologies with minimal iterations. The same process is also used when new requests or demands about some HB process or activity are identified. Continuously improving ontology according to new tacit and explicit knowledge corresponds to well-known knowledge spiral.

Regardless of the process's iteration number, "final" HB ontology is the most appropriate ontology that is then used in architectural part on Fig. 8. Architectural part provides system intended for use by end-users. It consists of three main parts: knowledge base engine, service engine and interface engine.

Knowledge base engine consists of knowledge base, which is triple store (subject-predicate-object) containing all gathered knowledge objects about HBs according to the schema induced by one or several ontologies from the HB data capturing process. In addition, it consists of core functionality for accessing and manipulating triple-store data.

Different interfaces can exists for different end-users and areas of usage. All requests for retrieval or manipulation of HB information are channeled through interface engine. Interface engine can directly use knowledge base engine for retrieval and manipulation of data, or can use service engine for more complex usage. Similar to different interfaces, service engine also can consist of different services for different usage. Core part of service engine is also reasoner for advanced usage of knowledge based HB data (e.g. using rules, fuzzy conditions, etc.).

Lastly, according to the "final" ontology and actual implementation of knowledge base engine, not all existing HB knowledge data may exist in this knowledge base system. Related knowledge data may exists in one or several other KBs, and therefore knowledge base engine is able to communicate and exchange knowledge with these KBs.

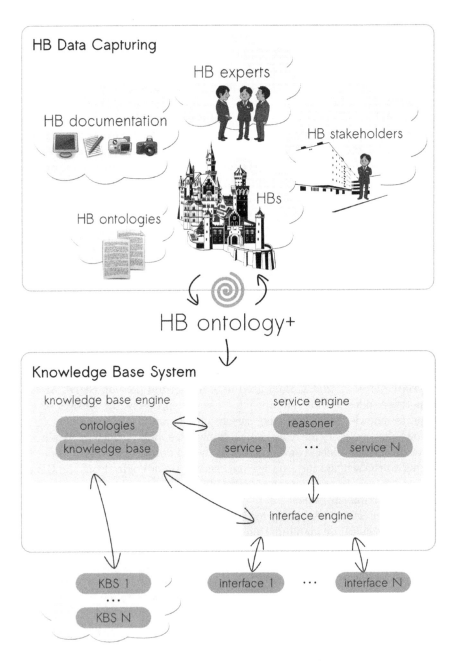

Fig. 8. Knowledge-based framework

3.2   Ontology

Ontology represents knowledge as a set of concepts within a domain, and the inter-relationships between those concepts, which enables the user to make a meaningful search without in-depth knowledge on a specific domain area [17].

Our ontology research was initially focused to documentation about building materials, specifically concrete, used during the reconstruction project for the Baroness' House. Figure 9 (left) shows an ontology with 49 concepts, 15 object properties and 15 data properties (Fig. 9, right) which was prototypically designed. The ontology was implemented in Protégé. The ontology also contains SWLR rules that infer fine aggregates, coarse aggregates, Mortar, MediumSand, CoarseSand, FineSand, Pebble, Pebble, Cobble. Some of the rules are defined in Table 1.

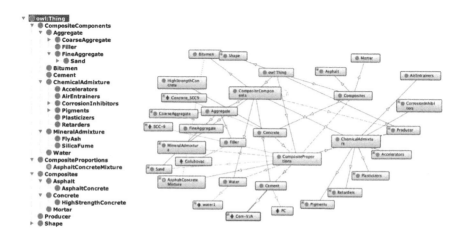

Fig. 9. Hierarchy of concepts (left) and their relations (right) for concrete ontology

Table 1. Rules for concrete production ontology

Rule for	SWLR rule
Coarse aggregate	Aggregate(?a1), hasSize(?a1, ?dm), greaterThan(?dm, 4.0) ->CoarseAggregate(?a1)
Fine Aggregate	Aggregate(?a1), hasSize(?a1, ?dm), greaterThan(?dm, 0.063), lessThan(?dm, 4.0) -> FineAggregate(?a1)
Mortar	hasConcreteMixProportions(?c, ?x)ˆConcrete(?c)ˆ hasSize(?a, ?sz)ˆlessThan(?sz, "4.0" ˆˆxsd:double)ˆ hasAggregate(?x, ?a) -> Mortar(?c)
Fine sand	Sand(?sd), hasSize(?sd, ?sz), greaterThanOrEqual(?sz, 0.063), lessThanOrEqual(?sz, 0.2) -> FineSand(?sd)

The concrete ontology is an open and therefore scalable repository of knowledge, which serves as a basis for development of further semantic applications for HB domain.

4 Conclusions

In the paper, we reviewed research and application of ontology-based data collection in the context of HB. Further, we presented a concept of knowledge-based framework that supports the process of incremental construction of ontology based on different domain sources.

A typical example that explains the use case for KBS in HB has happened on construction site where workers were in charge to connect new reinforcement to existing cured concrete using specific (Hilti) injection adhesives in drilled holes as designed by structural engineer (post-installed rebar connections). The workers replaced the planned system with (cheaper) alternative adhesive. At that moment, depth of the drilled hole had to be checked against the requirements of the alternative adhesive material. This is an unpredictable event and the information about the required depth of the hole for the rebar was not available. The goal is to transform such unpredictable events into predictable ones.

During reconstruction and maintenance of buildings we need to collect information about building in faster and easier way.

There is only little research literature published as intersection of ontologies and HB. One of the reasons for this is that, generally, application of ontologies to HB is out-of-scope for AEC researchers while IT researchers are more interested in basic IT research than applicative research. Luckily, construction informatics has growing interest in knowledge engineering in AECOO where the domain of HB belongs to.

It is our aim to continue with the research and development of the knowledge-based framework where collection of HB data can be automated thru linked data approach, i.e. ontology that can link complementary remote knowledge bases specializing in specific HB domains beyond building materials.

Future research will include integration of different complementary ontologies from the AECOO domain.

Acknowledgement. The paper is a work in progress in scope of the project COST TD1406 - Innovation in Intelligent Management of Heritage Buildings. Authors are grateful for the photos courtesy of dr. Bogdan Dugonik.

References

1. Ahmad, H., An, M., Gaterell, M.: KM model to embed knowledge management activities into work activities in construction organisations. In: Dainty, A. (ed.) Proceedings 24th Annual ARCOM Conference, 1–3 September 2008, Cardiff, pp. 309–318. Association of Researchers in Construction Management, UK (2008)
2. Andaroodi, E., Kitamoto, A.: Architectural heritage online: ontology-driven website generation for world heritage sites in danger. In: Ioannides, M., Fellner, D., Georgopoulos, A., Hadjimitsis, D.G. (eds.) EuroMed 2010. LNCS, vol. 6436, pp. 277–290. Springer, Heidelberg (2010). https://doi.org/10.1007/978-3-642-16873-4_21
3. Bullen, P.A., Love, P.E.D.: Adaptive reuse of heritage buildings. Struct. Surv. **29**, 411–421 (2011). https://doi.org/10.1108/02630801111182439
4. Dack.com: The excellent intranet cost analyzer. http://www.dack.com/web/cost_analyzer.html. Accessed 15 Sept 2017
5. De Luca, L., Busayarat, C., Stefani, C., Veron, P., Florenzano, M.: A semantic-based platform for the digital analysis of architectural heritage. Comput. Graph. **35**, 227–241 (2011)
6. Dvornik Perhavec, D.: Databases and data warehouses in a systemic approach for historical building reconstruction projects. In: Proceedings of the 12th International Conference on Computational Structures Technology. Civil-Comp Proceedings, 2–5 September 2014, Naples, Italy, vol. 106, pp. 1–11 (2014). ISSN 1759–3433
7. Dvornik Perhavec, D., Rebolj, D., Šuman, N.: Systematic approach for sustainable conservation. J. Cult. Herit. **16**, 81–87 (2015). https://doi.org/10.1016/j.culher.2014.01.004
8. eHeritage.si: Baroness House - Digital Cultural Heritage. http://www.eheritage.si/apl/real.aspx?ID=6174&IDC=6162&zoom=18&lat=5870424.65788&lon=1740576.458&layers. Accessed 15 Sept 2017
9. El-Diraby, T.: Domain ontology for construction knowledge. J. Constr. Eng. Manag. **139**, 768–784 (2012). https://doi.org/10.1061/(ASCE)CO.1943-7862.0000646
10. Hernández, F., Rodrigo, L., Contreras, J., Carbone, F.: Building a cultural heritage ontology for Cantabria. In: 2008 Annual Conference of CIDOC Athens, 15–18 September 2008
11. Hmida, H.B., Cruz, C., Boochs, F., Nicolle, C.: From 3D point clouds to semantic objects - an ontology-based detection approach. In: Proceedings of the International Conference on Knowledge Engineering and Ontology Development, pp. 255–260 (2011). https://doi.org/10.5220/0003660002550260
12. Idrus, A., Khamidi, F., Sodangi, M.: Maintenance management framework for conservation of heritage buildings in Malaysia. Mod. Appl. Sci. (2010). https://doi.org/10.5539/mas.v4n11p66
13. Khodeir, L.M., Aly, D., Tarek, S.: Integrating HBIM (Heritage Building Information Modeling) tools in the application of sustainable retrofitting of heritage buildings in Egypt. Procedia Environ. Sci. **34**, 258–270 (2016). https://doi.org/10.1016/j.proenv.2016.04.024
14. Lin, Y.C., Wang, L.C., Tserng, H.P.: Enhancing knowledge exchange through web map-based knowledge management system in construction: lessons learned in Taiwan. Autom. Constr. **15**, 693–705 (2006). https://doi.org/10.1016/j.autcon.2005.09.006

15. Liusman, E., Ho, D.C.W., Ge, J.X.: Indicators for heritage buildings sustainability. In: CESB 2013 PRAGUE - Central Europe Towards Sustainable Building 2013: Sustainable Building and Refurbishment for Next Generations, pp. 1–4 (2013)
16. Misic, D., Nahtigal, N., Kocutar, S., et al.: Baroničina hiša = Baroness' house: 1902–2015. University of Maribor, Faculty of Electrical Engineering and Computer Science, Maribor (2015)
17. Park, C.-S., Lee, D.-Y., Kwon, O.-S., Wang, X.: A framework for proactive construction defect management using BIM, augmented reality and ontology-based data collection template. Autom. Const. **33**, 61–71 (2013). https://doi.org/10.1016/j.autcon.2012.09.010
18. Tait, M., While, A.: Ontology and the conservation of built heritage. Environ. Plan. D Soc. Space **27**, 721–737 (2009). https://doi.org/10.1068/d11008
19. Tibaut, A., Jakoša, D.: Development of knowledge model for construction projects. In: Uden, L., Heričko, M., Ting, I.-H. (eds.) KMO 2015. LNBIP, vol. 224, pp. 248–259. Springer, Cham (2015). https://doi.org/10.1007/978-3-319-21009-4_19
20. Zhang, S., Boukamp, F., Teizer, J.: Ontology-based semantic modeling of construction safety knowledge: towards automated safety planning for job hazard analysis (JHA). Autom. Constr. **52**, 29–41 (2015). https://doi.org/10.1016/j.autcon.2015.02.005
21. Wetherill, M., Rezgui, Y., Lima, C., Zarli, A.: Knowledge management for the construction industry: the e-COGNOS project. J. Inf. Technol. Const. (ITCon) **7**, 183–196 (2002)

Linked Open Data as Universal Markers for Mobile Augmented Reality Applications in Cultural Heritage

John Aliprantis[✉], Eirini Kalatha, Markos Konstantakis, Kostas Michalakis, and George Caridakis

University of the Aegean, 81100 Mytilene, Greece
{jalip,ekalatha,mkonstadakis,kmichalakis,gcari}@aegean.gr

Abstract. Many projects have already analyzed the current limitations and challenges on the integration of the Linked Open Data (LOD) cloud in mobile augmented reality (MAR) applications for cultural heritage, and underline the future directions and capabilities. The majority of the above works relies on the detected geo-location of the user or his device by various sensors (GPS – global positioning system, accelerometer, camera, etc.) or geo-based linked data, while others use marker-based techniques to link various locations with labels and descriptions of specific geodata. But when it comes to indoor environments (museums, libraries) where tracking the accurate user's position and orientation is challenging due to the lack of GPS valid sensor data, complex and costly technological systems need to be implemented for identifying user's OoI (Object of Interest). This paper describes a concept which is based on image identification and matching between frames from the user's camera and stored images from the Europeana platform, that can link the LOD cloud from cultural institutes around Europe and mobile augmented reality applications in cultural heritage without the need of the accurate user's location, and discusses the challenges and future directions of this approach.

Keywords: Linked Open Data · Augmented reality · Cultural heritage
Image matching · Mobile applications

1 Introduction

Today, cultural heritage institutions like libraries, archives and museums (LAMs) are eager to find new ways to attract and educate new visitors, while also preserving and promoting their cultural heritage. Therefore, they are turning to solutions like ubiquitous mobile applications and augmented reality techniques in order to enhance user's perception, deliver a more complete touristic experience and promote interaction among users or between user and cultural artifact.

However, the augmented reality applications in culture have also their limitations and drawbacks, as their consistent use from users have made them quite familiar and acceptable, raising more and more the expectations and requirements for new interactive and visual discovery methods. Current applications are characterized rather static and

© Springer International Publishing AG, part of Springer Nature 2018
M. Ioannides (Ed.): ITN-DCH 2017, LNCS 10605, pp. 79–90, 2018.
https://doi.org/10.1007/978-3-319-75826-8_7

cannot be updated easily, due to the nature of the data that they process and display. Many of them use closed databases of information that are built and accessed only by a single application, while others depend on open but single databases disconnected from others, called channel (like Wikipedia). Nowadays, this is perceived as a limitation and drawback from users, as they demand access to more personalized, dynamic and adaptive information, in order to satisfy their personal interests and desires [1].

A possible solution to this issue is the usage of dynamic databases like the Linked Open Data (LOD) Cloud, which uses the infrastructure of the World Wide Web to publish and link datasets that can then be examined and processed by applications accessing to them, while also these datasets are continuously updated and linked with new assets [2]. Linked Data [3] is one of the most practical parts of the Semantic Web [4], as it is a model for representing and accessing data that are flexible enough to allow adding or changing sources of data, to link with other databases and data and to process the information according to its meaning. As a structured data model, linked data is also readable and editable by search engines and software agents, thus increasing importance for data interchange and integration. Despite that, the integration of LOD databases into augmented reality applications is not impeccable, as developers have to address other issues which mostly are derived from its open world consumption, leading to trust issues and data quality assessment [1].

In recent years, many cultural institutes have converted their cultural heritage information that was previously only used for internal purposes, to linked data in distinctive datasets which are linked to the LOD cloud, usually with the aid of web aggregators such as Europeana. In this way, structured data can benefit both the institution and the larger community by expanding the semantic web and establishing an institution as a trusted source of high quality data, while also giving the opportunity to develop new interfaces for users to experience cultural heritage, like the mobile augmented reality applications [5]. Mobile tourist guides, enriched storytelling and digital representation of cultural heritage monuments are only few of the many applications that have been developed in order to enhance user experience during their cultural interaction, combining successfully the augmented reality techniques with the large and open linked data resources. Nevertheless, the majority of these applications are strongly dependent on the geo-location of the user or geo-tagged data, as their function rely on identifying points of interest (PoIs) in user's field of view and adjust the context-sensitive information to be displayed in screen from geo-based linked data [2, 6].

Current research aims in proposing a prototype that uses linked cultural data from cultural institutions (museums, libraries, art galleries) in Europe which are stored in specific structured data standards (Resource Description Framework - RDF) and are freely available to the public for further processing (open data). Its main focus is cultural artifacts that are stored in indoor unprepared environments and thus user tracking is almost impossible. One of the main objectives of this research is the implementation and optimization of the image identification algorithm for mobile devices. Several works present various techniques to identify the field of view (FOV) of the user by matching frames from his camera to already existed databases of images [7], while others use point cloud databases to match images with 3D models (2D to 3D matching) [8]. In the proposed prototype, geographical information of the user's device (GPS sensor) is only used to narrow the number of the possible databases to be searched, by considering the latest value of the sensor and a certain range around it, thus improving efficiency and accuracy. This procedure however, not only decreases the computation time of the search algorithm, but also determines the ontologies to be matched by identifying the subject of the nearby cultural institutions. Then, the software queries the server requesting images of cultural objects located in this area (using SPARQL language), and if the image matching to the camera's frames is successful, the object that the user has in his field of vision is identified and the appropriate description and metadata from the LOD database (Europeana aggregator) are shown. A key attribute of the above prototype is the use of the Europeana API (Application Programming Interface) which allows developers to use these cultural data and implement applications for cultural heritage.

The paper is organized as follows. In Sect. 2, we present the current projects in culture that integrate linked data in augmented reality applications, whose basic characteristic is the location – based approach on the display of their content. Section 3 analyzes the positives of the LOD – AR integration and describes the issues that must be addressed. In Sect. 4, we illustrate the proposed concept and define the current issues in the LOD – AR integration that it addresses and the challenges that we have to overcome. Finally in Sect. 5, we discuss our future work based on this approach.

2   Related Works

The integration of Linked Open Data sources into augmented reality applications has emerged as an effective solution for static datasets of mobile applications, with many projects having already built several prototypes. Vert and Vasiu [1] developed a prototype that integrates user – generated linked open data and open government data in a mobile augmented reality tourist guide in Timisoara, Romania. In this model, the identification is accomplished with the aid of GPS sensors from user's devices, and PoIs stored in linked open data bases like DBpedia and LinkedGeoData that are verified with Google Fusion Tables.

ARCAMA-3D [2] is a mobile platform that overlays the surroundings of the user with 3d representation that highlights the objects of interest (OoIs), allowing users to interact with them and seeking more information through the Linked Open Data cloud. This platform is also strongly depended on geo-location data and embedded sensors like GPS and accelerometer in order to align the 3d content with the physical environment, using also methods like the Kalman filter [9]. Furthermore, its data is context-sensitive as it highlights the buildings with different colors if they contain interesting information for the user with respect to his interests.

Van Aart et al. [6] envision a mobile tourist guide application which will be able to dynamically combine information, navigation and entertainment. In this way, they propose the implementation of a mobile application which constructs dynamic walking tours in Amsterdam based on user's interests and geo-location of PoIs nearby, whose data are stored in linked datasets like DBpedia and LinkedGeoData. The proposed algorithm is quite efficient in outdoor environments, even if it has to deal with the significant discrepancies that exist between coordinates for the same location, but its accuracy might not be sufficient when it comes to an indoor augmented reality application.

Hegde et al. [10] argue about the importance of linked data and how can they enrich PoIs in order to enhance browsing experience in augmented reality applications. They claim that PoIs cannot give information by themselves and as far as there are no links to additional information through the common augmented reality applications, the offering experience may not satisfy the demanding users. Linking semantically additional content to enrich PoIs enables users to discover more information based on their interests.

In conclusion, the above research projects show the potential of using the Linked Open Data cloud as the main source dataset for a mobile application where the information access is based on the geo-location of the user. However, there is no sufficient research on mobile applications based on indoor environments such as museums and libraries, where the integration of LOD is not straightforward, as user's location and orientation regarding the artifacts is much more difficult to be tracked, especially in a non pre-prepared environment.

3   LOD – AR Integration: Benefits and Issues

As Vert and Vasiu [11] claim in their work about the LOD – AR integration, not only augmented reality applications benefit from the Linked Open Data cloud but the vice versa is equally important. As already mentioned, integrating linked open data in mobile applications has certain benefits, most of them related to the static and closed classical databases that are used widely in augmented reality applications, but on the other side, the LOD cloud can also profit from the raising amount of content created by the MAR applications that can be linked to it, increasing its diversity and size, which in turn favors the Linked Data application developers.

In recent years, augmented reality applications are in enduring popularity and widely accepted by users but this seems to reach its boundaries as there are some issues which need to be addressed directly. This is also due to the fact that state-of-the-art Augmented Reality browsers like Layar, Wikitude, Junaio and Tagwhat are based on the current version of the web (Web 2.0) which however is to be replaced by the Semantic Web (or Web of data, Web 3.0) [4], the new web version that changes the way we conceive and interact with web data, and therefore it affects the functioning of these AR browsers.

Reynolds et al. [12] argue about the limitations of current MAR applications with regards to the present web version, and conclude that there are 3 major issues of the architectures of existing augmented reality applications, as follows:

- **Selection and integration of data sources.** As we mentioned before, current MAR applications are based on static and closed databases. As a result, any update in application's dataset has to be done manually which is a rather demanding or sometimes impossible task, taking into account the massive information that many applications may contain. Furthermore, there is little or no interaction between individual databases as usually they are exclusively designed and constructed for the need of particular applications. That means there are no linked datasets (for example there are no hyperlinks or symbolic relationships between different but associated data) and developers have to create a new data set if they want to combine the purposes of two or more applications.

- **Utilization of contextual information.** The increasing amount of information that MAR applications can handle and display nowadays can satisfy even the most demanding users. Meanwhile, a mobile device such as smartphone or tablet, has a small screen that usually cannot display all the necessary information, or even worse may cause users to feel overwhelmed by the amount of data that appears on their screen. In recent years though, new mobile devices are equipped with a range of sensors like GPS and accelerometer, which facilitate the use of contextual information. Augmented reality applications can use the information taken from these sensors to estimate recent activity and tendency from users, in order to specify the desired data that users can require, thus minimize the possibility of displaying irrelevant or redundant information.
- **Browsing experience.** Web browsers link pages of data through hyperlinks, hence allowing users to navigate and explore new content based on their interests. Augmented reality browsers and applications don't support such functionality as their content doesn't include any links to data outside their data sets. As a consequence, current AR applications provide a rather fixed experience regarding to the information that they can display.

Linked Open Data principles are well-suited for addressing the above issues that hinder the ongoing progress of MAR applications. Until today (August 2017), the LOD cloud includes more than 1100 datasets from various fields such as social networking, science and government data, which are linked with each other [13]. Furthermore, it contains plenty of geo-location data entries, such as those found in data sets like GeoNames and LinkedGeoData, which not only provide the coordinates of many locations but also facts and events that characterize them. Meanwhile, many of the included datasets are linked to the DBpedia which stores general information for very common concepts in structured form, and been extracted by the data created in Wikipedia.

Integrating linked data in MAR applications can enhance augmented reality by addressing the three issues mentioned above. With the linked databases that are also open for update from developers and users, augmented reality applications are no longer static as data can be dynamically selected and processed theoretically from the entire LOD cloud. Furthermore, linked data can better exploit the sensor data from user's devices by specifying more efficiently the query for the desired data, thus enabling the utilization of contextual data. Also, due to the functioning of the linked open data items, augmented reality applications can display additional data inside the view of the application, without requiring the user to close the application and open a new one like a mobile browser, which aims towards enhancing the user's browsing experience [11].

Equally, LOD cloud is also benefited by its integration with augmented reality. The increasing amount of information that AR applications produce and handle, such as 3D models, can be linked to the LOD cloud, and help it grow in size and diversity, something that can be capitalized on by both developers and other users or linked datasets. Furthermore, linked data applications lack in user – friendly interfaces, as they have to display structured data in complex RDF triples, thus augmented reality applications can intervene as an already known interface which allow users to interact with linked data in a way that they are already familiar and in favor of.

Even though this integration has many benefits, there are some further issues that need to be taken into consideration. First of all, the size of the LOD cloud may be an advantage but it has to be used wisely, especially when it comes to mobile devices like smartphones with small screen, as there is a massive amount of data that can be displayed, which may upset or confuse the user. Filtering displaying data regarding the context and user's interests can be an effective countermeasure. Also, the fact that linked data are mostly open data that everyone can update or even add and link their own, raises trust, quality and privacy issues that developers must deal with.

Furthermore, queries of linked data are handled by powerful technologies such as RDF and SPARQL that also are complex and time consuming processes. As a result, they may slow down the functioning of a mobile augmented reality application or even worse, introduce incomparable barriers on its design and its normal features. Finally, not every linked data set has the same vocabulary and ontology, something that leads to matching issues, while data may be duplicated, with wrong coordinates or overlapped in different datasets, so developers have to implement more sophisticated queries and algorithms [12, 14].

In conclusion, linked open data seems to be an effective solution to enhance the emergence of augmented reality applications, due to its quantity of interlinked information, and also its dynamic selection and integration of data, while it can benefit from the data produced by AR applications that can be linked to it. Furthermore, this integration answers to the expectation of users nowadays to be able to use dynamic, adaptive and personalized technology applications that help them explore and interact with their content efficiently.

4   Proposed Concept Overview

Current work aims in proposing a new way of integrating linked data in mobile augmented reality applications that guide visitors in a cultural institution. One of its basic features is that it refers to indoor environment or locations where accurate values of GPS sensors are nearly impossible. We already mentioned that many of the current projects in the LOD – AR field are depended on the tracking of user's precise location, in order to query the appropriate geo-location data that will be displayed. That is major constraint if we consider that many cultural institutions such as museums and libraries are closed buildings where it is very difficult to track and link user's position with a internal PoI. Furthermore, there may not be concrete geo-data for every cultural artifact inside a building so it is tricky to specify with which object the user is interested. in order to fetch the correct data from the LOD cloud.

So, how can we track user's location and orientation inside a building effectively and recognize the PoI that user probable refers to? Many projects that incorporate augmented reality techniques in indoor environments and therefore track user's location amongst the cultural exhibits require the technical preparation and transformation of the area, with installation of specialized devices. Wireless technologies and indoor GPS, cooperating with the state-of-the-art smartphones with many sensors, are quite accurate methods but are rather costly and complex to be widely implemented [15, 16].

RFID (Radio – Frequency Identification) and BLE (Bluetooth Low Energy) technologies can be also effective and viable solutions but there are also certain technological and practical aspects that need to be addressed [17, 18]. Furthermore, QR codes and image tracking are the most low cost and simple methods but they require additional actions from users, which may be frustrating [19]. Finally, modern mobile devices have the capability to use their powerful camera and processing power in order to perform large-scale indoor 3D scene reconstruction based on cloud images and sensor data [20]. These techniques track effectively user's location in indoor environments but they have all in common one vital disadvantage, which is the need of a pre-prepared environment with complex and sometimes costly technological systems.

In our proposed concept we are going to implement an indoor tracking method based on image recognition and identification between frames retrieved from mobile device's camera and linked open data sets. The basic concept is that accurate user's tracking inside a room is not necessary once we identify which artifact user is currently examining through his camera. Taking advantage of the images that are usually associated with a cultural artifact in the LOD cloud, we can compare the frames taken by the camera with the appropriate image data set from the cloud. Upon successful identification, the system queries the rest of the information about the tracked object, and also its links from the linked data, and finally the user although being in an indoor environment has access to the LOD cloud through the PoI in front of him.

4.1 Architecture Description

The architecture of the proposed concept involves four key components: the LOD cloud, the augmented reality interface, user's mobile device and finally the cloud database of the application. The data flow and function sequence are pictured on the above figure (Fig. 1).

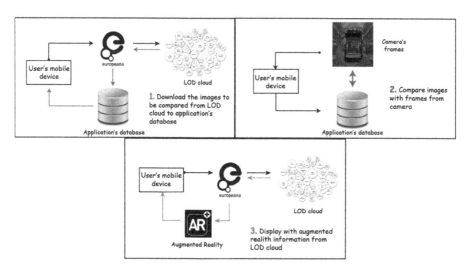

Fig. 1. The proposed architecture of the concept

In the first level of the architecture, the user's mobile device connects with the LOD cloud in order to query for cultural artifact images that are located in institutions near user's location. This procedure will be accomplished with the aid of linked data online portals such as Europeana aggregator, which allows free access to many European cultural databases. The selected images are stored in the application's cloud database where they are converted to the appropriate format with characteristic points, so afterwards they can be compared with the camera's frames.

After the application's database is formed, the second level involves the cooperation of mobile device's camera and application's database in order to identify the PoI that the user is currently looking at. To achieve this, specialized algorithms that detect same patterns in images must be implemented, taking into account various conditions that may alter current images of artifacts regarding to the images stored to the LOD cloud.

Finally, after the PoI has been identified, the user's device queries the LOD current database for more information about the cultural artifact and its links, and displays them in the user's screen with augmented reality techniques. The user then can interact with the information shown as digital content to the screen and navigate to the LOD cloud according to his interests.

4.2 Use Case Scenario

The proposed framework includes five major steps to be implemented, depicted in Fig. 2. It requires mobile user devices like smartphones and tablets, and can be functional only at cultural institutions that have shared their cultural heritage as linked open data in the LOD cloud, hence making it available to the public through online aggregators. Once user is inside the building and starts the application on his mobile device, the proposed framework follows the next steps:

1. The software retraces the last known GPS sensor value that indicates the city or region that the user is currently exploring. Since GPS is not available inside a building, we cannot track the user's location but we can still narrow the possible cultural institutes that the user may visit. That helps us minimize the linked data sets that need to be queried about the forthcoming image frames. In the best scenario, we can assume the exact building the user may currently be in, so we can have all the appropriate images from the equivalent cultural heritage of the institution, but on the worst case, we still can extract the city that user is visiting and the available linked data sets in this area, but it will surely affect the computation time of the matching images function later on.
2. After the identification of the cultural institutes that are nearby the user and maintain their heritage as structured data in the LOD cloud, the framework queries about images that represent their artifacts, and the result of the query is stored in the cloud-based database of the framework. For the query, we can use the powerful SPARQL language and the Europeana API, once the Europeana online platform is the EU digital aggregator for cultural heritage [21].
3. The next step is the image processing and preparation for the matching function. Images stored in system's database must be in a specific form which allows software

to compare and decide if two images are the same. This usually is achieved with the detection of characteristic points of an image [22] and the search for the same patterns among many images.

4. In this step, the framework compares the frames taken by the user's camera with the images from its database, and in case of matching it detects the artifact that the user is interested for. This seems to be the most demanding function of the whole procedure, as it requires a lot of processing power and the use of complex software. Frame rate and latency of the result are two issues that need to be addressed, but with the necessary filters this part of the procedure can be quite effective.

5. Finally, once the framework specifies the PoI from the LOD cloud that the user is currently interested in, it uses augmented reality techniques to display more information about it. Furthermore, the user can seek more data about the current object or relevant artifacts by using the links from the LOD cloud.

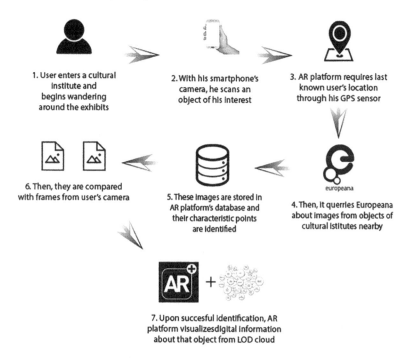

Fig. 2. Proposed framework - LOD and AR integration in indoor environments

The basic concept of the above framework is that it takes advantage of the large amount of images in the LOD cloud and treats them like image - "markers". A marker in augmented reality is an image with specific characteristics that figures a distinctive pattern, easily recognizable by the software. Upon successful detection, the system usually reacts by displaying a message or digital content, when others just link users to another website like QR codes. All the uploaded images that are associated with multiple cultural artifacts can be potential markers, thus these images can be tracked through image recognition.

Furthermore, the proposed framework needs to handle the possible data overload in the user's screen, as we already mentioned the significant size of the LOD cloud and the small screen of a mobile device. That's why context awareness techniques will be applied to display information according to user's personal interests and profile, based also on the metadata of the linked data sets.

In conclusion, the proposed framework aims in integrating linked data in augmented reality applications for indoor environments in a way that both benefit from each other. On the one hand, there will be a cross functional AR prototype for all cultural institutions that share their data in the LOD cloud without any preparation of environment (regionally restricted in Europe because of Europeana limitations as the used aggregrator). On the other hand, the proposed user interface will visualize LOD with AR techniques providing more familiar and friendly interaction ways with users.

4.3   Challenges and Limitations

Like the majority of the applications that integrate linked data with augmented reality techniques, the proposed framework has its own challenges. First of all, the size of data that needs to be displayed in the user's screen is way too big, as it is based on the LOD cloud, so context-awareness methods must be implemented in order to personalize the digital content and links that will be displayed. Also, the heterogeneity of the linked data sets must be addressed with specialized algorithms that consider the differences between languages and ontologies, coupled with structural ambiguities and misclassification of data.

Furthermore, this project faces a few more challenges which are related to its wide range of capabilities. As we already mentioned, the GPS sensor values cannot be valid in indoor environment thus won't be taken into account in tracking of the user's position inside a building. But previous values of the sensor are quite important in order to minimize the possible linked data sets that should be queried and therefore the number of images that need to be processed and compared. A potential incorrect value of the GPS sensor may lead to false data sets or too many images that will cause an endless processing time without the right outcomes. The same result will cause a disabled or uninstalled sensor in the mobile device.

Also, the computation time and the necessary processing power that is needed to perform the matching function between the stored images and the camera's frames may end up as a very challenging issue. That's why the GPS value is of importance for the decrease of the amount of processed data. Also, the matching function which compares the characteristic points of two images should require modern mobile devices capable of executing complex algorithms in limited time.

Moreover, the effectiveness of the proposed framework depends on the quality and reliability of the images that figure the cultural artifacts and are uploaded on the LOD cloud. Factors like brightness, angle of the image, changes of the artifact's location and background differences may affect the outcome of the matching function, thus misleading user to false information.

5   Conclusion and Future Work

In this paper, we introduced a new way of integrating linked open data sets in augmented reality applications for cultural heritage institutions. We argue that images stored in the LOD cloud could be potential "markers" for augmented reality tracking techniques, and we can exploit this feature to track user's PoI in an indoor environment. Considering that GPS sensors are not fully functional inside a building and indoor tracking can be accomplished only with the preparation of the corresponding room by using complex and costly equipment, we present a framework that can still recognize the cultural artifact that the user is currently interested in, by using image recognition techniques. The proposed method aims in matching images from the LOD cloud that are relative to cultural artifacts, with frames from the user's mobile device camera and after successful detection, it displays the information and links from the linked data set. Although it presents many issues as it requires a great amount of computing power to perform the matching function, it still has a lot of potential to become a universal augmented reality tool that incorporates linked open data functionalities.

Our next steps include the review of existing matching algorithms between two images and the evaluation of their effectiveness in our project. We also plan to design the database of the application appropriately in order to minimize the calculation time of the tracking process, a critical issue for the proposing system. Finally, our future plan involves the development of a prototype that will encompass the promised functionality and will successfully merge LOD and AR in a mobile application for a selected cultural institution.

References

1. Vert, S., Vasiu, R.: Integrating linked open data in mobile augmented reality applications-a case study. TEM J. **4**(1), 35–43 (2015)
2. Aydin, B., et al.: Extending augmented reality mobile application with structured knowledge from the LOD cloud. In: IMMoA (2013)
3. Bizer, C., Heath, T., Berners-Lee, T.: Linked data-the story so far. In: Semantic Services, Interoperability and Web Applications: Emerging Concepts, pp. 205–227 (2009)
4. Shadbolt, N., Berners-Lee, T., Hall, W.: The semantic web revisited. IEEE Intell. Syst. **21**(3), 96–101 (2006)
5. Marden, J., et al.: Linked open data for cultural heritage: evolution of an information technology. In: Proceedings of the 31st ACM International Conference on Design of Communication. ACM (2013)
6. van Aart, C., Wielinga, B., van Hage, W.R.: Mobile cultural heritage guide: location-aware semantic search. In: Cimiano, P., Pinto, H.S. (eds.) EKAW 2010. LNCS (LNAI), vol. 6317, pp. 257–271. Springer, Heidelberg (2010). https://doi.org/10.1007/978-3-642-16438-5_18
7. Bettadapura, V., Essa, I., Pantofaru, C.: Egocentric field-of-view localization using first-person point-of-view devices. In: 2015 IEEE Winter Conference on Applications of Computer Vision (WACV), pp. 626–633. IEEE (2015)
8. Chen, K.W., Wang, C.H., Wei, X., Liang, Q., Yang, M.H., Chen, C.S., Hung, Y.P.: To Know Where We Are: Vision-Based Positioning in Outdoor Environments. arXiv preprint arXiv: 1506.05870 (2015)

9. Kalman, R.E.: A new approach to linear filtering and prediction problems. J. Basic Eng. **82**(1), 35–45 (1960)

10. Hegde, V., et al.: Utilising linked data for personalized recommendation of POI's. International AR Standards Meeting, Barcelona, Spain (2011)

11. Vert, S., Vasiu, R.: Integrating linked data in mobile augmented reality applications. In: Dregvaite, G., Damasevicius, R. (eds.) ICIST 2014. CCIS, vol. 465, pp. 324–333. Springer, Cham (2014). https://doi.org/10.1007/978-3-319-11958-8_26

12. Reynolds, V., et al.: Exploiting linked open data for mobile augmented reality. In: W3C Workshop: Augmented Reality on the Web, vol. 1, June 2010

13. Abele, A., McCrae, J.P., Buitelaar, P., Jentzsch, A., Cyganiak, R.: Linking Open Data Cloud Diagram (2017). http://lod-cloud.net/

14. Vert, S., Vasiu, R.: Relevant aspects for the integration of linked data in mobile augmented reality applications for tourism. In: Dregvaite, G., Damasevicius, R. (eds.) ICIST 2014. CCIS, vol. 465, pp. 334–345. Springer, Cham (2014). https://doi.org/10.1007/978-3-319-11958-8_27

15. Khoury, H.M., Kamat, V.R.: Evaluation of position tracking technologies for user localization in indoor construction environments. Autom. Constr. **18**(4), 444–457 (2009)

16. Ta, V.-C., et al.: Smartphone-based user location tracking in indoor environment. In: 2016 International Conference on Indoor Positioning and Indoor Navigation (IPIN). IEEE (2016)

17. Tesoriero, R., et al.: Using active and passive RFID technology to support indoor location-aware systems. IEEE Trans. Consum. Electron. **54**(2) (2008)

18. Oosterlinck, D., et al.: Bluetooth tracking of humans in an indoor environment: an application to shopping mall visits. Appl. Geogr. **78**, 55–65 (2017)

19. Michalakis, K., Aliprantis, J., Caridakis, G.: Intelligent visual interface with the internet of things. In: Proceedings of the 2017 ACM Workshop on Interacting with Smart Objects. ACM (2017)

20. Chen, S., Li, M., Ren, K.: The power of indoor crowd: indoor 3D maps from the crowd. In: 2014 IEEE Conference on Computer Communications Workshops (INFOCOM WKSHPS). IEEE (2014)

21. Haslhofer, B., Isaac, A.: data.europeana.eu: The Europeana linked open data pilot. In: International Conference on Dublin Core and Metadata Applications (2011)

22. Mikolajczyk, K., Schmid, C.: Indexing based on scale invariant interest points. In: Proceedings of the Eighth IEEE International Conference on Computer Vision, ICCV 2001, vol. 1. IEEE (2001)

Semantic Representation and Enrichment of Cultural Heritage Information for Fostering Reinterpretation and Reflection on the European History

Andreas Vlachidis[1] [ID], Antonis Bikakis[1(✉)] [ID], Daphne Kyriaki-Manessi[2] [ID], Ioannis Triantafyllou[2] [ID], Joseph Padfield[3] [ID], and Kalliopi Kontiza[3] [ID]

[1] University College London, London, UK
{a.vlachidis,a.bikakis}@ucl.ac.uk
[2] Technological Educational Institute of Athens, Athens, Greece
{dkmanessi,triantafi}@teiath.gr
[3] The National Gallery, London, UK
{joseph.padfield,kalliopi.kontiza}@ng-london.org.uk

Abstract. The modern advances of digital technologies provide a wider access to information, enabling new ways of interacting with and understanding cultural heritage information, facilitating its presentation, access and reinterpretation. The paper presents a working example of connecting and mapping cultural heritage information and data from cultural heritage institutions and venues through the open technological platform of the CrossCult project. The process of semantically representing and enriching the available cultural heritage data is discussed, and the challenges of semantically expressing interrelations and groupings among physical items, venues, digital resources, and ideas are revealed. The paper also highlights the challenges in the creation of a knowledge base resource which aggregates a set of Knowledge Organization Systems (KOS): a carefully selected subset of the CIDOC Conceptual Reference Model, a set of application ontologies and an optimised classification scheme based on domain vocabularies.

Keywords: Digital humanities · Ontology · Knowledge representation
Semantic technologies · History reflection · CIDOC-CRM · SKOS

1 Introduction

Semantic Web technologies can ease access to Cultural Heritage content, facilitating new ways of engaging with heritage for the general public and experts that go beyond a simple interactive engagement. They enable capturing and describing the meaning and the connections among data, allowing an intelligent integration of resources via machine readable and human interpretable representations of domain knowledge that enables retrieval, reasoning, optimal data integration and knowledge reuse of disparate cultural heritage resources [1]. The benefits of Semantic Web technologies to Cultural Heritage

© Springer International Publishing AG, part of Springer Nature 2018
M. Ioannides (Ed.): ITN-DCH 2017, LNCS 10605, pp. 91–103, 2018.
https://doi.org/10.1007/978-3-319-75826-8_8

include harmonised view to disparate and distributed contents, semantic-based content aggregation, search, browsing and recommendation [2, 3].

The CrossCult[1] Project, taking advantage of the advances of digital technologies, particularly focused on the aspects of interactivity, recollection, and reflection, aims to demonstrate new ways for European citizens to appraise History. By facilitating interconnections between different pieces of cultural heritage information, public view points and physical venues, the project aims to move beyond the siloed presentation of historical data and foster the re-interpretation of history as we know it. Such connections allow reflection and reinterpretation of historical and societal views to be triggered. The project employs four flagship pilot cases, which are used to demonstrate how augmentation, data linking, semantic-based reasoning and retrieval across diverse cultural heritage resources can be achieved and contribute to its history reflection and re-interpretation aims.

This paper outlines the role of standard conceptual models for mediating semantic interoperability and discusses the role of Reflective Topics as a conceptual vehicle for fostering cross-border perspectives and reinterpretation of European history. Further sections present the rationale of the modelling choices for addressing the semantic requirements of the project in terms of facilitating interconnections among digital resources, and discuss the implementation pathway leading to the definition of the CrossCult Knowledge Base. The paper concludes with a discussion on the benefits of the adopted method and the future steps towards a greater application of semantic and knowledge representation technologies in cultural heritage.

2   Background

There is an abundance of tools for managing and semantically modelling cultural heritage data, such as the Dublin Core (DC)[2] Metadata Elements and DC Terms, the Simple Knowledge Organization System (SKOS)[3], the Functional Requirements for Bibliographic Records (FRBR)[4], the Europeana Data Model (EDM)[5], the CIDOC-CRM[6], the MIDAS Heritage[7] standard, the Lightweight Information Describing Objects[8] (LIDO) and the VRA Core[9]. These have been employed by numerous projects with varying degrees of success to aggregate and harmonise access to content across cultural heritage resources [4]. Among them, CIDOC-CRM, the Conceptual Reference Model (CRM) of the International Committee for Documentation (CIDOC) of the International Council of Museums, has become a well-established ISO standard (ISO

---

[1] http://www.crosscult.eu.
[2] http://dublincore.org/documents/dcmi-terms.
[3] https://www.w3.org/2004/02/skos/.
[4] https://www.ifla.org/publications/functional-requirements-for-bibliographic-records.
[5] http://pro.europeana.eu/page/edm-documentation.
[6] http://www.cidoc-crm.org/.
[7] https://historicengland.org.uk/images-books/publications/midas-heritage/.
[8] http://www.lido-schema.org.
[9] https://www.loc.gov/standards/vracore/.

21127:2006) for modelling cultural heritage information, due to its ability to handle the variability and complexity of cultural heritage data [5]. It provides an extensible semantic framework that any cultural heritage information can be mapped to, based on real world concepts and events for modelling data with respect to empirically surfaced arrangements rather than artificial generalisations and fixed field schemas [6]. The aptness of CIDOC-CRM in modelling cultural heritage data is evident by several large-scale projects that integrate vast datasets of classical antiquity, museum exhibits and archaeological research, such as, the Oxford University CLAROS project [7], the British Museum ResearchSpace[10] and the EU FP7 Ariadne Infrastructure [8].

Making use of such technologies, Semantic Web portals provide a range of user-centred services, enabling information seeking activities of serendipitous and relational search, personalisation and context awareness. But most importantly they are extendible to new types of information and new functionalities. Such portals are also very attractive from a publisher's/data provider's perspective by facilitating the distributed creation and maintenance of links and content, which significantly benefits reusability, enrichment and intelligent content aggregation. Semantic Web portals support user experiences that revolve around an orthogonal access of information, through conventional search and browsing activities with respect to the semantics (classes and attributes) of a conceptual data model.

A fundamental aim of CrossCult is to unleash the user experience from the conventional keyword search and hyperlink-based browsing of cultural heritage content by realising the advances of Semantic Web technologies in order to facilitate interconnections between pieces of cultural heritage information, public view points and physical venues. To this aim, the project integrates innovations from the intersection of Humanities with Computer Science in order to trigger substantial reflection on history as we know it, focusing on aspects that are cross-cultural and cross-border, as well as on grand societal challenges, such as population movements, access to health services, women's place in society, power structures and others. It is a multidisciplinary research endeavour between historians, archaeologists, information scientists and software engineers, seeking innovative experiences of engagement with cultural heritage that stimulate reflection and help European citizens appreciate their past and present history. By exploiting the abilities of Semantic Web technology, the project establishes interconnections among gallery items, museum exhibits, archaeological sites and urban spaces (POIs), aimed at fostering cross-border perspectives and a holistic understanding and reinterpretation of European history from multiple points of view.

To this aim the role of the Reflective Topic - a topic that people reflect on stimulated via groupings or narratives that link together different cultural heritage resources or POIs - becomes indispensable. The notion of Reflective Topic encompasses all those conceptual connections that can be made to create a network of points of view, aiding reflection and prospective interpretation over a historical topic. Such narratives can captivate user engagement and create long-lasting experiences based on interconnections among existing digital historical resources and by creating new ones through the participation of the public.

---

[10] http://www.researchspace.org/.

3 Methodological Approach

The CRM ontology provides a set of elements, which capture generic concepts related to the Cultural Heritage domain. The representation of domain-specific or application-specific concepts is possible via the instantiation of the E55 Type class, which enables connection to categorical knowledge commonly found in cultural documentation. In CrossCult, we adopted a common data modelling methodology, which consists of modelling the available knowledge via the standard CIDOC-CRM classes and further defining project-specific concepts as types (instance of E55) linked to SKOS-based thesauri concepts [9]. Simple Knowledge Organization System (SKOS) is a W3C recommendation designed for representation of thesauri, classification schemes, taxonomies, or any other type of structured controlled vocabulary. It builds upon RDF and RDFS, and its main objective is to enable easy publication and use of such vocabularies as linked. SKOS structures can be linked to CIDOC-CRM instances to provide a specialised vocabulary.

To address the semantic requirements of the project in terms of facilitating interconnections among digital resources and to relate such resources to Reflective Topics, we adopted two distinct but also complementary Knowledge Organization Systems (KOS): A domain ontology (CrossCult Upper-level Ontology); and a domain vocabulary (CrossCult Classification Scheme) in the form of a faceted classification of terms mapped to a set of specialised thesauri, which provide additional categorisations and groupings in the form of semantic short cuts. This combination accommodates a common layer of conceptual arrangements which we define as the CrossCult Knowledge Base, enabling semantic-based reasoning and retrieval across disparate data through an ontological structure and data enrichment and augmentation through a formally expressed classification of domain concepts. In this sense, the project focuses on the construction of an environment hosting and enhancing semantic representations emerging from cultural artefacts, monuments and places based on methods of data modelling and mapping with respect to well-defined interoperable semantics.

3.1 CrossCult Upper-Level Ontology Rationale

Based on the merits of comprehensiveness, specialisation and extensibility of CIDOC-CRM, the project adopts the W3C Web Ontology Language (OWL) version of CIDOC-CRM as defined by the Erlangen implementation (ECRM160714) [10]. The model guarantees the use of well-defined and interoperable semantics, which facilitate the definition of an ontology aimed at capturing formalisms that describe the "world" of CrossCult in terms of common conceptual arrangements and relationships between people, places, things, events and periods across a diverse range of cultural heritage resources.

Figure 1 presents the abstract model of the CrossCult Upper-Level ontology which describes the actual semantics of the top layer of the ontology, including the relationships among CIDOC-CRM and project-specific entities. The project-specific class *Reflective Topic* incorporates the semantics of reflection, enabling interconnection between physical or conceptual things of manmade or natural origin. It can be understood as an extension of the CRM *E89 Propositional Object* entity extended by the project-specific *reflects* property, which is a reversed and extended definition of the CRM property *P129 is about*. The property in its original form describes the primary subject of a propositional object. The *reflects* property definition sets an instance of a Reflective Topic as the primary subject of reflection of a physical or conceptual thing.

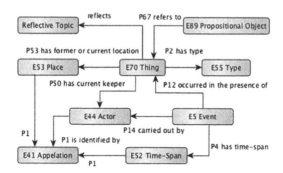

Fig. 1. Abstract schema of the CrossCult Upper-Level ontology

3.2 CrossCult Classification Scheme Rationale

CIDOC-CRM as a formal and generic structure of concepts and relationships is not tied to any particular vocabulary of types, terms and individuals. This level of abstraction, albeit useful for the semantics of the broader cultural heritage domain, does not cover the need for a finer definition of types, terms and appellations. The need for an additional level of vocabulary semantics is addressed by the CrossCult Classification Scheme. The CrossCult Classification Scheme, incorporated into the upper level ontology, aims at linking semantic concepts with: (a) subjects describing the art object referring to their meaning, depiction and/or symbolism (e.g. middle class – social class) as well as names as subjects (e.g. Apollo), and forms as subjects (e.g. basilicae, aqueducts); and (b) a broader and complex set of concepts that gear the visitor to stop and reflect during or after his/her visit to the venues. These concepts, broad in their scope, consist of abstract notions that are formed by several terms in order to produce a new notion of and stimulate "reflection in history" and social values, e.g. migration through history, healing power of water, religion and social development, etc.

The CrossCult Classification Scheme is a project specific tool that aims to organise in a faceted taxonomy terms connected by their use and function in the project: these may represent concepts, people as subjects and types or forms of works. The Scheme draws from the basic principles of organising knowledge in broad semantic areas and building within them narrower concepts. The idea of creating a simple scheme that will not have the full requirements of a complicated subject organisation tool such as a thesaurus, nor the simpler form of a "subject heading tool", has actually led us to base our concept on the principles of the basic SKOS concept elements.

The following steps were taken in constructing the CrossCult Classification Scheme:

(a) The contributing terms were derived from the specifications of the four pilots and the descriptions of the relevant cultural heritage objects.
(b) The terms were verified against three standard vocabularies, the Arts and Architecture Thesaurus of Getty (AAT)[11], EUROVOC[12] and the Library of Congress (LC) Subject Authorities[13], and mapped to the authority vocabulary resources, using the *skos:closeMatch* property. This secured compatibility and direct linking to the authority of the controlled vocabulary. Project specific terms that could not be verified in external sources were also included, documented (mimicking the process used within the existing classifications schemes) and incorporated within the classification scheme structure.
(c) Terms were organised in a faceted taxonomy, allowing the assignment of multiple classifications to each term. Terms of similar specificity were placed at the same hierarchical level. Broader and narrower term relationships were established based on the guidelines of AAT, EUROVOC and LC, whilst special effort was made to create sound hierarchical relationships of project specific terms.
(d) As with all authority files, the CrossCult Classification Scheme is subject to update, as new terms emerge through the development of the project and the introduction of new case studies. To simplify this process relevant guidelines for the addition of new terms were developed.

Apart from the standard facets that one can find in most common vocabularies (e.g. Activities, Culture, People, etc.), the CrossCult Classification Scheme contains two additional facets, which were created for the specific needs of the project: a facet for Types, accommodating the terms that are used to describe types of the entities defined in the ontology; and a facet for Reflective Topics, accommodating the terms that are used to describe topics of historical reflection. The ways that the vocabulary terms are linked to the elements of the ontology are described in Sect. 4.4.

4   Implementation

Four flagship pilot cases from eight venues across Europe participate in the project, comprising (as these are described in the project website): a *large multi-thematic venue*, *many small-venues*, *a single venue* (*non-typical transversal connections*), and *Multiple cities* (*Past-Present interplay*). Such a pluralistic environment of cultural heritage resources represents a considerable variety of cataloguing approaches and data structures. In order to connect these resources they were all mapped to the CrossCult Upper-level Ontology and the CrossCult Classification Scheme. This semantic alignment and mapping of the contributing resources to a common reference layer of was necessary for obtaining the benefits of interconnection, cross-searching, relational search, and context awareness of digital resources.

---

[11] http://www.getty.edu/research/tools/vocabularies/aat/.
[12] http://eurovoc.europa.eu.
[13] http://authorities.loc.gov/.

The available resources were modelled as ontology individuals (ontology population), the individuals were enriched with semantic definitions and linked to Semantic Web resources from DBpedia, Wikidata and elsewhere, along with the CrossCult Classification Scheme, to provide additional subject-based definitions to the ingested data.

4.1   CrossCult Pilots

A coordinated effort between historians, information scientists, and pilot representatives examined the objectives of reflection uses cases of the pilots and overviewed the contributing cultural heritage resources, in order to define the reflective topics for each pilot. In detail, the four pilots encompass the following combinations of data resources and reflection objectives.

Pilot 1, Large multi-thematic venue (National Gallery, UK). The collection contains information about paintings such as medium and support, dimensions, date of production, location in the gallery, information about the related artists, and other data explicitly related to each painting. There is also an extensive use of various types that describe paintings in terms of design techniques, styles and materials while a set of subject keywords is also available to refine the descriptions of the paintings and their relations to different concepts and themes. Reflection is encouraged by tailored recommendations that support engagement with the content based on user preference and knowledge. The user experience is advanced beyond a single choreographed route, allowing users to create their own virtual groupings and presentations, and compare their experiences with other users and the current presentation of a collection.

Pilot 2, Many small venues (Roman healing spa of Lugo, Spain and Chaves, Portugal, archaeological site of Aquae Tauri, Italy and the ancient theatre of Epidaurus, Greece). The pilot contributes data resources from four separate archaeological sites and as a result, data coverage ranges from extended descriptions of objects from the archaeological sites to simple, almost telegraphic entries of objects and their associated subject keywords. In addition, data contains references to entities other than physical objects, including monuments, physical features, activities, historical locations, and people. Reflection happens by exploring connections among items aided by experts' input to enable interpretative thinking, comparison and knowledge discovery.

Pilot 3, One venue, non-typical transversal connections (Archaeological museum of Tripolis, Greece). The pilot contributes data from a small Greek archaeological museum, containing descriptions about the temporal, geometrical, spatial and contextual characteristics of the exhibits. The descriptions do not vary significantly in terms of size and level of detail, albeit some descriptions are a little longer than others. The modelling requirements of this pilot draw some parallels with Pilot 1 in terms of semantically describing temporal, spatial and contextual information. Reflection is promoted by tailoring the narratives in a way that raises empathy among the participants, enabling prospective interpretation and unexpected learning, which may happen by relating elements from the narratives to aspects of the participant's life, as well as through meaningful comparisons between the past and his/her present.

Pilot 4, Multiple cities, "Past & Present" interplay (City of Luxembourg, Luxembourg and Valletta, Malta). The pilot contributes data from a sample of several Points of Interest (POI) located in contemporary urban spaces. The data focuses on the relationship of POIs with specific reflective narratives and multimedia that drive the narratives and navigate the users of a mobile app towards the location of POIs. The data describes attributes of the POIs, including spatial, geometric and temporal information as well as reflective narratives and relevant multimedia. The pilot aims at a collaborative reflection over key topics of population movement and immigration in order to provoke comparisons on the topic of immigrant integration in the present and the past and enable users to reflect over and reinterpret migration-related events under different situations than those of the original event.

4.2   Semantic Alignment and Mapping

The mapping process addressed common modelling requirements across the four pilots with regards to spatial, temporal, geometrical, and other associative interpretations of data. Attention was paid on the extensibility qualities of the proposed model for accommodating future potential uses, whilst catering for any particular specialisation requirements hinted by the pilots. In this respect, the CIDOC-CRM proved an invaluable instrument for capturing the common semantic definitions of the participating cultural heritage resources whilst providing a clear documented process for additional project specific extensions.

Figure 2 presents the modelling arrangements of the common semantics across the four pilots of the CrossCult project. At the core of the model resides the CIDOC-CRM entity *E18 Physical Item*, which comprises all persistent physical items with a relatively stable form, man-made or natural. The entity enables the representation of a vast range of items of interest, such as museum exhibits, gallery paintings, artefacts, monuments and points of interest, whilst providing extensions to specialised entity definitions of targeted semantics for man-made objects, physical objects and physical features. The arrangement benefits from a range of relationships between *E18 Physical Item* and a set of entities that describe the static parameters of an item, such as dimension, unique identifier, title, and type. The model also allows the description of more complex objects through a composition of individual items (i.e. P46 is composed of). Moreover, the well-defined semantics enable rendering of rich relationships between the physical item and entities describing the item in terms of ownership, production, location, and other conceptual associations. The project specific property *reflects* has been added to enable specific, direct connections between existing concepts and the CrossCult class Reflective Topic.

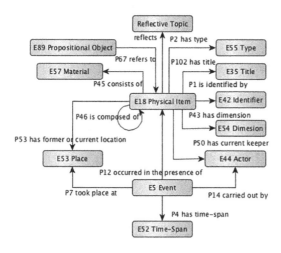

Fig. 2. Arrangements of common semantics across CrossCult Pilots

4.3 Population and Enrichment of the CrossCult Knowledge Base

The Population and Enrichment phase applied the conceptual arrangements and definitions of the CrossCult ontology to a range of disparate data resources originating from the four pilots of the project whilst linking a selected set of ontology individuals to Semantic Web resources and definitions. During ontology population, the tasks of data decoupling, cleansing and semantic enrichment were performed and a diverse range of cultural heritage data was mapped to a common layer of semantics complying to the CrossCult Ontology [15].

Three separate stages addressed issues affected by the heterogeneity of the available data. The Manual Data Extraction stage imposed a unified data structure across a range of unstructured sample data available in text format. The task identified textual instances of relevant types (i.e. type of exhibit and related material), temporal and spatial information, dimensions, and other features of interest such as inscriptions or visual representations. The Semi-Automatic Database Construction stage populated a set of relational database tables with structured data, from spreadsheets originating directly from the pilots. The Automatic OWL Generation stage, ingested the structured data of the relational database into the ontology. The process employed a series of PHP routines driven by SQL queries for retrieving selected database records and declaring them as ontology individuals using OWL class and property assertions. The routines cater for the automatic generation of statements with respect to individual(s) declaration, class assertion, object property assertion, and data property assertion.

The semantic enrichment phase enriched a selected set of ontology individuals with links to standard and well-known Semantic Web resources, such as DBpedia and the Getty Art & Architecture Thesaurus. The symmetric property *owl:sameAs* is employed for enabling linking of individuals to DBpedia resources. The process provided additional definition, consistent standardised descriptions, and enhanced connections improving utility and interoperability of content, as demonstrated in Fig. 3. The figure presents the classification and relationships of ontology individuals describing the National Gallery painting of Eustache Le Sueur, *Alexander and his doctor*, about 1648-9 (NG6576). The painting is modelled as an instance of E22.Man-Made Object uniquely identified by a National Gallery (UK) reference and associated with a conceptual type (Canvas painting). The information related to the production of the painting, such as date of production, artist and technique, is handled by the semantics of a production event.

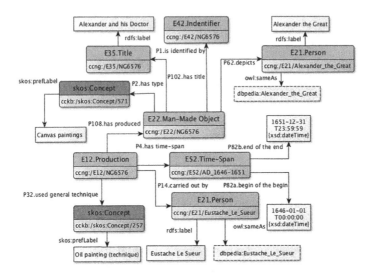

Fig. 3. Class definitions and relationships of ontology individuals

4.4   Vocabulary Integration and Association

The CrossCult Classification Scheme was integrated into the Upper-Level ontology delivering a unified Knowledge Base resource, as depicted in Fig. 4). Vocabulary terms were all defined as instances of the *skos:Concept* class, and connected to external vocabulary resources using appropriate properties, as described in Sect. 3.2. Terms referring to types were classified under *E55 Type* and were associated to the individuals they describe via the *P2 has type* property. Terms that represent subjects used to enrich the semantic description of cultural heritage objects or places, were classified under *E89 Propositional Object.* They were then associated to the objects/places/reflective topics they refer to via the *P67 refers to* property. Finally, vocabulary terms referring to Reflective Topics were classified under the project-specific ontology class *Reflective Topic,* and were associated to the entities that drive the corresponding reflection via the *reflects* property.

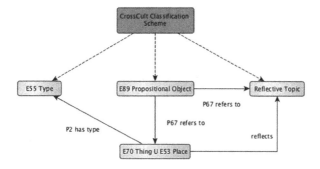

Fig. 4. Relationships between the Classification Scheme and the Upper-level Ontology

5   Discussion

CrossCult is now in its second year, during which the remaining parts of the CrossCult Knowledge Base are being finalised based on the same data modelling methodology and principles used for the Upper-level ontology. Specifically, our ongoing work includes: adding ontological definitions for other project-related concepts, such as the pilots' venues and the users of the pilot apps; further refining the scope and structure of Reflective Topics and their relation to keywords, narratives and other reflection proposals; augmenting the data with media content and narratives that enhance their reflection and re-reinterpretation qualities; further semantically enriching the resource descriptions with more links to external standardised Semantic Web resources. At the same time, the CrossCult platform and mobile apps for the four project pilots are being developed. The CrossCult platform consists of: front-end tools, which can be used by experience designers, museum experts/curators and external stakeholders, to develop market-ready applications; a back-end, which integrates technologies for the storage and management of the available information and digital resources as well as supporting any other necessary functionalities needed by the front-end and the mobile apps (e.g. route/path recommendation [11], personalisation [12], micro-augmentations [13], games [14], etc.).

The semantic-based design of the CrossCult Knowledge Base, presented in this paper, enhances the capabilities of the CrossCult platform and the mobile apps in many different ways. It enables the development of services, e.g. for search, navigation, route finding, etc., that (i) can be tailored to the needs and preferences of each user; (ii) can highlight associations between different cultural heritage resources or venues and form groupings of items from the venues' collections under certain historical topics, serving the history reflection and re-interpretation aims of the project; (iii) augment the user experience by linking the cultural heritage resources of a venue with external historical, geographical or other types of information or digital resources; (iv) support different kinds of visualisation of a venue's collection based on the temporal, spatial or any other kinds of contextual relationships; (v) are extendible to more types of information and, therefore, new functionalities. Moreover, given the growing popularity of CIDOC-CRM, and Semantic Web technologies, among cultural heritage institutions, the Cross-Cult Knowledge Base will contribute to the development of a broader knowledge-based network of museums, galleries and other cultural heritage venues, which in the future could enable the development of unified services for the visitors of their physical or virtual collections, built on top of a global knowledge base for cultural heritage.

Acknowledgements. This work has been funded by CrossCult: "Empowering reuse of digital cultural heritage in context-aware crosscuts of European history", funded by the European Union's Horizon 2020 research and innovation program.

References

1. Hyvönen, E.: Semantic portals for cultural heritage. In: Staab, S., Studer, R. (eds.) Handbook on Ontologies. IHIS, pp. 757–778. Springer, Heidelberg (2009). https://doi.org/10.1007/978-3-540-92673-3_34
2. King, L., Stark, J.F., Cooke, P.: Experiencing the digital world: the cultural value of digital engagement with heritage. Heritage Soc. **9**(1), 76–101 (2016)
3. Hyvönen, E.: Publishing and using cultural heritage linked data on the semantic web. Synth. Lect. Semant. Web Theor. Technol. **2**(1), 1–159 (2012)
4. Ronzino, P., Amico, N., Niccolucci, F.: Assessment and comparison of metadata schemas for architectural heritage. In: XXIIIrd International CIPA Symposium, Prague, Czech Republic, pp. 12–16, September 2011
5. Oldman, D., Doerr, M., de Jong, G., Norton, B.: Realizing lessons of the last 20 years: A manifesto for data provisioning & aggregation services for the digital humanities (a position paper). D-lib Mag. **20** (7/8) (2014). http://www.dlib.org/dlib/july14/oldman/07oldman.html
6. Doerr, M.: The CIDOC conceptual reference module: an ontological approach to semantic interoperability of metadata. AI Mag. **24**(3), 75–92 (2003)
7. Kurtz, D., Greg, P., David, S., Graham, K., Florian, S., Zisserman, A., Wilks, Y.: Claros-bringing classical art to a global public. In: e-Science 2009 Fifth IEEE International Conference, pp. 20–27. IEEE (2009)
8. Meghini, C., Scopigno, R., Richards, J., Wright, H., Geser, G., Cuy, S., Fihn, J., Fanini, B., Hollander, H., Niccolucci, F., Felicetti, A., Ronzino, P., Nurra, F., Papatheodorou, C., Gavrilis, D., Theodoridou, M., Doerr, M., Tudhope, D., Binding, C., Vlachidis, A.: ARIADNE: a research infrastructure for archaeology. J. Comput. Cult. Heritage (JOCCH) **10**(3), 18–27 (2017)
9. Tudhope, D., Binding, C.: Still quite popular after all those years–the continued relevance of the information retrieval thesaurus. Knowl. Organ. **43**(3), 174–179 (2016)
10. Goerz, G., Oischinger, M., Schiemann, B.: An implementation of the CIDOC conceptual reference model (4.2. 4) in OWL-DL. In: Proceedings of the 2008 Annual Conference of CIDOC-The Digital Curation of Cultural Heritage (2008)
11. Osche, P.-E., Castagnos, S., Napoli, A., Naudet, Y.: Walk the line: toward an efficient user model for recommendations in museums. In: 11th International Workshop on Semantic and Social Media Adaptation and Personalization (2016)
12. Deladiennée, L., Naudet, Y.: A graph-based semantic recommender approach for a personalised museum visit. In: 12th International Workshop on Semantic and Social Media Adaptation and Personalization (2017)
13. Theodorakopoulos, M., Papageorgopoulos, N., Mourti, A., Antoniou, A., Wallace, M., Lepouras, G., Vassilakis, C., Platis, N.: Personalized augmented reality experiences in museums using google cardboards. In: 12th International Workshop on Semantic and Social Media Adaptation and Personalization (2017)

14. Bampatzia, S., Bourlakos, I., Antoniou, A., Vassilakis, C., Lepouras, G., Wallace, M.: Serious games: Valuable tools for cultural heritage, games and learning alliance conference (2016)
15. Vlachidis, A., Bikakis, A., Kyriaki-Manessi, D., Triantafyllou, I., Antoniou, A.: The crosscult knowledge base: a co-inhabitant of cultural heritage ontology and vocabulary classification. In: Second International Workshop on Semantic Web for Cultural Heritage (2017)

Digital Cultural Heritage: Semantic Enrichment and Modelling in BIM Environment

Federica Maietti[1]([⊠]) (iD), Marco Medici[1] (iD), Federico Ferrari[1] (iD),
Anna Elisabetta Ziri[2] (iD), and Peter Bonsma[3] (iD)

[1] Department of Architecture, University of Ferrara,
Via Ghiara 36, 44121 Ferrara, Italy
{federica.maietti,marco.medici,
federico.ferrari}@unife.it
[2] Nemoris s.r.l, Via Decumana 67, 40133 Bologna, Italy
annaelisabetta.ziri@nemoris.it
[3] RDF Ltd., 25 Iskar str., Sofia, Bulgaria
peter.bonsma@rdf.bg

Abstract. The ongoing EU funded INCEPTION project proposes a significant improvement in the 3D modelling for the enhancement of Cultural Heritage knowledge by the use of a BIM approach for the semantic enrichment and management of models. Indeed, when used in the CH field, semantic BIM will be able to connect different users (e.g. scholars, technicians, citizens, governments), supporting the need for interpretation of the cultural heritage model.

The expectations on this are quite broad, but the architectural differences make the task quite difficult. Since every building is the final result of different influences and combinations in order to solve practical problems, as well as further additions and changes during time, the INCEPTION project is developing common parameters, setting a nomenclature or "glossary of names" as a starting point to semantic enrichment and modelling in BIM environment.

One of the main issues in creating a nomenclature is that there are many different active sources that all have very valuable information that would be interesting to be reused. Furthermore, this means both valuable but potentially competing information needs to be connected. Semantic Web technology and Linked Open Data principles make it possible to define an open H-BIM ontology. This state-of-the-art technology is developed by members of the W3C organization and is at the moment, a mature technology. INCEPTION makes use of the tools available, supporting these standards.

Keywords: Heritage buildings · Semantic modelling · Linked open data
Heritage documentation · H-BIM

© Springer International Publishing AG, part of Springer Nature 2018
M. Ioannides (Ed.): ITN-DCH 2017, LNCS 10605, pp. 104–118, 2018.
https://doi.org/10.1007/978-3-319-75826-8_9

1   Introduction

One of the main challenges in 3D modelling is related to an effective BIM approach for cultural heritage knowledge, semantic enrichment and model management. The ongoing EU funded INCEPTION project proposes an improvement in this methodology by recognizing that buildings are a set of elements, named by an architectural style nomenclature and organized by spatial relationships. Now, a shared library for historical elements does not exist. Starting from the so-called Heritage Building Information Modelling (H-BIM) approach the necessity of the libraries' implementation will be reached by INCEPTION, avoiding the oversimplification of the shapes. When used in models of cultural heritage, semantic BIM [1] will be able to connect different users (e.g. scholars, technicians, citizens, governments), supporting the need for interpretation of the cultural heritage model, in addition to the common BIM features of 3D visualization, technical specification and dataset [2].

Starting from a definition of concepts and their relationships, we can state that the first step in creating semantic BIM for cultural heritage is by defining the ontology: a formal representation of knowledge as a hierarchy of concepts within the cultural heritage domain. The linguistic definitions related to the ontology concepts can also be used as shared vocabulary to denote the types, properties and interrelationships of cultural heritage aspects [3].

The expectations on this are quite broad, but the architectural differences make the task quite difficult. Naming each architectural element that composes a building is not an easy task. If we look at classical architecture, we can find several books that deeply analyze and summarize rules which were fundamentally adopted in classical buildings. When mainly based on classical orders, ancient architecture is easier to understand and name, even if the building practice often differs from the theory. For instance, to list some of the most known theoretical books from the past, we can mention *De architectura (On architecture, published as Ten Books on Architecture)* by Vitruvio; *De re aedificatoria (On the Art of Building)* by Leon Battista Alberti; and *I quattro libri dell'architettura (The Four Books of Architecture)* by Andrea Palladio.

These are only some of the major treatises that influenced architectures all over the world for centuries. Nevertheless, local practices introduced several variations, including, many different constructive techniques, shapes and decorations that were not standardized. Every building is the final result of different influences and combinations in order to solve practical problems, as well as further additions and changes over time.

For this reason, aiming at the standardization in heritage documentation data handling and management, the INCEPTION project is developing common parameters, setting a nomenclature or "glossary of names" as a starting point to semantic enrichment and modelling in BIM environment [4]. The recognition of shapes, either manually or automatically performed, is possible only if single architectural elements (or their variations) are identified and univocally classified following a shared procedure.

Over the years, several architectural dictionaries have been produced. Thousands of architectural names have been collected and managed following a specific sorting. For instance, a traditional thematic dictionary collects names in alphabetical order, for a specific language, describing every single name and without the requirement of conceptually linking them together. Conversely, an architectural treatise explained by graphics gives more consistency to the nomenclature, setting up specific relation between elements (Fig. 1).

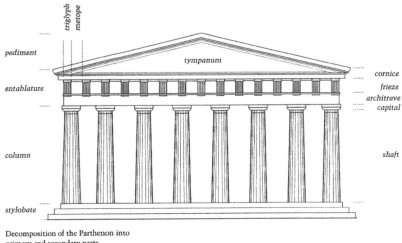

Decomposition of the Parthenon into
primary and secondary parts

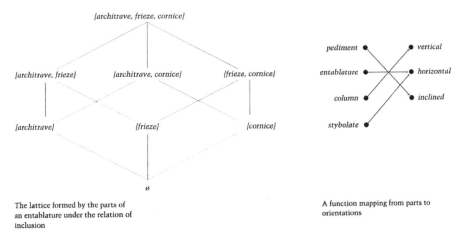

The lattice formed by the parts of
an entablature under the relation of
inclusion

A function mapping from parts to
orientations

Fig. 1. Example of "storage of values and proprieties" in data structure through the decomposition of the Perthenon into parts (source: W.J. Mitchel [5]).

This defines two different kind of issues within INCEPTION:

- setting up of a common glossary of names for all Demonstration Cases by involving scholars and experts;
- organizing names following a structure that could ensure the linking between elements which could be re-used in the IT development phase.

2   State of the Art in Heritage Nomenclature and Linked Open Data

The need for the definition of an international "glossary" for architectural heritage and by extension, for cultural heritage has arose. This need has originated from the fact that there are various methodologies regarding heritage documentation. Various vocabularies and thesauri are used in the field of conservation, while the variety of "uniqueness" of each cultural artefact turns its categorization into a difficult endeavor. In addition, not only spatial information needs to be standardized, but also the related metadata. Multilingualism, the translation of terms and the existence of many local words for the description of the same object, are the most important challenges when structuring vocabularies. Therefore, the attempt to describe an object with terms understandable to every culture and the adoption of a common "linguistic ground" meets a number of difficulties (Table 1).

Table 1. Vocabularies/Thesauri

Thesaurus name	Primary relevance
Herein	Architecture, Monuments
UNESCO Thesaurus	General
UK Archival Thesaurus	Archives
Centre National d' Archaeologie Urbaine	Sites, Archaeology
Pactols Thesaurus by Frantiq	Archaeology
Getty, The Art & Architecture Thesaurus	Art, Architecture
The Getty Thesaurus of Geographic names	Sites
Getty, The Union List of Artists Names	Actors, artists
Getty, The Cultural Objects Name Authority	Museums

The above vocabularies and thesauri provide an extensive list of object terms in different thematic areas and relate each object term to others within a hierarchical taxonomy. Due to the fact that the needs of each institution are diverse, some of these standardized vocabularies provide controlled flexibility, by allowing the specialized user to add new terms within the vocabulary, in order to express finer points of distinction among similar but subtly different objects. It is clear that the vocabularies establish only a convention for object names, in order to facilitate data retrieval, and in many cases, do not substitute for fuller descriptions. Thesauri provide terminological tools for the identification of terms and concepts in various fields of science. For example, the HEREIN thesaurus (2014) provides the aforementioned service in the field of CH, TGN thesaurus does likewise in the field of geographic names, AAT in the field of art and architecture etc.

One of the main issues with creating a nomenclature in general is that there are many different active sources that all have very valuable information that would be interesting to be reused. Furthermore, this means both valuable but potentially competing information needs to be connected. Since this information is constantly in development, linking is preferable rather than copying a "static" version at a certain date. This is even more true for Heritage nomenclature.

Semantic Web technology and Linked Open Data principles make it possible to define an open H-BIM ontology without having the complexity of defining the complete schema as a copy of external sources. This state-of-the-art technology is developed by members of the W3C organization and is at the moment a mature technology with mature supporting tools. INCEPTION makes use of the tools available supporting these standards.

The above named state-of-the-art vocabularies/thesauri define a nomenclature for the Cultural Heritage domain. Before this valuable knowledge can be used as linked open data the following steps need to be defined:

- translate the vocabularies/thesauri in a technology that supports linked open data;
- interlink the different vocabularies/thesauri and link them together;
- filter what is relevant for the H-BIM ontology within INCEPTION.

2.1 The Choice of the Getty Vocabularies

Analyzing the state of the art, Cultural Heritage data dictionary related to "names" connected to architectures and sites, different sources were browsed, considering primarily European policies in managing and sharing information on cultural heritage. Such as the HEREIN Thesaurus, a multilingual thesaurus that enables the identification of terms and concepts relevant to the field of heritage in 14 languages.

The UNESCO Thesaurus, for example, is a controlled and structured list of terms used in subject analysis and retrieval of documents and publications in the fields of education, culture, natural sciences, social and human sciences, communication and information. Continuously enriched and updated, its multidisciplinary terminology reflects the evolution of UNESCO's programs and activities.

The starting point for semantic organization and glossary definitions for cultural heritage buildings is the integration of the glossary with ifcOWL (in order to start working on H-BIM modelling defining specific parts of the model), ifcOWL as Semantic Web serialization on schema level for IFC schemas will be followed where possible for BIM content stored/exchanged via IFC. No useful connections were found with HEREIN (this is more related with the GIS aggregation level and less on product definition) or other thesauri. Anyway, the analysis of available nomenclatures will go on, according to activities of WP3, by analyzing national and international resources.

For the Web service set up, the Getty Vocabularies were chosen as a starting point, including AAT - Art & Architecture Thesaurus, TGN - Getty Thesaurus of Geographic Names and ULAN - Union List of Artist Names.

The Getty vocabularies contain structured terminology for art, architecture, decorative arts, archival materials, visual surrogates, conservation, and bibliographic materials. Compliant with international IT standards, they provide authoritative information for cataloguers, researchers, and data providers. In the new linked, open environments, the vocabularies provide a powerful tool to be adopted within the INCEPTION project, even if a filtering activity is required in order to make them suitable. Furthermore, where an existing vocabulary will not correctly cover a specific definition, it will be integrated. Current work is creating an ontology as a valuable base for possible upgrading about what is expected/required in H-BIM.

The AAT, TGN and ULAN contain structured terminology for art and other material culture, archival materials, visual surrogates, and bibliographic materials. Compliant with international standards, they provide authoritative information for cataloguers and researchers, and can be used to enhance access to databases and web sites. The Getty Vocabularies are produced by the Getty Vocabulary Program (GVP) and grow through contributions.

UNIFE, NEMORIS and RDF are extending the H-BIM ontology based on the classification available in Getty and are integrating this with the 'BIM' classification generated from the IFC schemas.

3   The INCEPTION Approach

This section focuses on the methodological explanation of how to filter and select the nomenclature for Cultural Heritage starting from the chosen vocabularies. The creation of a shared semantic field for Cultural Heritage will be reached through a wiki-like 3D parametric modelling approach. Anyway, the simple definition of a vocabulary of architectural elements is not sufficient to describe the complex relationship present in a H-BIM model. Those concepts have to be organized in a hierarchy and related through properties that describe more complex relationships than parent/child, like composition or geolocation (ontology).

Therefore, a specific hierarchical organization of European Cultural Heritage information about buildings is under development, based on a sematic approach to prevent restricted access to the knowledge. With a top-down approach, information about the target of the model will be organized in a semantic structure, adding to geometric information attributes such as architectural style, time frame, author, location, etc.

Semantic 3D reconstruction of heritage buildings and sites needs a multidisciplinary approach based on the collaboration of various experts towards the development of 3D models integrating semantic data [6]. The first step requires the identification of the Cultural Heritage buildings semantic ontology and data structure for information catalogue in order to integrate semantic attributes with 3D digital geometric models for management of heritage information. The ultimate goal of this process is the development of semantic 3D reconstructions of heritage buildings and sites, integrated with intangible information and social environment, to create models more accessible and implementable. Collection of semantic data associated to the models, enables the semantic information enrichment by users, sharing knowledge and allowing new interpretation and understanding of European cultural assets (Fig. 2).

The issue of semantic enrichment has been split into "how to retrieve the data" and "how to aggregate the data". If 3D data can be captured following a more commonly shared procedure. Terminology and interpretation have a large variety when looking at semantics, due to different competencies, skills and languages. On the other hand, making data aggregable asks for a Semantic Web structure [7] in order to give back to different users a new way to look at the information in a heritage context. A Semantic Web structure also means that the relations, properties and composition of the "nodes"

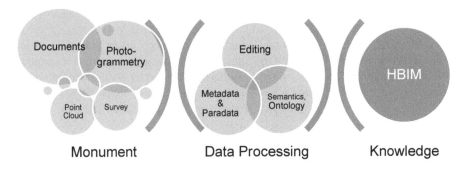

Fig. 2. The phase of *Data Processing* is the bond that ensures the successful development of H-BIM.

of information give a new insight which is different from a list of the same concepts or a database structure. At present, consistent structured data is missing for cultural heritage architectures.

The INCEPTION approach in the selection of the nomenclature for Cultural Heritage starts from classical architectural sources: the project is focused on historical architectures and sites, and the activities accomplished during the first year of the project defined the common framework for catalogue methodology. The outcomes from this work led to comprehensive considerations related to possible classifications of individual buildings and sites [8] according to international charts, recommendations and conventions.

The work done so far regarding the "taxonomy of monuments" according to holistic e-documentation needs, is the base to understand the approach on "names" to start a classification in Semantic Web in order to connect terms with H-BIM ontology. Additional future steps will allow adding further terms, definitions and different translations by means of automatic procedures. Therefore, the common glossary of names crossing all Demonstration Cases is under development. Names have been organized following a structure that could ensure the linking between elements and could be re-used in the IT development phase. In the new linked, open environments, the vocabularies provide a powerful tool to be adopted within the INCEPTION project, even if a filtering of activities is required in order to make them suitable. Current work is creating an ontology as a valuable base for possible upgrading about what is expected/required in H-BIM.

3.1   Filtering Getty Vocabularies

Focusing in particular on the AAT - Art & Architecture Thesaurus, a lot of names are unnecessary for our purposes and the complete and unfiltered adoption could result in being wasteful. By the use of SPARQL queries, it is possible to extract relevant information from Getty sources [9]. The query allowed extracting 2041 names from the concept of "architectural elements", asking for narrower concepts. The query goes in depth by seven levels, where we decided to stop because of too detailed object names.

The choice was made due to the results but could be easily extended in other directions (broader or narrower or including other types of classification if applicable).

The Getty Vocabularies approach was intended to identify a universal architectural approach, whilst a cross check with case studies was performed. Indeed, within the INCEPTION project, several historical Demonstration Cases were identified in order to achieve a significant variation in terms of size, location and historical period. On each building or architectural space, a modelling segmentation was carried out, identifying architectural components to be matched with their names (Table 2).

Table 2. Example table of collected names – the Spanish Demonstration Case of Castle of Torrelobatón, Spain

Level 1	Level 2	Level 3	Level 4	Level 5	Level 6	Level 7
Torre del homenaje (Tower keep)	Defensas (Forebuilding)	Garitón (Bartizan)	Balcón (Balcony)	Tronera (Embrasure)	Saetera (Arrow slit/Loophole)	Ladronera (Parapet)
Torre prismática (Square tower)	Cara (Face)	Flanco (Flank)	Tronera (Embrasure)	Saetera (Arrow slit/Loophole)	Ladronera (Parapet)	
Torre cilíndrica (Cubo) (Round tower)	Tronera (Embrasure)	Saetera (Arrow slit/Loophole)	Ladronera (Parapet)			
Baluarte (Bastion)	Tronera (Embrasure)	Saetera (Arrow slit/Loophole)	Ladronera (Parapet)			
Barbacana (Barbican)	Tronera (Embrasure)	Saetera (Arrow slit/Loophole)				
Muro (lienzo de muralla) (Curtain wall)	Barrera (Barrier)	Alambor (Scarp)	Contrafuerte/Espolón (Buttress)	Garita (Hut)	Tronera (Embrasure)	Saetera (Arrow slit/Loophole)
Columna (Column)	Base (Base)	Fuste (Shaft)	Capitel (Capital)			
Habitación/Dependencia (Room)	Espacio expositivo/Museo (Museum)					
Ventana (Window)	Reja (Bar iron/ Wrought iron)					

In order to proceed with the Glossary of Names, each partner responsible for a Demonstration Case was asked for the filtering of the extracted list of names by matching with names of architectural elements that could be identified in their Demonstration Case (Table 3).

3.2 Demonstration Cases Analysis

Nine Demonstration Cases are under development within the INCEPTION project, chosen in significant heritage sites, and are representative of different kinds of Cultural Heritage (archaeological sites, monumental complexes, castles, museums, etc.).

Starting from the holistic e-documentation and integrated 3D data capturing, each Demonstration Case is thoroughly defined in terms of semantics, including the glossary of names, in order to define the nomenclatures as the starting point for advanced

Table 3. Example table of links to AAT dictionary– the Spanish Demonstration Case of Castle of Torrelobatón, Spain

Names	AAT dictionary URL	Query depth level
arch, dome or vault components	http://vocab.getty.edu/aat/ 300076608	2
<floors and floor components>	http://vocab.getty.edu/aat/ 300052265	2
fencing (barriers)	http://vocab.getty.edu/aat/ 300299221	2
<bastions and bastion components>	http://vocab.getty.edu/aat/ 300100130	2
keeps	http://vocab.getty.edu/aat/ 300003694	2
buttresses	http://vocab.getty.edu/aat/ 300000891	3
corbels	http://vocab.getty.edu/aat/ 300003610	3
<coffered ceilings and coffered ceiling components>	http://vocab.getty.edu/aat/ 300076213	3
<windows and window components>	http://vocab.getty.edu/aat/ 300052375	3
loopholes	http://vocab.getty.edu/aat/ 300003018	3
moats	http://vocab.getty.edu/aat/ 300003716	3
barbicans	http://vocab.getty.edu/aat/ 300003628	3
scarps (fortification elements)	http://vocab.getty.edu/aat/ 300003713	3
columns (architectural elements)	http://vocab.getty.edu/aat/ 300001571	4
roofs	http://vocab.getty.edu/aat/ 300002098	4
<bases for columns>	http://vocab.getty.edu/aat/ 300233843	4
shafts (column components)	http://vocab.getty.edu/aat/ 300001754	4
parapets	http://vocab.getty.edu/aat/ 300002717	4
curtain walls (fortification elements)	http://vocab.getty.edu/aat/ 300002504	4
bartizans	http://vocab.getty.edu/aat/ 300003636	4

(*continued*)

Table 3. (*continued*)

Names	AAT dictionary URL	Query depth level
machicolations	http://vocab.getty.edu/aat/ 300002695	4
<capitals and capital components>	http://vocab.getty.edu/aat/ 300065036	5
<doors and door components>	http://vocab.getty.edu/aat/ 300052371	5
embrasures (battlement components)	http://vocab.getty.edu/aat/ 300002597	6
merlons	http://vocab.getty.edu/aat/ 300002601	6

modelling in Heritage BIM environment and the development of tailored tools and applications for a wide and inclusive access to European Cultural Heritage.

Demonstration Cases under analysis are:

- Istituto degli Innocenti in Florence, Italy;
- Saint Nicholas Chapel of the Church of Obergum, the Netherlands;
- Stone Villages in Croatia;
- Technical Museum "Nikola Tesla" in Zagreb, Croatia;
- Castle of Torrelobatón, Spain;
- Church of Panayia (The Virgin) Phorviotissa (Asinou), Cyprus;
- Acropolis of Erimokastro in Rhode, Greece;
- Villa Klonaridi in Athens, Greece;
- Historical Museum of Hydra, Greece.

Morphologies of buildings and sites have been described by listing descriptive terms hierarchically related. The morphological description of elements will allow advancements in H-BIM modelling starting from geometries up to the link of different semantic attributes and related contents. Therefore, how to name building descriptions was the preliminary step to link heritage digital documentation and representation toward semantic modelling.

In order to be compliant to the INCEPTION inclusive approach (forever, for everybody, from everywhere) the semantic H-BIM will allow interactions with the 3D models, advanced representations, integration of semantic metadata, and the management of changes undergone by buildings overtime (time-machine).

The adopted methodological workflow included the integration of different contributions from several sources, from the expertise by INCEPTION partners and stakeholders, to the literature review, with a specific focus on the most significant texts explaining the relation between architectural elements, their shape and their nomenclature.

Aiming at the creation of H-BIM models, the generic list of names of architectural elements were hierarchically organized, mapping a significant subset of the ifcOWL ontology whilst, at the same time, the matching with the Getty vocabulary was preserved. Thus, each identified element into a Demonstration Case was double connected, from one side to its possible geometrical description, as well as on the other side, to a wide linguistic resource providing an unambiguous description (Fig. 3).

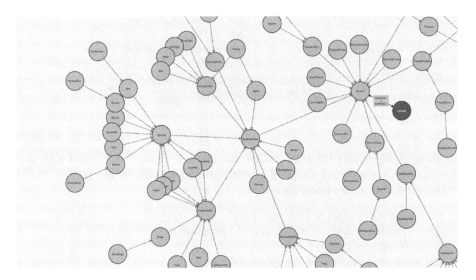

Fig. 3. Graphical representation of the INCEPTION H-BIM ontology.

Nevertheless, this approach allows forecasting the inclusive possibility of giving wide access to Cultural Heritage: the two-way connection between linguistic resources and the geometrical appearance opens, indeed, to the development of a platform and several applications where the user can enjoy a CH asset and its complexity both with technical or non-technical expertise.

3.3 Semantic Organization and Data Management Toward H-BIM Modelling

The 3D semantic models in the INCEPTION project will contain geometric information for 3D visualization, historical information for narration, and geo-technical as well as structural information for material conservation, maintenance and refurbishment. The 'intelligent' 3D models generated will be accessible for all types of users for multiple purposes depending on the needs and level of knowledge of the end-users.

Since 1994, the currently named IFC standard has been in development. While the actual roots point back towards 1985, the Building & Construction specific development started 10 years later. IFC is often seen as the reference open BIM standard and it is safe to say it is the most mature and widely adopted open standard for exchange of information about BIM in the broadest sense of the word. Many people see IFC as a geometry format. However, IFC is able to handle a large variety of geometrical representations, so it is much more than just geometry. It contains many structures, grouping mechanisms as well as a lot of semantics. Over the years, a lot of semantics has been integrated in the IFC schema definition in many different layers. Within the INCEPTION project, a tool has been developed in order to convert both the semantic information from the IFC schema into parts of the H-BIM ontology as well as being able to convert real data files (tested up to 500 Mb files) towards project content according to the H-BIM ontology.

The tool is able to convert the schema IFC 2x3 TC1 (the mainstream version), IFC 4 ADD2 (latest version of the latest official schema) and IFC 4x1 (latest IFC version with integrated infra structure elements).

The tool creates part of the H-BIM ontology on request (as soon as a revision is released this can be adapted automatically). Any instance of files created/available for a specific project can also be converted and the content is correctly defined against the defined H-BIM Ontology. It is possible to integrate any other ontology like Getty without losing correct links with the generated project content.

At the moment, mainly the IFC object classification (entities inheriting from IfcObject) is converted together with some small other parts from the IFC schema for non-geometrical data. Within INCEPTION, H-BIM uses for geometry a geometric ontology independent from IFC with $\pm$ 100 classes where conversion from all IFC geometry as well as from Collada will be available as a service. Based on what is needed by projects this can be extended or reduced in a generic way (Fig. 4).

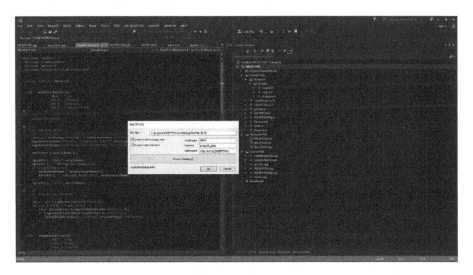

Fig. 4. Screenshot of the software tool for IFC schema conversion and H-BIM ontology creation.

3.4   Next Steps

The bsddOWL development is definitely something to keep an eye on, but seems to be less mainstream. A good reusable first step could be the development of a SPARQL end-point on top of the current bSDD solution.

Within the IFC world, two of the main items of development at the moment are the linked data/Semantic Web approach and the infra extensions. The linked data/Semantic Web approach is followed as much as possible and covered by the developed application. The infra extensions also cover local roads and therefore could be relevant for INCEPTION also. The solution as developed for INCEPTION is generic, this means H-BIM ontology parts coming from IFC could directly contain newly proposed extensions, the proposed extensions for IFC 4x1 (currently Release Candidate 3) is already working and part of the H-BIM ontology.

The major challenges and areas of research to be faced are:

- The automation of data capture and H-BIM creation.
- The update and maintenance of information in H-BIM.
- The handling and modelling of uncertain data, objects and relations occurring in historic buildings.

The approach of the INCEPTION project on data management in H-BIM models should help to solve some of these challenges by adding semantic information (intelligence) to raw data and providing a platform able to effectively manage all available information. The main objective is the sharing and the portability of H-BIM models from different people and different capacities, to a wider user community with different purposes.

4   Achieved Results

The current work is to create an ontology as a valuable base for possible upgrading about what is expected/required in H-BIM [10]. However, it is important to understand the difference between BIM standards and the Semantic Web technologies. Indeed, the ifcOWL is defined as a serialization of an IFC schema definition [11], in order to enable the use of contents semantically managed. For this reason, within INCEPTION, H-BIM is meant to be an ontology to support storage of semantic knowledge available for Cultural Heritage buildings and architectural complexes, as well as their related information [12]. The integration of Getty vocabularies and ifcOWL is a complex but feasible task, focusing on the actual queries, communications and current H-BIM work. Furthermore, within INCEPTION, we have the chance to test such integration, achieving positive results as well as beginning an implementation, thanks to the use of a "glossary of names" gathered by the Demonstration Cases analysis.

5   Conclusions

Developing an H-BIM is a complicated "reverse engineering" process. According to the INCEPTION workflow, it starts with documenting user needs, including and engaging not only experts but also non-experts. The demand is leading us to "how" and "what" surveying information we should include in H-BIM. The surveying produces a variety of different data, formats and outputs. It is essential to process the data without losing important information like metadata and paradata while editing and developing the digital elements of the H-BIM. A methodology of archiving digital data and linking them to the final product is one of the main outcomes. Before and during the creation of H-BIM, semantics and ontologies must be defined. In that phase, nomenclature (vocabularies, thesauri, etc.) are critical to maintain a common typology and to support interoperability.

Starting from the standardization for H-BIM modelling, the methodology for merging IFC models and semantic data has been defined. The identification of the Cultural Heritage buildings semantic ontology and data structure for information catalogue will allow the integration of semantic attributes with hierarchically and mutually aggregated 3D digital geometric models for management of heritage information. The development of a semantic 3D reconstruction, integrated with intangible information and social environment, structuring digital representation of buildings and sites will lead to the creation of models more accessible and implementable in a Heritage-BIM environment, based on Open BIM standard (IFC, IFD, etc.).

Acknowledgements. The project is under development by a consortium of fourteen partners from ten European countries led by the Department of Architecture of the University of Ferrara. Academic partners of the consortium, in addition to the Department of Architecture of the University of Ferrara, include the University of Ljubljana (Slovenia), the National Technical University of Athens (Greece), the Cyprus University of Technology (Cyprus), the University of Zagreb (Croatia), the research centers Consorzio Futuro in Ricerca (Italy) and Cartif (Spain). The clustering of small medium enterprises includes: DEMO Consultants BV (The Netherlands), 3L Architects (Germany), Nemoris (Italy), RDF (Bulgaria), 13BIS Consulting (France), Z + F (Germany), Vision and Business Consultants (Greece).

The INCEPTION project has been applied under the Work Programme Europe in a changing world – inclusive, innovative and reflective Societies (Call - Reflective Societies: Cultural Heritage and European Identities, Reflective-7-2014, Advanced 3D modelling for accessing and understanding European cultural assets).

This research project has received funding from the European Union's H2020 Framework Programme for research and innovation under Grant agreement no 665220.

References

1. Pauwels, P., et al.: Integrating building information modelling and semantic web technologies for the management of built heritage information. In: Digital Heritage International Congress (DigitalHeritage), vol. 1. IEEE (2013)
2. Arayici, Y., Counsell, J., Mahdjoubi, L. (eds.): Heritage Building Information Modelling. Taylor & Francis, Oxford (2017)

3. Achille, C., Lombardini, N., Tommasi, C.: BIM and cultural heritage: compatibility tests in an archaeological site. Int. J. 3D Inf. Model. (IJ3DIM) **5**(1), 29–44 (2016)

4. Logothetis, S., Delinasiou, A., Stylianidis, E.: Building information modelling for cultural heritage: a review. ISPRS Ann. Photogrammetry Remote Sensing Spat. Inf. Sci. **2**(5), 177 (2015)

5. Mitchell, W.J.: The Logic of Architecture: Design, Computation, and Cognition. MIT press, Cambridge (1990)

6. Maravelakis, E., Konstantaras, A., Kritsotaki, A., Angelakis, D., Xinogalos, M.: Analysing user needs for a unified 3D metadata recording and exploitation of cultural heritage monuments system. In: Bebis, G., et al. (eds.) ISVC 2013. LNCS, vol. 8034, pp. 138–147. Springer, Heidelberg (2013). https://doi.org/10.1007/978-3-642-41939-3_14

7. Lodi, G., et al.: Semantic web for cultural heritage valorisation. In: Hai-Jew, S. (ed.) Data Analytics in Digital Humanities. MSA, pp. 3–37. Springer, Cham (2017). https://doi.org/10.1007/978-3-319-54499-1_1

8. Münster, S., Pfarr-Harfst, M., Kuroczyński, P., Ioannides, M. (eds.): 3D Research Challenges in Cultural Heritage II: How to Manage Data and Knowledge Related to Interpretative Digital 3D Reconstructions of Cultural Heritage. LNCS, vol. 10025. Springer, Cham (2016). https://doi.org/10.1007/978-3-319-47647-6

9. Saygi, G., et al.: Evaluation of GIS and BIM roles for the information management of historical buildings. ISPRS Ann. Photogramm. Remote Sens. Spat. Inf. Sci. **2**, 283–288 (2013)

10. Bonsma, P., Bonsma, I., Maietti, F., Sebastian, R., Ziri, A.E., Parenti, S., Martín Lerones, P., Llamas, J., Turillazzi, B., Iadanza, E.: Roadmap for IT research on a heritage-BIM interoperable platform within INCEPTION. In: Borg, R.P., Gauci, P., Staines, C.S. (eds.) Proceedings of the International Conference "SBE Malta 2016". Europe and the Mediterranean: Towards a Sustainable Built Environment, pp. 283–290. Gutenberg Press, Malta (2016)

11. Logothetis, S., Stylianidis, E.: BIM open source software (OSS) for the documentation of cultural heritage. Virtual Archaeol. Rev. **7**(15), 28–35 (2016)

12. Cheng, H.-M., Yang, W.-B., Yen, Y.-N.: BIM applied in historical building documentation and refurbishing. Int. Arch. Photogrammetry Remote Sensing Spat. Inf. Sci. **40**(5), 85 (2015)

Building Information Modeling for Cultural Heritage: The Management of Generative Process for Complex Historical Buildings

F. Banfi[1,2(✉)], L. Chow[1], M. Reina Ortiz[1], C. Ouimet[3], and S. Fai[1]

[1] Carleton Immersive Media Studio (CIMS), Carleton University, Ottawa, Canada
`{lchow,sfai}@cims.carleton.ca,`
`MiquelReinaOrtiz@cmail.carleton.ca`
[2] ABC Department, Politecnico di Milano, Piazza Leonardo da Vinci 32, Milan, Italy
`fabrizio.banfi@polimi.it`
[3] Heritage Conservation Services, PSPC, Quebec, Canada
`Christian.Ouimet@tpsgc-pwgsc.gc.ca`

Abstract. Building Information Modeling (BIM) enhances the sharing of information during the traditional process for new construction, but most of the time, it requires high levels of knowledge management for the historical digital model (H-BIM). The innovation in the Digital Cultural Heritage (DCH) domain is supported by the development of Information and Communications Technologies (ICT) and modern tools that are able to transmit morphological characteristics of the buildings in all their uniqueness. The latest research in the field of H-BIM shows a significant emergence of innovative methods and management initiatives for the generation of complex historical elements, leading to the confrontation of the paradigm of regularity (simple geometric shapes) with the new paradigm of complexity (historical building elements). This paper proves the benefits of the BIM for project management of the Centre Block of the Canadian Parliament in Ottawa, Ontario Canada, and shows the results obtained by the introduction of Advanced Modeling Techniques (AMT) during the generative process, reducing time and cost for the creation of the complex architectural and structural elements. The uniqueness of the forms of historical buildings is a real value to be transmitted throughout the building's lifecycle with high Levels of Detail (LOD). Proper management of geometric primitives and Non-Uniform Rational Basis Spline (NURBS) models have guaranteed the conversion of spatial data (point clouds) from laser scanning and photogrammetry (geometric survey) into parametric applications. This paper explores the generative process of one of the most complex spaces within The Centre Block building of Parliament Hill—Confederation Hall.

Keywords: Historic building information modelling (HBIM)
Advanced modeling techniques (AMT)
Non-Uniform rational basis spline (NURBS) · Level of detail (LOD) · Accuracy

© Springer International Publishing AG, part of Springer Nature 2018
M. Ioannides (Ed.): ITN-DCH 2017, LNCS 10605, pp. 119–130, 2018.
https://doi.org/10.1007/978-3-319-75826-8_10

1   Introduction

Building Information Modeling (BIM) is an innovative modelling methodology able to improve the management of new construction projects and assemble large amounts of information during the lifecycle of the building. In recent years, BIM has also become viable in the field of built heritage, favouring the restoration and management processes of historic buildings in a digital environment [2, 8]. Although BIM is typically best suited for new construction, the development of a historical model (HBIM) for historic buildings and complex existing structures can also benefit from the uses of this emerging technology.

The intricate reality of the built heritage and the growing need to represent the actual geometry using free-form modeling collide with the new paradigms of complexity and accuracy, opening a novel operative perspective for the management of historic building with the different type of technologies and BIM-based analysis [3]. Thanks to laser scanning technology and photogrammetry for a BIM specialist is easier to create the as-built BIM (AB-BIM). This study presents an Advanced Modeling Technique (AMT) for historic heritage buildings, which integrate the free-form modeling and NURBS algorithms with additional parameterization to orientate the BIM to the correct level of detail (LOD) and accuracy (LOA).

The Carleton Immersive Media Studio (CIMS), a Carleton University Research Centre dedicated to using digital technologies for architectural rehabilitation and heritage conservation, developed a building information model for Centre Block – one of Canada's most significant heritage assets. Confederation Hall — a celebrated interior heritage space of Centre Block — has been an appropriate research subject for studying the improvement of Advanced Modeling Techniques (AMT) and the creation of specific databases composed of historical structural detailed 3D objects.

1.1   Parliament Hill: The History of Centre Block

The Parliament Hill National Historic Site comprises the Library of the Parliament, Centre Block, West Block, and East Block. These four buildings are considered exemplary models of the gothic revival style. Centre Block, the central building on Parliament Hill, is the home to Canada's parliamentary democracy – housing both the House of Commons and the Senate.

In 1916, the original Centre Block building was destroyed by a fire, and the design for a new Centre Block was started promptly by architects Jean Omer Marchand and John A. Pearson. The new design was a six-story building with the ninety-two meter Peace Tower as its centrepiece. The building was constructed as a hybrid structure of structural steel framing and load-bearing masonry, a new technology at the time that improved fire protection and allowed for taller and lighter buildings.

In 1986, Centre Block (see Fig. 1) was designated as a Classified Federal Heritage Building primarily for its significance as a national landmark and its architectural value.

Fig. 1. Historical Picture of the Centre Block under construction. Date: 1918-09-18 Source: Library and Archives Canada, Image#e010865984

1.2   The Centre Block Rehabilitation Project

The century-old Centre Block building (see Fig. 2) will undergo a major rehabilitation program commencing in 2018. In preparation for the Centre Block Rehabilitation Project program of work, CIMS developed a Building Information Model (BIM) in partnership with Heritage Conservation Services (HCS) and the Parliamentary Precinct Directorate (PPD) of Public Services and Procurement (PSPC). The upcoming rehabilitation project will be PSPC's largest and most complex rehabilitation project to date (Government of Canada, 2017).

The ten-year-long rehabilitation project includes updating mechanical, electrical and plumbing systems, security, and communications technology, as well as restoring masonry, seismic upgrades, stabilising existing windows and replacing roofing [9].

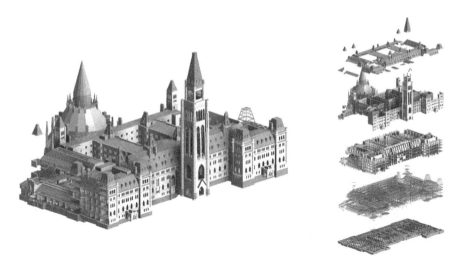

Fig. 2. Building Information Model of Centre Block. Parliament Hill, Ottawa, Canada. Source: Carleton Immersive Media Studio 2017

1.3   The Centre Block: A BIM-Based Solution for Built Heritage

Included within the project mandate for the Centre Block Rehabilitation Project was the creation of existing conditions BIM. The intention of creating a BIM was to facilitate an integrated project delivery (IPD) method for the Centre Block Program of Work. According to the American Institute of Architects (AIA), IPD is defined as "a project delivery approach that integrates people, systems, business structures, and practices into a process that collaboratively harnesses the talents and insights of all project participants to optimise project results" (AIA National, 2007) [1].

Although not required for IPD, the use of BIM can help facilitate the early collaboration of all project parties resulting in increased efficiency and the reduction of errors (Kent, Becerik-Gerber, 2010). In addition to capturing the existing conditions of the building, the model was developed in anticipation of specific model uses that follow industry best practice including, but not limited to, the generation of drawings, site analysis, design coordination, and design authoring.

In order to meet the goals mentioned above, the level of detail (LOD) and level of information (LOI) required for each building element category required specification. The level of detail – relating to the graphical information within the model – ranged from LOD 300–500. The LOI – related to the non-graphical information – for each building element varied based upon the availability of information for in situ building elements [6, 7]. The Centre Block BIM required the synthesis of heterogeneous data sets, including geo-referenced point cloud data, photogrammetry, archival drawings, historical structural steel catalogues, and historical photographs. The geo-referenced point cloud data was the primary source of data, with the remaining sources of data acting as secondary sources for when point cloud data was not available.

2   The Research Case Study

2.1   The New Paradigm of Complexity for HBIM: The Confederation Hall

The Confederation Hall is the case study developed in this paper. It is the central space just beyond the main entrance that symmetrically divides the Centre Block.

The octagonal chamber is organised in two different levels: the ground floor and the upper gallery. Limestone clustered columns divide the perimeter; themselves subdivided by dark green syenite pillars. A vaulted ambulatory supports the upper gallery. The arcaded arches are supported on one side by the hall's fan-vaulted ceiling and on the other on a single column in the centre of the room—a stone carved element with an image of Neptune (see Fig. 3).

Fig. 3. The Confederation Hall of the Centre Block. Source: Carleton Immersive Media Studio 2017 (Color figure online)

The Confederation Hall was the last part of the Centre Block's interior to be completed. This structure is adorned with stone carvings including the coats of arms of Canada and the provinces and prominent symbols from Canadian life. This space was considered significant as a case study due to its importance within the whole construction and history of the building as its high level of detail in craftsmanship.

2.2 Problem Statement: Challenge in BIM Generation

BIM applications are characterised by internal databases made up of object families. Each family includes different types of 3D objects. Each 3D object matches architectural and structural elements in reality such as the wall, ceiling, ceiling, pillar, roof, etc. The absence of 3D objects corresponding to complex historical elements in BIM database requires the creation of three-dimensional objects through a set of modeling commands. The latter is limited to a number of commands, including but not limited to, extrusion, sweep and swept blend. These commands allow users to create any shape and object, but the generative process requires long production times.

The free-form modeling differs from parametric modeling because it allows creation any form thanks to mathematical logic based on NURBS algorithms.

The main challenge for the implementation of the digital model of the Confederation Hall has been the integration of primary data sources (point clouds), secondary data sources (archival and CAD drawings, historical documents) and NURBS elements into BIM application with high levels of accuracy and detail.

Specifically, the following study emphasises the need for NURBS algorithms into BIM application. The novel generative method of the Confederation Hall has reached an automatic interpolation of the points that make up each 3D scan, transferring complex NURBS 3D elements from modeling software such as Rhino, Maya, etc. into BIM applications such as Revit and Archicad and structural analysis applications such as Midas, Abaqus, Teckla, etc. [4, 5].

2.3 Research Objectives

The development of a parametric model of the Confederation Hall for structural analysis has required the following research objectives:

- The lack of existing object libraries required the development of specific 3D objects by Advanced Modeling Tools (AMT) based on different type of data such as historical documentation and geo-referenced survey data.
- Integration of Non-Uniform Rational Basis-Splines (NURBS) into parametric applications (Autodesk Revit) in order to reduce the time and cost of the generative process of Historic Building Information Modeling (H-BIM)
- Improve the Level of Detail (LOD) and the Level of Accuracy (LOA) of each structural 3D object of the Confederation Hall with a deviating value of 1/2 mm between Point Cloud and 3D elements.
- To achieve an Automatic Verification System (AVS) of the Deviation Value between accurate point - clouds and 3D Objects to favour a precise description of how the model has been generated.

3 The Generative Process for Complex Structures

3.1 The Real Value of HBIM

In recent years, different studies have proposed innovative solutions to improve the quality of digital models for historic buildings [10]. The tangible and intangible values of the built heritage represent a cultural value for our modern society. The HBIM has allowed a holistic management of different types of information and has guided high levels of knowledge through the use of databases, table and schedules [5].

This integrated system has allowed the creation of a model that considers the building's richness of every single element and to share information through a Revit-shared project over time. Laser scanning and photogrammetry (primary data source) have allowed the definition of the outer part of each architectural and structural element, on the other hand, historical drawings, reports, etc. (secondary data source) have allowed the identification of the historical constructive techniques of the main vaulted system, lancet arches and stone decorations. As the point clouds reflect the geometric complexity of the historic construction, the digital model has reflected the geometric irregularity without an excessive standardisation of structural elements. This has been a fundamental aspect of this study oriented to improve structural simulation based on irregular and complex elements. The uniqueness and authenticity of historic buildings have preserved towards a more exhaustive simulation with a limited extra-cost in terms of processing time.

3.2 Primary and Secondary Data Sources: Laser Scanning, Photogrammetry and Historical/2D CAD Drawings

The integration and use of existing heritage building's documentation for 3D digital reconstruction is an innovative challenge that typically involves a management of heterogeneous datasets such as 3D survey data, CAD and historical drawings, tables and schedules, 3D non-contact imaging data and photographs. BIM can incorporate semantic data pertaining to physical characteristics such as structural materials, stratigraphic data, the behaviour of the material, etc. On the other side, HBIM needs to be given the resources to enable it to accomplish its tasks as a matter of urgency. BIM-based analysis requires high LOD and LOI in order to improve the test results and advanced simulation. The primary data source was georeferenced point cloud data from terrestrial laser scanning and photogrammetry (see Fig. 4). The data was captured by CIMS in partnership with Heritage Conservation Services (HCS), PSPC, using a Leica C10 and P40 (exterior and large interior spaces) and a Faro Focus (small to mid-sized interior spaces). Significant heritage interiors including the Senate, Senate Foyer, House of Commons, House of Commons Foyer, Rotunda, Hall of Honour and the exterior of the Peace Tower were also captured by HCS using photogrammetry. Secondary sources such as archival drawings, photographs, historical steel catalogues, and technical reports were referenced in cases where point cloud data was not available (see Fig. 5).

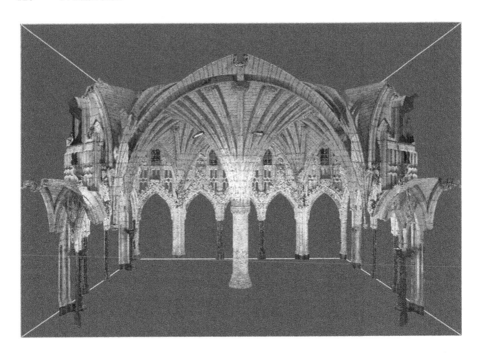

Fig. 4. Dense Point cloud of Rotunda. Centre Block. Photogrammetry from Heritage Conservation Services, PSPC 2017

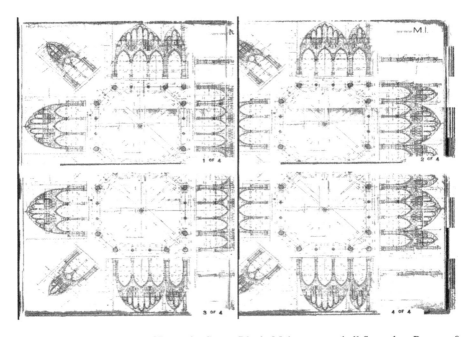

Fig. 5. Historical drawings of Rotunda. Centre Block. Main entrance hall floor plan. Pearson & Marchand Architects. Date 1920-05-20. Source: National Archives 1999, Reference#3890.

3.3 BIM Generation for Complex Structural Elements: Advanced Modeling Techniques and NURBS Algorithms

The accuracy of forms detected by using laser scanning, photogrammetry, drones and total station (3D data capture) clashes with the standardisation of 3D objects in the BIM databases. Each single structural element has its characteristics both in morphological and typological terms. The latter has been enhanced thanks to the proper use of NURBS interpolation algorithm which has allowed the automatic and semi-automatic extraction of geometric primitives (splines, polylines, etc., slices) directly from point clouds [9].

Non-Uniform Rational B-Splines (NURBS) algorithms have allowed the generation of complex elements and link difference structural application such as Midas FEA, Abaqus, SAP 2000 etc. NURBS interpolation algorithms for spline and complex surfaces has been employed to construct an exact geometric model.

As shown in Fig. 6, the proposed method is characterised by four steps:

1. The determination of the point cloud portion exactly matches the element to be generated. Thanks to the integrated use of the latest generation software such as Context Capture, Pointools, Scene, and Recap, it has been possible to orient, clean and decimate the point clouds with the aim of obtaining an appropriate base ready to be used for the model generation.
2. Many CAD programs use the term spline to describe an interpolated curve. Later it is obtained thanks to the application of the NURBS interpolation. Free-form modeling software like Mc Nell Rhinoceros has allowed the automatic extraction of geometric primitives from the point cloud. This second step has been crucial to determining the boundary conditions of the each structural element. After the first phase of automatic extraction of the perimeter, a second phase enabled the semi-automatic closing of the perimeters.
3. The closed perimeter and the internal points have allowed the NURBS interpolation for complex surfaces. This third step has been determined for the automatic creation of surfaces with subdivision UV 32x32. This specific parameter has allowed the generation of complex elements with a high level of precision and parametrization, avoiding traditional techniques such as 2D drawing and slicing. Thanks to exchange formats such as dwg, sat, aci etc., it was possible to transfer complex 3D objects into structural applications which that can convert NURBS model into detail meshed model for structural simulations.
4. The automatic generation of complex NURBS surface required the definition of a control system. The Automatic Verification System can automatically calculate the average distance between all the points used and the object being achieved. Figure 6 shows the AVS of the Structural Pillar of the Confederation Hall.

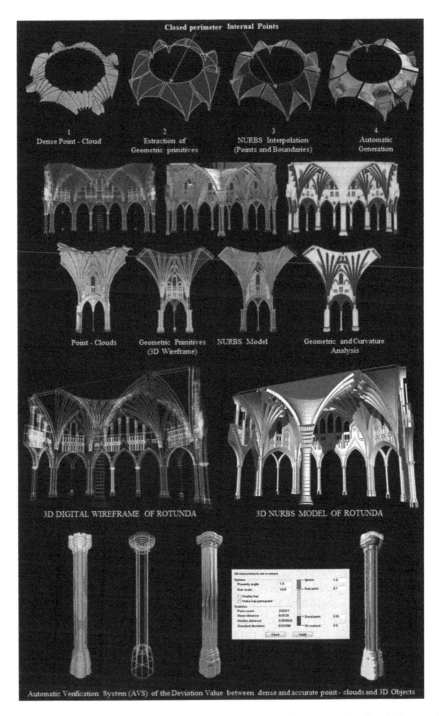

Fig. 6. The generative process for complex structural elements and related Automatic Verification System. The Deviation value between point clouds and the 3D object is 1-2 mm.

The median distance is 1.39 mm. This value was obtained from each structural element located in the point cloud.

3.4 Result and Conclusion

The generation of complex historic 3D objects has required Advanced Modelling Tools (AMT) to manage the structural and architectural elements of the Confederation Hall of the Centre Block with a high level of detail (LOD). The case study has been an important research field to improve the integration of Non-Uniform Rational Basis-Splines (NURBS) into the parametric logic of the HBIM of the Center Block.

The study has shown that NURBS modeling represents a real need for the generative process of complex elements in parametric applications. They can reduce time and cost of the generation of the digital model for existing heritage buildings. At the same time, FEA applications are state of the art software which define advanced nonlinear and detail analysis for civil and structural engineering applications. They are specialised for refined method analysis, which requires the real geometry of each complex structural element and the related material parameters. The NURBS model of the Confederation Hall has achieved a proper definition for structural analysis and finite element analysis (FEA) with a level of accuracy around 1/2 mm.

The level of accuracy (LOA) of the digital model has been verified by an automatic tool (Point/Surface Deviation) able to measure the point count (the number of points of the point clouds), the mean distance between the selected points and the selected surface,

Fig. 7. The NURBS model of the Confederation Hall's complex vaulted system. The generation of each 3D object (highlighted in yellow) allows the digital management of each structural element such as arches, vaults, stones, non-vertical and complex decorations with high levels of accuracy (LOA)/information (LOI) in BIM application and in finite element analysis (FEA) software. (Color figure online)

the median distance between the selected points and the selected surface and finally, the standard deviation between the selected points and the surface.

This analysis has been a useful Automatic Verification System (AVS) of the Deviation Value between Dense point - clouds, and 3D Objects could become a requirement to attest the quality of existing models (AS-found BIM) (Fig. 7).

Acknowledgments. This work was supported by Carleton Immersive Media Studio (CIMS), a Carleton University Research Centre, in Ottawa (Ontario). CIMS is working with Heritage Conservation Services (HCS) and the Parliamentary Precinct Directorate (PPD) of Public Services and Procurement Canada (PSPC) on the documentation and the creation of a Building Information Model (BIM) in Autodesk Revit.

The work has also been supported by the project New Paradigms/New Tools for Heritage Conservation in Canada, funded by the Social Sciences and Humanities Research Council (SSHRC) of Canada, Partnership Grants.

    Social Sciences and Humanities   Conseil de recherches en
                    Research Council of Canada   sciences humaines du Canada

References

1. AIA National|AIA California Council: Integrated Project Delivery: A Guide. Version 1, 25 May 2017. https://info.aia.org/SiteObjects/files/IPD_Guide_2007.pdf
2. Banfi, F.: Building information modelling – a novel parametric modeling approach based on 3d surveys of historic architecture. In: Ioannides, M., et al. (eds.) EuroMed 2016. LNCS, vol. 10058, pp. 116–127. Springer, Cham (2016). https://doi.org/10.1007/978-3-319-48496-9_10
3. Banfi, F.: BIM orientation: grades of generation and information for different type of analysis and management process. Int. Arch. Photogrammetry Remote Sensing Spat. Inf. Sci. **42** (2017). https://doi.org/10.5194/isprs-archives-xlii-2-w5-57-2017
4. Banfi, F., Fai, S., Brumana, R.: BIM automation: advanced modeling generative process for complex structures. ISPRS Ann. Photogrammetry Remote Sensing Spat. Inf. Sci. **4** (2017)
5. Barazzetti, L., Banfi, F., Brumana, R., Gusmeroli, G., Previtali, M., Schiantarelli, G.: Cloud-to-BIM-to-FEM: structural simulation with accurate historic BIM from laser scans. In: Simulation Modelling Practice and Theory, vol. 57, pp. 71–87 (2015)
6. CanBIM: AEC (CAN) BIM Protocol. CanBIM (2014). http://www.canbim.com/canbim-documents
7. Chow, L., Fai, S.: Developing verification systems for building information models of heritage buildings with heterogeneous datasets. Int. Arch. Photogrammetry Remote Sensing Spatial Inf. Sci. **42**, 125 (2017)
8. Della Torre, S.: Shaping tools for built heritage conservation: from architectural design to program and management: learning from 'Distretti culturali'. In: Community Involvement in Heritage, pp. 93–102, Garant (2015)
9. Government of Canada. Following the Rehabilitation of the Parliamentary Buildings (2017). https://www.tpsgc-pwgsc.gc.ca/citeparlementaire-parliamentaryprecinct/rehabilitation/index-eng.html

Innovative Business Plans for H-BIM Application Related to Alternative Financing Opportunities for Cultural Heritage

Klaus Luig[1(✉)], Dieter Jansen[1], Federica Maietti[2] ⓘ, Luca Coltro[3], and Dimitrios Karadimas[4]

[1] 3L Architekten, Horlecke 46, 58706 Menden, Germany
{klaus.luig,dieter.jansen}@3-l.de
[2] Department of Architecture, University of Ferrara, via Ghiara 36, 44121 Ferrara, Italy
federica.maietti@unife.it
[3] 13BIS Consulting SARL, 13bis rue St Exupéry, 83120 Plan de la Tour, France
lmcoltro.13bis@gmail.com
[4] Vision Business Consultants, 10 Antinoros Street, 11634 Athens, Greece
d.karadimas@vbc.gr

Abstract. Within the EU funded project "INCEPTION – Inclusive Cultural Heritage in Europe through 3D semantic modelling", the use and application of H-BIM data is focused at. The project realizes innovation in 3D modelling of cultural heritage through an inclusive approach for time-dynamic 3D reconstruction of built and social environments.

The methods and tools will result in 3D models that are easily accessible for a wide range of user groups and interoperable by different hardware and software tools. One of the main aims of the project is to develop an open-standard Semantic Web Platform for Building Information Models for Cultural Heritage (H-BIM) to be implemented in user-friendly Augmented and Virtual Reality applications on mobile devices.

The Innovative Business Models for H-BIM applications related to alternative financing opportunities for cultural heritage is under development in order to exploit the results of the project. Nevertheless the innovative business modelling process is transferable on other cultural heritage driven projects. The objective is to achieve a sustainable viral reach of the data Platform and relevant apps by means of free of charge and open access applications, free use of general information, technical information and premium data at a reasonable price, involvement of large commercial and institutional players.

Keywords: Heritage BIM applications · Business modeling
Interoperability and data sharing

1 Introduction

The EU project INCEPTION - Inclusive Cultural Heritage in Europe through 3D semantic modelling, funded under the call *Reflective Societies: Cultural Heritage and*

M. Ioannides (Ed.): ITN-DCH 2017, LNCS 10605, pp. 131–143, 2018.
https://doi.org/10.1007/978-3-319-75826-8_11

European Identities, Advanced 3D modelling for accessing and understanding European cultural assets, is developing new research avenues in the field of heritage 3D data acquisition and modelling.

The INCEPTION project main aim is focused on innovation in 3D modelling of cultural heritage through an inclusive approach for time-dynamic 3D reconstruction of heritage sites and on the possibility to create an inclusive understanding of European cultural identity and diversity by stimulating and facilitating collaborations across disciplines, technologies and sectors.

Within this overall structure, the project is divided into five main steps: setting up of a common framework and knowledge management; advancement into the integrated 3D data capturing methodology; semantic modelling for Cultural Heritage buildings in H-BIM environment; development of the INCEPTION Platform; deployment and valorization through different on-site and off-site applications for a wide range of users.

The project, lasting four years, started in June 2015 and it is now approaching the third year of development. The first stage related to the enhancement in 3D acquisition processes has been accomplished by improving first of all integrated data capturing methodologies, while the enhancement of technologies is under development. In the meanwhile, the research is dealing with the creation of interoperable 3D models in H-BIM environment to be shared by an open standard Platform. Simultaneously to the achievement of the main technical results, the deduction and development of a business plan is intended to prove the economic opportunities and the market relevance of the developed solutions. In the third phase of the project, the exploitation plan will be finalized and case-related business plans will validate the created business plans.

2   The INCEPTION Project: An Overview

As part of 3D integrated survey applied to Cultural Heritage, digital documentation is gradually emerging as effective support of much of different information in addition to the shape, morphology and dimensional data. The implementation of data collection processes and the development of semantically enriched 3D models is an effective way to enhance the connection between ICT technologies, different Cultural Heritage experts, users and different disciplines, both social and technical. The possibility to achieve interoperable models able to enrich the interdisciplinary knowledge of European cultural identity is one of the main outcomes of the European Project "INCEPTION - Inclusive Cultural Heritage in Europe through 3D semantic modelling", funded by European Commission within the Programme Horizon 2020. The project ranges from the overall digital documentation and diagnostic strategies for heritage protection, management and enhancement, to the 3D acquisition technologies. The development of hardware, software and digital platforms is aimed at representation and dissemination of cultural heritage through ICT processes and BIM addresses to Cultural Heritage assets, up to the implementation of semantic information to a wider and more extensive use of 3D digital models [1].

2.1 Inclusive Cultural Heritage Through 3D Semantic Modelling

The overall concept and project methodology of INCEPTION is based on five main Actions [2].

The first one, achieved during the first year of the project, is related to the development of a common framework for catalogue methodology, basically by mapping the stakeholder's knowledge demands and targeted implementations by scholars, technicians, citizens and governments through the identification of key requirements that contribute to meet Europe's societal objectives related to Cultural Heritage. The implementation of an effective, cross-disciplinary and collaborative work methodology allowed to define the data collection process, case studies setup, selection and utilization of system and instruments, implementation of semantically enriched models and exploitation in education and business.

The second Action is related to the integrated 3D data capturing through a protocol to be followed during the planning and performing of a 3D laser scanner survey of Cultural Heritage, and it is referred to an architectural, archaeological, urban and site scale.

Action 3 started during the second year of project development with the identification of the Cultural Heritage buildings semantic ontology and data structure for information catalogue. Integration of sematic attributes with hierarchically and mutually aggregated 3D digital geometric models is indispensable for management of heritage information.

Action 4 is the development of the INCEPTION Semantic Web Platform. The interoperable Semantic Web H-BIM Platform allows achieving the widest accessibility and interoperability, the use of three-dimensional models by researchers from different disciplines and non-expert users, minimizing the difficulties of interaction with this kind of data, now accessible only by experts through the use of dozens of different software.

Action 5, Deployment and Valorization, is based on a wiki-like approach to share and enrich models' information and interpretation by users; the 3D models will be delivered in different Apps for numerous of purposes. The "browsing and query interface" will be defined allowing contributions by researchers and experts that actually do not deal with 3D data, and enabling a wide and easy access to the data by citizens, non-expert users and public at large.

Demonstration activities are pursuing three main goals: to gather practical inputs from the stakeholders; to setup a relevant environment for testing and validation of the research outcomes; and to disseminate the preliminary results through real examples with direct involvement of the stakeholders.

Within the INCEPTION Platform, every user will be able to upload 3D models (following the specific INCEPTION standard), semantic data, documents (i.e. pictures, maps, literature), leave comments or other material necessary to improve the scientific knowledge [3].

The user applications and model deployment will be done remotely, simultaneously or in different moments, from the heritage site, such as in labs, museums, classrooms, or even in personal homes or offices. Deployment of 3D models with integral narratives on the heritage sites [4]. This will provide the users (i.e. visitors/tourists, scholars/researchers) with an interactive possibility to access the knowledge about the sites and objects, to exchange the knowledge between each other, and to enrich the knowledge with their findings and complementary (or contradicting) insights.

2.2 INCEPTION Approach Towards Business Strategies

Quite often research and development projects are suffering from appropriate ideas and fitting actions on the exploitation of results in the project duration and afterwards. Often a missing strategy that is developed as an ongoing monitoring process in order to upgrade the exploitable results and to adjust the principal business modeling strategies continuously is the cause. In order to avoid these failures INCEPTION embedded activities for business modeling in different project phases starting with the identification of key exploitable results already at month 12 of the project. The following chapter will give an insight in the activities performed and the process foreseen for further development.

3   Business Modelling and Cultural Heritage

3.1 The Platform Oriented Approach

In order to create and store qualified digital data of cultural heritage that is applicable and usable for different user groups the solution for an easy and free of charge access of such a Platform that needs funding is ambitious. The Description of Action of the EU funded project is providing a generic overview of the action included in the creation of business modelling and the INCEPTION core Business Plan for the Platform. This will constitute the project's main business plan covering all commercially viable project developments and results

The objective is to achieve a sustainable viral reach of the data Platform and relevant apps by means of:

– Implementing the Platform as a free of charge and open access application;
– Allowing free use of general information;
– Supplying technical information and premium data at a reasonable price;
– Involving large commercial and institutional players by negotiating partnerships;
– Involving for financial support and event financing.

3.2 Market Strategy

An initial market strategy can be summarized in the following building blocks:

Open access:	the Platform will represent an innovative and premium tool with continuous technical upgrading and with an open access approach.
Free online users:	students, professional and general public have free access to main general data.

Paid subscription:	specific technical data for professionals and other interest groups are available and can be downloaded for a limited charge or with a periodic subscription.
Events:	specific events will be charged such as tenders based on Platform data or one-off conferences, seminars and other specific uses of the Platform and database information.
Indirect revenues:	exploitation of users' data, data collected by cookies, geo-location data (in accordance with the privacy terms and conditions in force).
Onsite revenue streams:	onsite visitors who acquire fee-based audio-guides and case specific apps making use of the Platform database.
Strategic partnerships:	with institutional partners (such as UNESCO, governmental institutes, national agencies, etc.) and killer-apps partnerships with mass online engines, social networks and mass commercial sites (as Google Maps, HP, Leica, Trip advisor, etc.) to boost the "reach".

The intention is to use the stakeholders (many of them potential users or clients) to support the commercialization of the Platform and to approach potential clients. The demo cases of the project -e.g. museums- provide relevant information as frequency of visitors and other commercialization related facts and figures. These facts and figures are the basis of the revenue calculation of the case related business plans.

During INCEPTION the willingness of the large public to pay a limited fee for specific information will be investigated, as well as the potential income from sharing visitors' information with interested parties.

The original intention has been for the Platform to be implemented and managed by different project partners responsible for:

- Platform implementation and management + server hosting, implementation and maintenance of software for end users,
- Business development, dissemination, contracts management and financial management.

The qualified partners are committed to initiate the Platform and take responsibility for the initiative, implementation and initial exploitation. When successful, they will involve other commercial partners that are better equipped at that point in time.

The initial exploitation and business plan is under elaboration. No project related budget will be used for the initial implementation and investment costs. Preliminary financial projections have been made to show that the Platform could be self-supporting after five years. This aim seems to be feasible; initial financial projections and model outcomes have been included in the project's scope.

3.3   Business Modeling Alternatives

Following the principles of individual business model generation as described by Oster-walder and Pigneur [5] under the headline of Canvas the start from scratch while creating a business model is foreseen. Canvas is an appropriate tool if the product to sell is not complex (e.g. a book) and the targeted customer group is homogeneous. This approach is often used in EU funded R&D projects as it is easy to apply by semi-experts. In case of the INCEPTION core business Platform the product is extremely complex and demanding and the targeted customer group is heterogeneous. Therefore an innovative process or a new methodology is needed in order to fulfill these characteristic and complex demands of the Platform being used and applied by different user groups from tourists to experts.

Today innovative business modeling is extremely important in order to raise the success factor of any kind of business activities. Referring to Prof. Oliver Gassmann, University of St. Gallen, head of the Business Model Innovation Lab, the creator of the business model navigator approach [6], 90% of today's successful operating business models are built just out of 55 existing patterns of business models and the innovation creating successful breakthrough business models is just to combine 2 or 3 of these patterns to build up a new successful business model instead of developing self standing ones in a smart way.

Figure 1 below shows different patterns that are developed as parallel actions focusing on a time related basis. The junctions show the fusion and combination of patterns that strengthen the original business model and add up innovation and create success.

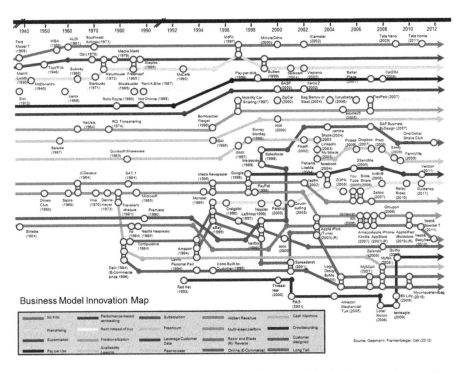

Fig. 1. Business model innovation map. Source: Gassmann, Frankenberger, Csik (2012).

Furthermore, it is foreseen to follow two different ways of business modelling strategy:

1. Economically driven and more RoI (Return of Investment) focused knowing about the economic risks.
2. Impact Investment driven, social growth oriented and less RoI focused but looking for a combination of financial + environmental + social sustainability.

As case 1 is well introduced and following the principles of regular market mechanisms there is no need to explain the principal business model. The funding company has to prove a RoI and a margin based on the business idea and related to a running time of the company. Based on forecasts of revenues and margins the profitability is proofed.

3.4   Impact Investment Oriented Business Modeling

Case 2 "Impact Investment" is following a different approach which is less profit oriented in the short-term but it focuses on a wider concept of sustainability that includes environmental issues and social values enhancing the results of the investment by providing extra value for the society.

In this note the significance of seeking Impact Investing sources of funding along with (not instead of) the traditional capital markets in order to fund the scale up of the platform is highlighted.

First of all, laser scanning has become an important impact as 3D model + basic BIM translation becomes almost automatic. In this situation the operational costs to upload a new site would be limited to the variable cost of laser scanning and the insertion of specific info of the site.

In order to scale up fast there is a need to address a customer base that has a large network of CH sites under the same governance. Most of these aggregations will probably be public networks of CH sites or associations of a mix of public and private managed sites. The involved partners of the consortium believe that there will be a significant interest to participate in the platform not only for commercial reasons (i.e. to achieve a better and innovative offer) but also to pursue scientific and preservation goals. Most likely these networks - mostly public entities or non-profit associations - will not have the funds available to enable the upload of several CH sites on one hand and on the other hand they will probably also have strict rules to increase their offering of paid services.

Because of the above, it is unlikely to assist to a snowball effect generated by a crowd of CH networks jostling one another to jump on the platform even if they might have enjoyed the effectiveness of the tool through the application to the demo-cases. In other words a period of intensive self-investment must be foreseen before there is a chance to appreciate the snowball effect. Also the strategy of a partnership with a large player (e.g. Google) cannot be imagined with a product at a too early stage of development.

The search of funding required to scale up the platform will necessarily lead to approach the private capital markets. If presented as a general investment target the Platform would be considered exclusively for its projected Internal Rate of Return (IRR) and compared to all other investment opportunities. In the venture capital radar screen, the platform may be probably compared to products such as war-drones and - if we look only at online apps - it may have to battle against an adult-dating platform. But a particular aspect of the INCEPTION product is that the platform concerns the protection, conservation and dissemination of CH; in other words, it is not a mere business initiative with the only objective to make money and one only valuation parameter: its projected IRR. Instead, the platform has been created, above all, with scientific and ethical purposes for the benefit of all the people across geography and time. The investors that will invest in the platform know that they are seeking positive returns but also that they are doing good deeds for humanity.

3.5 The Asset Class Impact Investing and Its Specific Demands

The asset class that seeks responsible investments is called Impact Investing. The impact investors are always looking for new products in this sector and they are also ready to give up some basis points of yield to pursue the good deeds. The INCEPTION Platform is – in our understanding – potentially eligible to enter this asset class. Thanks to the presence of foundations that have this very objective of philanthropic investing one could imagine to upload sites that may never become profitable on their own but that may be of a great scientific and cultural interest; additionally one could approach the large networks of CH sites cited above and push to upload the majority of their sites without the pressure of a quick IRR with a high hurdle rate. Above all the objective is to access a large and growing asset class of capital investments which, at the moment, is still confined to a limited range of target investments. Though, in order to be able to access this asset class though we have to:

(a) become eligible and work so that the CH preservation becomes *de iure* an Impact Investing category and
(b) elaborate our offering and business plan approach to meet the Impact Investing requirements (Fig. 2).

Impact Investing has grown in the last years and it has been recognized as a new asset class by the capital markets. In fact, according to the latest survey of the Global Impact Investing Network (GIIN), collectively, as of the end of 2016, 208 respondents managed USD 114 billion in Impact Investment assets and they plan to increase capital invested by 17% in 2017 also encouraged by the fact that their impact investments have performed either in line with or exceeded both impact and financial expectations.

Concerning the first point, we acknowledge that some industry sectors are identified as appropriate to Impact Investing such as: Microfinance and related Financial Services, (Renewable) Energy, (Social) Housing, Health, Education, etc. As anticipated above, one of our adjacent goal within INCEPTION is to promote the Cultural Heritage Protection and Conservation (CHPC) as an Impact Investment sector *de iure*. This will enable the INCEPTION Platform to be an eligible investment target for 2i fund managers.

Concerning the second point, it is necessary to adopt a (recognized) way of quantifying social impact in the business plan of the Platform. In fact, impact investors together with the standard financial parameters of evaluation they request a computation of the social impact of their investments (Fig. 3).

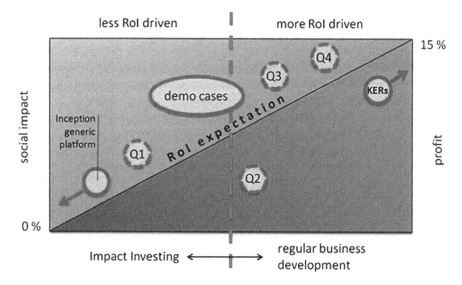

Fig. 2. RoI expectation and generic relation to social impact. Ref. 3L © 2017.

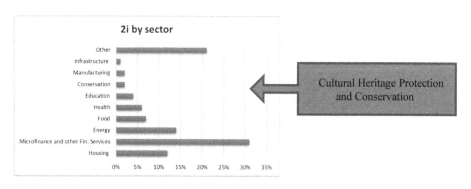

Fig. 3. Allocation by sector – GIIN.

3.6 Outlook on Further Business Modeling Activities Based on the Business Model Navigator Created by Prof. Oliver Gassmann, University of St. Gallen, Switzerland

The core business plan modeling of INCEPTION will focus on these two generic options mentioned above and it is not yet decided how the combination of these two options might be realised. Following the ideas of the DoA as shown above the translation into the business model navigator development is described as follows:

"Pattern 18 Freemium, Choosing between free basic and paid premium versions: Good samples of the Freemium pattern are Hotmail, Survey monkey, Skype, Spotify or Dropbox. The nature of Freemium is to offer a basic use for free and an enhanced quality of use balanced. The Freemium pattern is popular with internet based businesses with marginal production costs approaching zero and the benefit of external network effects. In the past these kind of companies have used

the Freemium model to test user acceptance of new software releases or business models. The pattern works even better when coupled with a strong customer focus [6]."

The description of the pattern is 100% fitting to the needs of the core business plan for the INCEPTION Platform. The quality level distinction following the different needs of the user groups and the strategy of even upgrading the user to a higher information level combined with a paid offer is an appropriate business modeling idea. Possible combinations with other patterns and ideas for offers related to target groups are:

"Pattern 1: Add-on, additional charge for extras: In the Add-on business model, while the core offer is priced competitively, numerous extras drive up the final price. In the end customer pay more than originally anticipated, but benefit from selecting options that meet their specific needs. Airline tickets are a well-known example: customers pay a low price for a basic ticket, but the overall costs are increased by 'add-on' extras such as credit card fees, food and baggage charges. The Add-on pattern generally requires a very sophisticated pricing strategy. The core product must be effectively advertised and is often offered at very low rates [6]."

Add-ons that are applicable for the core data Platform offer related to the qualification and needs of the different user groups are:

Q1 level tourists/citizens: ideas for add-on's are: VIP services of any kind (e.g. travel booking, parking, accommodation, special areas visits that are originally closed to the public, extra print brochures, app for virtual guided tours via smartphone, personal guided tours, special event participation, cultural flat rate offer).

Q2 level technicians: extra data material for qualified maintenance planning (e.g. data of qualified craftsmen for tendering and operating issues or building supply industry connection for qualified application support, CH BIM models for upgraded maintenance planning e.g. 4D/5D preparation).

Q3 scholars: extra material following extra educational needs (e.g. connection support between the requested and other stored projects that are reasonably connected by smart data).

Q4 Scientific data base users: extra material following extra scientific needs (e.g. connection support between the requested and other stored projects that are reasonably connected by smart data) (Fig. 4).

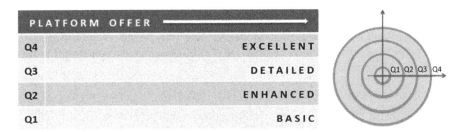

Fig. 4. Qualification of INCEPTION target customers related to knowledge conditions and requests, and information level needs. Ref. 3L © 2016.

The Add-on offer will be created using existing platforms as e.g. booking.com or tripadvisor.com and combine and link them at a single marketplace to focus on the targeted customer needs. Furthermore, the idea is to ease their interest following behavior requests. At the same time as the Add-on is accepted following a price value related offer strategy the clients are well trained in this scheme of business.

"Pattern 7: Cross selling, killing two birds with one stone, Cross-selling involves offering complimentary products and services beyond a company's basic product and service range with the aim of exploiting existing customer relationships to sell more goods [6]."

The Add-on examples above show a lot of potential of Cross-selling opportunities at the same time.

"Pattern 8: Crowdfunding, taking finance by swarm. The Crowdfunding business model involves outsourcing the financing of a project to the general public. Its intention to limit the influence of professional investors. It starts with announcement designed to raise awareness of projects looking for possible backers [6]."

Especially case 2 shows big potential for Crowdfunding as crowd funded projects are often based on social impact. The share of the investment costs for raising and running the Platform is the target. The preparation of a crowdfunding pitch presentation is not complicated and there are platforms at the internet looking for proposals for projects and matching the project needs with targeted investors.

"Pattern 15: Flat rate, 'All you can eat'- unlimited consumption at a fixed price. With this business model customers purchase a service or a product for a lump sum and then use as much as they wish. The main advantage for them is unlimited consumption with full control of their costs [6]."

A CH platform flat rate use is a promising option if the offer is targeted exactly to the needs of the addressed customers differing from Q1 to Q4 ambitions and requirements.

"Pattern 15: Leverage customer data, making use of what you know, Leveraging customer data is one major area benefitting from present-day technological progress and the possibilities it opens up in the fields of data collection and processing. Companies whose main activities centre on the acquisition and analysis of data are already thriving abundantly and illustrate the enormous demand in this segment. The concept is mirrored in increasingly frequent statements such as 'data is the new oil' [6]."

As the INCEPTION Platform is collecting and storing different kind of information at project and customer level – Q1 to Q4 – anyway the smart handling of customer data is a task of filtering the information collected and not of collecting the information. This creates an extra value. Regular customer data are sold for 5 € per data set. The Platform has an extra value for lot of companies that are providing services and products for the different target groups and the stakeholders at the same time. Providing a critical mass of customers is attracting interest groups in terms of placing advertisement or special services that add value to the Platform offer.

Considering the different customer groups and their specific needs it is obvious that a suite solution consisting of apps related to different offers and topics is a good business scheme that will be modeled related to the above mentioned patterns. The core Platform is planned as a structured database and the apps will enable the different user groups to filter the appropriate information related to their customer profile.

3.7   Summary Business Modeling Strategy and Intermediate Results

Within the above mentioned exploitation activities, some important preliminary steps have been accomplished, including: 1. Development of INCEPTION's core business plan for the platform and 2. Identification of 16 Key Exploitable Results (KERs) at early project stage. Having noticed that at least 6 to 8 KERs show an impact of creating a valuable business model for itself these intermediate results are very promising even knowing that CH and profitable business are often not creating a well balanced partnership. Furthermore, case related Business Plans (BP) will be developed. This is done additionally as a follow up activity in order to validate the profitability of the single demonstration cases that are associated with the core INCEPTION platform and its functionalities. Different stakeholders from municipalities to monuments or museums will profit from associating them to the INCEPTION platform.

4   Conclusions

In the near future based on two input tables distributed to the partners and the stakeholders involved in the demo-cases an ongoing inductive data-gathering process will enable us to feed the business plan with critical market data. Subsequently, in order to enrich these findings, we will launch a research of existing broad market databases and, potentially, a survey among a broader base of clients to better understand the market landscape.

On the construction costs side instead, we will intensively study the split between pure variable costs and Platform's development costs with a marginal decreasing rate; about the latter, we will try to establish a mathematical distribution that will enable us to evaluate the investments of uploading new categories to the Platform.

Innovative business models for H-BIM application related to alternative financing opportunities as a cross-over of innovative business modeling for cultural heritage offer a great opportunity to enrich the share of information of cultural heritage at an enhanced level.

At the same time, innovative financing tools offer the possibility of covering the needed expenses without additional funding. Impact investment provides an innovative way of creating a win-win situation for CH driven projects of any kind. INCEPTION provides key exploitable results and manifold exploitation opportunities for different stakeholders representing profit and non-profit organizations. The professional treatment of business modeling at any project stage starting from the kick-off is a promising way of assuring the exploitation quality for the benefit of all CH project partners.

Acknowledgements. The INCEPTION project is under development by a consortium of fourteen partners from ten European countries led by the Department of Architecture of the University of Ferrara.

Academic partners of the Consortium, in addition to the Department of Architecture of the University of Ferrara, include the University of Ljubljana (Slovenia), the National Technical University of Athens (Greece), the Cyprus University of Technology (Cyprus), the University of Zagreb (Croatia), the research centers Consorzio Futuro in Ricerca (Italy) and Cartif (Spain).

The clustering of small medium enterprises includes: DEMO Consultants BV (The Netherlands), 3L Architects (Germany), Nemoris (Italy), RDF (Bulgaria), 13BIS Consulting (France), Z + F (Germany), Vision and Business Consultants (Greece).

The INCEPTION project has been applied under the Work Programme Europe in a changing world – inclusive, innovative and reflective Societies (Call - Reflective Societies: Cultural Heritage and European Identities, Reflective-7-2014, Advanced 3D modelling for accessing and understanding European cultural assets).

This research project has received funding from the European Union's H2020 Framework Programme for research and innovation under Grant agreement no 665220.

References

1. Di Giulio, R., Maietti, F., Piaia, E.: 3D documentation and semantic aware representation of Cultural Heritage: the INCEPTION project. In: Proceedings of the 14th Eurographic Workshop on Graphics and Cultural Heritage, pp. 195–198. Eurographic Association (2016)
2. Di Giulio, R., Maietti, F., Piaia, E., Medici, M., Ferrari, F., Turillazzi, B.: Integrated data capturing requirements for 3D semantic modelling of cultural heritage: the INCEPTION protocol. In: ISPRS International Archives of the Photogrammetry, Remote Sensing and Spatial Information Sciences, pp. 251–257 (2017)
3. Maietti, F., Di Giulio, R., Balzani, M., Piaia, E., Medici, M., Ferrari, F.: Digital memory and integrated data capturing: innovations for an inclusive cultural heritage in Europe through 3D semantic modelling. In: Ioannides, M., Magnenat-Thalmann, N., Papagiannakis, G. (eds.) Mixed Reality and Gamification for Cultural Heritage, pp. 225–244. Springer, Heidelberg (2017)
4. De Luca, L., Busayarat, C., Stefani, C., Véron, P., Florenzano, M.: A semantic-based platform for the digital analysis of architectural heritage. Comput. Graph. **35**(2), 227–241 (2011)
5. Osterwalder, A., Pigneur, Y.: Business Model Generation. Campus, Frankfurt (2011)
6. Gassmann, O., Frankenberger, K., Csik, M.: The Business Model Navigator. Pearson, Harlow (2015)

3D Models of Ancient Greek Collection of the Perm University History Museum

Creation and Use

Nadezhda Povroznik[✉] (iD)

Perm State National Research University, Perm 614990, Russian Federation
povroznik.ng@gmail.com

Abstract. Exhibits of the ancient collection of the Perm University History Museum have a significant historical and cultural value. The purpose of this article is to demonstrate the experience to implement low budget digitization, creation and use of 3D models of the antique collection of the Perm University History Museum. The article describes the technological process of 3D models' creation. It also shows ways how to overcome the limitations of the automatic digitization process (correction of a polygonal mesh, texture, etc.), examines ways to verify the correspondence between the created digital copy of the exhibit and the original, and shows the possibilities of using the created collection of 3D models in scientific research, education and popularization of historical and cultural heritage. The creation of 3D photogrammetric models of exhibits and their publication online improve access to historical and cultural heritage items for their subsequent use. Perspective directions for the secondary use of digital items are scientific study of exhibits, use in educational activities in the training of specialists in the field of Digital History and as illustrative material, as well as solving the problems of historical reconstruction of objects' domestic use and popularization of historical and cultural heritage among various categories of the population.

Keywords: 3D model · Photogrammetry · Ancient greek collection
Low cost digitization · Access · Usage

1 Introduction

Perm State University was founded in 1916 as Perm Department of Saint Petersburg State University. The status of the Imperial University suggested the existence of museums with exhibits for the purpose of demonstrating to students. So the Museum of Antiquities and Arts was established to support the educational process among the students of History and Philology Faculties. The museum's collections were formed in various ways, including unique items, which were bought from collectors in Moscow and St. Petersburg. During the Second World War part of Hermitage collections was evacuated to Perm. After the war, when the funds were returned to Leningrad, the leadership of the Hermitage decided to present with the part of the exhibits the Museum of

© Springer International Publishing AG, part of Springer Nature 2018
M. Ioannides (Ed.): ITN-DCH 2017, LNCS 10605, pp. 144–154, 2018.
https://doi.org/10.1007/978-3-319-75826-8_12

Antiquities and Arts at Perm University. Today the Museum has more than 25 thousand storage units. The Museum's storage facility includes the following subject collections of historical and cultural heritage items, that is "Ancient Egypt", "Ancient Greece", "The Fine Arts of Europe" and some others.

Digitization of the museum's exhibits is caused both by the need to make the museum items more available for their use in scientific research and education, and it is also connected with the training of specialists in the field of creating digital information resources of historical and cultural heritage.

At the moment we create 3D models of exhibits of the Ancient Greek collection, which is represented by objects of ancient Greek life from the 6th century BC up to the 2nd century AD.

The most important factor in the project's realization is the implementation of low-budget digitization, which has affected the technical and technological basis of the process. The choice of software was also caused by the special conditions of the developers for the implementation of non-commercial projects in the field of preservation and representation of historical and cultural heritage.

The purpose of this article is to demonstrate the experience to implement low budget digitization, creation and use of 3D models of the antique collection of the Perm University History Museum. The article describes the technological process of 3D models' creation, it also shows ways how to overcome the limitations of the automatic digitization process (correction of a polygonal mesh, texture, etc.), examines ways to verify the correspondence between the created digital copy of the exhibit and the original, and shows the possibilities of using the created collection of 3D models in scientific research, education and popularization of historical and cultural heritage.

2   Related Work

Creation of high-quality 3D photogrammetric models of objects of historical and cultural heritage appears to be at the center of researchers' attention [1–4]. 3D modeling of isolated objects using photogrammetry technology is very relevant with regard to value of sources [5, 6]. Most methods and technologies for creating high-quality 3D models with a high degree of automation are costly, due to the price of equipment (laser scanners) and software. Nevertheless, very low cost digitization technologies with high quality of 3D models are very popular. Recent reviews of low-budget digitization technologies have been published [7, 8], the software based on SfM and IM technologies has been analyzed [9], their advantages and disadvantages have been examined [10]. Some of the identified limitations can be overcome by using the methods described in this paper.

The development of the information environment in the field of historical and cultural heritage is accompanied not only by the increase in the quantity and quality of these resources, but also by the creation of digital cultural heritage services related to heritage documentation, data organization, and the simplified search for the necessary resources with the help of aggregators (for example, Europeana [11]). Recent questions about the ways to use in the future the created digital resources of historical and cultural heritage have become more urgent [12]. Among these methods one can single out the scientific direction of use (including reconstruction), educational, social, including the popularization of history and historical and cultural heritage, commercial as well as creative directions, which are becoming more and more in demand [13]. The project, realized at Perm University, connected with the creation and use of 3D models of exhibits from the collection of the History Museum has a high potential for diversified use, which is shown in this article.

3   3D Model Creation

3.1   The Center for Digital Humanities. Educational Courses in Preservation and Representation of Historical and Cultural Heritage

The Center for Digital Humanities at Perm State University [14] deals with the application of information technologies in humanitarian research and education. The staff of the Center have developed and now conduct a whole range of educational courses on the topic of preservation and representation of historical and cultural heritage based on information technologies. The basic course "Information technologies in Humanities research" is taught at all faculties of the university. One of the sections of the course is devoted to the preservation and representation of the historical and cultural heritage on the basis of ICT, which also includes the demonstration of the possibilities of 3D modeling technology to address these issues. So students learn to create models on the basis of real valuable objects from the collections of the Perm University History Museum.

Perm State University also ensures a program for the preparation of masters in "Digital technologies in sociocultural and art practices" in the direction "Culturology". The curriculum provides several courses related to the preservation and representation of historical and cultural heritage based on information technology. In particular, the course "Fundamentals of 3D modeling and virtual reconstructions", related to the creation and visualization of 3D models of cultural heritage, has been created. The approbation of this course was connected with the experience of creating 3D models of the antique collection's exhibits.

The important condition for the development and implementation of the training course was the realization of low-budget digitization, which influenced the choice of software and technological basis of the process.

3.2   The Program-Technological Basis of the 3D Modeling Process

To create 3D models, photogrammetry technology was chosen [15], based on the principle of constructing realistic 3D models based on photographic images of the subject.

As a specialized software for creating 3D models, 3DF Zephyr Lite Steam Edition1 and Agisoft Photoscan have been chosen. While choosing software, the quality of 3D capture played a decisive role, as well as the special conditions for acquiring licenses for non-commercial use when implementing projects in the field of historical and cultural heritage.

The following equipment has been used for shooting:

- digital camera Canon EOS 600D Kit 18-135 (on a tripod);
- three LED lamp installations (left, right and top);
- rotating platform with a linear surface;
- softbox.

The usage of LED SMD projectors "Soyuz" allowed us to minimize the thermal impact on the exhibits.

Necessary items when shooting were also clean gloves to protect the subject from possible exposure to grease and dirt from the hands.

3.3 Photogrammetric Image Acquisition and Data Processing

The process of creating 3D models is determined by the selected technology and includes several stages, the first of which is photographing the object.

The fundamental requirement for photographic images for subsequent photogrammetric processing is a high degree of overlap to ensure the full coverage of the source image, since points in a sparse point cloud are created from coincidences of similar pixels identified simultaneously in several photographs.

Exhibits of collections refer to isolated objects, and they have been shot from several camera positions to match the model better to the original. Photographing has been conducted by a 360° rotating platform with a graduated and graded surface.

The basic settings of the camera for shooting were as follows:

- Minimum ISO value (400);
- size image (RAW) 5184 × 3456.

After the photography, the photos of the objects were uploaded for photogrammetric processing of digital images, and then the cameras were calibrated and aligned in automatic mode (Fig. 1).

In some cases, the automatic camera alignment process did not yield positive results, and it was required to set the markers for re-alignment manually and to obtain a more accurate location of the points.

The process of aligning the cameras is accompanied by the construction of the initial sparse point cloud, on the basis of which the process of dense point cloud generation goes on. Dense point cloud was edited, for example, extra points were removed.

The next step is to calculate the data of dense point cloud and the formation on this basis of a geometric polygonal mesh.

The last stage of the model construction is the creation of a texture and the acquisition of a realistic model based on the data of 2D photographic images.

Some of the created models required correction of the external geometry because there were inaccuracies in the formation of a polygonal mesh. So, for example, the greatest difficulty was represented by the construction of a three-necked neck of an antique vessel of oenochoe and the external geometry of the vessel was corrected in the program for editing 3D models of MudBox. With the tools of the application, the surface of the neck was smoothed and the thickness of one of the petals was increased to match the original.

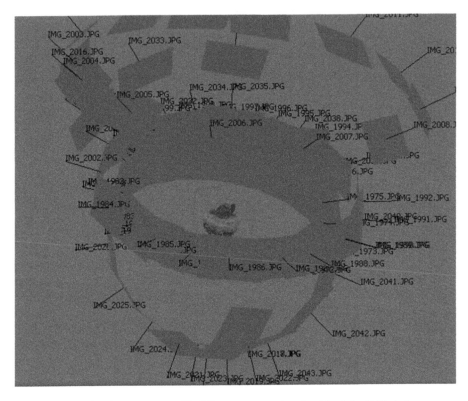

Fig. 1. Aligning cameras and building a sparse point cloud in Agisoft PhotoScan

3.4 The Accuracy of the 3D Models. Problems of Digital Reconstruction of Historical and Cultural Heritage Objects

The maximum correspondence of a digital copy to the original is a significant task of 3D reconstruction of historical and cultural heritage objects. However, the solution of this problem has a number of difficulties that require a special approach. We enumerate some of them.

The photogrammetric modeling technology based on photographic images of the object allows us to reconstruct the external shape of the object with high accuracy. However, the complexity of the external geometry of ancient Greek vessels often makes it impossible to make a series of photographs with 100% capture of all parts of the object, since the part the object's surface remains in the "blind" zone. Most often, such zones are in places difficult to photograph. For example, the upper part of the aryballos with the image of the deer has a complex geometric shape in the form of a notch under the visible part of the neck. The survey of the vessel in the horizontal position did not allow full fixing of this part. Therefore, it was required to use the 3DF Zephyr tool to close holes in a hard-to-reach zone, and MudBox to smooth the surface and correct the shape of the part of the "blind" zone (Fig. 2).

Fig. 2. Mesh of aryballos under correction

Another problem is the technological limitations of the photogrammetric technology based on image acquisition, when black, shiny, lacquer and some other objects can not be correctly counted by the program. It is more effective to use the photogrammetric technology with a 3D laser scanner that partially removes these limitations, but we cannot use such equipment because it is too expensive for a low-budget project.

However, there are low-budget methods that partially allow to overcome the difficulties with the processing of black and lacquered items without using a scanner [16]. So, we used talc while processing and photographing black lacquer products. It reduced the surface glitter and obtained better images. The experiment showed ambiguous results. On the one hand, it was possible to build a 3D model with a sufficiently high quality of external geometry. On the other hand, the texture of the vessel was less realistic and different from the original. This discrepancy was corrected somewhat with the help of the Adobe Photoshop graphics editor.

Vessels are complex objects for 3D modeling, because we have to recreate both their external and internal geometry. So the task is to reconstruct the invisible (inner) part of the object. Most of the information resources created for the representation of the historical and cultural heritage represent vessels with inaccessible inner contents (vessels with narrow necks, for example) only in the form of 3D models with a reconstructed exterior. Reconstruction of the inner part in these cases is not carried out, visible holes in the form of a model either close [17] or leave opened [18].

Another important problem of matching a digital copy to the original is the quality of the color rendition, tint and contrast, which must be controlled during 3D modeling. Color quality control, tone mapping and contrast control are subjective in nature, since visual colour comparison of a digital copy and the original is carried out by a person. For these purposes, a color scale is used, which reflects the system of colour shades.

Thus, the created 3D models have a high degree of compliance with the originals.

4 Publication of 3D Models

The creation of 3D models is accompanied by the export of a polygonal mesh and the texture of objects in formats intended for publication of models and their review by the user. 3D models were exported as a package of formats - OBJ (file with 3D geometry data), MTL (which completes OBJ file with information about the materials used in this model) and JPEG (image texture model). During the export process, the 3D model was saved with the resolution that is optimal for online publication and subsequent comfortable download by the user. A master copy of the model with the highest resolution was also exported.

Our approach is to use existing free platforms for the publication of 3D models to maximize the availability of digitized items of historical and cultural heritage.

The created models are published on the Sketchfab platform [19], which has a whole set of functions for displaying objects. Some of the functions are control of the main parameters of the scene (the orientation of the object, field of view, background, etc.), the possibility of operating with light when the 3D model is displayed. The important function is the adjustment of materials, which provide the ability to manipulate the intensity of color and glitter, which allows you to display the luster of lacquered objects more realistically. Other settings for displaying the 3D model allow you to operate with the image grit, sharpness, to change the color balance, etc.

It is also possible to arrange annotations describing the details and features of the model elements, which is a significant tool for working with historical and cultural heritage and allows the user to familiarize themselves with the subject and its features.

The information resource has been developed on the website of Perm University Museums [20] to demonstrate the created digital museum objects on the Sketchfab platform.

5 The Usage of 3D Models' Collection

5.1 Usage the Collection in Humanitarian Research

The creation of the exact model, the most appropriate to the original, is a scientific task. The process of creating an external geometry is described above, while the reconstruction of internal geometry is still in the process of searching for optimal solutions. The restoration of the internal geometry of the vessels is carried out on the basis of the study of scientific literature devoted to the analysis of antique vessels of various types [21]. Verification of the internal structure is also possible on the basis of the exhibits with missing fragments stored in the Museum, and these fragments can be recovered due to the high accuracy of the internal geometry of vessels of different types. Accuracy for constructing the internal geometry of the vessel will allow recreating the whole appearance of a real vessel, and will also become the basis for the accuracy of the conducted experiments of the object's domestic usage.

The possibilities of scientific use of the created collection of 3D models are related both to the study of individual subjects and the collection as a whole. The study of museum subjects is important because of the lack of information about the objects and their origin. The creation of a collection of 3D exhibits, which are available online, allows these exhibits to be introduced into scientific circulation as historical sources for a broader research audience. The analysis of the vessels' symbolism, the study of the origin, the interrelationships of the objects of the collection in the world context with similar objects in other collections will allow to answer many important questions about ancient history, culture and its distribution in the world.

5.2 Educational Process

There are several basic methods of application of these 3D models in the educational process. The original purpose of creating the Museum of Antiquities and Arts at Perm University was an object demonstration of collections to students. 3D modeling, the availability of online collections allow this process of demonstration to be more detailed and convenient in studying.

The 3D models can also be used to study real domestic use of objects, reconstruction of the everyday life of an ancient Greek two thousand years ago. In this regard, the study of the everyday history becomes more vivid and lively.

The process of creating 3D models of the collection's exhibits is important in the training of specialists, who work with historical and cultural heritage - historians, restorers, creators of scientific digital content based on historical resources. It is important to study modern standards for the creation of historically-oriented information resources, to train how to work with specialized software, including those related to 3D modeling. The experience of the Center for Digital Humanitarian Studies at Perm University shows the effectiveness of this approach.

5.3 Historical Reconstruction of Object's Everyday Use

The ancient collection of the Perm University History Museum contains real items of ancient Greek life, including lamps, vessels of different types, shapes and sizes, having different purposes. The use of certain objects is obvious, whereas the ways in which others were used are not so obvious and cause many questions about its usage, traditions and application.

One of such items is the oenochoe, the 3D model of which has already been created and it is situated in a virtual collection on the museum's website [22]. This vessel was used for drinking wine and served for pouring wine mixed with water into kylikes for its direct consumption. Oenochoe has a three-petalled structure of the corolla (the top of the vessel). We cannot clearly explain the purpose of these petals. It is possible to assume several variants of its practical designation. First, such a structure can be explained from an aesthetic point of view, at the time when beauty and grace of execution were of great importance. On the other hand, the main difference between oenochoe and other vessels is that three-petalled structure of the neck.

Therefore, one can assert the practical significance of this particular structure. The question arises, how the pouring out of liquid from the petals of the vessel took place. Perhaps the oenochoe served for simultaneous pouring into three other vessels, or the liquid was poured into the vessels in turn, and this order depended on the inclination of the person's hand. At the same time, it was important not only how the liquid came from one vessel to another, but also the pose of a person who poured and other circumstances, the study of which was an important and interesting part of the history of ancient Greek's everyday life.

Another everyday item is a lamp, the 3D model of which is also created and available online [23]. Obviously, the lamp was used for lighting. At the same time, there are many questions about the appointment of the lamp, its wick, its material and thickness, the quantity and quality of oil, the time and intensity of combustion, the size of the illuminated space, etc.

A series of experiments with imitation of its real household usage will help to answer all these questions.

Reconstruction of antique objects' everyday life requires a comprehensive study of these processes with the involvement of scientific literature and historical sources, as well as a materialized copy of the subject. 3D printing of objects of historical and cultural heritage is one of the possibilities to create such copies. Modern 3D printing technologies allow you to copy not only the subject itself, but also the image on it.

5.4 Popularization of Historical and Cultural Heritage. Printing 3D Models on a 3D Printer

The creation of 3D models' collections opens wide opportunities for popularization of historical and cultural heritage among various categories of the population - schoolchildren of different ages, students, various categories of adults. Such opportunities include carrying out various activities with demonstration of models, including public lectures and interactive activities.

3D printing of exhibits will allow us to carry out public events with demonstration of real use of subjects of Ancient Greek way of life. Different forms of interaction between researchers and museum visitors are possible. A special role is played by the possibility of discovering the historical and cultural heritage for a visually impaired audience, when one can touch objects and try them in action.

The essential complexity of 3D printing of 3D models is the search for suitable materials for printing, so that the printed model is close to the original not only in form but also in appearance (color, texture, etc.) and other characteristics (weight, for example). Existing 3D printers allow us to use gypsiferous materials and it is possible to print colour images on them. However, gypsum is short-lived, it is not resistant to external environment (heat, moisture). Therefore, it is necessary to solve a whole complex of questions about suitable equipment and materials used.

6   Conclusion

Exhibits of the ancient collection of the Perm University History Museum have a significant historical and cultural value. The creation of 3D photogrammetric models of exhibits and their publication online improve access to historical and cultural heritage items for their subsequent use. Prospective directions for the secondary use of digital items are scientific study of exhibits, use in educational activities in the training of specialists in the field of Digital History and as illustrative material, as well as solving the problems of historical reconstruction of objects' domestic use and popularization of historical and cultural heritage among various categories of the population.

References

1. 3D Research Challenges in Cultural Heritage. A Roadmap in Digital Heritage Preservation. In: Ioannides, M., Quak, E. (eds.) Information Systems and Applications, incl. Internet/Web, and HCI, vol. 8355, pp. 1–142. Springer (2014). https://doi.org/10.1007/978-3-662-44630-0
2. Ioannides, M., Fink, E., Moropoulou, A., Hagedorn-Saupe, M., Fresa, A., Liestøl, G., Rajcic, V., Grussenmeyer, P. (eds.): EuroMed 2016. LNCS, vol. 10059. Springer, Cham (2016). https://doi.org/10.1007/978-3-319-48974-2
3. Callieri, M., Cignoni, P., Ganovelli, F., Impoco, G., Montani, C., Pingi, P., Ponchio, F., Scopigno, R.: Visualization and 3D data processing in David's restoration. IEEE Comput. Graph. Appl. **24**(2), 16–21 (2004)
4. Livio de Luca, M.: 3D Modelling and semantic enrichment in cultural heritage. In: Fritsch, D. (ed.) Proceedings of Photogrammetric Week 2013, pp. 323–333. Wichmann/VDE Verlag, Belin & Offenbach, Berlin (2013)
5. Levoy, M., Pulli, K., Curless, B., Rusinkiewicz, S., Koller, D., Pereira, L., Ginzton, M., Anderson, S., Davis, J., Ginsberg, J., Shade, J., Fulk, D.: The digital michelangelo project: 3D scanning of large statues. In: Proceedings SIGGRAPH Computer Graphics (2000). https://graphics.stanford.edu/papers/dmich-sig00/dmich-sig00-nogamma-comp-low.pdf. Accessed 10 Sept 2017
6. Gonizzi, B.S., Caruso, G., Micoli, L.L., Covarrubias, R.M., Guidi, G.: 3D visualisation of cultural heritage artefacts with virtual reality devices. In: Yen, Y.-N., Weng, K.-H., Cheng, H.-M. (eds.) The International Archives of the Photogrammetry, Remote Sensing and Spatial Information Sciences, vol. XL-5/W7, 2015, 25th International CIPA Symposium, Taipei, Taiwan, pp. 165–172 (2015)
7. Waas, M., Zell, D.: Practical 3D photogrammetry for the conservation and documentation of Cultural Heritage. In: Börner, W., Uhlirz, S. (eds.) International Conference on Cultural Heritage and New Technologies, Vienna (2013). http://www.chnt.at/wp-content/uploads/Waas_Zell_2014.pdf. Accessed 10 Sept 2017
8. Shults, R.: New opportunities of low-cost photogrammetry for cultural heritage perservation. In: Tucci, G., Bonora, V. (eds.) The International Archives of the Photogrammetry, Remote Sensing and Spatial Information Sciences, vol. XLII-5/W1, 2017 Geomatics and Restoration. Conservation of Cultural Heritage in the Digital Era, Florence, Italy, pp. 481–486 (2017)
9. Guidi, G., Micoli, L.L., Gonizzi, S., Brennan, M., Frischer, B.: Image-based 3D capture of cultural heritage artifacts an experimental study about 3D data quality. IEEE Digit. Heritage **2**, 321–324 (2015)

10. Hassani, F.: Documentation of cultural heritage techniques, potentials and constraints. In: Yen, Y.-N., Weng, K.-H., Cheng, H.-M. (eds.) The International Archives of the Photogrammetry, Remote Sensing and Spatial Information Sciences, vol. XL-5/W7, 2015 25th International CIPA Symposium, Taipei, Taiwan, pp. 207–214 (2015)
11. Europeana Collections. http://www.europeana.eu. Accessed 10 Sept 2017
12. Cultural Heritage: Reuse, Remake, Reimagine. Europeana Space, Best Practice Network. Spaces of possibility for the creative reuse of digital cultural content. Third European Conference, Berlin (2016). http://www.europeana-space.eu/conferences/berlinconference2016. Accessed 10 Sept 2017
13. Europeana Fashion. http://www.europeanafashion.eu. Accessed 10 Sept 2017
14. Center for Digital Humanities Homepage. http://dh.psu.ru. Accessed 10 Sept 2017
15. Foster, S., Halbstein, D.: Integrating 3D Modeling, Photogrammetry and Design. Springer (2014). https://doi.org/10.1007/978-1-4471-6329-9
16. Porter, S.T., Huber, N., Hoyer, Ch., Floss, H.: Portable and low-cost solutions to the imaging of Paleolithic art objects: a comparison of photogrammetry and reflectance transformation imaging. J. Archaeol. Sci. Rep. **10**, 859–863 (2016)
17. 3D Models of vessels in collection of Ure Museum of Greek Archaeology. https://sketchfab.com/uremuseum. Accessed 10 Sept 2017
18. 3D Models of vessels in collection of Museo Arqueológico Nacional. https://sketchfab.com/man. Accessed 10 Sept 2017
19. Center for Digital Humanities of Perm University, 3D models. https://sketchfab.com/DH_PSU/models. Accessed 10 Sept 2017
20. Perm University Museums, Collections. http://museum.psu.ru/collections. Accessed 10 Sept 2017
21. Gómez, H.H.: 3D reconstructing of vessels using CGView. In: Descargado de e-Archivo, repositorio institucional de la Universidad Carlos III de Madrid. https://e-archivo.uc3m.es/bitstream/handle/10016/16955/PFC_Hector_Hernandez_Gomez.pdf. Accessed 10 Sept 2017
22. 3D Model of Oinohoa, Collection of the Perm University History Museum. http://museum.psu.ru/object/oinohoa. Accessed 10 Sept 2017
23. 3D Model of Lamp, Collection of the Perm University History Museum. http://museum.psu.ru/object/svetilnik. Accessed 10 Sept 2017

Towards a Digital Infrastructure for Illustrated Handwritten Archives

Andreas Weber[1]([X]) (iD), Mahya Ameryan[2] (iD), Katherine Wolstencroft[3] (iD), Lise Stork[3] (iD), Maarten Heerlien[4], and Lambert Schomaker[2] (iD)

[1] BMS-STePS, University of Twente, 7500 AE Enschede, The Netherlands
a.weber@utwente.nl
[2] ALICE, University of Groningen, Nijenborgh 9, 9747 AG Groningen, The Netherlands
{m.ameryan,l.r.b.schomaker}@rug.nl
[3] LIACS, Leiden University, Niels Bohrweg 1, 2333 CA Leiden, The Netherlands
k.j.wolstencroft@liacs.leidenuniv.nl
[4] Naturalis Biodiversity Center, PO Box 9517, 2300 RA Leiden, The Netherlands
maarten@heerlien.net

Abstract. Large and important parts of cultural heritage are stored in archives that are difficult to access, even after digitization. Documents and notes are written in hard-to-read historical handwriting and are often interspersed with illustrations. Such collections are weakly structured and largely inaccessible to a wider public and scholars. Traditionally, humanities researchers treat text and images separately. This separation extends to traditional handwriting recognition systems. Many of them use a segmentation free OCR approach which only allows the resolution of homogenous manuscripts in terms of layout, style and linguistic content. This is in contrast to our infrastructure which aims to resolve heterogeneous handwritten manuscript pages in which different scripts and images are narrowly intertwined. Authors in our use case, a 17,000 page account of exploration of the Indonesian Archipelago between 1820–1850 ("Natuurkundige Commissie voor Nederlands-Indië") tried to follow a semantic way to record their knowledge and observations, however, this discipline does not exist in the handwriting script. The use of different languages, such as German, Latin, Dutch, Malay, Greek, and French makes interpretation more challenging. Our infrastructure takes the state-of-the-art word retrieval system MONK as starting point. Owing to its visual approach, MONK can handle the diversity of material we encounter in our use case and many other historical collections: text, drawings and images. By combining text and image recognition, we significantly transcend beyond the state-of-the art, and provide meaningful additions to integrated manuscript recognition. This paper describes the infrastructure and presents early results.

Keywords: Deep learning · Digital heritage · Natural history
Biodiversity heritage

Mahya Ameryan and Andreas Weber share the first authorship of this paper.

© Springer International Publishing AG, part of Springer Nature 2018
M. Ioannides (Ed.): ITN-DCH 2017, LNCS 10605, pp. 155–166, 2018.
https://doi.org/10.1007/978-3-319-75826-8_13

1   Introduction

Many heritage collections and archives consist of documents in which handwritten text in different languages and scripts are interspersed with images. In order to open up and interlink such multimedial collections, heritage institutions typically resort to manual enrichment methods such as keyword tagging and full-text transcription [1–3]. Often, these methods rely on crowdsourcing, where volunteers take large parts of the work upon themselves [4–6]. Although such practices produce high-quality data, it is a labour-intensive, time consuming and therefore costly way of opening up heterogeneous collections [7]. Furthermore, these methods require an advanced level of expertise from professionals and even from volunteers. One can neither transcribe illustrated handwritten manuscripts without thorough knowledge of palaeography, a dying expertise, nor can one add useful subject information to a document or drawing without having knowledge about its context and semantic structure [8]. The disclosure of scientific manuscript collections, for instance, heavily depends on the availability of domain-specific background knowledge [9]. Multimedial manuscript collections cannot be enriched, if one is unable to situate notes and hand-drawn sketches and drawings in their historical context.

Traditionally, humanities researchers treat text and images separately. This separation extends to traditional handwriting recognition systems [10–12]. Many of them use a segmentation free OCR approach which only allows the resolution of homogenous manuscripts in terms of layout, style and linguistic content [13, 14]. This is in contrast to our infrastructure which aims to resolve heterogeneous handwritten manuscript pages in which different scripts and images are narrowly intertwined. Authors in our use case, a 17,000 page account of exploration of the Indonesian Archipelago between 1820–1850 ("Natuurkundige Commissie voor Nederlands-Indië) tried to follow a semantic way to record their knowledge and observations, however, this discipline does not exist in the handwriting script. The use of different languages, such as German, Latin, Dutch, Malay, Greek, and French makes interpretation more challenging. On many pages, handwritten text is also intermixed with sketches and drawings. Owing to this complexity, the paper heritage of the Natuurkundige Commissie (further referred to by the acronym NC) has remained largely inaccessible to scholars and the general public.

Since the reliable semantic interpretation of illustrated handwritten heritage collections requires an integrated approach to text and image recognition, this paper describes the basic layout of a user-centred infrastructure which is developed in the context of the research project Making Sense of Illustrated Handwritten Archives (2016–2020). By integrating text and image interpretation, we aim at providing meaningful additions to integrated manuscript recognition. To address this challenge, our infrastructure takes the state-of-the-art word retrieval system MONK as starting point and augments it with page layout and image analysis, and semantic integration. Owing to its visual approach, MONK can handle the diversity of material we encounter in our use case and many other historical collections: text, drawings and images [15]. This paper also entails initial results on the active learning performance of MONK in the context of the NC collection. Combining image and textual recognition into one digital infrastructure, allows for an integrated study of underexplored heritage collections and archives in general. In our opinion, this is the most promising way to achieve the required level of accuracy for handwritten illustrated collections. Our work is financed by the Netherlands Organization for Scientific Research (NWO) and the Dutch publishing house Brill.

2   Use Case: The Archive of the Committee for Natural History of the Netherlands Indies (1820–1850)

In order to realize the digital infrastructure, we utilize the notes and illustrations of the NC archive as its use case. This extensive corpus, which was composed by 17 naturalists and draftsmen contains a rich account of scientific exploration in the Indonesian Archipelago in the period 1820–1850 (see Fig. 1). The NC charted the natural and economic state of the Indonesian Archipelago, in the nineteenth century a Dutch colony, and returned a wealth of scientific data and specimens which are stored in the archive and depot of the Naturalis Biodiversity Center in Leiden [16, 17]. In addition to the thousands of handwritten notes and drawings, the collection comprises tens of thousands of biological and geological specimens and a four-volume publication on the commission's findings [18, 19]. Owing to its high scientific and cultural value, Naturalis restored and digitized the NC's paper legacy and specimens between 2007 and 2015 with funds from the Metamorfoze and the FCD programme[1].

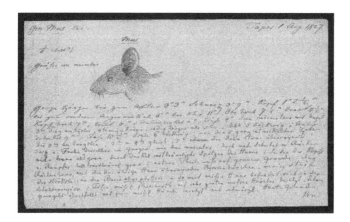

Fig. 1. Illustrated field note by H. Boie (1797–1827). It is composed in a mix of German, Latin, Dutch, Greek, and Malay. Naturalis BC, NNM001001061_020. Public Domain Mark 1.0.

Though the paper heritage of the NC collection is digitally preserved, it remains inaccessible to scholars and the general public, also due to its heterogeneous structure as discussed in the introduction of this paper. In order to establish links between handwritten field notes, drawings and specimens, our digital infrastructure must be able to

---

[1] The Metamorfoze programme funds the preservation of paper heritage that is deemed to be of national importance for the Netherlands. The FCD programme (FES Collection Digitization, 2010–2015) digitized a significant part of the specimens preserved by Naturalis.

cope with a number of challenges. The biggest challenge on a semantic level is the evolution of concepts; in the case of the NC the evolution of toponyms and taxon names in particular. Since locality names and scientific species names have often changed over time, due to conceptual, political and linguistic shifts, our infrastructure must also be able to deal with background knowledge in the form of controlled vocabularies (e.g. biological taxonomies, gazetteers) and context information as it is provided by publications on individual naturalists [20, 21] and databases [22]. The labels of historic specimens only provide general information on collection localities and collectors (e.g. "Java, Boie"). Until now, only initial attempts were made to disclose and connect the material manually [23].

While authors in our use case tried to follow a structured way to record their knowledge and their observations, however, this discipline does not exist in the handwriting script. Figure 2 show three samples of fully connected, mixed cursive and isolated handprint on a same line of our data. Also, Fig. 3 shows some different binarized labelled word images of NC manuscript showing common problems. Moreover, different languages used in fieldnotes, including German, Latin, Dutch, Greek, Malay and French makes interpretation more challenging. The multi-layered character of the NC collection makes it thus the perfect use case to realize a technologically advanced and usability-engineered digital infrastructure for interpreting illustrated handwritten archives in general.

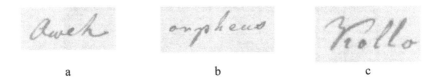

a   b   c

Fig. 2. Multiple writing styles on the same line of a NC manuscript: (a), (b) and (c) show fully connected, mixed cursive and isolated handprint styles exist on the same line.

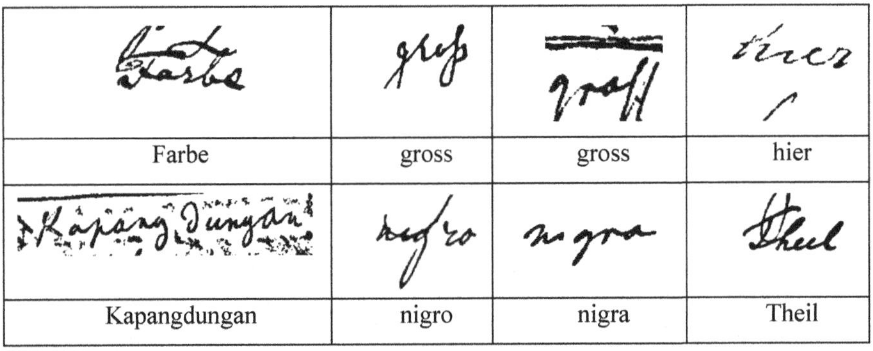

Farbe	gross	gross	hier
Kapangdungan	nigro	nigra	Theil

Fig. 3. Binarized labelled word images of NC manuscript showing common problems.

2.1 MONK: A Solid Point of Departure

The infrastructure proposed here, takes the state-of-the-art word retrieval system MONK, as a starting point and augments it with page layout, image analysis and semantic integration. MONK achieves a high accuracy on a wide range of script styles [24–26]. It is used by humanities researchers from well-known institutes around the globe (e.g. National Archive and National Library in The Hague, Czech National Archive, Harvard University Yenchin (Chinese handwritten) collection, the Dead Sea Scrolls, in cooperation with Israel Antiquity Authority). MONK was developed in SCRATCH (SCRipt Analysis Tools for the Cultural Heritage), a project in the context of the NWO-funded CATCH programme (Continuous Access to Cultural Heritage, 2004–2014), and its follow-up valorisation project SCRATCH4ALL. The system was scaled up to the 'Big Data' level in TARGET, a project funded by the European Regional Development Fund. Because of its visual approach, MONK can handle the diversity of material that one encounters in many historical collections: text, drawings, and images [15]. The large majority of related systems are designed to handle only a single homogenous manuscript in terms of layout, style and linguistic content.[2]

Internationally, the most noteworthy project aimed at automated historical handwriting recognition is the READ project, a high profile EU e-Infrastructure project funded by the European Commission that is aimed at resolving a small number specific documents in toto [14, 27]. This is in contrast to our goal, where we aim to recognize and semantically interpret pages in a large document collection with a wide variety of writing styles. Since the tool which the READ consortium (Transkribus) is developing needs a single language model, it cannot process different languages and scripts on one page. With our approach, different languages and scripts may be intermixed with images, as the active learning system of MONK does not require prior training and can cope with heterogeneous pages. In our opinion, the tabula-rasa approach of MONK is much better suited for our use case and other historical collections. MONK differs from Transkribus and other systems which follow a segmentation free OCR approach in three ways.

1. The MONK system uses shape-based feature vector methods that have very few assumptions concerning the content or style of the material. The range of different handwriting types, languages and styles that MONK can handle is consequently much broader than that of other handwriting recognition systems. Examples of manuscripts that have been successfully processed by MONK are medieval Western texts, 18th century captain's logs, the Qumran Dead Sea scrolls, Arabic, and Chinese texts. MONK was able to adapt to process Chinese text from scratch, with zero labels within a two-week period [28]. The system currently handles 25 k character classes, processing three hundred manuscripts in wood-block printed and handwritten styles.
2. The reason for this success is the avoidance of the traditional OCR (optical character recognition) approach which assumes that individual characters are essentially legible [15]. This assumption only holds for a fraction of handwritten material and a limited number of scripts. Even where individual characters are seen, by human

---

[2] An exception is: https://kogs-www.informatik.uni-hamburg.de/projekte/IMPACT.html, last accessed 2017/09/02.

visual inspection, the poor image quality usually requires the full-word pattern to be used for reducing the number of alternative classifications. Several traditional systems, make use of Hidden Markov modelling [29]. This technique has a number of fundamental and practical disadvantages for handling highly diverse image data. We mention three of them. (1) Whilst Markov models work successfully in the one dimensional domain of speech, the two dimensional pixel domain is in many ways much more complex. (2) The amount of labelled data is extremely limited in historical handwriting compared to speech, and (3) hidden-Markov requires model design by highly skilled researchers. This leads to handwriting recognition systems that are manually tuned to a particular application [25]. Live training of such systems by ordinary users is not possible.

3. In the MONK system, active-learning methods are used to allow the system to learn quickly from the input of experts. The system presents a number of word-zone images to the user, who has to confirm their text label, or provide a meaningful label for them. As the system can decide which images to show to an expert, it can collect feedback for those images from which it can learn the most. By combining active learning with learning methods that do not require a large number of labelled examples, such as nearest-neighbour methods, MONK can learn to recognize novel document collections in a relatively short time. As the number of harvested labels increases, increasingly advanced and more 'label-greedy' Machine-Learning methods are employed, such as SVMs, Convolutional Neural Networks, and Multidimensional Long Short-Term Memory (MDLSTM) [30]. This allows MONK to keep improving its performance once more examples become available. Alternative methods suggest that by labelling the first few hundred pages of a large collection, you can model the data and you can process the rest of the collection. If the collection is 10,000 or 50,000 pages, however, the initial pages, which are often neatly written, may not be representative of the rest of the collection. A random sampling across the dataset is more suitable for training the model. For this paper, we used MDLSTM for word recognition [31].

The experimental dataset contains 6286 word images with 121 word classes with an alphabet of 37 different characters. Each word class contains 19 to 259 examples. To generalize our results to be independent of the chosen train and test datasets, we used 10-fold cross validation. In order to increase the variation of the training set, they were morphed, two times [32]. For each fold, the original, morphed and two-time morphed images were used for the training set, whilst each of the validation and also test sets contained one of 10 original subsets. We used three configurations for MDLSTM (Table 1). The input block is 2×10, the hidden block size is 3×4 and 2×4; the learning rate is e^{-4}; momentum is 0.9. These architectures differs in hidden and subsample sizes (Table 1). Training was stopped after 30 consecutive evaluations without improvement on the validation set. In order to ensure lexically valid responses, the output strings are corrected by word matching using the Levenshtein distance. The lexical entry with the lowest distance is considered to be the final output. Apart from looking at the most likely hypothesis (top 1), we also counted the number of times a correct word was found among the top-5 candidates. Table 1 shows the mean and standard of deviation of word recognition rate (%) derived by MDLSTM for 10-fold validation on our dataset. It should be noted that tests such as these are subject to a large number of factors and selection criteria: for classes with many labels, the results will be high, while difficult words usually also have fewer labels, and lower accuracy.

Table 1. Mean and standard of deviation of word recognition rate (%) for three different MDLSTM neural networks, using 10-fold validation.

Arch.	Hidden size	Subsample size	Training	Test (top1)	Test (top5)
A14	8, 40, 80	8, 50	100 ± 00	70 ± 3	83 ± 2
A28	20, 50, 100	8, 4	100 ± 00	73 ± 2	85 ± 1
A30	2, 10, 50	6, 20	92 ± 8	61 ± 2	77 ± 2

2.2 Towards a Digital Infrastructure: Next Steps (2017–2020)

The success of our infrastructure crucially depends on the accurate recognition as well as semantically structuring and interlinking content from handwritten illustrated documents. Our use case is representative of many other cultural heritage collections. In order to achieve this goal MONK, the pattern-recognition basis of which is already solid, is enriched with three new systems which will be discussed separately below.

System I: Layout Analysis System. A layout-analysis system is required that improves the ability to identify and segment visual and textual elements in an image. This entails the inclusion of new, adapted methods for layout analysis, pattern recognition and machine learning. The system ensures that elements in the layout of digitized images are detected and segmented. In order to carry out this task, the system relies on a locally operating segmentation procedure [33] which will be tuned to this type of document data in combination with smart pre-processing to avoid effects of the "background" of the document affecting the quality of the segmentation.

Of special interest in the NC document collection is that many documents have a well-defined, consistent layout; on different pages, images and text may appear at the same place. Moreover, there is often a separation between pictorial material and text in the form of a 'white', i.e. paper-coloured boundary. Initial developments and experiments focus on pre-processing structured documents of which the layout, use of underlines, etc. is consistent through the documents.

The MONK system will subsequently be used to identify potential words, assigning a probability that a word is recognized in each region. The recognition accuracy can be improved by exploiting the recognized images. It is a tremendous advantage to be able to make use of multimodal combinations of text and images: the probabilities of structural elements in pictures are much more reliable (i.e., have a large raw count), than the probabilities for linguistic patterns that have a long-tailed distribution (occurring a few times). The underlying biological structure (has_wings, has_beaks), for example, creates common pictorial themes that can be exploited by infrastructure. These pictorial elements can be recognized separately and combined in a model using attribute learning which is an effective way to transfer knowledge between different labelled instances.

System II: Integration of Background Knowledge. This system functions as a bridge between bottom-up hypotheses that the computer generates from the illustrated hand-written pages and existing semantic bodies of knowledge. The bridge includes a mechanism which brings statistically inferred (deep learned) semantics in a fruitful dialogue with (formally coded) ontologies. While the labelling interface does not impose any limits on the labels, we can prompt users to favour terms from existing ontologies and vocabularies, using techniques such as auto-complete and by displaying extra context through synonyms and alternative spelling. The advantage of using standardized terms is that once words have been linked to standardized terms, background knowledge concerning the context of these terms can be used to bias the recognition of the scanned pages.

For instance, we know that most field note records from the NC collection are biodiversity observations. Consequently, we know that they contain a similar set of basic metadata required to describe such biodiversity observations. This includes (i) the name of the observed species, (ii) the researcher who identified it, (iii) the geographic location, (iv) the date of observation.

Many documents have a typical structure in which these metadata elements occur in specific positions. If MONK is uncertain about the term that corresponds with a word candidate, knowledge about the specific position and category that the multiple word candidates belong to, can help to make the right choice, especially for words that occur only a few times throughout the manuscripts. Consider the recognition of dates and place names. Drawings and sketches of zoological specimens often contain a toponym and the date of a sighting in the lower left corner (see Fig. 4). Place names are followed by a comma, and the month is represented in Latin characters followed by the year in Arabic

Fig. 4. Field drawing of a red-throated Barbet (*Begalaima mystacophanos*), Buitenzorg, Java, May 1827. Figure created by Andreas Weber and Maarten Heerlien, licensed under CC-BY-SA 4.0. Drawing: Naturalis BC, NNM001000144_002.

digits. While the place and date are separate words, their proximity in a specific place on the page helps their identification as dates and place names [34]. Besides layout structure, ontological information such as hierarchical structures can be used to assist the word-recognition. Figure 4, for instance, was drawn in Java of which amongst others 'Buitenzorg' is a second level subdivision. Word recognition can use this information to bias the labelling towards 'Buitenzorg' instead of other, visually similar words.

The position and proximity of related words and ontological information can also be used to identify the names of observed species, which can be found in field drawings as well as in field notes. In field drawings, species names are noted at the bottom of the document (see Fig. 4). While species names typically consist of multiple words, these names follow the rules of (i.e., taxonomic) nomenclature. Regardless of the language of an individual field note, taxonomic names are represented according to the Linnean system of binominal nomenclature. It consists of a capitalized genus name, followed by a non-capitalized species name (e.g. *Burro multicolor Boie)*. Taxonomic names are written in italics in printed texts and are underlined in handwritten texts. Although the taxonomic classification of species may have changed since the early nineteenth century, these basic taxonomic categories can be used by MONK: order, family, genus, and species [35]. Species names will be the more useful, as they are always binomen, followed by author name, unless it is a new species (genus+species, (author)). If multiple adjacent word candidates possibly represent taxonomic terms, this knowledge can therefore be used to prioritize taxonomic names over other possible interpretations.

System III: Organization, Linking and Serving of Content. The accurate extraction of named entities such as person, species, and place names from handwritten illustrated collections is essential for making such collections available for researchers and a wider public. However, in order to enable algorithms to reason over the data to bootstrap or aid the word-recognition process, or to compare the extracted content with other resources, the data must be organized, structured and interlinked in a standard way. This will enable researchers to ask complex questions across the whole collection. Some projects, such as the Field Book Project,[3] already use standards for linking field books and other collections to their metadata, but none aim to link content. To do so effectively, we build on accepted community metadata standards, rather than developing a bespoke solution for this particular collection [36]. In this way, the work on the NC content serves as a proof of concept for other cultural heritage collections. The core resources we have adopted, for example, include the Darwin Core (DwC) standard for describing biodiversity data and the Dublin Core (DC) standard for describing data sources on the web.

The relationship between metadata entities is defined in an application ontology, represented in OWL,[4] which allows the semantic enrichment and integration of extracted archive content (e.g. species observations are made in a particular place, by a particular person). These relationships can be used to assist human and machine labelling as well as allowing the formulation of rich queries through the interface. For example, researchers could retrieve all bird species observed by a specific naturalist outside of

---

[3] http://biodivlib.wikispaces.com/The+Field+Book+Project, last accessed 2017/09/01.
[4] https://github.com/lisestork/NHC-Ontology, last accessed 2017/09/01.

Java, in South East Asia. The ontology also allows the consolidation of synonyms that are expressed with multiple different words or languages throughout the collection, such as place names, species names, or abbreviations, into single semantic concepts. Semantically integrated data will be stored in RDF (Resource Description Framework, the W3C standard for data interchange on the web), which will allow the content to be served as Linked Data, and more importantly, open the possibility of integration with other cultural heritage resources already available as Linked Data.

3 Discussion

This paper introduces a new digital infrastructure which allows curators of historical archives and manuscript collections to disclose and connect handwritten illustrated archives. Moreover, it presents initial results on the active learning performance of MONK on the NC collection, without the development of a prior language model. Owing to its visual approach, it is able to handle heterogeneous collections. Our use case offers a rich landscape of challenging visual material which we use to develop, synchronise and refine the infrastructure. In order to scale up MONK, the Making Sense project enriches it on three levels – recognition techniques, textual post-processing, and the querying of extracted results. On the level of recognition techniques we propose adapted methods for layout analysis, pattern recognition and machine learning. On the level of textual post-processing, we develop a system that functions as bridge between bottom-up hypotheses that the computer creates from the illustrated handwritten pages and existing semantic bodies of knowledge. This involves combining the use of ontologies and controlled vocabularies (for labelling text and images) and deep learning for image recognition. On the level of querying of extracted results, we semantically structure and link the extracted content in a standardized format, drawing on existing community standards and background knowledge to produce a resource that is interoperable with other collections. In sum: by combining handwriting recognition, layout segmentation, image recognition and ontological data annotation our infrastructure has the potential to significantly improve the automated extraction, classification and linking of knowledge from historical manuscript collections. It thus opens up new opportunities for scientific research, heritage institutions and publishers, while reducing the need for costly human intervention.

References

1. Heerlien, M., Van Leusen, J., Schnörr, S., De Jong-Kole, S., Raes, N., Van Hulsen, K.: The natural history production pine: an industrial approach to the digitization of scientific collections. J. Comput. Cult. Herit. **8**, 3:1–3:11 (2015)
2. Pethers, H., Huertas, B.: The Dollmann collection: a case study of linking library and historical specimen collections at the Natural History Museum, London. Linnean **31**, 18–22 (2015)
3. Ogilvie, B.: Correspondence networks. In: Lightman, B. (ed.) A Companion to the History of Science, pp. 358–371. Wiley (2016)
4. Ridge, M. (ed.): Crowdsourcing Our Cultural Heritage. Ashgate, Farnham (2014)

5. Franzoni, C., Sauermann, H.: Crowd science: the organization of scientific research in open collaborative projects. Res. Policy **43**, 1–20 (2014)
6. Terras, M.: Crowdsourcing in the digital humanities. In: Schreibman, S., Siemens, R., Unsworth, J. (eds.) A New Companion to Digital Humanities, pp. 420–438. Wiley, New York (2015)
7. Causer, T., Tonra, J., Wallace, V.: Transcription maximized; expense minimized? Crowdsourcing and editing The Collected Works of Jeremy Bentham. Lit. Linguist. Comput. **27**, 119–137 (2012)
8. Causer, T., Terras, M.: 'Many hands make light work. Many hands together make merry work': Transcribe Bentham and crowdsourcing manuscript collections. In: Crowdsourcing Our Cultural Heritage, pp. 57–88. Ashgate, Surrey (2014)
9. Orli, S., Bird, J.: Establishing workflows and opening access to data within natural history collections. Collections **12**, 147–162 (2016)
10. Mitchell, W.J.T.: Picture Theory: Essays on Verbal and Visual Representation. University of Chicago Press, Chicago (1994)
11. Kusukawa, S.: Picturing the Book of Nature: Image, Text, and Argument in Sixteenth-Century Human Anatomy and Medical Botany. University of Chicago Press, Chicago (2011)
12. Kwastek, K.: Vom Bild zum Bild - digital humanities jenseits des textes. In: Baum, C., Stäcker, T. (eds.) Grenzen und Möglichkeiten der Digital Humanities (= Sonderband der Zeitschrift für digitale Geisteswissenschaften, 1) (2015)
13. van der Zant, T., Schomaker, L., Zinger, S., van Schie, H.: Where are the search engines for handwritten documents? Interdisc. Sci. Rev. **34**, 224–235 (2009)
14. Mühlberger, G.: Die automatisierte Volltexterkennung historischer Handschriften. In: Digitalisierung im Archiv: Neue Wege der Bereitstellung des Archivguts, pp. 87–116. Archivschule Marburg, Marburg (2015)
15. Schomaker, L.: Design considerations for a large-scale image-based text search engine in historical manuscript collections. Inf. Technol. **58**, 80–88 (2016)
16. Mees, G., van Achterberg, C.: Vogelkundig onderzoek op Nieuw Guinea in 1828. Zoologische Bijdragen **40**, 3–64 (1994)
17. Klaver, C.J.: Inseparable Friends in Life and Death: The Life and Work of Heinrich Kuhl (1797–1821) and Johan Conrad van Hasselt (1797–1823). Barkhuis, Groningen (2007)
18. Temminck, C.J., Müller, S., Schlegel, H., de Haan, W., Korthals, P.W.: Verhandelingen over de natuurlijke geschiedenis der Nederlandsche overzeesche bezittingen. Luchtmans, Leiden (1839–1847)
19. Roberts, T.R.: The freshwater fishes of Java, as observed by Kuhl and van Hasselt in 1820-23. Zoologische Verhandelingen **285**, 1–93 (1993)
20. Fransen, C.H.J.M., Holthuis, L.B., Adama, J.P.H.M.: Type-catalogue of the Decapod Crustacea in the collections of the Nationaal Natuurhistorisch Museum, with appendices of pre-1900 collectors and material. Zoologische Verhandelingen **311**, 1–344 (1997)
21. Hildenhagen, T.: Heinrich Kuhl - Das Leben eines fast vergessenen Naturforschers aus Hanau. Neues Magazin für Hanauische Geschichte, pp. 110–214 (2013)
22. See for instance the digital Cyclopaedia of Malaysian Collectors. http://www.nationaalherbarium.nl/FMCollectors/Introduction.htm. Last Accessed 08 Sep 2017
23. Hoogmoed, M.S., Gassó Miracle, M.E.: Type specimens of recent and fossil Testudines and Crocodylia in the collections of NCB Naturalis, Leiden, the Netherlands. Zoologische Mededeelingen **84**, 159–199 (2010)
24. van der Zant, T., Schomaker, L., Haak, K.: Handwritten-word spotting using biologically inspired features. IEEE Trans. Pattern Anal. Mach. Intell. **30**, 1945–1957 (2008)

25. Van Oosten, J.-P., Schomaker, L.: A Reevaluation and benchmark of hidden Markov models. In: 2014 14th International Conference on Frontiers in Handwriting Recognition (ICFHR), pp. 531–536 (2014)
26. Van Oosten, J.-P., Schomaker, L.: Separability versus prototypicality in handwritten word-image retrieval. Pattern Recognit. **47**, 1031–1038 (2014)
27. READ project website. https://read.transkribus.eu/. Last Accessed 27 July 2017
28. He, S., Wiering, M., Schomaker, L.: Junction detection in handwritten documents and its application to writer identification. Pattern Recognit. **48**, 4036–4048 (2015)
29. Günter, S., Bunke, H.: HMM-based handwritten word recognition: on the optimization of the number of states, training iterations and Gaussian components. Pattern Recognit. **37**, 2069–2079 (2004)
30. Hochreiter, S., Schmidhuber, J.: Long short-term memory. Neural Comput. **9**, 1735–1780 (1997)
31. Graves, A.: RNNLIB: a recurrent neural network library for sequence learning problems. http://sourceforge.net/projects/rnnl/. Last Accessed 01 Sep 2017
32. Bulacu, M., Brink, A., van der Zant, T., Schomaker, L.: Recognition of handwritten numerical fields in a large single-writer historical collection. In: 2009 10th International Conference on Document Analysis and Recognition, pp. 808–812 (2009)
33. Yan, K., Verbeek, F.J.: Segmentation for high-throughput image analysis: watershed masked clustering. In: Margaria, T., Steffen, B. (eds.) ISoLA 2012. LNCS, vol. 7610, pp. 25–41. Springer, Heidelberg (2012). https://doi.org/10.1007/978-3-642-34032-1_4
34. Shi, Z.: Handwritten document images based on positional expectancy, Master thesis, Artificial Intelligence, University of Groningen, the Netherlands, May 2016
35. Gassó Miracle, M.E.: On whose authority? Temminck's debates on zoological classification and nomenclature: 1820–1850. J. Hist. Biol. **44**, 445–481 (2011)
36. Stork, L., Weber, A.: A linked data approach to disclose handwritten biodiversity heritage collections. In: Presented at the Digital Humanities Benelux Conference 2017 (2017)

Anchoring Unsorted E-Sources About Heritage Artefacts in Space and Time

Gamze Saygi[✉], Jean-Yves Blaise, and Iwona Dudek

UMR CNRS/MCC 3495 MAP Modèles et Simulations Pour l'Architecture et le Patrimoine,
Centre National de la Recherche Scientifique,
Campus CNRS Joseph Aiguier - Bât. Z' 31 Chemin Joseph Aiguier,
13402 Marseille Cedex 20, France
{gamze.saygi,jean-yves.blaise,iwona.dudek}@map.cnrs.fr

Abstract. Thanks to citizen-side contributions, heritage scientists can now quite often gather large amount of spatio-temporal data about heritage artefacts. In the context of *minor heritage* collections, which often slip through large-scale heritage programs, accessing such data sets may be a decisive turn in uncovering important clues, or significant relationships in and across collections. In other words, the "citizen science" paradigm seemingly opens a whole new range of opportunities at research level (e.g., enrichment of data, comparative analyses, multidisciplinary annotations) and for collection holders (e.g., networking, "intangible" museums).

Yet, due to the nature of such data sets (e.g., heterogeneity in the wording, in the precision, verifiability issues, contradictions), these opportunities also raise challenges, in particular when wanting to foster cross examinations by heritage scientists. The global objective of our research is to better weigh how the nature of citizen-side contributions can impact the way information can be recorded, formalized, and visualized. In this paper a clear focus is put on the space and time parameters: geo-visualization, and spatio-temporal data visualization. The paper introduces a series of open-source geo-visualization solutions that have been designed for use in the context of information sets harvested from citizen-side e-sources, and that help document minor heritage assets.

The results we present show that hybrid visualizations can act as a basis for comparative reasoning and analysis, but also that the *core service* we should manage to offer is definitely an infovis one: *getting to understand (at last) what we really know (and ignore).*

Keywords: Information visualization · Spatial data · Temporal data
Cartography · Geo-visualization · Information filtering · Cultural heritage
Citizen science

1 Introduction

Minor heritage comprises edifices/objects/landscapes, in other words vernacular heritage artefacts which are the result of past actions carried out by local society/inhabitants, by know-how, artisanship, acquired and transmitted from one generation to

© Springer International Publishing AG, part of Springer Nature 2018
M. Ioannides (Ed.): ITN-DCH 2017, LNCS 10605, pp. 167–178, 2018.
https://doi.org/10.1007/978-3-319-75826-8_14

another. Indeed, they were important components of everyday life at a time, but of today, they generally slip through large heritage programs or documentation initiatives. It is a particular research topic as items are usually not well documented, or documented in a very erratic way.

Heritage scientists and cultural actors cannot really count on existing and comprehensive research work when they want to analyze minor heritage. Nevertheless, as of today, there is a large number of citizen-side contributions (e.g., personal or associative web sites, blogs, or crowdsourced data sets) dedicated to the minor heritage. However, when looking at these contributions, there is neither any connection between them nor any structure. So, what if we pull those information sets together in such a way that cultural/scientific professionals can better analyze them? Moving from this point forward, this research focuses not only on "minor" heritage, but also on citizen science and its potential, in an attempt at deciphering the context of "human" beyond the artistic value of heritage artefacts. Correspondingly, our research effort questions the relevance and benefits of the citizen science paradigm in the context of minor heritage with a specific focus on spatial and temporal information. The aim of this research is not to depict one particular artefact but to gain some understanding of information trends in a large collection of artefacts, i.e., spotting patterns in the data sets that can then be analyzed and ultimately related to historical, geographical, climatic or other factors, and to cross-examine evidence about heritage collections.

On the other hand, one could think that a visual model in terms of three-dimensional rendering seems to be the nature of cultural heritage visualization, [1] but there is a large amount of (often ill-defined) spatio-temporal information hidden beyond the imagery. Consequently, a complementary formalism is required for a comprehensive understanding of spatial characteristics of heritage edifices, their evolution, and more generally to address the *why* and *how* questions that need to be examined when trying to recount the stories of artefacts and of their interrelations in what Kienreich [1] calls an *information space*. In that context, information visualization (infovis), which is defined as "computer supported, interactive, visual representation of abstract data to amplify cognition" [2], its potential to do cross-examination, and uncover illiterate information. Intersecting *infovis* and carto/chrono-graphy, this paper puts a clear focus on the space and time parameters: geo-visualization, and spatio-temporal data visualization. It introduces a series of open-source geo-visualization solutions that have been designed for use in the context of information sets harvested from citizen-side e-sources, and that help document minor heritage assets.

Yet, one thing has to be stated clearly: this paper's claim *is not* that the visualization solutions we propose help analyze the heritage artefacts themselves. Our claim is that the emergence of the citizen science paradigm requires pushing to the fore solutions helping to analyze and cross-examine the data behind these artefacts, with its heterogeneity, lacks, and contradictions. The contribution focuses on an early-stage possibility: distributing the data in time and space, and trying to highlight the informational patterns such a visualization bias allows for.

2 State-of-the-Art

Recent research in spatio-temporal information visualization has found application platforms in a wide spectrum of fields, some of which extends to temporal data visualization with a physical spatial reference. Some researchers in the geographical domain initiated the joint use of information visualization and cartographic representation (contour lines, relief shading, or orthoimages) by superimposing vector graphics [3], color-coded notation [4, 5], combination of the two former [6, 7] or animated colored graphs [8, 9] as spatio-temporal information layers supporting enhanced information visualization. Similar to those, many innovative visualization techniques are applied in the context of flow analysis [10, 11]. The work of [12] for instance analyses the potential benefits of animation on both static maps and the space-time cube, whereas the study of [13] visualizes spatio-temporal information dynamically as 3D animation superimposed on a cartographic background. In Beaude [14] travel times of commuters are analyzed by means of a combination of three visuals solutions: a geo-tagged topographic map, a "topological space" in which durations are represented by distances to the center point, and a time series represented as a histogram. The noteworthy contribution of Boyandin [15] brings a novelty to flowmaps by combining the potentials of geo-visualization and abstract temporal information visualization as a hybrid solution. The study results in an easier interpretation of spatio-temporal patterns and of their mutual relations. In parallel to this approach, some interactive platforms [16, 17] offer an integrated visualization of choropleth mapping and geotagging based on the temporal queries defined by users in order to analyze diverse regional dynamics. This integration is reinforced in some other studies [18, 19] by embedding graph and chart displays coupled with temporal animations or interactive navigation [20].

There is also a growing interest for diverse spatio-temporal information visualization techniques embedded in a cartographical solution. As an exemplification, Goovaerts [21] criticizes the use of three-dimensional visualization applied to cartography, Thakur [22] introduces a "data vases" visual metaphor based on kite diagrams in order to visualize multiple time, Bell [23] reuses the "data rose" visualization introduced by Huang [24] to superimpose geo-visualization and ringmaps. Similarly, Zhao [25] deciphers the potential of integrating multiple visualizations, i.e. cartographic representation with ringmaps, horizontal and vertical views in different scales (national, regional, etc.) by adding extrusion value for temporal events. In addition, Tominski [26] employs color coded 3D trajectory bands embedded on a 2D map and complements the visualization with a circular time display. And, Slingsby [27] experiments a link between treemaps, spatial treemaps, raster maps and road maps. The above mentioned interactions allow cross-filtering of information by applying different spatial and temporal variable combinations.

A few applications [28, 29] have also targeted data sets in relation with historical sciences: they appear as very promising for geo-localizing information, and [30] adds a simultaneous visualization of temporal events. Nevertheless, these examples incorporate spatial anchoring of information in-forms of geo-localization, but they consider the temporal dimension only in the context of a linear, punctual and determined actions. More specific to the cultural heritage domain, geo-localization of information proved its importance with a number of examples [31–34] in the field, some of which offering enhancement with simultaneous temporal information visualization. Nevertheless, detaching spatial information from temporal information bounds the understanding of cultural heritage information. In fact, spatio-temporal information visualization is a challenging issue in that application field due to the heterogeneous, imperfect, fuzzy and sometimes uncertain nature of temporal data. Some studies [35, 36] already take into consideration uncertainties and heterogeneity of temporal data, and Blaise [37] explored a number of visualization options, i.e. combination of two-dimensional spatial representations with diverse temporal visualization (timeline, concentric time) in order to represent architectural changes of a group of edifices throughout the time. Although those studies draw attention to the particularities of spatio-temporal visualization for cultural heritage studies and their prospected needs, they do not offer a generic framework that would match a variety of use cases.

Thorough evaluation of the in-house approaches shows that most visualization solutions in which both spatial and temporal data are of concern to analysts, there is a general tendency to segregate them in different views. Our contribution in comparison to the aforementioned studies focuses on experimenting a hybrid *space + time* visualization solution, adapted to information sets extracted from citizen-side unsorted e-sources, and concerning a large amount of minor heritage artefacts.

3   Implementation and Interactive User Platform

The global objective of our research is to better weigh and assess how the nature of citizen-side contributions can impact the way information about minor heritage can be recorded, formalized, and visualized. One of the first developments we have engaged is a series of open-source geo-visualization solutions that have been designed for use in the context such information sets, and that help document minor heritage assets. The idea was to try to see what how unsorted raw data as available in web content (whatever the origin and target of the web pages) can act as a tool for the (re)interpretation of minor heritage. The research process started with the cumbersome task of analyzing and pulling together large and unsorted data sets (web pages mainly). That first task lead to a structuring of the data that offers a level of flexibility suitable to the harvesting context (e.g., heterogeneity, lacking elements), and focusing on the "localization" or "anchoring" of the information in time and space.

In a second stage we designed open-source geo-visualization solutions allowing for what the whole process is about: comparative reasoning. Shortly said, the ambition of these open-source visual solutions is to support analysts in their effort to pull together and make sense of unsorted, raw evidence. The visualization platform builds on the famous mantra of Shneiderman [38]: "overview first, zoom and filter, then details-on-demand", and aims to do implicit data filtering through user interaction. It does not only distribute (in space and time) e-sources systematically, but allows analysts to uncover expected or unexpected patterns and correlations among the information set. In this section we first present the test case and in particular the data we cope with, and then comment on some of the visual solutions.

3.1 Harvesting and Structuring the Data

The research encompasses three heterogeneous collections: edifices, movable objects (ethnographic collections from the MuCEM, Museum of European and Mediterranean Civilizations) and intangible heritage (practices, craftsmanship). Naturally the way

Fig. 1. Imagery representing archetype of (some) edifices within the collection.

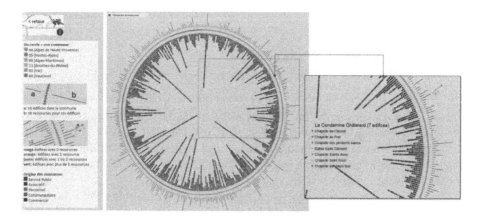

Fig. 2. A visualization of e-sources distributed by commune. Each commune is represented by a small circle composing the overall circular diagram, the colors of these circles differentiate the administrative structure communes belong to. Lines running from the circles outbound measure the number of edifices per communes (the longer the line, the highest amount of edifices). The small squares making up the lines inward have a color code according the e-source category, and length of the lines show the amount of e-sources. A selection by the user of one the circles results in the opening of a list of edifices per commune, with for each of them a number of e-sources. Significant remarks can be made when analyzing the visualization: no systematic relation of the number of edifices to the number of sources, a detectable difference in the origin of sources between communes on the right (green circles) and communes on the left-down quarter (blue circles), substantial differences across edifices of the same commune, *etc.* (Color figure online)

items of these three collections are localized (in time and space) is uneven, and an issue as such, but in this paper we shall focus on the first aforementioned collection, composed of 1066 rural chapels (Fig. 1) located in the south-east of France (Southern Alps, *région Provence-Alpes-Côte d'Azur*), distributed in 340 communes[1]. The spatio-temporal data brought together is quite significant in terms of quantity (over 2500 e-sources), and can be described as imperfect, incomplete, and heterogeneous both in terms of determinacy and of origin. Besides, there is neither any connection between them nor any predefined structure since most of the e-sources originate from scattered local initiatives (e.g., individuals recounting a journey, group of persons interested in the local history). E-sources are stored with typological markers showing the origin of the producers, from "official" web sites to individual blogs (Fig. 2).

The harvesting task aimed at providing for each edifice the following indications:

- Geospatial characteristics: geographical location, with an assessment of quality (0–4 scale), typological markers, orientation, altitude, toponymical variations.
- Temporal characteristics: anchoring in time of the artefact's creation or foundation, with an assessment of contradictions and a data model storing on one hand the verbal indication as found in the source and a transfer to a tuple of integers, and a recording of cyclic events (e.g., votive festivals).
- Imagery and other qualitative indications such as alternative names.

It has to de said that these indications are not always available, can be worded in an imprecise way (e.g., *...the edifice was located along the narrow valley close to the stream...*) or can be contradictory, hence it created one of the next challenges: creation of explicit graphical semiology.

3.2   The Visualization Effort

The aim of the visualization effort goes beyond the localization of artefacts on maps: what is targeted is to support information analysis and data quality assessment, as an overly above a background cartography. In terms of technology, the platform combines RDBMS, HTML/js scripting, and a cartography part developed over the *leaflet* web library [39]. The whole platform thereby remains fully "in line" with the very essence of citizen science initiatives.

The resulting interactive geo-visualization facilitates exploration by information filtering in various zoom levels and offers the following services: (i) examining each edifice individually, (ii) evaluating groups of edifices focusing on a specific commune, (iii) comparing individual edifices or communes with each other by applying different spatial and/or temporal information filters, (iv) interpreting the overall dataset by detecting relations, similarities and differences in regional scale. Table 1 summarizes the various visual solutions we have developed and tested.

---

[1] The communes are the lowest level of administrative division in the French Republic.

Table 1. Comparison of the available information layers in different geo-visualization solutions

| a | b | c | d | e |

Available information layers/access options	a	b	c	d	e
Geographical location	✓	✓	✓	✓	✓
Quality of localization	✓	✗	✓	✗	✗
Implantation (relation with a setting)	✗	✗	✗	✗	✓
Orientation	✓	✓	✓	✓	✗
Altitude	✓	✓	✓	✓	✗
Visual (thumbs)	✓	✓	✗	✓	✗
Ordinal/linear time	✓	✗	✓	✗	✓
Cyclic time	✓	✗	✓	✗	✗
Amount of e-sources	✓	✗	✓	✗	✓
Origin of e-sources	✓	✓	✓	✓	✗
Quality of information	✓	✗	✓	✗	✓
User-side free interaction	✗	✗	✓	✗	✗
Pre-defined controlled zoom levels	✓	✓	✗	✓	✓

The solutions we have experimented implement the concept of implicit filtering at two levels: using the geographical localization itself, and using the representation of that localization (zoom level). Shortly said, several issues have been at the heart of our developments: the age-old question of combining space and time in a unique visual component, the use of alternative models of time and of alternative filtering by zoom levels, the notion of information patterns, and of course pitfalls to overcome when facing incomplete or ill-defined pieces of data (e.g., contradictory temporal information, imprecision of localization). The following figure (Fig. 3) illustrates (some of) the actual services provided.

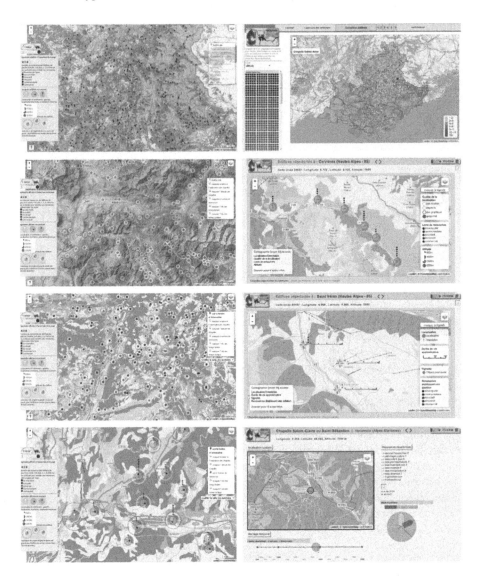

Fig. 3. Examples of open-source geo-visualization solutions in two main variations: on the left-hand side a user can superimpose all or some spatio-temporal information for cross comparison according to his/her preference, whereas on the right-hand side, target information is predefined and information layers are displayed/hidden following zoom level change by the user. The background cartography is subject to change in both cases.

4 Evaluation and Limitations

The overall implementation process has been straightforward to handle, and found convenient for organizing interaction between a map and other components of the web interface. Nonetheless, it derives the necessity for the designer to invest time on programming interactions. In addition, some limitations need to be made clear:

- The platform allows enhancing cartographical layer with other components but it has a rather limited graphic vocabulary.
- The readability of the "abstract" semiology representing overlaid spatio-temporal information patterns is significantly impacted by the cartographic background layer selected by the user. For instance, some layers may be visible in black and white Open Street Map (OSM) background while they are not in regular OSM.
- We experimented embedding multiple cartographic backgrounds, named "tiles" in the leaflet architecture (OSM, OSM B&W, IGN's géoportail, Wikimedia, etc.). It can be seen as an advantage for different readings of information patterns but alters the performance when adding numerous tiles (downloading time becomes costly).
- We faced an inconsistency problem regarding the different projections provided by diverse open-source repositories. For instance, the boundaries of communes provided by public sources do not persistently overlap with OSM.
- The overlapping of symbols – also an age-old problem in cartography - remains an open issue. At this stage, we offer user-side interaction that allow resizing of the semiology, typically in the case of close vicinities. The state-of-the-art seems to prove that an ideal solution remains to be found for redistribution/masking/grouping of the overlapping symbols.
- The density of the information layers added on top of the cartographic background leads to large files, embedding an important set of client-side events handling and js functions. At this stage, the scalability of the implementation remains questionable: the reuse of the technological pipeline should be a concern if wanting to extend the experiment to significantly larger collections.

Finally, we also carried out an experimental evaluation of the main cartographic solutions in order to investigate the coherency of the system with human cognition, i.e., its efficiency as a *communication channel*. It allowed us to compare two approaches for information filtering, i.e., predefined controlled zoom levels (the zoom level implicitly filters the information layers) and a classic user-side free interaction (user-side selection of information layers to display).

Seven human evaluators, used to heritage as a domain but with different back-grounds, were asked to spot information patterns (comparing the amount of sources for a set of edifices for instance), to carry out basic tasks (finding an edifice with a given information pattern for instance), and in the case of maps with predefined controlled zoom levels to associate information layers with a given zoom level.

In user-side free interaction mode, the majority of the rates show that readability of ill-defined localization was more convenient than the readability of ill-defined temporal data. Ultimately testers were asked to rate the readability and efficiency of the carto-graphic products in a more flexible way, and here the variety in background of testers was an important and positive aspect of the evaluation as it showed that beyond some specific shortages of the platform, named by most testers, a number of choices and designs are diversely judged. The relevance, the information retrieval capabilities of the platform clearly would require different "ways of doing" matching the different types of understanding of the testers. Naturally we need to say that the overall evaluation should be seen as a preliminary one, we acknowledge the necessity to further evaluate, and develop overall implementation accordingly.

5   Conclusions and Future Works

This research aims at answering to the question of how information harvested from citizen-side contributions about time and space, given their very nature (e.g., imperfections, heterogeneity), can be profitable for comprehensive analysis by heritage scientists such as cross-examination. It is found out that although there is a growing interest on applying visualization solutions/models for evaluating spatial and temporal information, most segregate spatial information from temporal information, which might create misconceptions especially concerning heritage spaces' dynamic characteristics which continuously evolve in time. Our contribution differs from the aforementioned approaches by providing a hybrid information retrieval platform, designed to allow for the identification of information patterns in a wide *minor heritage* collection. This requires a comprehensive solution allowing both evaluating peculiarity of each artefact and comparisons with one another.

The introduced space + time geo-visualization solutions targeted minor heritage assets for which there is a lack of comprehensive analytical information. Evaluation results show that provided open-source visualization solutions embedding various spatial and temporal attributes in a platform, can allow scientists to benefit from hybrid visualizations as a basis for comparative reasoning and analysis. By this way, one can uncover illiterate information patterns and correlations in the information by filtering and combining spatio-temporal variables.

We now plan to experiment collaborative 3D data acquisition in connection with the developments carried out in our research unit. What is ahead is also collecting real-life experiences and testimonies, beyond existing sets of e-sources, through crowdsourcing-like initiatives.

Acknowledgements. This research is funded by the *région Provence-Alpes-Côte d'Azur* regional authorities, under the program entitled Territo*graphie* (www.map.cnrs.fr/territographie), conducted in co-operation with MuCEM (Museum of European and Mediterranean Civilizations). The authors are indebted especially to Édouard de Laubrie from MuCEM for his continuous support and collaboration.

References

1. Kienreich, W.: Information and knowledge visualisation: an oblique view. MIA J. **0**(1), 7–17 (2006)
2. Card, S.: Information visualization. In: The Human-Computer Interaction Handbook: Fundamentals, Evolving Technologies, and Emerging Applications, pp. 509–543. Lawrence Erlbaum Assoc Inc. (2007). https://doi.org/10.1201/9781410615862.ch26

3. Kääb, A., Huggel, C., Fischer, L., Guex, S., Paul, F., Roer, I., Salzmann, N., et al.: Remote sensing of glacier- and permafrost-related hazards in high mountains: an overview. Nat. Hazards Earth Syst. Sci. **5**, 527–554 (2005). https://doi.org/10.5194/nhess-5-527-2005

4. Pritchard, H., Murray, T., Luckman, A., Strozzi, T., Barr, S.: Glacier surge dynamics of Sortebræ, east Greenland, from synthetic aperture radar feature tracking. J. Geophys. Res. **110** (2005). https://doi.org/10.1029/2004jf000233

5. Lang, O., Rabus, B.T., Dech, S.W.: Velocity map of the Thwaites Glacier catchment, West Antarctica. J. Glaciol. **50**, 46–56 (2004). https://doi.org/10.3189/172756504781830268

6. Star, C.: Jakobshavn Glacier Flow in the Year 2000. NASA Scientific Visualization Studio, SVS Image Server (2006)

7. Joughin, I., Howat, I.M., Fahnestock, M., Smith, B., Krabill, W., Alley, R.B., et al.: Continued evolution of Jakobshavn Isbrae following its rapid speedup. J. Geophys. Res. **113** (2008). https://doi.org/10.1029/2008jf001023

8. Robert, S.: Le paysage visible de la Promenade des Anglais à Nice: essai d'une représentation cartographique dynamique. Mappemonde, No. 86 (2007)

9. Kobben, B., Becker, T., Blok, C.: Webservices for animated mapping: the TimeMapper prototype. In: Peterson, M. (ed.) Lecture Notes in Geoinformation and Cartography, pp. 205–217. Springer, Berlin (2012). https://doi.org/10.1007/978-3-642-27485-5_14

10. Geertman, S., de Jong, T., Wessels, C.: Flowmap: a support tool for strategic network analysis. In: Geertman, S., Stillwell, J. (eds.) Planning Support Systems in Practice, pp. 155–175. Springer, Berlin (2003). https://doi.org/10.1007/978-3-540-24795-1_9

11. Konjar, M., Boyandin, I., Lalanne, D., Lisec, A., Drobne, S.: Using flow maps to explore functional regions in Slovenia. In: 2nd International Conference on Information Society and Information Technologies - ISIT 2010 (2010)

12. Biadgilgn, D.M., Blok, C.A., Huisman, O.: Assessing the cartographic visualization of moving objects. Momona Ethiop. J. Sci. **3**(1), 80–104 (2011). https://doi.org/10.4314/mejs.v3i1.63687

13. Antoni, J.P., Klein, O., Moisy, S.: La discrétisation temporelle. Une méthode de structuration des données pour la cartographie dynamique. Cartes & Géomatique, Revue du Comité Français de Cartographie **213**, 27–31 (2012)

14. Beaude, B., Guillemot, L.: Commuting scales. Cartographie dynamique d'accessibilité temporelle. Mappemonde; no. 105 (2012)

15. Boyandin, I., Bertini, E., Bak, P., Lalanne, D.: Flowstrates: an approach for visual exploration of temporal origin-destination data. In: Eurographics/IEEE Symposium on Visualization (EuroVis 2011), vol. 30(3), pp. 971–980 (2011). https://doi.org/10.1111/j.1467-8659.2011.01946.x

16. Interactive mapping of American presidential political votes. http://dsl.richmond.edu/voting/interactive/

17. Interactive library of regional population dynamics. http://stats.oecd.org/OECDregionalstatistics/#story=0

18. Banos, A., Lacasa, J.: Spatio-temporal exploration of SARS epidemic. Cybergeo: Eur. J. Geogr. Systèmes, Modélisation, Géostatistique, document 408 (2007). https://doi.org/10.4000/cybergeo.12803

19. de Oliveira, M.G., de Souza, B.C.: GeoSTAT – a system for visualization, analysis and clustering of distributed spatiotemporal data. In: Proceedings XIII GEOINFO, 25–27 November 2012, Campos do Jordao, Brazil, pp. 108–119 (2012)

20. Kapler, T., Wright, W.: Geo time information visualization. Inf. Visual. **4**(2), 136–146 (2005). https://doi.org/10.1109/infvis.2004.27

21. Goovaerts, P.: Three-dimensional visualization, interactive analysis and contextual mapping of space-time Cancer data. In: 13th AGILE International Conference on Geographic Information Science (2010)
22. Thakur, S., Rhyne, T.-M.: *Data Vases:* 2D and 3D plots for visualizing multiple time series. In: Bebis, G., Boyle, R., Parvin, B., Koracin, D., Kuno, Y., Wang, J., Pajarola, R., Lindstrom, P., Hinkenjann, A., Encarnação, M.L., Silva, C.T., Coming, D. (eds.) ISVC 2009. LNCS, vol. 5876,   pp.   929–938.   Springer,   Heidelberg   (2009).   https://doi.org/ 10.1007/978-3-642-10520-3_89
23. Bell, K.: Visualizing crime – a "Data Rose" Blooms. Dir. Mag. (2011)
24. Huang, G., et al.: Geovisualizing Data with Ring Maps. Esri ArcUser (2008)
25. Zhao, L., Forer, P., Harvey, A.S.: Multi-scale and multi-form visualisation of human movement patterns in the context of space, time and activity: from timeline to Ringmap. In: AGILE 2008 Conference, Girona, Spain (2008)
26. Tominski, C., Schumann, H., Andrienko, G., Andrienko, N.: Stacking-based visualization of trajectory attribute data. In: IEEE Transactions on Visualization and Computer Graphics 18, vol. 12, pp. 2565–2574 (2012). https://doi.org/10.1109/tvcg.2012.265
27. Slingsby, A., Dykes, J., Wood, J.: Using treemaps for variable selection in spatio-temporal visualisation. Inf. Visual. **7**, 210–224 (2008). https://doi.org/10.1057/palgrave.ivs.9500185
28. The Growth of Newspapers across the U.S.: 1690-2011. http://web.stanford.edu/group/ ruralwest/cgi-bin/drupal/visualizations/us_newspapers
29. MyHistro/the Hundred Years' war. http://www.myhistro.com/story/the-hundred-years-war/ 34325/1#!war-during-the-rule-of-charles-v-67299
30. Visualizing emancipation. http://dsl.richmond.edu/emancipation
31. World Heritage List interactive map. http://whc.unesco.org/en/interactive-map/
32. Cultural Heritage Map of Turkey. http://turkiyekulturvarliklari.hrantdink.org/en/
33. An interactive geo-spatial visualization tool for GLAM (Galleries, Libraries, Archives, Museums). http://glammap.net/
34. Philippine Inventory of Cultural Properties and Historic Events. http:// www.philippineheritagemap.org/map
35. Blaise, J.-Y., Dudek, I.: Concentric time: enabling context + focus visual analysis of architectural changes. In: Kryszkiewicz, M., Rybinski, H., Skowron, A., Raś, Z.W. (eds.) ISMIS 2011. LNCS (LNAI), vol. 6804, pp. 632–641. Springer, Heidelberg (2011). https:// doi.org/10.1007/978-3-642-21916-0_67
36. Kauppinen, T., Mantegarib, G., Paakkarinena, P., Kuittinena, H., Hyvonena, E., Bandinic, S.: Determining relevance of imprecise temporal intervals for cultural heritage information retrieval. Int. J. Hum.-Comput. Stud. **68**, 549–560 (2010). https://doi.org/10.1016/j.ijhcs. 2010.03.002
37. Blaise, J.Y., Dudek, I.: Can infovis tools support the analysis of spatio-temporal diffusion patterns in historic architecture? In: 40th Annual Conference of Computer Applications and Quantitative Methods in Archaeology. CAA Series Computer Applications and Quantitative Methods in Archaeology, March 2013, pp. 367–378. Amsterdam University Press, Southampton (2013)
38. Shneiderman, B.: The eyes have it: a task by data type taxonomy for information visualizations. In: Proceedings IEEE Symposium on Visual Languages, pp. 336–343 (1996). https://doi.org/10.1016/b978-155860915-0/50046-9
39. Leaflet open-source JavaScript library for mobile-friendly interactive maps. http:// leafletjs.com/

Using Innovative Technologies in Preservation and Presentation of Endangered Archives

Aleksandar Jerkov[1] and Vasilije Milnovic[2(✉)]

[1] University Library, Belgrade, Serbia
jerkov@unilib.bg.ac.rs
[2] Scientific Center, University Library, Belgrade, Serbia
milnovic@unilib.rs

Abstract. This paper presents an in depth review on the project "Safeguarding the fragile collection of the private collection of the Lazic family". Namely, University Library in Belgrade (ULB) received a grant of the British Library in the framework of Endangered Archives Programme for this project. The aim of this project primarily was to digitize and thus preserve for posterity extremely valuable private collections. However, our intention was also to introduce the possibility of using new digital technologies in the preservation and presentation of vulnerable archival materials of historical importance in adequate physical space and to provide opportunities for the general public active participation in such activities. This cutting-edge technology is suitable for interactive presentation of materials which are too fragile to leaf through. Fully aware of the importance of the availability and open access to cultural and scientific heritage for achieving the knowledge society and the role of academic libraries in its dissemination, these extremely vulnerable materials are also presented in the open access repository, which will include research papers based on the materials available within the project. So, the objects can be analyzed both "on the outside" via the metadata and with the help of the software for editing digital repositories and "on the inside" via a concise overview of the content of individual objects. Digital objects structured in this way will grab users' attention and bring back the historical content into focus.

Keywords: Innovative technologies · Digitization · Digital technologies
Vulnerable archival material · Project

1 Introduction

There are three main reasons for the digitization of a nation's cultural heritage. The first is that it provides access to academic material for a much wider constituency than solely professional academics. Conservation is the second reason. In theory, digitizing documents reduces the need to handle the originals and thus slows down the pace of deterioration. However, the act of copying can itself damage original documents. For this reason, it is important to keep to a minimum the number of times a particular collection is digitized. The third rationale for digitization is to create new methodologies for the study of primary sources [5].

© Springer International Publishing AG, part of Springer Nature 2018
M. Ioannides (Ed.): ITN-DCH 2017, LNCS 10605, pp. 179–188, 2018.
https://doi.org/10.1007/978-3-319-75826-8_15

Whenever we talk about the cultural heritage of a region and the study of it, as well as the promotion and presentation of such materials, the main issue is the transparency of the material, because it is the best way to witness the common cultural heritage of Europe and the world. This is obviously reflected in projects such as this one, whose transparency and the abundance of authentic and unbiased materials, enable any interested researcher to make their own judgment about different cultural, historical and socio-political issues in accordance with their own critical mind and common sense. Therefore, this paper presents an in depth review on the project "Safeguarding the fragile collection of the private collection of the Lazic family". Namely, University Library "Svetozar Markovic" in Belgrade received a grant of the British Library in the framework of Endangered Archives Programme for this project.

The aim of this project primarily was to digitize and thus preserve for posterity extremely valuable private collections owned by the non-governmental organization "Adligat" [4] which is also a library and a museum. It means that the whole project is a collaborative effort between an academic institution and non-governmental sector. This form of cooperation is valuable as the academic libraries go beyond their primary functions and meet the needs of other types of organizations which is generally important for the advancement of a society.

The preservation of Digital Cultural Heritage is an ongoing action, to be periodically revised, in order to update data sets and metadata formats. These are time consuming activities, in particular if carried out independently by each cultural institution. Common procedures and workflows would reduce the cost both in terms of time and money to be allocated to this task and would contribute to the general interoperability and openness of data which is stated as the priority for the global knowledge society [1].

Given the fact that the implementation of this project is still ongoing, our intention is to introduce the possibility of using new digital technologies in the preservation and presentation of vulnerable archival materials of historical importance in adequate physical space and to provide opportunities for the general public active participation in such activities. Fully aware of the importance of the availability and open access to cultural and scientific heritage for achieving the knowledge society and the role of academic libraries in its dissemination, these extremely vulnerable materials are also presented in the open access repository, which will include research papers based on the materials available within the project.

2 Description of Project Organization

The University Library "Svetozar Markovic" as the central scientific library in Serbia, which has up to now gained invaluable experience in several versatile digitization projects, most notably ICT-PSP CIP 2007–2013 European Commission projects Europeana Libraries: Aggregating digital content from Europe's libraries and Europeana Newspapers: A Gateway to European Newspapers Online is the coordinator of the current digitization project "Safeguarding the fragile collection of the private collection of the Lazić family".

Here we present in short the phases of the project and their duration. The main phase, i.e. the digitization process has had the following stages: research and the selection of the materials (2 months), equipment transfer and setting up (1 month), scanning (4 months), metadata processing of the scanned selected publications (1 month). Simultaneously with the aforementioned stages, the website which will enable reading the metadata of the scanned objects and raise interest of the audience through entertaining quizzes about the scanned content has been constructed. To disseminate the project results we have planned a six-month promotion of the digitized materials in the media and on the social networks and presentations at two international expert conferences. At the moment, three specialist courses on digitization, metadata and cloud storing are being held on the project. Three experts from the University Library in Belgrade are training people from "ADLIGAT" to transfer knowledge and good practice in the aforementioned fields. The aim of this project activity is to equip more people with the necessary knowledge and skills so that they can standardize their efforts in digitization and promote successful digitization models. At the end of the project a scientific conference on the highest level will be held in Serbia where both local and international stakeholders and experts will gather to contribute to the topic and discuss project's sustainability and potential future development. One of the topics motivated by the project results will be standardization of the process of digitization on the national level as so far there have not been clear and determined standards in this field in Serbia. Standardization of digitization would provide unification of digital objects and create possibility for the construction of a unique repository on the national level. National policies about cultural preservation need to re-use best practices, to share solutions and to avoid duplication of efforts, in particular in the current context of economic crisis where the resources available are often smaller. The use of the e-infrastructures is a pillar in this direction and the cultural heritage sector should progress towards its full integration in the new concept of open science [1].

The very process of scanning was done at the private archive of the Lazić family due to the vulnerability of the materials. The digitization process lasted for four months and 12.500 pages were scanned each month. Two scanners, Robotic book scanner and Flatbed color image scanner, owned by the University Library "Svetozar Marković" were used at this stage to ensure both speed of scanning and possibility for scanning of physically delicate materials.

3   Collection Content

The collection of the private library owned by the Lazić family which is digitized in the aforementioned project coordinated by the University Library in Belgrade has several sub-collections. The digitized collection, which is the result of the project, has 50.000 pages.

3.1 Law Books (Part 1)

The first group of materials that was digitized was published by Geca Kon who was the most important Serbian and later Yugoslav publisher at the beginning of the 20th century. At certain periods, his publishing activity was on a much larger scale compared to other publishers in Serbia altogether. Many of the most important titles of Serbian literature, history and law were published at the time thanks to him. However, considering his participation in the First World War against the German and his Jewish origin, his publications were massively destroyed during the Second World War when the German used him as an example of anti-Jewish propaganda, and the books from his bookstore were confiscated and transferred to Vienna. During the Second World War his publishing company was taken over by a fascist publishing company "Jugoistok", which, when communists came to power, became "Prosveta". However, due to the support of the monarchy and capitalist system, Geca Kon's publications were even after the war unpopular and considered to be published by the "class enemy" which is why very often only a small number of publications was saved. We chose to digitize law publications due to the fact that these publications, being expert literature, were published in a much lower circulation when compared to fiction and historical literature for the general public, which altogether makes these publications quite rare. Moreover, notes on books, stamps, Ex Libris etc. are in themselves invaluable and quite rare. For some of these important libraries the only trace of their existence is the Ex Libris on these books. Here we list only some of the most exclusive materials that were digitized:

- Political and Legal Discussions (Serbian: Političke i pravne rasprave), by Slobodan Jovanović published in 1910 represent an extremely rare document as the author was the president of the Press Bureau in the Serbian government in exile during the First World War, the president of the Government in exile during the Second World War, the president of the Serbian Royal Academy, rector of the University of Belgrade, Public Law Professor at the Faculty of Law and its dean.
- Bill of Sale, lectures at the Faculty of Law (Serbian: Ugovor o prodaji i kupovini, predavanja na Pravnom fakultetu), by Živojin M. Perić published in 1920 is an extremely rare publication by the most renowned Serbian layer between the two world wars, published in extremely low circulation.
- Original Slavic Law before the 10th century (Serbian: Prvobitno slovensko pravo pre X veka), by Dr Karlo Kadlec is an extremely rare law study and generally there is only a small number of studies and documents about this type of law.

The total number of publications that were published by Geca Kon digitized in the project is 132. None of these publications has ever been digitized even though they raise a lot of interest among the readers. Therefore, their digitizations is justified and will be welcomed by scientific, expert and general audience.

3.2   Law Books (Part 2)

These publications are the second part of the collection of law books that was digitized. They were not published by Geca Kon. There are 29 books and some of the most rare and valuable are the following:

- Amendments of the regulations on disabled veterans and other regulations on the disabled (Serbian: Izmene i dopune uredbe o ratnim invalidima i drugi propisi o invalidima), published in Belgrade in 1938 is an extremely rare publication important for the retrospective overview of the position and treatment of a great number of war veterans, which was one of the burning issues and a big social problem.
- Yugoslav Social Legislation, social service handbook (Serbian: Jugoslavensko socijalno zakonodavstvo priručnik za socijalnu službu), by Ilija P. Perić, published in Belgrade in 1931 is also a very rare publication as it is an internal handbook for social workers.
- Collection of laws of the new age, proclamation of His Royal Highness the King as of January 6 1929 (Serbian: Zbirka zakona novog doba proklamacija NJ.V. Kralja od 6. januara 1929. godine), printed by Dr. Časlav M. Nikitović is one of the very rare publications as the laws in it remained in force even after the introduction of monarchist dictatorship.

3.3   War Publications

Serbian war publications (1914–1918) are very specific considering the tragic events that happened to Serbian people at the time. After winning the battles at Cer and Kolubara, Serbia was attacked on three sides. After the tough battles it was decided that Serbian state, government, parliament, military and a large number of Serbian people should retreat to Greece. They retreated via Albanian mountains during winter, so there were less than 200 000 people who finished this journey. Serbian state continued to exist in exile with its government and the people, but without its territory, which is a specific case in history. One of the important evidence of the continuity of the Serbian state is the Serbian publishing activity in exile which, due to the aforementioned circumstances, is historically significant. All the publications printed in Corfu, where the seat of the Serbian government was, in Bizerte (Tunisia), where the great number of the wounded was, and in Thessaloniki have the status of national heritage of great importance according to the Serbian law. This is also applied to some of the rare publications of the Serbian emigration printed in Geneva, Nice, London and in the USA. Some of the most valuable publications are the following:

- English–Serbian dictionary by Đorđe A. Petrović, published in Thessaloniki in 1918 is an extremely rare publication used by the soldiers to communicate with the English medical staff.
- Law on the amendments of the National bank law (Serbian: Zakon o izmenama i dopunama zakona o Narodnoj Banci) published in Corfu in 1916 extremely rare as there is no a library in Serbia that possesses this document.

- Secret subversive organization, a report from the trial at the military court to the officers in Thessaloniki (Serbian: Tajna prevratna organizacija izveštaj sa pretresa u vojnom sudu za oficire u Solunu po beleškama vođenim na samom pretresu), printed in Thessaloniki in 1918 is an extremely rare publication as the officers were charged for an attempt to kill Serbian crown prince and previously they organized the overthrow and assassination of the royal family in 1903. This is the most important legal process held during the war.
- Serbian school day in France 13/26 March 1915 (Serbian: Srpski školski dan u Francuskoj 13/26 marta 1915 godine), published in Niš in 1915 is a very rare publication written during the retreat of the Serbian army. The role of this publication was to show that Serbian army and people were supported by the Allies.

3.4 Periodicals

- "Pregled listova" is an extremely rare publication of an informative journal for the membres of the Serbian government, printed in Geneva in low circulation (most probably less than 50 copies, 3 are only known to exist), on different types of paper, on a hectograph, depending on the war atmosphere. "Pregled listova" is actually an overview of war publications, the selection of the most important texts of the allies and enemies with the aim to inform the Serbian government about the media picture of Serbia and current war activities. Marked "confidential", it was available only to the highest state and war officials. The greatest number of copies were destroyed. By digitization, the periodical has become available to the public for the first time.
- "Misao" is an extremely rare Serbian war journal published in England. There were only four volumes and it was edited by the immigrants and intellectuals in England.
- "Krfske novine", a very rare publication, a symbol of Serbian periodicals published during the war. It is important as Serbian literary works were published there, poetry in particular, which was later considered a classic and the most important work about the war created during the war.

3.5 Calendars

Calendars were favourite periodicals, printed once a year, on a low quality paper, in a form of a book which comprised different areas of science and entertainment, dedicated to all generations so as to be read throughout the whole year. In addition to low quality paper, the calendars were not preserved but thrown away which is why they are extremely rare nowadays. Digitization of some calendars from the 19th century is a real challenge considering the fact that paper falls apart and that the very leafing through is quite difficult.

- "Vardar" – a calendar for 1898, printed by the bookstore Lj. Jokisimović in 1897 is an extremely rare calendar which cannot even be found at the National Library of Serbia.

- "Orao" – an illustrated calendar for 1889 which has 365 days, printed in Novi Sad, is a very rare publication as Serbian writers at the time contributed to it with their texts.
- Entertainment calendar for 1855 by Svetozar Stojadinović, written before the reform of the Serbian alphabet in 1868. It is extremely rare and it is considered national treasure according to the Serbian law.
- "Srpkinja" – an illustrated calendar for women from 1896, is one of the rarest publications from this collection as it was written for women.

3.6 Archival Material

Archival material about the First World War which includes several letters, notes, postcards and other documents such as an original war poster – a call for help to Serbia in 1916, a photograph of a soldier on the day of Bulgarian capitulation, several short letters, extremely rare war postcards-photographs of Serbian Refugee Theatre from Bizerte (Tunisia), etc. is especially important. There is an extremely valuable collection of letters and telegrams addressed to the family of Field Marshal Živojin Mišić, one of the most renowned Serbian commanders who led Serbian army in the Battle of Kolubara, when at the very beginning of the War much weaker Serbian army defeated Austro-Hungarian army. Telegrams and letters sent on the occasion of his death in 1921 include the speech held on Živojin Mišić's funeral. The majority of these materials have never been published and the wider and scientific public is not familiar with their content.

4 Using Innovative Digital Technologies in Preservation and Promotion of Vulnerable Materials Within the Project

Extremely fragile materials, which are a part of the aforementioned project, will be presented to the library users in the physical space via the new digital technology recently acquired by the University Library "Svetozar Marković". This cutting-edge technology is suitable for interactive presentation of materials which are too fragile to leaf through. Users can browse digital content in a transparent way via a touchscreen while simultaneously looking at the particular publication behind the screen in the physical space. In addition to the digitization of printed publications, this device can be used for the presentation of photo galleries, 3D objects and videos. It provides a completely new and unique experience to all those interested in rare or fragile publications whose access is usually restricted. The University Library "Svetozar Marković" is the first institution in East Europe and the third library in the world to have acquired this new digital technology. In order to introduce wider audience with the materials digitized in the project and with this new technology, we plan to visit the libraries in the network of academic libraries in Serbia where the cabinet display will be installed for certain period of time and the public enabled to use it (Picture 1).

Picture 1. Magic box

At the same time, all the materials and expert research papers based on it are available in open access on the project website. Digitized materials which can be displayed in this "virtual-physical" box, in addition to the sets of metadata of connected with the individual objects have a detailed content structure of the object and in that way they create a unique presentation of the very object which is easily searchable and accessed. Namely, the objects are analyzed both "on the outside" via the metadata and with the help of the software for editing digital repositories and "on the inside" via a concise overview of the content of individual objects.

In addition to the final editing of the very sets of photos, i.e. scans for the presentation, this software includes a detailed content analysis, which relies on the most contemporary OCR technology and which enables full access to the object. With the help of the software the object will be internally structured following the principle of the precise analysis of content and zoning, so that in the final presentation we get the detailed picture as regards an individual chapter or an article (Picture 2).

Picture 2. Mets/Alto

PDFs offer only very limited keyword searching. Valuable metadata elements like headline, sub-headline, author (or byline), dateline, and the geometric contours of individual articles are unnecessary in the PDF-to-plate process and thus are not embedded in the PDF. Searching a PDF shows the highlighted search term in the text but not on the image of the page, making locating the article on the page oftentimes difficult. For these reasons and others, the newspaper and library communities developed the Mets/Alto standard some years ago. Mets/Alto has already proven itself for preservation of digitized newspapers and although metadata indicating article, photo, or illustration boundaries, authors, etc. can be added to a PDF file, existing software systems would have to be modified to search it, whereas Mets/Alto is an already widely supported standard [2].

Following these standards, the Library will, with the help of the software for processing scanned materials, zone digital objects and improve their web presentation with data about the author, publishing stm. or page numbers, photos from the publication, and other more detailed data such as captions, continual headlines, subheadlines or advertisements.

Digital objects structured in this way will be much operative and will provide for a unique search with concise results which will give users a detailed overview of the collection content and enable them to quickly and easily search through the content by a search term. The Internet Archive employs what is known as 'image-front' digitization, which begins with photographic capture. Once the scanner has captured all of the pages, the many individual photographs are submitted to various image processing programs which prepare those images for later recombination into a tidy book-like presentation for online reading. A book is not only digitized; it is also 'datafield'. Books become 'data sets' or 'text corpora'. Words become 'data points'. Machines become 'readers' [3].

By creating a special digital repository and website with the digitized materials from this project, the Library strives to open another window into the digital world, where other smaller and bigger institutions will have an opportunity to present themselves and where only time will dictate values, aspiring to spread the view through this unique informative window into the cultural heritage in and after the project.

5   Conclusion

The use of new technologies in preservation and promotion of national cultural heritage is only a first step towards reviving valuable archival and library materials in this region, which with the help of new technologies can provide great insights to all interested researchers and simplify achievement of scientific and research results. At the same time, the importance of such heritage is promoted in a modern and technologically superior way. Bearing in mind that this process is a part of an international project, it becomes clear that this fact is confirmed in a comparative and transparent way.

This content is connected with the necessity of establishing wider and more specific scientific cooperation on the territory of the Balkans and Europe as well, on the foundation of the global process of digitization. This digital cultural and scientific cooperation should offer a great breakthrough in the various scientific fields through the open access academic records with no precedents in the past.

References

1. Fresa, A.: Digital cultural heritage roadmap for preservation. J. Humanit. Arts Comput. J. Digital Humanit. **8**, 107–123 (2014)
2. Geiger, B., Snyder, H., Zarndt, F.: Preserving and accessing born digital newspapers. In: Newspapers: Legal Deposit and Research in the Digital Era, pp. 31–36. De Gruyter Saur, Berlin (2011)
3. Murrell, M.: The datafied book and the entanglements of digitization. Anthropol. Today **30**(5), 3–6 (2014)
4. Non-governmental organization "Adligat". http://www.adligat.rs/
5. White, A.: Digital Britain: new labour's digitisation of the UK's cultural heritage. Cult. Trends **20**(3/4), 317–325 (2011)

Analysis, Documentation and Proposal for Restoration and Reuse of the "Chrysalis" Silk Factory in Goumenissa, Kilkis, Northern Greece

Stavros Apotsos[✉], Athanasios Giamas, Leandros Zoidis, Despoina Ioannidou, Nikolaos Karagiannis, Zoe Kokkinou, Eleni Marinakou, Vasiliki Masen, Maria Miza, Effrosyni Bilmpili, Dimitrios Papadimitriou, Christina Papaoikonomou, Athena Siafaka, Ioannis Tavlarios, and Kiriaki Vasteli

Aristotle University of Thessaloniki, Thessaloniki, Greece
stavros_apotsos@hotmail.com, giamasathanasios@gmail.com,
lzoidis2014@gmail.com, dioannidu@yahoo.com,
nikaragiann@gmail.com, zoe_kokkinou@yahoo.gr,
eleni_marinakou@hotmail.com, vasiliki.masen@gmail.com,
miza_maria@yahoo.com, effrossyni@gmail.com, dpapajim@gmail.com,
christinapapaoiko@hotmail.com, a.siaf@hotmail.com,
tavlariosioannis@gmail.com, kvasteli@hist.auth.gr

Abstract. "Chrysalis" simultaneously reflects the upsurge in industrial activity in northern Greece in the early 20th century and the social, economic, and political conditions in the wider area of Goumenissa and the region of Central Macedonia. The complex was studied in the context of the Interdisciplinary Collaboration Seminar, a key component of the Interdisciplinary Program of Postgraduate Studies "Protection, Conservation and Restoration of Cultural Monuments", Faculty of Engineering, Aristotle University of Thessaloniki, during the academic period 2014–2016. The postgraduate students' team consisted of archaeologists, architects, civil engineers, a rural and surveying engineer, and a mechanical engineer. The project includes a series of studies covering historical research and documentation, surveying, architectural and structural analysis, identification, interpretation, proposal for reuse, structural reinforcement, exhibition of industrial machinery, museological study, and lighting design.

Keyword: Industrial heritage · Industrial machinery and equipment
Research in archives · Structural engineering analysis
Proposal for restoration and reuse

1 Introduction

The building complex of the "Chrysalis" silk factory, its surviving mechanical equipment and archival material constitute a unique example of Greece's industrial heritage. It was built between 1928 and 1930 as the third industrial establishment of one of the country's major silk companies. "Chrysalis" simultaneously indicates the upsurge in industrial activity in northern Greece in the early 20th century and the social, economic

© Springer International Publishing AG, part of Springer Nature 2018
M. Ioannides (Ed.): ITN-DCH 2017, LNCS 10605, pp. 189–198, 2018.
https://doi.org/10.1007/978-3-319-75826-8_16

and political conditions in the wider area of Goumenissa and the region of Central Macedonia. The factory was the largest industrial establishment ever built in the region. Even more remarkably, most of its initial equipment is preserved. For these reasons, the Greek Ministry of Culture listed the complex as a historic monument in 1985 (Figs. 1 and 2).

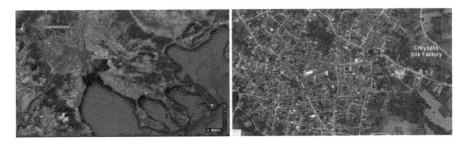

Fig. 1. Location of Goumenissa in northern Greece and location of the "Chrysalis" silk factory in Goumenissa (Source: https://maps.google.gr)

Fig. 2. The industrial complex, present state (Source: personal archive)

2   Analysis and Documentation

2.1   Historical Analysis

Historical analysis followed the selection, processing, output and recording of data to provide complete documentation of the monument [1, 2]. More specifically, documentation involved a selection of various data relating to the monument, including bibliographical references, initial designs and old pictures, data from historical sources and prior interventions, onsite research and oral interviews (Fig. 3). All the above were digitized to make them easy to preserve, access, and share.

The results of documentation provided necessary information about the operational process as well as the building's construction, technical characteristics, various interventions and other historical facts such as earthquakes, damage and deterioration.

Fig. 3. "Chrysalis" silk factory in the 1930s, inner courtyard and sample of correspondence (Source: Athanasiadis archive)

2.2   Topographic Survey

Several methods were combined to represent the geometry of the building complex and its surrounding area in 3D space. A total station and a GPS were used for surveying the site and building footprint. Elevations and building details were created using Photogrammetry, and a 3D model was created with images taken by a drone (Fig. 4). A laser scanner was used for a detailed representation of mechanical equipment inside the reeling hall. Both the digital model and the orthographic images have led to accurate architectural drawings.

Fig. 4.   3D model created from drone images

2.3   Architectural Analysis

The factory consists of three wings joined together in order to form an asymmetrical U shape. The southern wing, which is the longest, reaches a length of 110 m. The site encompasses 12.628 m^2, of which 2.416 m^2 are occupied by the building.

The wings of the complex create an inner courtyard. The engine-house is located in the center and contains the engines, boiler and auxiliary rooms (Fig. 5). The articulation of different spaces was imposed by the production process and consequent disposition of equipment.

Fig. 5. Inner courtyard (Source: personal archive)

The complex has experienced a large number of alterations since initial construction, including expansions, equipment reinforcement, adaptations to new technologies, shrinkages and additions, all of which form a unique history.

The factory's facilities included the following: delivery of raw material, distribution and boiling cocoons, reeling hall, spinning-room, engine room, boiler room, warehouses, administration offices and auxiliary spaces (kitchen, dining room, dormitories) (Fig. 6).

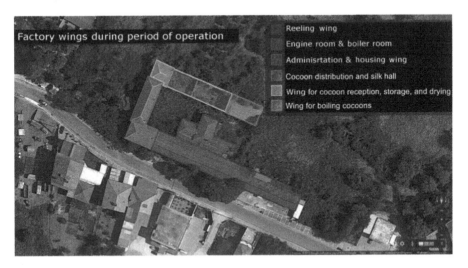

Fig. 6. Factory wings during period of operation (Source: https://maps.google.gr)

2.4 Documentation of Mechanical Equipment

The surviving mechanical equipment illustrates the evolution of the process of silk production and transition from domestic sericulture to industrial silk production (Fig. 7) [3, 4]. In the early 20th century, western technology and the local workforce combined to augment preexisting production activity. This transition is reflected in the machinery still standing in the abandoned factory. In light of the importance of the mechanical equipment, a laser scanner was used for the detailed survey.

Fig. 7. Interior of the reeling hall (Source: personal archive)

Analysis included the full documentation of mechanical equipment and flow of the production process, and also investigated issues relating to energy sources and motion transmission.

2.5 Structural Analysis

The structural analysis followed specific regulatory frameworks (Eurocode 1, 2, 5, 6 & 8). The detailed survey provided valuable information about the building's construction and existing condition and enabled an accurate computer simulation of the bearing structure. Simulations were conducted using the finite element method (FEM). In addition, laboratory tests were carried out to determine the mechanical characteristics of existing building materials (Fig. 8).

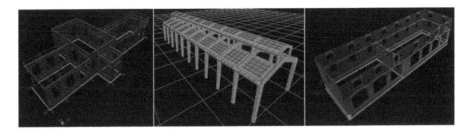

Fig. 8. Simulation models of bearing structure

3   Proposal for Restoration and Reuse

3.1   Objectives and Goals of the Project

The restoration and reuse proposal aims to highlight the "Chrysalis" silk factory as a note-worthy example of 20th-century industrial architecture. The derelict complex may once again play a vital role in the Goumenissa area by boosting local economic and social life.

3.2   Program

Briefly, the program for new uses includes a silk museum in conjunction with a space for weaving workshops, a conference center, a restaurant venue and an administration office for the new establishment (Fig. 9).

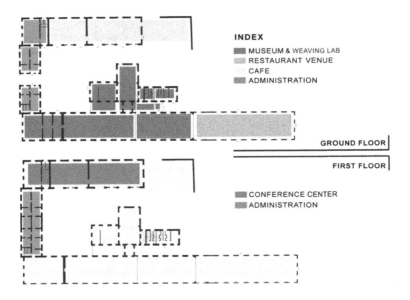

Fig. 9. Reuse proposal for the building complex

3.3   Design and Project Criteria

The primary aim in restoring the complex is to maintain and promote its architectural industrial character as well as its unique equipment, while retaining the volume, typology and morphology of the buildings. The type of interventions, however, varies in different parts of the factory. In particular, in the wing for boiling and drying cocoons, which was destroyed by fire, the idea of the intervention is to maintain the building in its current "derelict" state. A new structure that will host the conference center will be set inside the ruined shell (Fig. 10).

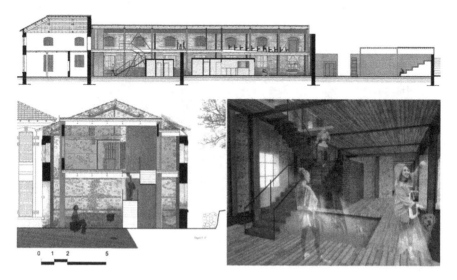

Fig. 10.   Conference hall, proposal

The proposed interventions for the structural restoration include the following: repair and reinforcement of foundations, ensuring of diaphragmatic function, jackets of shot-crete reinforced cement, grout injections, partial additions, maintenance and restoration of roofs and floors as well as restoration of all wooden and metal parts.

Given that they contain the most important industrial equipment, it was decided to house the Silk Museum in the engine-house and reeling hall. All the equipment elements were classified according to their importance and conservation status. Those deemed of greatest importance will be exhibited in situ (Fig. 11). Laser scanning produced during the documentation phase will be used to restore damaged parts of the equipment with 3D printing technology. And 3D simulation of the machinery will allow an in-depth understanding of the production process. Finally, the museological proposal, taking full advantage of existing digital technology, will provide a virtual tour of the museum and a number of museum applications to ensure a rich multimedia experience.

Fig. 11. The reeling hall, museological proposal

The outdoor space of the factory is a large area extending over approximately 12.8 hectares. Open-air space assumes major importance in the restoration and reuse proposal. It supports new uses and at the same time functions independently as a public space for the community of Goumenissa. It is a vital green area with promenades and modest, reversible configurations which blend in with the landscape and the industrial complex while meeting the criteria of accessibility (Fig. 12).

Fig. 12. Proposal for the entire complex and open space of the site (Color figure online)

4   Conclusion

The present study encompasses the analysis and documentation of the "Chrysalis" silk factory as well as a proposal for its restoration and reuse. Rescuing, utilizing and reviving this notable industrial monument will not only enrich the history of our industrial heritage, but also contribute substantially to the economic revival of Goumenissa by offering new compatible uses demonstrating the greatest respect for its identity.

The project aims at an innovative proposal under actual conditions, while one of its main aspects is digitality. Just as our cultural heritage was received from previous generations, we must prepare to deliver it to future generations. The connection between the future and the past is an issue of the present which can only be addressed using all available means. In a digital age where everything is recorded, studied and evaluated with digital media, our mission was to enhance both tangible and intangible cultural goods and convert them into social goods.

Acknowledgements. The project was undertaken in the context of the Interdepartmental Program of Post-Graduate Studies: "Protection, Conservation and Restoration of Cultural Monuments," Faculty of Engineering, Aristotle University of Thessaloniki. Supervisors of the Interdisciplinary Collaboration Seminar project: Alexandra Alexopoulou, Professor, School of Architecture A.U.TH & Director of I.P.P.S., Aris Avdelas, Emeritus Professor, School of Civil Engineering A.U.TH., Christos Ignatakis, Emeritus Professor, School of Civil Engineering A.U.TH., Aris M. Klonizakis, Dipl. Architect A.U.TH./MSc U.C.L., Styliani Lefaki, Assistant Professor, School of Architecture A.U.TH., Konstantinos Tokmakidis, Professor, School of Rural and Surveying Engineering A.U.TH., Thomas Xenos, Professor, School of Electrical and Computer Engineering A.U.TH. Special thanks are owed to Eleni Athanasiadi, current owner of the property.

References

1. Agriantoni, C.: The Beginnings of Industrialization in 19th Century Greece, Historical Archive, Commercial Bank of Greece, Athens (1986). (in Greek)
2. Polyzos, Y., Panagiotopoulos, V., Agriantoni, C., Belavilas, N.: Historical Industrial Equipment in Greece, Odysseas Publishers, Athens (1998). (in Greek)
3. Portal, M.L.: Silk production in soufli. A contribution to Greek industrial archaeology. Archaeol. Arts **89**, 53–58 (2003). (in Greek)
4. Athanasiadou, E.: Athanasiades Family Archive, Chrysalis Silk Factory, Goumenissa, Kilkis (1930–1984). Accessed Nov 2014

The Loom: Interactive Weaving Through a Tangible Installation with Digital Feedback

Anastasios Dimitropoulos, Konstantinos Dimitropoulos, Angeliki Kyriakou,
Maximos Malevitis, Stelios Syrris, Stella Vaka, Panayiotis Koutsabasis ⓘ,
Spyros Vosinakis(✉) ⓘ, and Modestos Stavrakis ⓘ

Department of Product and Systems Design Engineering, University of the Aegean,
84100 Hermoupolis, Syros, Greece
spyrosv@aegean.gr

Abstract. The design of hybrid interactions, which involve both tangible and digital aspects, is a recent trend in interactive systems for cultural heritage because it adds physicality to the interaction and affords sociality of experience. The paper presents the approach for the design, prototyping and evaluation of an interactive loom at an industrial museum with which visitors can experiment and play to gain awareness about the weaving process. The system comprises of a small-scale (shoebox-sized), simplified loom replica made of wood that is connected through appropriate (Arduino) sensors to an interactive application (Unity) that digitally recreates and enhances the outcomes of user interaction onto a multitouch screen. We found that hybrid interaction is important for educational reasons because it supports constructivist learning, which favors exploration, active learning and experimentation over passive consumption of information. Also, the approach is suitable for engaging younger people, who often do not find much interest in museum visits.

Keywords: Tangible interaction · Physical interaction · Hybrid interaction
Loom · Interactive weaving · Cultural heritage · Museum · Arduino · Unity

1 Introduction

A recent trend in museum installations is the use of hybrid approaches that combine tangible interactions with digital content. Traditionally, museum visits have been enriched with augmented content that presents additional information about the exhibits or the related context through static or mobile digital devices, such as audio guides, info kiosks, multitouch tables or mobile apps. However, the overuse of such solutions might lead to a disassociation between the actual artifacts and the digital content, divert visitor attention from the 'actual' exhibition, and leave less room for reflection [1]. A notable path to avoid the aforementioned issues and still retain the benefits of enhancing a museum visit with useful content is the use of tangible interactive artifacts that are linked with digital information. This approach, if properly designed, can lead to more playful and thus engaging experiences, and increase social enjoyment and sharing. Although it is usually not feasible to let users touch and experiment with the original exhibits, it is

© Springer International Publishing AG, part of Springer Nature 2018
M. Ioannides (Ed.): ITN-DCH 2017, LNCS 10605, pp. 199–210, 2018.
https://doi.org/10.1007/978-3-319-75826-8_17

however possible to construct physical replicas or simplified models and enhance them with digital/interactive affordances to offer a more holistic experience.

The design of usable and effective hybrid physical/digital artifacts for museum visitors is an issue that needs further research and experimentation. As a design task, it is quite complex and requires a lot of testing and reiterations. It involves a number of experts from various fields, it needs the active participation and feedback from a range of users, and, most important, one has to focus not only on the usability of the physical parts and the digital components, but also of the system as a whole; there has to be a good interplay between the physical and digital content that positively contributes to the user experience. Currently there are no generalized design patterns, approaches or guidelines to be found for this type of installations. Thus, there is a need for study of the design process and of the effect of successful paradigms to help shed more light on the prospects and pitfalls of this design field.

In this paper, we present the design, implementation and early evaluation of a hybrid interactive installation at an industrial museum, focusing on the design process and the lessons learned. The aim of our research is twofold: (a) to design an effective solution for the interactive and embodied understanding of the operation of a loom in a museum and, (b) to reflect on the design process used and critically review the design of such systems. The implemented system is comprised of a simplified small-scale model of a loom and a multi-touch screen presenting related digital content[1]. Visitors of the museum can experiment, play and gain awareness about the weaving process through interacting with the loom model whilst observing the results of their actions on screen. Additionally, a multimedia interface presents information about the loom exhibits of the museum and the textile industry (Fig. 1). The installation is designed to be placed next to an actual loom, which is a permanent exhibit of the industrial museum. The main motivation behind our work was the fact that visitors, especially younger ones, tend to spend little time in examining the complex machines presented in the museum. We examined whether their engagement with an interactive replica that lets users actively experiment and learn about their operation and usage, positively affected the user experience.

Fig. 1. Left: the hybrid (digital and physical) prototype of the loom. Right: The homepage of the multimedia interface of the system.

---

[1] A video presentation of the design process and system is available at: https://www.youtube.com/watch?v=TPBCTI9GX5w.

2   Related Work

The physicality of a museum visiting experience is considered a major issue. Visitors want to be able to stand close and study important exhibits with attention in order to reflect on the emotional, socio-economic and contextual conditions of their creation. Of course, it is not common practice to allow users to touch or use the real artifacts that are often sensitive to damage, wear and tear. It is however possible to construct accurate physical replicas and enhance them with digital/interactive affordances to offer a more holistic and experiential visit. This approach has been adopted by various museums and exhibitions. For example, the Prado Museum in Madrid, Spain, offers a touchable exhibition of paintings from Da Vinci and other famous artists, which all visitors – including the blind and the visually impaired - can touch and sense in a new way [2]. Another example is the work of Anagnostakis et al. [3] who create 3D printed replicas of Cycladic figurines that are enhanced with Arduino sensors to let blind users touch and feel the replicas in order to hear respective audio descriptions.

Furthermore, the public exhibition of artwork and its placement on display is a wider issue that has been extensively discussed in the area of curatorship and museums from many perspectives such as fidelity of reproduction [4]; visitor perception and issues of authentic objects vs. replicas [5]. In the cases where the original object may not be touched or it is not available, it has been suggested that "3D multi-visualization augments the perception of physical characteristics of the artifacts allowing a more embodied experience with these objects" [6].

Modern science museums usually contain several tangible interactive installations, that let users actively play and experiment with scientific concepts [7]. This approach follows the constructivist perspective, which favors exploration, active learning and experimentation over passive consumption of information. Several studies in science museums have shown that the augmentation of physical experiments with digital content leads to significant conceptual gains. For example, in [8], an exhibit device called Be the Path, which consists of two fixed metal spheres (one foot apart) with wires connecting them to a battery and a light bulb, was digitally augmented to illustrate electrical conductivity and the flow of electricity through circuits. Visitors attempt different configurations to complete the circuit—by using their body to close the gap between the metal spheres—and light the bulb by touching the metal spheres. Their embodied interaction with the device and the augmented illustration of electrons' flow around the circuit enhances visitor understanding and learning. Currently, we are witnessing interesting novel approaches that combine tangible artifacts and digital content for science learning like the work in [9] which developed a tangible museum exhibit for exploring bio-design by utilizing active and concrete tangible tokens to allow visitors to experience a playful biodesign activity through complex interactivity with digital biological creations.

A similar approach can be applied in museums exhibiting complex devices or processes related to technology and industry. In these cases, the aim is not only to observe the physical artifacts (e.g. machines of the past), but also to be able to actively use them and understand their operation. For example, in the Tower of London visitors can interact with a half-sized replica of a cannon in a hybrid tangible-digital environment [10].

3   Iterative Design Approach

Our work focused on an industrial museum[2] that includes many exhibits of machinery and small industry. To increase visitor understanding and engagement, it is important not only to present the original machines but also to illustrate or convey their internal structure as well as the human operation. In order to approach these goals for the visitor experience, we sought to identify new ways of interaction that were not merely digital but would afford user operations onto a physical loom model (thus afford embodied user interactions with the model). In addition, we had to avoid a toy-like experience, therefore we decided to enhance the outcome of user interaction with the loom by displaying it onto an interactive multi-touch surface with the idea that this surface would also allow users to search for more information about the interactive exhibit as well as pursue explanations to possible queries.

In order to elaborate and refine these basic ideas and framing into a working proto-type, we followed an iterative design approach that includes several design methods in context and close cooperation with museum curators and other experts, as well as visitor observation and interviews. The iterative design approach followed for the development of the interactive exhibit of the loom can be described with the following intertwined phases (Fig. 2):

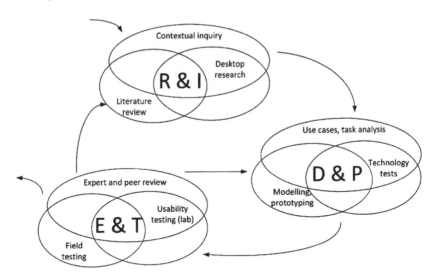

Fig. 2. The iterative design approach followed.

Research and inquiry (R&I). This includes various methods and activities with most important those of contextual inquiry, desktop research and literature review. Contextual inquiry is the most important activity because it helps the design team to gain under-standing about the particular situation, context, people, place, exhibits, etc. Desktop

---

[2] Industrial museum of Hermoupolis, Syros island, Greece: http://www.ketepo.gr/en/.

research and literature reviews complement contextual inquiry with information and knowledge about trends and developments in similar contexts, worldwide.

Design and prototyping (D&P). This includes several activities that largely depend on the project at hand. For this project we focused on use cases, scenarios and task analysis, since the visitors had to be able to make use of the loom replica without prior knowledge of operation. Furthermore, we conducted several technology tests of microprocessors, sensors, conductors, and their connectivity to a computer system in general and a 3D visualization engine in particular. In addition, consecutive modelling and prototyping of the loom artefact and the interactive application took place.

Evaluation and testing (E&T). This phase includes several evaluation and testing activities that generally occurred in the classroom, in the lab and in the field. In the classroom, expert and peer review took place by other students, tutors, domain and technology experts with earlier models and prototypes. In the lab, usability was the main focus of the tests, in order to ensure that the system could be used by peers and other students. Field studies took place in the museum with the working prototype and the participation of real users.

We have followed this generic approach in several design projects interactive systems for cultural heritage like [3, 11, 12]. These projects explore the use of contemporary interaction technology to convey cultural heritage and to be applied in museums and other cultural sites. The projects stem from an interaction design & engineering studio course and are carried out by students at their final year of study in cooperation with cultural heritage professionals and sites. In these projects, we follow a problem-based [14], studio-centred [15] approach to interaction design and learning which lasts for an academic semester that is reviewed by tutors twice a week in co-located meetings as well with intermediate reports and online cooperation tools.

3.1   Research and Inquiry

Contextual inquiry. The concept of contextual inquiry typically refers to a focused interview with the client in the workplace, during working hours [13]. We have conducted contextual inquiries inside the museum with two museum curators and one marine engineers (who is domain expert knowledgeable of the machines exhibited at the museum). We also conducted two contextual inquiries with two loom weavers who owned looms and showed us the weaving process (some photos from contextual research are depicted in Fig. 3). Furthermore, we undertook several sessions of observations of museum visitors (including children) and a semi-structured interview with a teacher of a primary school to explore the design space and identify requirements. The main outcomes of this contextual research gave us further detail of requirements (and ideas and provided information for design decisions mainly about the space where the machine was located and the size of the machine as well as how the visitors would approach the interactive exhibit.

Fig. 3. Left: Photograph of a piece of machinery from the industrial museum. Centre: Photograph of a loom from the industrial museum. Right: A woman illustrating the weaving process onto an operating loom.

Desktop research. Desktop research is about finding relevant information over the web, especially on videos of similar systems or projects, open access/source software that can be downloaded and tested, open designs of loom models, etc. Desktop research is important to avoid re-inventions that others may be providing with rights of free use or reproduction. We did not find any project similar to our one, but we did find useful material, such as videos about how to operate a loom, as well as about connecting microcontroller sensors to physical models.

Literature review. Literature review is about finding scientific papers about relevant and related topics. In the context of this project, we did not address this as a formal written report but as a collection of works that were related to hybrid interactive installations for cultural heritage. From the literature review, we identified the trend of making hybrid interactive installations for various purposes but we did not find any work on a project about interactive loom and weaving.

3.2   Incremental Modelling and Prototyping

Use cases and task analysis. There were many ideas about the use cases and scenarios, including: instructional avatar mediated interactions (to allow learning); game-like interactions in the form of assignments i.e. create a particular piece of (digital) garment or pattern; free exploration and creation of a garment pattern, intertwining of user actions with narratives about the cultural value of the loom or the textile industry, etc. From the very start of this project, a central question was the nature of the tasks and actions that the users would be able to perform with the interactive exhibit, and throughout the research and inquiry phase we kept exploring ideas. But, as the design proceeded we gradually developed the specification of use cases and tasks in the form of detailed task analyses which included pairs of user actions (with the loom model) and system responses (with the multitouch surface).

Technological tests. These tests were about the microcontrollers, sensors and their connectivity to the computer-based system; the creation of the digital loom model with animations and touch-based interactions; the implementation of an accompanying multimedia interface with additional information about the loom exhibits of the museum and the textile industry. Technological tests were carried out very early in the project since it was essential to realize the technical feasibility of ideas in the given timeframe.

Consecutive production of loom models and prototypes. From the beginning of the design phase it was clear to the design team that a simplified model of the loom would have to be constructed. To realize the form, materials and operation details of the loom model, a series of rough models were constructed (Fig. 4). The main design decisions about the loom model construction were: (a) for reasons of convenience, speed and durability, the final model would be made of wood (instead of cardboard or a 3D printed model that were other alternatives); (b) the model would comprise of six string heddles and support three colors, (c) the user should use a simplified model of a loom comb, in the form of a pen-like interface, to touch the strings; beforehand, the user would have picked a color.

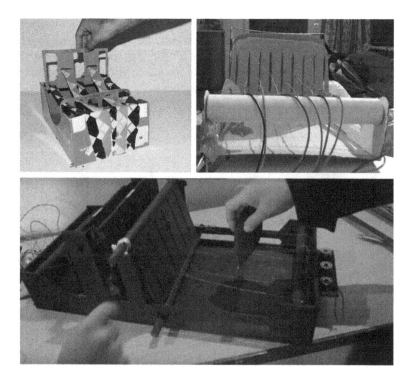

Fig. 4. Top left: The first model of the loom, made of cardboard and nylon (for strings). Top right: A subsequent model of the loom (cardboard and wire strings, with a comb) connected to Arduino sensors. Bottom: The final model of the loom made of wood and wire strings.

3.3 Evaluation

Expert and peer review. During the lifetime of the project, expert review of ideas, models and rough prototypes, took place on a weekly basis. Expert review was carried out by the course tutors in terms of comments and questions aimed at stimulating students' thinking and approach. Additionally, peer review took place in terms of constructive comments and ideas by other student teams. Furthermore, the process followed was inherently open to feedback from other domain experts since it included exploratory and confirmatory observation, interviews and contextual inquiries.

Usability testing. As soon as a first working system was constructed, usability testing sessions were organized in the classroom and the computer lab (Fig. 5). The participants were other students who played the role of museum visitors. The goals of the usability test were to identify qualitative and quantitative issues during instrumental (i.e. task-based) interactions. A total of 24 users (ages 15–48) were provided with particular tasks to carry out and they were observed during the process, while at the end they provided the team with their comments. The team also took notes of observed behaviors as well as spontaneous verbal comments. The main results of the usability test led to the following recommendations for changes and corrections to the design: (a) add textual labels onto the 3D model of the loom for clarity and learning; (b) improve readability of the user interface; (c) reduce information on each web page; (d) change the visual angle of the digital model of the loom to allow a better and more convenient view; (e) several minor corrections to the physical loom model, (f) adjust timings of responses between Arduino sensors and the digital loom model. These changes were included in the final version of the system.

Fig. 5. Left: Peer review of the first sketches and model of the loom (classroom). Right: Field testing and evaluation at the museum, with users (school students).

Field testing and evaluation. The hybrid loom installation was setup in the industrial museum as a new interactive exhibit for several days. The installation was placed next to a real loom and it was also connected to a projector for visitors to see the output of the screen. Several visitors played with the interactive exhibit and provided positive comments. In addition, a field test was organized with the participation of 15 pupils during an educational visit. Pupils were asked to develop a simple (digital) garment pattern by making use of the physical model of the loom as their 'interface'. All pupils expressed enthusiasm with the system and they provided comments mainly about possible future extensions (e.g. 'more patterns', 'more colors', 'to add stamps', 'to print the pattern onto a t-shirt', etc.)

4 Discussion, Results and Lessons Learnt

Interaction design is inherently about the conceptualization and creation of new inter-actions and systems and requires creativity, making, research and thinking aiming at purposeful innovation from the customer/user perspective. Particularly in the field of cultural heritage, over the last few years we are witnessing an increasing number of 'high-tech' interactive systems (made up of various contemporary and emerging tech-nologies, like mobile apps, interactive multi-touch public displays, online and mobile games, virtual/augmented reality systems, etc.) to the service of enhancing the user experience of visitors at museums, exhibitions, archaeological sites and various other places of cultural interest including cities and places with a historic or cultural tradition [16]. The design of these interactive systems is knowledge- and labor-intensive, and it may be characterized as a learning process for designers themselves, since they need to research and learn about new technologies, users and application contexts.

In this paper, we have outlined the design process and methods followed to develop an interactive exhibit of a loom that can be operated by museum visitors to create awareness about the weaving process. We have outlined the approach in practical terms and in the context of this particular project, in order to present a case study of interaction design methods for the domain of cultural heritage and interactive museum exhibits. From the beginning of this project, a number of design issues emerged and respective design decisions had to be made.

Perhaps the first of these design issues was *about the most appropriate technologies and materials to be used*. Given the fact that the main concept (of the interactive loom exhibit) was identified through contextual research and inquiry, we had to identify the technology and materials that would transform the concept into a working system. The design-led approach allowed for use of applied research methods, as well as experi-mentation and incremental development from rough initial ideas to working solutions. In this project various iterations, models and prototypes were developed: for example, the loom model gradually evolved from a cardboard and nylon model into model made of wood (Fig. 4). Overall, the interactive exhibit was developed with the adoption and integration of various technologies: Arduino, Unity, 3D Studio Max, Web technologies (HTML, CSS, Javascript), Creo Parametric. Thus, from the methodological perspective, *it is critical to rapidly make and test prototypes, experiment with technologies in order to ensure a working solution of a novel system*.

Another important design question was about the *purpose and goal of user interac-tions*, for which there were many initial ideas (presented in Sect. 3.2. Use cases and task analysis). In general, there are many purposes and goals for interactive systems in cultural heritage from the user perspective, including [16]: play (game), virtual or phys-ical exploration, presentation of digital content, user-generated content, simulation or operation, soundscapes, etc. The main focus and contribution of this work is the design and development of *hybrid interactions with interactive exhibits, which involve both tangible and digital aspects*. This is an identified trend in interactive systems for cultural heritage that is expected to develop considerably in the next few years.

An essential aspect of the design approach was the *reflection on formative user testing and evaluation results before moving to the next phases of design and development*. Contemporary design thinking acknowledges the importance of getting timely feedback from various users and stakeholders in order to inform the design process [17]. During the lifetime of this project, there were many open sessions of user testing that occurred in the classroom, the lab, and the field (also outlined in Fig. 5).

Regarding the *instrumental use* of the interactive exhibit, we have provided the user with a set of tasks that can be performed in order to either re-create a given textile pattern, or to create a new pattern from scratch. Certainly, there are many more options to user interactions and further extensions of the system, that can add more gamification (e.g. competition, score, leaderboard, sharing of results, etc.) and personalization elements (e.g. user identity, avatar, take-aways of creations, personalized help and adaptation of tasks to user pace or preferences, etc.). The results obtained from user and field testing were very encouraging. In the field testing, the *usability of the system was high*, since that users achieved in task performance with no supervision as well as to recover from errors. Also, *users showed much enthusiasm about the interactive exhibit* as it drew their attention immediately and they all expressed intense interest in play, exploration and interactive weaving. However, there is of course room for extension and improvement, since some participants expected a form of haptic feedback (onto the loom, rather than on the screen), while the need to look at both the prototype and screen resulted in discomfort/confusion for a few users. These issues will have to be addressed in future versions of the system.

One last important design issue was about the *location of the exhibit within the museum and its relationship to other exhibits*. This is an issue that also affects the cultural value and awareness created by the visit in general, therefore it was a joint decision with the curators of the museum. To allow for more in this respect, we have developed a multimedia web system that presented users with historic information, photographs and videos of interviews of loom weavers (Fig. 1). During the field testing, several users did not explore the multimedia part of the application in favor of tangible interaction and creation of digital patterns. The multimedia subsystem needs to be better integrated into the primary task of interactive weaving in a gamified approach that will provide challenges and rewards.

5   Conclusion

We expect that the value of interactive exhibits for museums which offer hybrid interactions, i.e. of both tangible and digital nature, will be widely acknowledged in the next few years; especially in museums that are related to science, technology and industry, where the demonstration of exhibits and the active participation of visitors in learning programs is of the essence. The development of hybrid interactions is a creative process with no standards or methods to be followed. Even the technology to be employed might be unknown to some extent to the design team.

In this paper, we have presented a design approach and a working interactive exhibit of an interactive loom that allows museum visitors to experiment and play by creating simple garment patterns to gain awareness about the weaving process. We envisage that the design approach presented can serve as a generic guide for other designers who aspire to develop novel, hybrid interfaces. In addition, the interactive exhibit of the loom might serve as an inspiring example or analogy for museum curators, technology designers and cultural professional experts to commission development of interactive exhibits of this sort for other science, technology and industrial museums.

Acknowledgements. We thank Dr. Jenny Darzentas for providing comments and proofreading of the paper.

References

1. Petrelli, D., Ciolfi, L., van Dijk, D., Hornecker, E., Not, E., Schmidt, A.: Integrating material and digital: a new way for cultural heritage. Interactions **20**(4), 58–63 (2013)
2. Delaware, B.: 3D printing allows the blind to experience famous artwork, Paste Magazine (2015). https://www.pastemagazine.com/articles/2015/04/3d-printing-allows-the-blind-to-experience-famous.html. Accessed 22 Aug 2017
3. Anagnostakis, G., Antoniou, M., Kardamitsi, E., Sachinidis, T., Koutsabasis, P., Stavrakis, M., Vosinakis, S., Zissis, D.: Accessible museum collections for the visually impaired: combining tactile exploration, audio descriptions and mobile gestures. In: Workshop on Mobile Cultural Heritage, Mobile HCI 2016 (18th International Conference on Human-Computer Interaction with Mobile Devices and Services), Florence, Italy, 5–9 September 2016. ACM (2016)
4. MacDonald, L., Morovič, J., Saunders, D.: Evaluation of colour fidelity for reproductions of fine art paintings. Museum Manag. Curatorship **14**(3), 253–281 (1995)
5. Hampp, C., Schwan, S.: Perception and evaluation of authentic objects: findings from a visitor study. Museum Manag. Curatorship **29**(4), 349–367 (2014)
6. Galeazzi, F., Di Giuseppantonio Di Franco, P., Matthews, J.L.: Comparing 2D pictures with 3D replicas for the digital preservation and analysis of tangible heritage. Museum Manag. Curatorship **30**(5), 462–483 (2015)
7. Allen, S.: Designs for learning: studying science museum exhibits that do more than entertain. Sci. Educ. **88**, S17–S33 (2004)
8. Yoon, S.A., Elinich, K., Wang, J., Steinmeier, C., Van Schooneveld, J.G.: Learning impacts of a digital augmentation in a science museum. Visitor Stud. **15**(2), 157–170 (2012)
9. Okerlund, J., Segreto, E., Grote, C., Westendorf, L., Scholze, A., Littrell, R., Shaer, O.: SynFlo: a tangible museum exhibit for exploring bio-design. Presented at TEI 2016: Tenth International Conference on Tangible, Embedded, and Embodied Interaction. ACM (2016)
10. Tower of London: Armoury in Action. http://www.hrp.org.uk/tower-of-london/visit-us/top-things-to-see-and-do/armoury-in-action#gs.NZB7sVw. Accessed 22 Aug
11. Georgiadi, N., Kokkoli-Papadopoulou, E., Kordatos, G., Partheniadis, K., Sparakis, M., Koutsabasis, P., Vosinakis, S., Zissis, D., Stavrakis, M.: A pervasive role-playing game for introducing elementary school students to archaeology. In: Workshop on Mobile Cultural Heritage, Mobile HCI 2016 (18th International Conference on Human-Computer Interaction with Mobile Devices and Services), Florence, Italy, 5–9 September 2016. ACM (2016)

12. Vosinakis, S., Koutsabasis, P., Makris, D., Sagia, E.: A kinesthetic approach to digital heritage using leap motion: the cycladic sculpture application. In: 8th International Conference on Games and Virtual Worlds for Serious Applications (VS-GAMES). IEEE (2016)
13. Holtzblatt, K., Jones, S.: Contextual inquiry: a participatory technique for system design. In: Participatory Design: Principles and Practices, pp. 177–210 (1993)
14. Vosinakis, S., Koutsabasis, P.: Problem-based learning for design and engineering activities in virtual worlds. Presence: Teleoperators Virtual Environ. 21(3), 338–358 (2012)
15. Koutsabasis, P., Vosinakis, S.: Rethinking HCI education for design: problem-based learning and virtual worlds at an HCI design studio. Int. J. Hum. Comput. Interact. 28(8), 485–499 (2012)
16. Koutsabasis, P.: Empirical evaluations of interactive systems in cultural heritage: a review. Int. J. Comput. Methods Herit. Sci. (IJCMHS) 1(1), 100–122 (2017)
17. Löwgren, J., Stolterman, E.: Thoughtful Interaction Design: A Design Perspective on Information Technology. MIT Press, Cambridge (2004)

Design of 3D and 4D Apps for Cultural Heritage Preservation

Dieter Fritsch[1]([⊠]) and Michael Klein[2]

[1] Institute for Photogrammetry (ifp), University of Stuttgart,
Geschwister-Scholl-Str. 24D, 70174 Stuttgart, Germany
`dieter.fritsch@ifp.uni-stuttgart.de`
[2] 7reasons GmbH, Baeuerlegasse 4-6, 1200 Vienna, Austria
`mk@7reasons.net`

Abstract. The design of three-dimensional and four-dimensional Apps, running on the main operating systems Android, iOS and Windows, is the next challenge in Digital Cultural Heritage (DCH) preservation. The enrichment of 3D virtual reality models, derived from computer graphics, computer vision, laser scanning, and aerial and close range photogrammetry by audio and video information acts as an excellent basis for App design.

Based on experiences developing Apps for archaeology and architecture, the paper presents general workflows for data collection, storyboard design and App developments. The 4th dimension, time, can be injected into App content through the use of old photographs, sketches and paintings.

The software package Unity is used as a cross-platform engine, offered by Unity Technologies, to create 3D/4D Apps for PCs, mobile devices and websites. One of the main results of the European Project "4D-CH-World" are two Apps of the Testbed Calw: the App "Calw VR" and the App "Tracing Hermann Hesse in Calw". Both Apps are using the 3D models created by interactive 3D modeling in Autodesk 3ds Max, with 3D data resulting from airborne LiDAR, terrestrial laser scanning, Structure-from-Motion (SfM) and Dense Image Matching (DIM). The geometric 2.5D reference surface is a LiDAR DSM, further improved by DIM results of georeferenced aerial photography with GSD@20cm.

Keywords: Laser scanning · Structure from motion · Dense image matching Data fusion · Digital Cultural Heritage · Close range · Surface reconstruction 3D and 4D App developments

1 Introduction

The development of 3D and 4D Apps presenting Cultural Heritage content on mobile devices is a new challenge to be overcome, in science and development. This new way of presenting tangible and intangible Digital Cultural Heritage content will create awareness at different age groups: (1) Kindergarten kids, (2) Primary and High School pupils and teenagers, (3) students at universities, who are the future decision makers and academics, (4) Adults, who are interested in virtual tourism and home-based learning, and (5) Elderly and handicapped persons, who may suffer for some mental

© Springer International Publishing AG, part of Springer Nature 2018
M. Ioannides (Ed.): ITN-DCH 2017, LNCS 10605, pp. 211–226, 2018.
https://doi.org/10.1007/978-3-319-75826-8_18

diseases. Digital Cultural Heritage is so important, that we ought to boost it using all available channels.

Digital Cultural Heritage preservation is a formal endeavour to document the physical dimensions of the sites and objects. It is a method of keeping digital material alive so that it remains usable, as technological advances may render the original hardware, which is inaccessible (Kacyra 2009). Recently, it has become very important to digitally preserve the heritage and historical places in reference scaled models, as various natural and human agents of destruction currently threaten many heritage sites. For instance, weather erosions, earthquakes, chemical contamination and warfare pose significant hazards to heritage sites in such far-flung regions as the desert of Jordan (Al-Kheder et al. 2009) and Antarctica (Bathow and Breuckmann 2011). Moreover, many historical places such as the Monumental Arch linking the East and central sections of the collonade at Palmyra in Syria, built in the second and third centuries, have already disappeared forever (see Fig. 1). Additionally, Nimrud city, the ancient Assyrian city in Iraq was completely destroyed in 2015.

Fig. 1. The Monumental Arch Palmyra: before (left) and after the destruction by ISIS 2015 (right)

In order to use the most recent technologies in Digital Cultural Heritage preservation, the professionals working in this field ought to be linked to each other. This means the data collectors, data processors and data presenters should collaborate closely, for example, we may link photogrammetry and computer vision with geoinformatics and building information modeling on the one hand, and with computer graphics and serious gaming on the other hand. In more detail, archeological research is linked with landscape reconstruction and architectural modeling, interchanging data collection methods and 2D, 2.5D and 3D modeling procedures (see Fig. 2).

Geospatial App developments must take into account real data: photographs, point clouds, 3D virtual reality models, panoramic images, audio and videos. Therefore testbeds are needed that can provide the core data for the set-up of realistic 3D and 4D models and their semantic enrichment. For this paper, the Testbed Calw is used, a medieval town located in the Northern Black Forest, Germany.

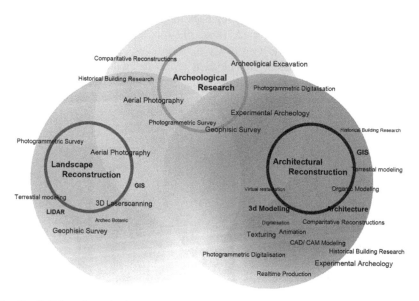

Fig. 2. Collaboration of scientific fields and methods for the benefit of DCH preservation

The structure of this paper is as follows: after the introduction the required databases of the Testbed Calw are outlined. This leads to additional in-situ data collection and data harmonization, to be presented in Sect. 3. Data postprocessing and interactive 3D modeling is given in Sect. 4. As we are dealing with 2D and 3D data, suitable data transformations are given. App design is presented in Sect. 5, introducing storyboard definitions using all data and models available. The characteristics of the Apps are given in detail. The paper is concluded by a summary of the main findings and an outlook to future work.

2   The Testbed Calw

One of the main testbeds chosen for the European Union 4D-CH-World project is the historic Market Square in Calw, a town located 40 km southwest of Stuttgart, Germany. The on-going data collection using terrestrial laser scanning, close-range photographs and aerial imagery and its resulting 3D modeling is serving not only the interests of the researchers of the 4D-CH-World project, but also the public, as this town has thousands of visitors every year.

Calw is also famous for being the birth town of the Nobel Prize winner in literature 1946, Hermann Hesse, who was born 2. July 1877 and lived here until 1895. In some of his work he described locations of Calw in great detail, linking it with his childhood memories.

The reason for Calw having been chosen as testbed for the EU 4D-CH-World project is simple: there is a huge amount of data for any 3D and 4D modeling approach available. First of all, an existing 3D virtual reality model of about 200 buildings can be rendered with an image data archive dating back to the 1850s and 1860s, when the first glass-plate photographs were collected. Those photo collections are made available by the Calw city archive and have been partly digitized. As Calw is a tourist attraction, thousands of photos can also be downloaded "from the wild" using Flickr, Picasa, Panoramio and many other sources. Figures 3a and b represent contemporary Calw (2015) by a photo and a 3D model, while Figs. 3c and d represent Calw from the year 1957 and 1890.

Fig. 3. Calw Market Square (a) Photo 2015, (b) Virtual Reality Model 2012 (c) Square upper part 1957 (d) Square lower part 1890

Besides many modern and old photos the following geospatial databases of Calw are available and used in this paper: a LiDAR Digital Surface Model with Ground Sampling Distance (GSD) of 1 m, for which the bare Digital Elevation Model (DEM) was derived by filtering vegetation and urban environments (see Fig. 4). Furthermore, ALKIS building footprints could be used for quality control and georeferencing. Airborne photography with a GSD of 20 cm was processed by Dense Image Matching (Hirschmueller 2008) obtaining a high resolution DSM (see Fig. 5) to be filtered and merged with the LiDAR DEM. The outcome of this fused 2.5D reference data is the final reference surface for creating the 3D and 4D Apps.

It is important to note, that the street levels are important to align the 3D building models with the 2.5D reference surface. This alignment is manually approved, otherwise too much alignment errors would occur.

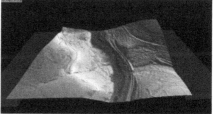

Fig. 4. LiDAR DSM@1m GSD, LiDAR DEM@1m DEM

Fig. 5. Airborne Photo@20cm GSD, 3D dense image matching point cloud

3 In-situ Data Collection and 3D Modeling

Using the merged 2.5D DEM as reference surface, about 150 fully textured 3D building models of the Market Square and surrounding streets are available, produced by a combination of terrestrial laser scanning, and aerial and close range photogrammetry. Further 3D building silhouettes were created manually (Debevec 1996) to complete the town's building infrastructure.

The workflow for the generation of 3D fully textured building models is given in Fig. 6. In total 10 Master's Theses in the GEOENGINE Master's Program of the University of Stuttgart have been supervised to train the students collecting, modeling and visualizing 3D building models.

After collecting the point clouds, mainly by terrestrial laser scanning and close range photogrammetry, every model is made up of different model elements such as points, lines, surfaces, bodies, cylinders, cones and cuboids – also a cube is introduced. The main body of the model is made from extruding a patch. To be more specific, only the objects which are larger than 20 cm, are included in this modeling approach. Therefore, the level of detail of the models is only restricted to the overall shape of the facades, without considering any windows or wall trimmings on it. In order to start reconstructing the model for a building the first step is fitting planes to the point cloud. Automatic methods, as presented in Fritsch (2003) and Fritsch et al. (2013), cannot be applied here, as we require high quality 3D virtual reality models. Leica's Cyclone software delivered the 3D CAD models as first outcomes of the Master's Theses (see Fig. 7). It was demonstrated that the accuracy of the façade reconstruction is very

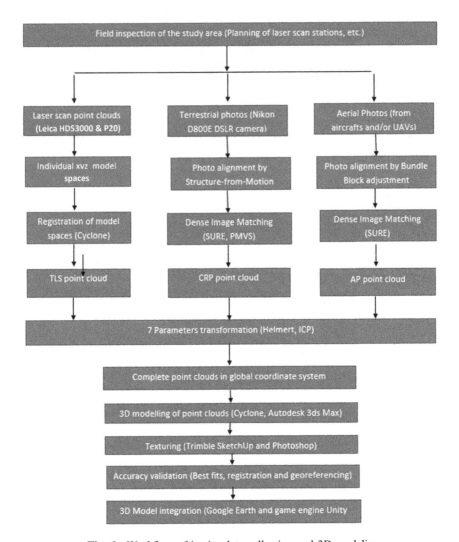

Fig. 6. Workflow of in-situ data collection and 3D modeling

high - almost all root mean squares are close to 0.01 m. It proves that Cyclone is reliable and effective when using point clouds to reconstruct the object surfaces. However, the reconstruction of the roof landscapes using DIM is not as precise as the façade reconstruction. Specifically, the RMS in the Master's Theses was about 0.3 m, because of the coarse GSD, which was 20 cm. Therefore, the accuracy of the point clouds from aerial photogrammetry is weak compared with terrestrial laser scanning.

The simple and easy-to-use 3D modeling technique using Leica's Cyclone for 3D CAD models and Trimble's SketchUp or SketchUp Pro for texturing has been applied

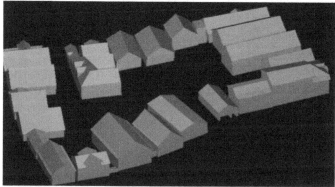

Fig. 7. 3D building models: TLS point clouds (above), 3D CAD models (center). 3D VR models (below)

by the GEOENGINE Master's students. Although it seems that the building models look quite complete, some extrusions in the facades are still missing, especially for the floors of the timbered houses dating back to the 16th and 17th centuries. Another drawback is the data volume of the texture, which amounts for some buildings up to 10 MB of texture memory or more. Having in mind the creation of Apps, which are limited for about 100 MB in total data volumes we have to look for economic data volumes and geometrically accurate building models.

4   Data Postprocessing and 3D Modeling

The workflow for interactive Structure-from-Motion and 3D modeling as mainly used in the tangible and intangible DCH preservation is given in Fig. 8. First of all suitable images have to be chosen, to be downloaded "from the wild" (Flickr, Picasa, Panoramio, etc.) or taken in a photo shooting. Afterwards the pose of the camera(s) is reconstructed manually by computational geometry using vanishing lines and points, or automatically by Structure-from-Motion. Quite often, ortho-rectified facade imagery is available, maybe the building footprints as well, also allow for the generation of 3D extrusions.

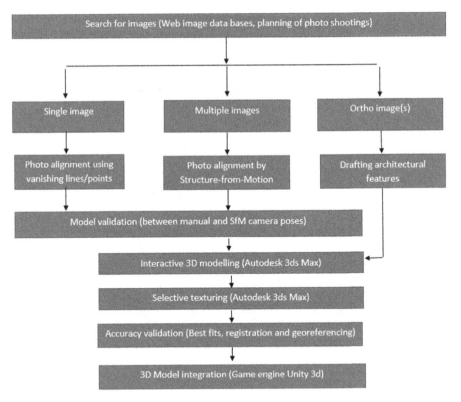

Fig. 8. Workflow of interactive 3D modeling

Through the manual alignment of the vanishing points in an image its distortion and perspective can be used to calculate the position of the camera during exposure (Tutzauer and Klein 2015; Fritsch and Klein 2017). Using the camera pose the geometry can be adjusted to fit to the camera matched image in the background through orthogonal translations and extrusions respecting the coordinate system of the modeling environment, modeling out the features of the desired structure. Figure 9 demonstrates the quality of the workflow of interactive modeling, using Autodesk 3ds Max for professional 3D Virtual Reality model generation of models of the Testbed Calw.

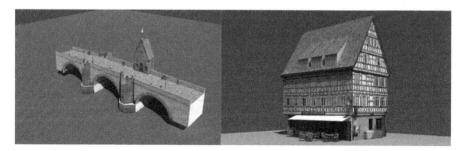

Fig. 9. Professional interactive 3D Virtual Reality models (a) Nikolaus Bridge (b) Café Wendland

Generating 3D VR models using the workflow of in-situ data collection and 3D modeling and/or the interactive workflow calls for *data integration*. Data integration in 3D modeling can also be rewritten as *data fusion* or *data transformation* (Zahib and Woodfill 1994). To merge point clouds a 7 parameter transformation with at least 3 control points is used, which is expressible as

$$X = X_o + \mu Rx \tag{1.1}$$

with X the $(3 \times 1)_u$ vector of world coordinates of u control points, X_o the $(3x1)_u$ vector of the 3 translation parameters (X_o, Y_o, Z_o), μ is the scale, R the $(3x3)_u$ rotation matrix depending on the unknown rotation angles α, β, γ and x the $(3x1)_u$ vector of the local u control point coordinates. This non-linear transformation is linearized considering only differential changes in the three translations, the rotations and the scale, and therefore replacing (1.1) by

$$dx = S\,dt \tag{1.2}$$

S is the $(3 \times 7)_u$ similarity matrix resulting from the linearization process of (1.1), given as

$$S = \begin{bmatrix} 1 & 0 & 0 & \vdots & 0 & -z & y & \vdots & x \\ 0 & 1 & 0 & \vdots & z & 0 & -x & \vdots & y \\ 0 & 0 & 1 & \vdots & -y & x & 0 & \vdots & z \end{bmatrix} \tag{1.3a}$$

and

$$dt' = [dx_o, dy_o, dz_o, d\alpha, d\beta, d\gamma, d\mu] \tag{1.3b}$$

representing the seven unknown registration parameters. If no scale adjustment is necessary, we set $\mu = 1$. In order to estimate also the precision of the datum transform, a least-squares Gauss-Helmert model (Fritsch 2016) must be solved, for $u \geq 3$ and $B := S$ leading to

$$\boxed{1^{\text{st}} \text{ order: } Av + Bx + w = 0, \text{ and } 2^{\text{nd}} \text{ order: } D(v) = D(l) = \sigma^2 P'} \tag{1.4}$$

Solving (1.4) with respect to x, v and the Lagrangian λ we use Gaussian error propagation for getting the desired dispersion matrices. With $D(w) = \sigma^2 AP^{-1}A'$ the precision of the datum transformation parameters is propagated to

$$D(x) = \sigma^2 \left[B' \left(AP^{-1}A' \right)^{-1} B \right]^{-1} \tag{1.5}$$

As an example, when we merged 11 point clouds of terrestrial laser scanning and close range photogrammetry we obtained precisions of about 1 cm. When using additionally the point clouds from airborne photography (see Fig. 10) we got about 10 cm.

Fig. 10. Point clouds from airborne photography using DIM

5   App Design and Implementation

Computer games have been used for real-time visualizations for the past three decades (Harrison 2003). For the development of Apps the software package Unity is used. It is a cross-platform engine developed by Unity Technologies and is used to develop video games for PCs, mobile devices and websites. With an emphasis on portability, the engine targets the following APIs: Direct3D on Windows and Xbox 360; OpenGL on Mac,

Linux, and Windows; OpenGL ES on Android and iOS; and proprietary APIs on video game consoles. Unity allows specification of texture compression and resolution settings for each platform that the game engine supports, and provides support for bump mapping, reflection mapping, parallax mapping, screen space ambient occlusion (SSAO), dynamic shadows using shadow maps, render-to-texture and full-screen post-processing effects. Unity's graphics engine's platform diversity can provide a shader with multiple variants and a declarative fallback specification, allowing Unity to detect the best variant for the current video hardware and, if none are compatible, to fall back to an alternative shader that may sacrifice features for performance.

In the 4D-CH-World Project Unity has been used to develop two Apps:

(1) The App "Calw VR"
(2) The App "Tracing Hermann Hesse in Calw"

The overall aims for the App development are given as follows: (1) Use Operating Systems Android, iOS and Windows, (2) provide real-time 3D environments using OpenGL ES 3.0, (3) the GUI should offer autoscaling and orientation, (4) allow for additional steering using embedded accelerometers and gyroscopes, (5) all text, audio and video narration must be available for at least two languages (English, German), (6) allow for augmentation through target tracking, (7) triggering scenes by using GPS sensors, (8) provide an interactive map display with turn-by-turn directions, and (9) overlay original site artefacts with reconstructions.

Before designing and implementing an App, a storyboard has to be defined. Storyboards are graphic organizers in the form of illustrations or images displayed in sequence for the purpose of pre-visualizing a motion picture, animation, motion graphic or interactive media sequence. The storyboarding process, in the form it is known today, was developed at the Walt Disney Studio during the early 1930s, after several years of similar processes being in use at Walt Disney and other animation studios. Figure 11 displays an excerpt of the Main Menu of the storyboard for the App Calw VR.

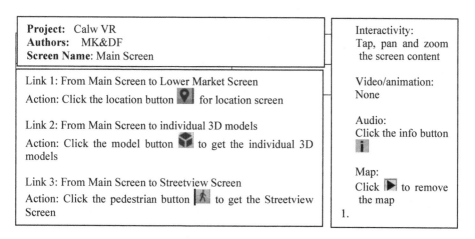

Fig. 11. Excerpt of the storyboard's main menu of the Calw VR App

Designing a storyboard for an App is a very time-consuming process, but very important, as it creates for the programmer an outline of which features and functions must be fulfilled.

Figure 12 presents the Main Screen of the Calw VR App and a closer view of the Calw Lower Market Square with the town hall.

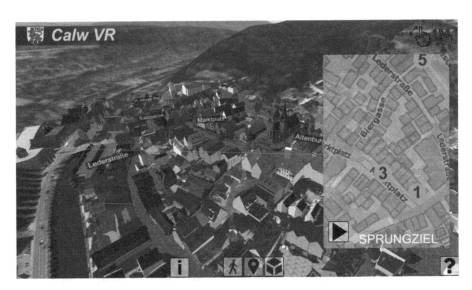

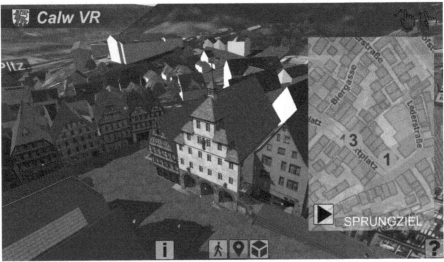

Fig. 12. Main screen (above) and closer view to town hall (below) of the App Calw VR

The 3D models of the past are generated by interactive modeling. Using vanishing line geometries, also implemented in Autodesk 3ds Max, the pose of a virtual camera supports the generation of 3D models, to be exported to Unity for providing App

Fig. 13. Time-slider in the App Calw VR

content. To view models from different eras in the App Calw VR a time-slide function is offered (see Fig. 13).

The virtual visitor can do walk-throughs and may visit building reconstructions, which are augmented by audio files and text semantics, according to the storyboard design (see Fig. 14).

The buttons of the App Calw VR allow for viewing the individual buildings, of the present and the past. For this reason time buttons on the 3D Building Screen refer to several dates or time epochs. The map on the ride hand side of Fig. 14b provides a fast switch between the individual 3D models. On the left hand side is text which can be displayed either English or German. This text is made available as audio content as well.

The second App "Tracing Hermann Hesse in Calw" uses the 2.5D and 3D contents of the App Calw VR. It refers to the time when Hermann Hesse lived his childhood in Calw, from 1877 to 1895. The storyboard for this app describes a pathway through the city center, between the birth building, his Latin school, his "Grandparents" house and the Schuetz Building, today the Hermann Hesse Museum. The virtual walkthrough textures the buildings along the pathway in black&white in order to add to its sense of authenticity.

The Apps are still "open" and can be augmented any time. Here we think that indoor panoramas and laser scans may provide more contents of special details, such as objects of the Hermann Hesse Museum or the room, in which he was born. The only limiting factor are the 100 MB for the App's data volume, thus data compression is an issue.

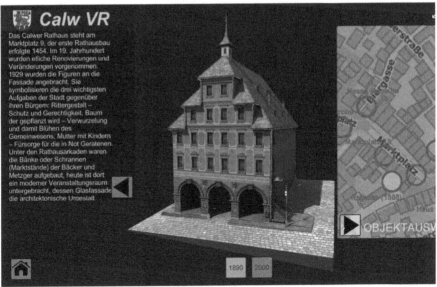

Fig. 14. Screen views of (a) A Virtual Walk and (b) The Town Hall around 1890

6 Conclusions

The design and development of 3D geospatial Apps is a demanding task. Here, the cooperation between several fields is required: spatial data collection of photogrammetry plays an important role delivering raw data, that is, laser scan point clouds and photos to be processed for dense image matching and texture mapping. Computer Vision in parallel offers fast and efficient image processing pipelines to be used by non-photogrammetrists. Interactive 3D modeling is used quite often in Computer Graphics and Serious Gaming. Thus collaboration is very important.

3D and time integration to allow for the fourth dimension is simple, but very efficient. The resulting Apps are creative tools, running on mobile devices of all kinds, and may be used in automotive Augmented Reality (AR) as well as environments for computer games.

Cultural Heritage is so important for all age groups. Thus we have not only to foster its content, but also to boost DCH using all available channels. For the next 3–5 years Apps might be right products to be used for these purposes. Recent years have given rise to fascinating new technologies, such as VR and AR; we should make the best possible use of them.

The story telling part must be adapted to the user's level of education. Therefore we should provide semantic contents with varying levels of detail. A child in Kindergarten may play with the App purely for fun, the school pupil might use it to learn about their home town and its history, while students and adults might expect more complex and dense information. Here comes ontology into the game.

Considering all aspects given above the DCH Apps offer great "Edutainment". It is worth all the effort, as CH is the backbone of every society. Thus, such investments will pay back in the long term.

Acknowledgements. Most of the buildings of the Testbed Calw have been reconstructed by the work of students of the International Master's Program Geomatics Engineering (GEOENGINE) of the University of Stuttgart. In particular, the work of the following Master's students is acknowledged, as contribution to the 4D-CH-World project: Ariel Bustamante, Bo Feng, Yuanting Li, Zelong Lian, Aozhi Liu, Abdull Munim, Yiwen Wang, and Ning Zhai.

The 4D-CH-World Consortium is also very grateful to the support of the City of Calw for delivering all information about the city's development over centuries, and the Landesamt fuer Geoinformation und Landentwicklung, Stuttgart, Baden Wurttemberg for offering topographic data, LiDAR data and building footprints of the Testbed Calw, free of charge. Otherwise, the Testbed Calw could not be realized.

Finally the financial support of the EU Projects "4D-CH-World" and the Marie Curie "ITN DCH" is gratefully acknowledged. Both project teams could collaborate closely and successfully.

References

Al-kheder, S., Haddad, N., Fakhoury, L.: A GIS analysis of the impact of modern practices and polices on the urban heritage of Irbid, Jordan. Cities **26**(2), 81–92 (2009)

Bathow, C., Breuckmann, B.: High-definition 3D acquisition of archaeological objects: an overview of various challenging projects all over the world. Paper presented at the CIPA Congress, Prague (2011)

Debevec, P.: Modelling and rendering architecture from photographs. Ph.D. thesis, University of California at Berkeley (1996)

Fritsch, D.: 3D building visualization – outdoor and indoor applications. In: Fritsch, D. (ed.) Photogrammetric Week 2003, pp. 281–290. Wichmann, Heidelberg (2003)

Fritsch, D., Becker, S., Rothermel, M.: Modeling facade structures using point clouds from dense image matching. In: Proceedings of International Conference on Advances in Civil, Structural and Mechanical Engineering, pp. 57–64. Inst. Research Engineers and Doctors (2013). ISBN 978981-07-7227-7

Fritsch, D.: Ausgleichungsrechnung damals und heute. In: Baumann, E. (ed.) Johann Gottlieb Friedrich Bohnenberger. Verlag W. Kohlhammer, Stuttgart (2016)

Fritsch, D., Klein, M.: 3D preservation of buildings – reconstructing the past. Multimed. Tools Appl. (2017). https://doi.org/10.1007/s11042-017-4654-5

Kacyra, B.: CyArk 500 – 3D documentation of 500 important cultural heritage sites. In: Fritsch, D. (ed.) Photogrammetric Week 2009, pp. 315–320. Wichmann (2009)

Harrison, L.T.: Introduction to 3D Game Engine Design Using DirectX and C#. Apress, Berkeley (2003)

Hirschmüller, H.: Stereo processing by semi-global matching and mutual information. IEEE Trans. Pattern Anal. Mach. Intell. **30**(2), 328–341 (2008)

Tutzauer, P., Klein, M.: The 4D-CH Calw Project – spatio-temporal modelling of photogrammetry and computer graphics. In: Fritsch, D. (ed.) Photogrammetric Week 2015, pp. 207–211. Wichmann & VDE, Berlin & Offenbach (2015)

Zabih, R., Woodfill, J.: Non-parametric local transforms for computing visual correspondence. In: Eklundh, J.-O. (ed.) ECCV 1994. LNCS, vol. 801, pp. 151–158. Springer, Heidelberg (1994). https://doi.org/10.1007/BFb0028345

Digital Heritage and 3D Printing: Trans-media Analysis and the Display of Prehistoric Rock Art from Valcamonica

Marcel Karnapke[1] and Frederick Baker[2(✉)]

[1] Bauhaus University, Weimar, Germany
marcel@karnake.com
[2] McDonald Institute for Archaeological Research, Cambridge University, Cambridge, UK
fb346@cam.ac.uk

Abstract. This paper examines the creation and use of 3D prints as an archaeological methodology of preservation, interpretation and public presentation. In their local Lombard dialect, the 150,000 rock engravings of Valcamonica (BS), are known as Pitoti or 'little puppets'. 3D printing methods have been used to transform digital scans of the engraved southern Alpine rock art into 3D puppets [1]. This methodology can be understood as solidifying air. The printed plastic resin replaces the air in the void created by the Copper, Bronze and Iron Age artists' stone hammer blow's. A practice based transmedia research stratergy used 3D printing combined with dance and shadow work to examine the potential meanings of a particularly enigmatic Hermaphrodite rock art figure, coming up with diverse interpretations.

Keywords: 3D printing · Rock art · Valcamonica · Trans-media
Hermaphrodite · Pitoti

1 Introduction

Modern 3D printer systems based on the principles of additive manufacturing present us with the perfect set of options as well as opportunities to realize the scans in physical form. While there are many different technologies when it comes to 3D printing, we used the RepRap 3 printing solution. Compared to other systems like the Z-Printer this printer is rather cheap and can still deliver a high level of detail in the prints. The printer supports a large variety of materials that are sent through a heating element and then applied to the printing bed, layer by layer. In this way the printer can slowly build up real physical 3D models based on prepared sets of data. Depending on size and complexity of these models a print may take between 4–7 h until it is finished. Due to the layered printing approach most printed models are durable and overall study [2]. This was tested in the course of the exhibition "Pitoti Digital Rock-Art from Ancient Europe" held in the Triennale, Milano and the University Museum of Archaeology and Anthropology, Cambridge [1]. In a Trans-media research strategy, 3D prints were compared as both relief and positive (sculptures) with the human bodies of dancers so as to develop and test different theories as to what the meanings of an ambiguous piece

© Springer International Publishing AG, part of Springer Nature 2018
M. Ioannides (Ed.): ITN-DCH 2017, LNCS 10605, pp. 227–238, 2018.
https://doi.org/10.1007/978-3-319-75826-8_19

of rock art dubbed the Hermaphrodite might be. This practice takes 3D printing beyond just documenting engravings, into the realm of theory development and the exploration of the possible artistic meanings attached to the works found all over the glaciated rocks of Valcamonica.

2   Reproducing the Original

The first challenge was to try to reproduce the engravings as accurate as possible. These prints could then be used to study the engravings at home as well as comparing the overall quality of the representations. In order to realize a model in 3D print it has to be edited and prepared in several ways. This tool chain as seen in Fig. 1 is the basic description of the applied software.

Meshlab   ▷   3ds Max   ▷   Meshmixxer   ▷   Netfabb   ▷   Skeinforge

Fig. 1.   Software products used in the Toolchain

The Meshlab software is used for the basic triangulation of the points as well as optimization with regards to point depth and possible scan errors Meshlab 2011 [3]. The second stage for editing the material was using Autodesk 3Ds Max as a 3D modeling tool. It was applied in order to add both shapes and geometric forms as well as to transform objects and to scale them in uniform and non-uniform ways. An integrated check up tool was also used to assure water tightness and remove general geometrical errors in the model Autodesk 3Ds Max 2012 [4]. After basic modelling, Meshmixxer was applied to refine meshes and edit problematic parts for printing [5]. Autodesk Meshmixxer 2012 [5]. Netfabb was used as final check-up and editing stage. Netfabb checks not only geometries and falsely oriented triangles, it automatically repairs holes in the structure and highlights editing errors in the editing stages that happened before Netfabb 2012 [6]. The final stage before the print is the Skeinforge application. Skeinforge converts the model in machine-readable go-code that is basically telling the printer where to move when and how much material to release through the extruder. Skeinforge is also the place in the tool chain where many different options can be set to alter the final result of the printing process.

2.1   First Prints

The first prints were modelled in a way to be printed in flat position inside the printer. Figure 10 shows on the left the initial print position. However testing the first prints in this position created serious irritations. For example, at various points the plastic material was spilled over edges and created disturbances in the material and therefore the overall print result was not satisfying. The only upside was that prints in this position took only about two hours to be finished. Changing the position of the print to what you can see in Fig. 2 on the right hand side proved to deliver a better result in respect to resolution as well as disturbances the plastic material created during the printing process. The only downside of switching position was that the amount of time needed for printing moved up to an average of four hours.

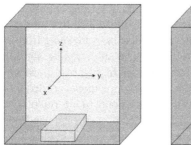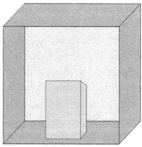

Fig. 2. 3D prints inside the printer in horizontal position (left) and vertical position (right)

2.2 Level of Detail

The first challenge was trying to print the engravings in their original spatial dimensions. Due to the fact that the so-called Hermaphrodite engraving is very shallow, the printer needed to operate at a millimetre level to reproduce a convincing result. Initial testing was done by rescaling the original z-depth four times. This way general characteristics of the engraving where enlarged and the capabilities of the printer could be tested. The next iterations of the print where then successively scaled less and less until the original scaled scan could be tested in print. Figure 3 illustrates the different stages of Z-scaling.

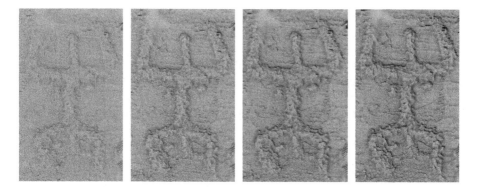

Fig. 3. From left to right – original z-depth scaled 2×, 3× and four times

The printer is perfectly capable to reproduce the original millimetre depth of the scanned engraving. Also visible on the left hand side is the fact that not only the features of the engraving are amplified but the overall geometry of the surrounding material as well.

Another important aspect concerning the level of detail was the polygon depth of the initial scan. Approximately one million polygons were used. Editing such a large number of faces can be challenging using current hardware and software. Therefore the question was – could the printer handle the amount of data and would it make sense to use the large data density when the printer would not be able to produce such a level of detail? The process to test this was comparable to the scaling that took place before. The first prints where reduced to about a fifth in data density meaning from about 1 million polygons reduced to 200.000. Due to the efficient subsampling algorithm the drastic changes in the reduction of density was barely visible. Figure 4 shows on the right hand a reduced model printed compared to the full resolution model printed on the left. Again, the printer was able to not only process the large amount of information but also showed a distinctly higher quality in the final print. The details on the left hand side maybe minor but even small irritations in the rock surface are now visible in the print.

2.3 Material

PLA was used as the primary printing material. In short PLA is poly-lactic acid, a material that is a thermoplastic, meaning it can be easily deformed by temperatures around 200 °C. These materials are also nontoxic and biodegradable. PLA comes in many different colours and can also be translucent in varying degrees. However only two materials were used in the final printing process: one being translucent with overall plastic characteristics and high temperature PLA that is more comparable with plaster and was not penetrable to light. The overall costs of this material are very low as it only costs about four cent per gram making most prints depending on solidity range from 1 to 5 Euros.

2.4 Infill Solidity

Another option in 3D printing is the solidity of the object being printed. Infill solidity determines the amount of material that is placed inside as the filling of the print. The first models for the representational prints where basically boxes with the engraving printed on the front face of them. A high value of infill solidity meant that the print became a solid object with a rather high amount of weight. Since the first prints were meant to be an exact copy of the original scan the weight added to the effect of actually holding a piece of solid rock in one's hand. However setting the infill solidity ratio to zero also proved to be of interesting effect since the printed object was now hollow. It gave rise to the opportunity to study the negative image on the other side of the printed face.

As Fig. 6 clearly shows the novelty of being able to study the negative side of the rock engraving could now be brought directly into the final print. However printing the scan in such a fashion meant branching off from purely trying to recreate the original engraving to representations and alternative ways of depicting the original.

Fig. 4. 3D relief prints – front (left) backside negative (right)

3 Making Theories Graspable

3.1 From 2D Surface to 3D Sculpture

In the course of the field season 2010, Alberto Maretta, Christopher Chippindale and Frederick Baker of the Prehistoric Picture Project [7] uncovered a Hermaphrodite looking Pitoti figure At the Bauhaus Virtual Reality Lab engineers were introduced to by showing them different images shot with and without directional flash photography. They also informed them about the issues that occur when trying to reproduce three-dimensional bodies out of two-dimensional depictions and working across different media in a Trans-media manner. Working with Professor Ben Sassen of the Bauhaus, Baker and Chippindale asked each student for his or her personal theory what the Hermaphrodite could depict in real life. 17 theories were amassed, ranging from rock-climbing, dancing and praying.

Before any pose struck by the students could be realized as 3D print, a major problem had to be solved: the fact that the engraving of the Hermaphrodite had very little depth to its three- dimensional body. In order to solve this problem, the basic idea was to use the novel negative side of the scan to weld together two mirrored scans. Consequently, the resulting model would actually have enough of a body to be put into various poses and body positions.

Figure 5(a) shows the natural state of the scan. As one can easily observe rock material is clearly visible around the scanned engraving. The first step was to roughly remove all the area of the rock in the scan that contained no material of the Hermaphrodite figure. This resulted in Fig. 5(b) showing only a square selection containing the important

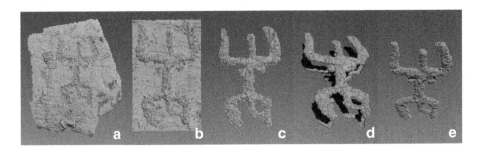

Fig. 5. 2D to 3D editing process – from left to right (a), (b), (c), (d), (e)

information. The next step was to release the figure from the surroundings by carefully removing non-elevated areas around the body of the figure. The elevated depth areas were used as a clue to isolate the important outline. As a result Fig. 5(c) illustrates the Hermaphrodite now free of any rock material that was discarded in the process of isolation. Figure 7(d) displays the positioning of two mirrored Hermaphrodite engravings that can now be welded at their border region to create the final result: A three-dimensional sculpture of the Hermaphrodite with phallus and attached breasts Fig. 5(d). This novel sculpture was now the body that could be reshaped and modified to test out the probability of theories. Such practise is a form of Trans-media research in which the same design is examined across different media, from the engraved relief, to a printed sculpture, to the human body and shadows.

Test printing of these first sculptures had to be done in a careful manner since objects like the phallus and the breasts were quite difficult to print without support materials. In Fig. 8 on the left is the initial attempt shown as gender neutral sculpture while the figure on the right is complete with breasts and phallus. The figure on the right is also scaled to the correct height of the Hermaphrodite as depicted in the original engravings.

3.2 Prayer Theory

As a proof of concept it was decided on realising two sculptures inspired by the theory that the Hermaphrodite might show a scene of a praying person or Orant. This is the technical term used for a praying figure coming from the Latin orans – to pray. The prayer itself is not a single pose but a complete motion from a lying to a kneeling upright position. The underlying question could be framed as follows: Would it be possible to recreate this pose by manipulation the arms and legs of the body of the sculpture to resemble it as close as possible?

3.3 Modelling

After arranging all the limbs the figure underwent one procedure necessary to clearly distinguish between this heavily edited and processed figure and the original Hermaphrodite. A filter was applied that moved all points closer together and hence reduced the details on the surface of the figure. It only left the most prominent characteristics intact.

In this way the recipient could clearly perceive the final figure as novel and somewhat alien compared to the original engraved structures.

Fig. 6. Comparison between video snapshot and final 3D model

Figure 6 shows the video freeze frame of the first pose in comparison to the filtered final 3D model. Printing the sculpture would prove to be challenging since most of the structures where not flat and oriented at steep angles. The next step was using a so-called support-raft (Fig. 7 left) that would be needed to stabilise critical structures during the printing process. The rafting process would be the next critical step for the realization of all other sculptures in 3D printing.

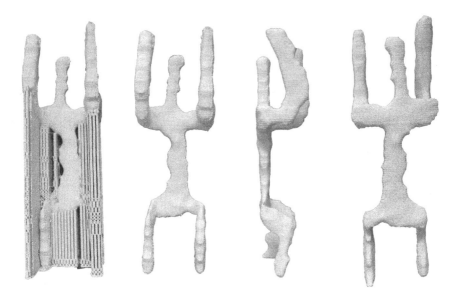

Fig. 7. 3D printed sculptures with support material (left) and after removal (right)

4 Preliminary Results

The previous sections have shown that using 3D printing to render theories into physical shape can not only be practically archived, but also helps understanding the translation of two dimensional objects into three dimensions and vice versa. Therefore the physical representation or translation of theories into this new medium enables new perspectives and observations in respect to probabilities and properties of various geometrical shapes.

4.1 Transfiguration

The theories applied to the Hermaphrodite in the previous section were mainly focused on depicting several human activities. Yet, there are theories that cannot be embodied or have a symbolical origin. This section documents the transfiguration of the Hermaphrodite into two hypothetical objects.

4.2 The Lizard

The lizard theory was developed during the video workshop at the Studio Bauhaus. Out of 17 ideas most of them were considering the figure as depicting a human or human activity. Yet the shape of the phallus and the head as well as the body rather reminded me of a lizard. It was also noticed that between the left upper leg and the right lower leg the figure seemed to be symmetrical. Both looked bigger compared to the others as if they were somewhat closer to the observer. This is a typical pose for a lizard when cooling two legs while standing on the other two remaining limbs.

4.3 Mesh Manipulation

The basic modelling process did not differ from the procedures shown before. Again only sharp rotation angles were used in the manipulation of the figure. Removing the surface details proved very effective for creating a curvy and round body for the lizard. The only part of the body that needed to be altered was the phallus or tail section of the figure. Autodesk Meshmixxer was used to enlarge the structure of the tail and make it longer, overall more fitting to the look of a lizard. However this meant generating a new mesh and therefore adding new information not part of the original dataset.

4.4 The Hermaphrodite

Transforming the figure into a physical hermaphrodite was only logical. Since almost all figures were gender neutral and resembled natural human beings it was finally time to transfigure the geometries into a real hermaphrodite with phallus and breasts directly attached to the body in anatomical correct positions.

4.5   Mesh Manipulation

The main body of the figure was kept exactly as it was. The only three objects that were manipulated were both breast and the phallus itself. Editing the phallus was not different from rotating a limb into the correct position. In contrast, editing the breast proved to be rather complicated since the breasts were not directly attached to the figure. Instead they were placed next to the main body and space was left above as well as next to them. This meant first isolating both breasts and cutting them out of the surrounding material followed by reattaching them afterwards to the central part of the upper body.

4.6   Shadow Mapping

Both shadow maps created by the lizard as well as with the hermaphrodite figure proved to be completely different from the previous praying figures. The lizard itself proved to have symmetries on the upper arms (Fig. 8 left) while the other part of the body was non-symmetrical. Trying to map the shadow of the tail to the shape of the original engraving proved to be also impossible. No position could be found that would resemble it even only in part.

The hermaphrodite in Fig. 8 on the right however proved to be a natural match considering the general shape of the body. Trying to match the breasts or the phallus turned out to be impossible. It has to be mentioned though that the phallus that is depicted in most Orants, as shaped in one vertical line, can be observed perfectly.

Fig. 8.   Shadow maps of the 3D printed lizard (left) and hermaphrodite (right)

4.7   Museum Gallery Use

The 3D prints proved to be one of the most popular and durable parts of the digitally created exhibits in Fig. 9. Despite being visited by 25,000 visitors in one month in the Triennale in Milan. Two types of prints were used. One was Hand-sized slabs of plastic with the engraving as an indentation just as it is found on the rocks in Valcamonica [8].

Fig. 9. 3D relief prints for interaction in Milan and Cambridge

This had a label "Please touch" and was very popular. Is work particularly well for visually impaired visitors. This is one visitor group that can benefit immensely from such 3D printing. The second prints where the sculptures that represented the inverse of the engravings, i.e. the air that replaced the rock when the engravings were cut. These were more fragile and so had to be placed in glass cases. These works made it possible for us to place the Pitoti within the minimalist tradition of artistic expression that has

Fig. 10. Sculptural 3D prints in the exhibition displays in Milan and Cambridge

echoes of the modernist masters such as Alberto Giacometti. In fact the engravings can now be clearly seen as from part of an ancient minimalist artistic tradition that developed in parallel to the more famous naturalist tradition of Classical Greek sculpture [9].

5   Conclusions

One might even say that as long as the engravings reside in surfaces they are not truly free and open to interpretation. Taking them out of surfaces like the computer screens and the printed image is a breakthrough, in the literal sense of the word. Once the engravings entered the third dimension the possibilities and their applications became vast. Future applications could help researchers in the field to quickly scan objects with devices as tiny as their mobile phone. At home cheap 3D printers could well be used to print out these objects by other researchers, schools or even museums to gain access to a highly detailed artefact that once was only reachable by walking hours through harsh climates and terrain. Printed artefacts could also help as interface mediators seeing as they are clear and direct references to the actual object. Advanced forms of modelling would use multiple engravings and fuse them together to create new objects for comparison. These objects could then be used to directly illustrate these ideas to other researchers without any cables, electricity or computers needed. It is important to highlight that 3D printing puts the materials back into human hands and the tactility of engraved rock art can again come to the forefront. While this has a clear advantage for groups like the visually impaired, it is also an advantage for the sighted uses, since the sense of touch cam be added to the sense of sight in the appreciation of this art.

3D printing can also be seen as a special form of Trans-media storytelling, in which the same design is transmitted across a range of platforms, each of which has its own aesthetic qualities [10]. For example this research has used each quality of the hermaphrodite: as relief, as outlined freestanding sculpture and as shadow, to interrogate the original design intention of the Prehistoric artist or artists. Whereby the outcomes (relief, sculpture and shadow) are all analogue, none would be possible in the same way without the digital medium of the 3D scan/data set as a media between the two of analogue stages of the art i.e. the original and its copies.

This is an important message for the newly developing field of digital heritage, because the question is not about an either or between the analogue original and a digital copy, but the use of the digital as a catalyst or a bridge between a chain of analogue objects, that form a cycle of reproductions across media and materials, that allow for an exciting form of Trans-media research and storytelling that use the key advantages of the digital: exactitude, multiplicity and scalability. It is the potential of this qualitative from of practice based methodology, that we have sought to demonstrate in the analysis of one rock art figure, but it is clear that its potential goes far beyond.

In our own work the 3D prints became the models for the 3D stereoscopic 360° animated film "Pitoti Prometheus" [11] that was produced from 2015 onwards, using the 3D data scans [12] similar to those that produced these prints. In this Virtual Reality film work for the GearVR both sound, colour and movement, were added to increase the Trans-mediarity yet further. It was a journey that started with the conceptual leap of transferring the prehistoric designs through a range of media and the modulated approach of manipulating the material to explore the multiplicity of meanings embedded in the 3D art forms.

Acknowledgements. Thanks to the Virtual Reality Lab, Professor Jens Geelhaar, Professor Bernd Fröhlich and Dr Alex Kulik and particularly Professor Ben Sassen and all his students who helped in this experiment at the Bauhaus University, Weimar. Our special thanks to the Prehistoric Picture Project co-director Christopher Chippindale who also curated the exhibition "Pitoti – Digital Rock-Art from Ancient Europe". We are especially grateful to Albert Marretta (Archeocammuni) for his expert assistance both in and outside the field. We are also thankful to Paolo Medici and Tiziana Cittadini at the Centro Camuno di Studi Preistorico (CCSP) in Capo di Ponte for their support for the field research as well as the Rock Art Natural Reserve of Ceto, Cimbergo and Paspardo, and the Ministero per I Beni e le Attivita Culturali, Soprindenza per I Beni Archeologici della Lombardia. The exhibition research was funded under the EU Education and Culture DG Culture Programme 2011.

References

1. Chippindale, C., Baker, F.: PITOTI: Digital Rock-Art from Prehistoric Europe: Heritage, Film, Archaeology. Skira, Milano (2012)
2. RepRap: Product Information RepRap. www.bitsfrombytes.com. Accessed May 2012
3. MeshLab: Software Information. meshlab.sourceforge.net. Accessed May 2012
4. Autodesk 3ds Max: Software Information. www.autodesk.de/3dsmax. Accessed May 2012
5. Autodesk Meshmixxer: Software Information. www.meshmixer.com. Accessed May 2012
6. Netfabb: Software Information. www.netfabb.com. Accessed May 2012
7. Prehistoric Picture Project. www.pitoti.org. Accessed May 2017
8. Marretta, A.: The rock art natural reserve of Ceto, Cimbergo, Paspardo. In: Marretta, A., Cittadini, T. (eds.) Valcamonica Rock Art Parks, pp. 84–98. Edizione di Centro, Capo di Ponte (2011)
9. Baker, F.: Prehistorischer Minimalismus. Pitoti-Felgravierungen auf der Schwelle zwischen Analogem und Digitalem. In: Kohl, K.-H., Kuba, R., Ivanoff, H., der Vorzeit, K. (eds.) Texte zu den Felsbildern der Sammlung Frobenius, pp. 107–117. Forbenius Institute an der Goethe Universität, Frankfurt am Main (2016)
10. Beck, A.: Die Felsgravierungen in Valcamonica. Bildgebende Verfahren und mediale Aneignung in der Wissenschaft. all-over: Magazin für Kunst und Ästhetik, Wien-Basel, April 2015
11. Baker, F., Karnapke, M.: Beyond stereoscopic: combining spatial acquisition technologies in real-time engines to produce immersive virtual reality film experiences for the dissemination of archaeological research. In: International Conference on 3D Imaging (IC3D), Liege, 13–14th December. IEEE Xplore (2016). Electronic ISSN 2379-1780. https://doi.org/10.1109/ic3d.2016.7823466
12. 3D-Pitoti Project. www.3d-pitoti.eu

The Conservation of Cultural Heritage in Conditions of Risk, with 3D Printing on the Architectural Scale

Sara Codarin[✉] [iD]

Department of Architecture, A>E Research Centre, Ferrara University,
via Ghiara 36, 44121 Ferrara, Italy
sara.codarin@unife.it

Abstract. Nowadays we are witnessing several demonstrations of damage, destruction, and loss of collective Heritage. Among these, according to the UNESCO *List of World Heritage in Danger,* we can mention ongoing conflicts around the world, environmental issues due to natural disruptions, and substantial vandalism.

Therefore, effective response capability and quick turn out applications are required in order to satisfy the current and future demand for environmental, social and economic sustainability.

The latest building site automation systems and 3D printing technologies (rapid prototyping) represent an applied experimentation of the effective realisation of three-dimensional volumes at different scales, from the design object to the building component, obtained by processing digital data with appropriate software.

Indeed, the coordination of specific tools for the three-dimensional survey, digital modelling, and additive manufacturing now eases the production of components or architectural components, aiming to elaborate new constructive settings that will contribute to update the modalities of management, conservation, and use of the Cultural Heritage.

At an international level, significant case studies bear testimony to how 3D printers allow the construction of free-forms structures or conventional multi-level buildings, by using the most common additive implementation systems, namely: powder bed deposition and cold extrusion layering.

The refining of these technologies can offer a useful contribution to building site security management, reconstruction time rate, interventions cost, and innovative design, within Heritage restoration and conservation frameworks.

Keywords: Cultural Heritage · 3D printing · Reconstruction

1 Introduction

1.1 Scientific Background

The current lack of innovation within the building process highlights the need to identify new methodologies in order to enhance established construction procedures, which

© Springer International Publishing AG, part of Springer Nature 2018
M. Ioannides (Ed.): ITN-DCH 2017, LNCS 10605, pp. 239–256, 2018.
https://doi.org/10.1007/978-3-319-75826-8_20

innovative characteristics are often the result of technological transfers from other applications, including naval and aeronautical engineering. Researchers are now attempting to demonstrate the applicability of automation technologies in architecture and aiming to industrialise the building process, not so much as a standardisation of the outputs but as the modernisation of each stage of execution, taking into account culturally rooted craftsmanship [1]. As a result, a simplified organisation on the building site, a crosscheck of planned phases, a replicability of process under different circumstances, and a reliability of outcome (standard elements or unique pieces) over time are expected.

Today, some typical aspects of prefabrication in building construction refer to materials and components that are executed off-site under controlled environmental conditions, to ensure high quality and certified performance. The advancement of the research, however, is deepening on-site automation procedures to increase the effectiveness of operations on the building site. Among the most advanced systems, we can mention valuable examples such as software-guided cranes for soil moving [2], robotic arms to install building elements [3], flying robots to displace and position construction materials [4], and large-scale 3D printers to create architectural components [5].

The application of the aforementioned innovations is worthwhile in contexts of emergency which require high-quality interventions, appropriate costs/benefit balances, and short reconstruction times, for example after landslides and earthquakes, and during armed conflicts. 3D printing [6], a technology with low operating costs and little material waste, for instance, has already been tested for the production of temporary housing modules to be used in post-emergency situations (*Unacasatuttadunpezzo*, by *Dshape* Company [7], *Technological Village*, by *Wasproject* [8]). It falls into the category of additive systems, which create volumes by adding overlapping layers of apposite printable materials, instead of subtracting portions from an initial compact volume - the usual procedure in industrial production.

The ability to change material *case-by-case,* depending on the circumstances and the result sought (required dimensions or load-bearing properties), has opened the possibility of using additive manufacturing for interventions on existing buildings, that may include volumetric additions or new insertions to fill envelopes or wall gaps (see Fig. 1).

At an international level, the collective Cultural Heritage is subject to risk events, from environmental, social or political turmoil. These occurrences may produce different damage at different scales, from objects of high historical value to architectural constructions, and to entire urban fabrics. Specifically, the phenomena of danger that affect buildings implicate a set of difficulties to be faced during the restoration procedures, which may include structural deficiencies, deterioration of the external envelope, and the absence of volumetric unity. The present study was undertaken with the purpose of analysing these criticalities and addressing a possible intervention methodology where reconstruction works are required, supported by technological progress.

In 1972, in the frame of the *World Heritage Convention,* the UNESCO defined a *List of World Heritage in Danger* [9], to keep track of ongoing worldwide risk episodes facing the world's Cultural Heritage. Following precise criteria (such as imminent or potential danger, based on social-political and environmental stability), and constantly updated over the years, the *List* "informs the international community of conditions which threaten the very characteristics for which a property was inscribed on the *World*

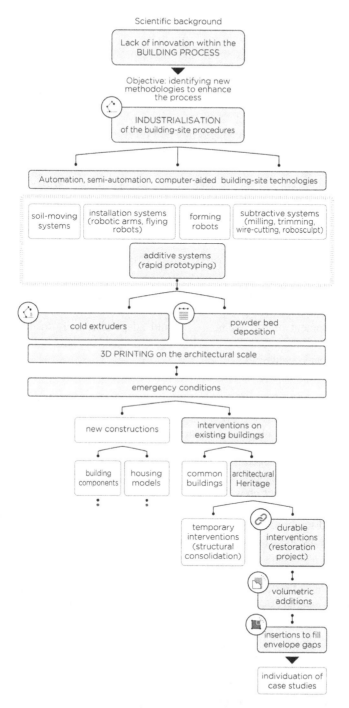

Fig. 1. Diagram summarising the individuation process of the subject under study (scheme edited by Sara Codarin).

Heritage List and in order to encourage corrective action". For this reason, the committee has drawn up a sequence of articles to clarify in which terms a property can be included among the under-protection resources and the respective procedures to be followed. According to the Art. 11 of the *Convention*, "the list may include only such property forming part of the cultural and natural Heritage as is threatened by disappearance caused by accelerated deterioration; (...) abandonment for any reason whatsoever; the outbreak or the threat of an armed conflict. Calamities and cataclysms; serious fires, earthquakes, landslides; volcanic eruptions; changes in water level, floods, and tidal waves".

Currently, the database includes 54 sites - 38 cultural and 16 natural - located worldwide. Among them, we can find historical centres, architectural buildings, and archaeological excavations. The impending risks identified for each location may cause punctual or diffuse damage, along with partial loss of volume or total destruction. Recovery must make use of conservation procedures designed to preserve the historical good for future generations and restore the formal unity of the work with appropriate reconstruction operations [10].

Thus the potential of large-scale 3D printing, in light of its compatibility with experimental performative materials and its ability to generate customised volumes with no geometric constraints, suggests the elaboration of a new construction methodology for restoration that takes sustainability into account.

The development of this technology could adapt effectively to different design requirements, with the possibility of achieving comparable results to those obtainable through traditional processes.

2   Innovative Intervention on CH and Cultural Background

2.1   The Role of Technological Advancement Within the Charters of Restoration

The development of new construction technologies opens a debate on the legitimacy of their application for restoration projects on the Architectural Heritage. Technical advancements in construction was a topic discussed during the elaboration of the Charters of Restoration, which was established in the twentieth century to support the development of the discipline.

In 1931, during the *First International Congress of Architects and Technicians of Historic Monuments,* the drafting of the *Athens Charter* laid down the basic principles for the conservation of Architectural Heritage [11]. Ever since, from a technical point of view, philological restoration was preferred to stylistic interventions (art. II) and the use of modern materials such as reinforced concrete for consolidation was admitted (art. V). However, anastylosis - the replacement of dismembered parts with a minimal amount of neutral elements to represent the image in its integrity and ensure its preservation - was the only proposed option for archaeological restoration (art. IV).

Conversely, the *Italian Restoration Charter* - the first official Italian guideline in this field - adopted in 1932 [12] showed a greater openness towards using the latest technologies for scientific restoration (art. 2). However, the Charter remained unmovable on the subject of anastylosis, as it viewed archaeological ruins as too remote from our traditions and our present civilisation (art. 3).

This concept is also expressed in the *Venice Charter* of 1964 [13], a post-war document where the concepts of tangible and intangible Heritage were introduced. Article 15 states: "all reconstruction work should, however, be ruled out *a priori*. Only anastylosis (…) can be permitted. The material used for integration should always be recognisable and its use should be the least that will ensure the conservation of a monument and the reinstatement of its form". The international committee, which gave the text a non-Eurocentric character, determined technical aspects as contributors to post-intervention recognisability for conservation purposes, and emphasised the idea that "the process of restoration must stop at the point where conjecture begins" (art. 9).

The terminology expressed up to this point, especially with regard to the possible modernisation of reconstruction processes in any work of art - pictorial, sculptural or architectural - was further refined in the *Italian Restoration Charter* of 1972 [14], issued as a circular by the Ministry of the Public Education. Given the cultural context of that time, the Charter of 1972 effectively prevented any "stylistic or analogical completions even in simplified forms, demolitions erasing the past, and patina removals" (art. 6). Instead, for the reintegration of small parts, "the reparation of properties that have volumetric gaps should be conducted with techniques and neutral materials that can be easily recognisable and without inserting crucial elements that may influence the figurative image of the object" (art. 7). The Charter accepted the use of new procedures and innovative materials - preferably already tested - for restoration works on Architectural Heritage, but only if minimised in comparison with the volume of pre-existence (art. 9).

Later, the *Declaration of Amsterdam* of 1975 [15], adopted by the Ministers Committee of the European Council only three years after the UNESCO *List of World Heritage in Danger* was drafted, took into account the risk conditions that specifically threaten the European Cultural Heritage, and represented a partial step back in conservation theories. A central paragraph of the manuscript states: "steps should be taken to ensure that traditional building materials remain available and that traditional crafts and techniques continue to be used. (…) Every rehabilitation scheme should be studied thoroughly before it is carried out. (…) New materials and techniques should be used only after approval by independent scientific institutions".

The official papers written in the following years provide an in-depth exploration of methods for recovering historical urban centres (the *Washington Charter on the Conservation of Historic Towns and Urban Areas* of 1987 [16]), archaeological sites (*Lausanne Charter for the Protection and Management of the Archaeological Heritage* of 1990 [17]), and built Heritage and landscape (Cracow Charter of 2000 [18]).

In 2003, the *ICOMOS 14th General Assembly* in Zimbabwe produced a document of international relevance: the *ICOMOS Charter, Principles for the Analysis, Conservation and Structural Restoration of Architectural Heritage* [19]. A synthesis of the principles previously outlined, the document favours an openness towards new constructive technologies, as long as they are consistent and compatible with pre-existing conditions. Article 3 is particularly important because it proposes detailed guidelines for Heritage restoration, remedial measures, and proper supervision of projects. First, "the choice between *traditional* and *innovative* techniques should be weighed up on a *case-by-case* basis and the preference is given to those that are least invasive and most compatible with Heritage values, bearing in mind safety and durability requirements" (art. 3.7).

Moreover, "where possible, any measures adopted should be reversible so that they can be removed and replaced with more suitable measures when new knowledge is acquired. Where they are not completely reversible, interventions should not limit further interventions" (art. 3.9). The characteristics of these techniques, especially new ones, "used in restoration and their compatibility with existing materials should be fully established. This must include long-term impacts so that the undesirable side-effects are avoided" (art. 3.10). Finally, bearing in mind the concept of cultural consistency, "each intervention should, as far as possible, respect the concept, techniques and historical value of the original or earlier states of the structure and leaves evidence that can be recognised in the future" (art. 3.12).

In this regard, we can assume that the Charters drafted at the beginning of the century postulated the basic principles of restoration and addressed the discipline mainly for conservative purposes; this is particularly evident if we consider that the committees members were solely European. On the other hand, recent Charters are better disposed toward the use of new technologies - even experimental - within the construction industry.

New technologies do not only represent an ordinary improvement to existing restoration methods; rather, they are substantially upgrading the traditional construction processes when they can meet the Charters requirements.

The verifiability of additive manufacturing leads us to imagine the effects of using 3D printing in the field of Heritage conservation. As will be explained in the next section, these manufacturing systems are adaptable in terms of printable materials, processing techniques, and installation modality of the outcomes. Indeed, they inspire discussion and debate about the consistency of applying experimental techniques that are different from the processes that led to the construction of the historical building. In fact, these techniques are more easily accepted for volumetric additions as independent objects that can be treated discontinuously with the existing, rather than for restoration interventions.

Given that 3D printing takes advantage of constructive principles derived from the past and reinterprets the traditional realisation and installation methodologies, it can then be used to produce construction elements - loading bearing or not - in order to fill gaps in damaged envelopes or structures. To support this concept, we present references to various case studies, taking into account different scenarios in which architectural reconstructions or volumetric integrations are required. The selected examples (buildings that are already damaged or under risk conditions) will be useful to compare *case-by-case* the proposed interventions using additive manufacturing with the methodologies outlined in the restoration theories, and then verify that the application of these technologies ensures compliance with the parameters set out in the Charters.

3   3D Printing Systems: Advantages, Limitations, and Potentials

3.1   State of the Art of Large-Scale Additive Manufacturing

The architectural design on pre-existent buildings requires high precision. The improvement of digital survey processes, three-dimensional modelling, and data management has addressed, for this purpose, the experimentation of computer-guided machines programmed to handle, install and assemble construction components [20]. Among the building site automation technologies (see Fig. 2), 3D printing systems (developed over the last few decades to optimise the design of prototypes within the industrial production chains and recently applied on the building scale) open scenarios for a possible application in the framework of existing building design. Unlike the subtractive technologies, which are commonly used for the production of design objects or technical components, 3D printing (also called rapid prototyping for its qualities to create results in a short time) allows the realisation of complex volumes through an additive processing. The printer mechanism provides the overlapping of consecutive thin layers of printable material (formulated to solidify instantly and support structural loads) with minimal material waste [21].

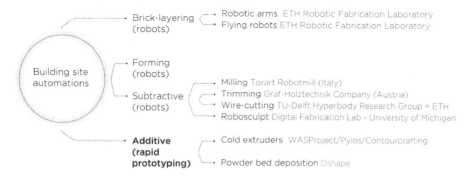

Fig. 2. Diagram of the most recent building site automation systems. 3D printing is an additive construction technology (scheme edited by Sara Codarin).

3D printed objects (previously digitally modelled) can be monolithic elements or plural objects (to be carried and placed on-site, after a possible pre-assembling phase

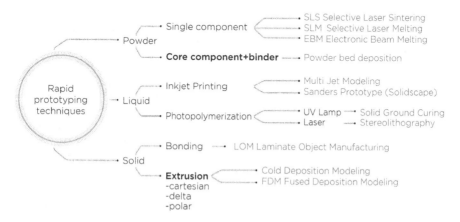

Fig. 3. Classification of the 3D printing techniques, based on materials processing. Currently, the construction industry is experimenting powder bed deposition and cold extrusion to print building elements (scheme edited by Sara Codarin).

off-site) composed of a homogeneous material that can be sand, plaster, clay or cement based. The most widespread innovative techniques (see Fig. 3) suitable for large-scale applications are machines that work by powder bed deposition processing or by cold extrusion.

Powder bed deposition works by layering on the printing area alternatively a base material (generally sand or gypsum) and an inorganic binder (see Fig. 4). This technique allows obtaining free-form monolithic shapes with no geometric limitations on any axis.

Fig. 4. Powder bed deposition 3D printer that allows the creation of free-form volumes. It consists of a sequence of nozzles that translate along the Cartesian area depositing sand and consequently the binder in all zones that are to be solidified. At the end of the process, the exceeding material is aspirated from the cavities in order to be reused (courtesy of *Dshape*).

The cold extrusion 3D printing technology consists of three arms connected to one point and moving in any direction (see Fig. 5). In this case, 3D printers are equipped with an extruder designed to deposit overlapping layers of a viscous mixture (commonly, based on raw soil or concrete conglomerates) able to solidify in a short time [22].

Fig. 5. 3D printers composed by an extruder programmed to deposit overlapping layers of a mixture that solidifies instantly (courtesy of *Wasproject*).

3.2 Reasons for Using Additive Manufacturing

Economic sustainability and innovation. Over the last decades, 3D printing has played a key role within the development of circular business models [23]: rapid prototyping can be an effective tool to extend the life of products (repairing not standard-shaped items that are already out of production) and to reduce resources consumption (recovery of waste materials in new printing mixtures). Recent research has also highlighted the economic and environmental potential of this technology also for large-scale constructions in terms of topological optimization, cost containment, and environmental impact reduction [24].

The prevailing cost component is the initial investment for the acquisition of the machine. Then, the production expense relates only to the value of the printable material, although nowadays it is relatively expensive. As a consequence, unlike the industrial production, the price of each produced element does not decrease depending on the quantity, but it does not increase based on its complexity or scale (part, component, module, or unit) [25].

3D printing allows working on-site, off-site and near the construction site, with the advantage of efficiently managing construction sequences (it avoids on-site storage of construction material that happens when the different construction phases are not well coordinated because of technical delays) without installing scaffolding or wet casting cartridges. Experts agree that this technology is not mature yet, as some aspect are still not controllable. Nevertheless, we can anticipate how it could be used once optimised, according to future regulations, and made accessible for architectural constructions.

Rapid prototyping - along with subtractive, moving, forming, and installing building site automations - represents an innovation that, in the coming years, could support or even substitute traditional construction tools [26]. This technological upgrading trend can be seen in *Foster's curve of innovation* of 1986 on the development and replacement of technologies according to the time variation (see Fig. 6).

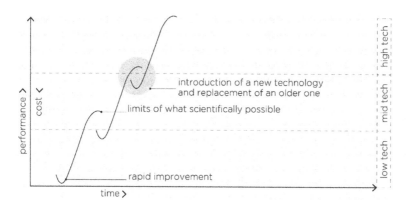

Fig. 6. *Foster's curve of innovation* showing that when a technology reaches its mature stage, it becomes increasingly vulnerable to substitute technologies (image edited by Sara Codarin).

Application potentials on existing buildings. Large-scale 3D printed objects can be used to fill wall gaps caused, for instance, by natural disasters, insufficient maintenance, or armed conflicts, in order to enhance reconstruction procedures in emergency situations. This methodology could help securing building structures hit by earthquakes, solving wall cracks that let the atmospheric agents enter the construction, and adding new components or entire structural systems essential for the future reuse of buildings.

The additions, which could be realised by a mechanical arm designed to deposit material (replacing workers in dangerous areas), can be punctual elements, new entire walls or new volumes inserted in the original historical envelope. The production of components matching perfectly with the gaps is possible by using as a starting point a digital survey (specifically performed to allow the recovery operation) and then taking into consideration the geometric tolerances. Both for structural and non-structural interventions, the printable material (raw soil, conglomerates, sand) has to be physically and chemically compatible with the historical building (generally made of brick, wood or stone) under study. In case of catastrophic events, the use of recovery materials obtained by grinding rubble could be an option: the rubble collected from damaged buildings, for example, could influence positively the cost of material transportation (especially when emergency areas are not accessible and the construction resources cannot be found locally). The definition of this process involves the analysis of further aspects such as the cost for moving the grinding machines and the difficulty of rapidly generating a printable homogeneous material.

Structural performances. A missing part of an architectural envelope can be replaced by a 3D printed component realised, as an example, on-site with a mechanical arm programmed to extrude a quick hardening mixture. After an earthquake or a disaster, for instance, an arch keystone may not be right-sized to be repositioned (following the anastylosis principles) and therefore achieve again the load-bearing capacity. So, if a new piece with a different shape has to be printed in substitution, before any intervention, all gaps and broken elements should be surveyed. The integration should not create a negative influence on the pre-existence (mainly on the interface between the new insertion and the original building system) or modify stiffness and ductility levels. If it is too soft, its mechanical features come into play only when the structure undergoes irreparable deformations. Conversely, if too rigid, it might crack even before the structure does. A load-bearing 3D printed element should not be weaker or stronger than the existing system. Instead, ported structures (such as a cornice or a curtain wall) can be lightened by using alveolar masses and therefore improving the mechanical reaction to seismic events.

The more advanced 3D printing processes can realise each three-dimensional point (*voxel*) with different mechanical characteristics. However, resistance tests are strictly necessary in order to decide whether the printing process, to achieve reliable results, should take place in a protected environment (off-site) or directly on-site.

Accuracy of the results. The choice of the language to be achieved within a conservative recovery process is essential to decide the most appropriate tool (machine and material) to be used. *Case-by-case*, it is necessary to understand how to face the reconstruction of missing parts. It is possible by imitating the original elements or making them fully identifiable. The first strategy works with inert, binder and additives materials that favour the integration of the reconstructed part, which is recognisable only through an expert and close analysis. The second approach aims at providing an integration with the original portions, but at the same time, it excludes the complete mimesis. The resulting readability of the figurative image can be compared (in this case at the three-dimensional and not coplanar level) with the pictorial integration techniques as the *tracing* method [27], or the chromatic abstraction/selection technique consisting of the application of uniform tonal macro-spots on damaged surfaces. We can chose such options for conservative integrations or new envelope additions (when new insertions are clearly different from the original building system).

Through 3D printing, indeed, it is possible to elaborate organic shaped geometries (to be managed by using digital software) in order to express a duality through an evident differentiation of volumes.

Contemporary approach. Interventions on existing buildings, that means on a given context, through innovative techniques and materials, transfer a message of ongoing cultural transformation and declare today's historical era, "according to criteria that regulate new renovation constructions such as minimum intervention, reversibility, and expressive distinctiveness". In particular, new materials are defined to optimise the performance of each prototyped components and thus to take advantage of the maximum of their static and figurative possibilities. Therefore, new scenarios and innovative design paradigms can be foreseen [28].

4   Possibility of Use for CH Conservation and Methodology

Technical procedures. In this section, we want to propose an innovative intervention programming on Cultural Heritage, using 3D printers and experimental materials [29]. Preventively, a database of three-dimensional models obtained possibly by a precautionary non-invasive survey should be provided. Moreover, given the lack of significant 3D printing realisations on the architectural scale (that means not only sculptural, pictorial or decorative apparatuses) in the field of restoration, this procedure ought to be justified by the elaboration of a pilot case which foresees:

- a choice of the most appropriate 3D printing technology on the basis of the size and morphology of the building lack;
- processing of a three-dimensional model, in order to select and elaborate the building damaged component, with minimal waste of resources, as long as the procedure consists of additive rapid prototyping;
- individuation of an eligible printable material which could be selected from a database of certified and compatible mixtures;
- on-site definition of a 3D printed reversible matrix to recreate the missing part of the architectural system. It could ensure structural performances and improved responsiveness to seismic stresses, thanks to the possibility to manage specifically material mass, density, and weight with a fast realisation timing;

- delineation of a specific interface area with possible punctual connections to merge the existing building to the reconstructed component.

Damaged construction parts can be realised either on-site by using the cold extrusion technology or off-site (eventually near the construction site) with a powder bed deposition 3D printer.

In the first case, mechanical arms on a truss cage can be used to consolidate the gap and to avoid further collapses. A printer with a mechanical arm, lifted at a specific level, working with quick-drying and rapid hardening material can be used for this kind of intervention. Oscillations, overhead works of the mechanical arm, and positioning of the nozzles have to be precisely controlled. Quick-drying and rapid hardening materials once extruded are able, in a very short time, to reach a sufficient load bearing capacities to support the following extrusions. To increase the adhesion of the mixture to the masonry, the extruder could also remove dust and non-coherent materials through a washing procedure or air blowing.

The use of powder bed deposition, instead, is preferable off-site or near the construction site, but the procedure can also be applied for on-site prefabrication.

Comparison with the constructive tradition. 3D printing on the architectural scale has revolutionised the hitherto construction rules but at the same time allows defining design intervention by taking into account the cultural background of each historical building. It can improve the quality of the whole process, especially with regard to the realisation of tailored building elements, with a reduced margin of constructive error that often occur in constrained or emergency conditions.

The outcomes of rapid prototyping procedures (technical details), if designed with accuracy, are compatible with the pre-existence from the structural and the formal point of view (volumetric completeness and chromatic similarity). The same result is achievable through traditional or innovative (additive production) systems, in compliance with the Charters requirements. A checklist of fundamental key points extracted from the Charters should be used to verify the legitimacy of 3D printed projects, in contexts where reconstruction is needed and where the monuments state of degradation does not allow the anastylosis. It may be considered:

- minimum intervention (1931 *Athens Charter*, 1932 *Italian Charter*, 1964 *Venice Charter*, 1972 *Italian Charter*, 2000 *Cracow Charter*, 2003 *ICOMOS Charter*);
- intervention reversibility (1972 *Italian Charter*, 2000 *Cracow Charter*, 2003 *ICOMOS Charter*);
- compatibility of the new integration (1972 *Italian Charter*, 2000 *Cracow Charter*, 2003 *ICOMOS Charter*);
- recognisability of the new insertion (1931 *Athens Charter*, 1972 *Italian Charter*, 1964 *Venice Charter*, 1972 *Italian Charter*, 2003 *ICOMOS Charter*);
- readability of the formal unity (1931 *Athens Charter*, 1972 *Italian Charter*, 2003 *ICOMOS Charter*);
- case-by-case approach (1931 *Athens Charter*, 1932 *Italian Charter*, 1972 *Italian Charter*, 2003 *ICOMOS Charter*);

– use of modern materials and construction techniques (1972 *Italian Charter*, 2003 *ICOMOS Charter*).

5 Intervention Scenarios and Cases Study

Recalling the article 11 of the *World Heritage Convention* of the 1972, as references for possible future scenarios we can use examples of Cultural Heritage at risk because of "outbreak or threat of an armed conflict", "calamities and cataclysms occurrences", and "accelerated deterioration" caused by the lack of maintenance on buildings.

This framing will be the starting point to propose innovative restoration interventions through the realisation processes so far described.

5.1 Outbreak or Threat of an Armed Conflict

Historical architectures, monuments, or archaeological excavations are not always accessible in contexts subjected for short or long periods to political or social tensions.

Under these circumstances, it is not possible to keep controlled the status of the constructions or to intervene immediately in case of damage or destructions. Therefore, because of the inability to visit the original architectural work, the primary objective should be the attempt to transfer its formal unity and, above all, its symbolic value (even though extrapolated from the historical and environmental context in which the work is located) in order to transfer its cultural importance. Any divulgation of information about historical buildings that are being destroyed or damaged by armed conflicts can be a key point to promote the collection of data (photos, 3D models obtained by digital surveys of photogrammetry technique) that will be fundamental to accelerate post-emergency construction or securing interventions. Nevertheless, database creation should always be a preventive procedure, especially in areas where conflicts are expected to happen.

The archaeological site of Palmyra, which is included in the UNESCO *List of World Heritage in Danger*, has suffered irreversible damages after recent conflictual events. Researchers from the Oxford University in collaboration with the *Institute of Digital Archaeology* [30], through an information campaign, has collected a large number of photographs of the site taken in different periods, that helped creating a three-dimensional model of all monuments of the location. Afterwards, they decided to create a scaled-down copy of the Arch of Palmyra as a symbolic element of the whole site, to diffuse its cultural message and keep promoting data documentation (see Fig. 7).

The prototype, realised by *Dshape* and *Torart* Companies, was obtained by adopting a numerical controlled subtractive technology on marble blocks, guided by a digital model input, obtained through photogrammetric technique. However, in a second phase, the procedure could be optimised using additive processes: the printers could be installed directly at the intervention areas with the objective of employing local resources (e.g. sand or ground soil) for the definition of 3D printable mixtures (after analysing the mechanical properties on material samples), to obtain an effective integration with the context. The configuration of the site is compatible with the application of on-site cold extrusion or off-site powder bed deposition.

Fig. 7. The realisation of Palmyra's arch through subtractive processing (courtesy of by *Dshape*) and the final three-dimensional model (photo by Sara Codarin).

The language used for the new added components can be expressed in pure forms or with decorative design hints (depending on the resolution of the printer), maintaining the possibility to recognise the printed components compared to the pre-existing elements. However, this procedure depends on the presence of conflicts, which are not always predictable. It may take years before a site gets secured.

5.2 Occurrence of Calamities and Cataclysms

Natural disruptions as earthquakes, landslides, floods, may damage historical buildings, which are not always responsive to these occurrences. If we focus our attention on Italian territory, for instance, in recent times it has been repeatedly hit by seismic events that have caused the irreparable destruction of historical centres, monuments, buildings of architectural relevance (usually made of load-bearing bricks or stones walls) and works of art. Following the earthquake that struck the Emilia Romagna region in 2012, numerous buildings have collapsed and historical architectures were condemned. There are further examples in which the seismic activity has damaged the decorative and structural apparatus of the buildings, though without blocking their use.

The Saint George Cathedral of Ferrara (UNESCO cultural property together with the historic centre of the city itself since 1999), for instance, has suffered numerous degradations, especially of the stone elements of the facade, which are currently under restoration. The collapsed decorative columns are about to be replaced with new elements, made with a numerically controlled subtractive technique (removal of material from an initial marble block) to obtain the resulting shape. The damage to which the cathedral is subjected is fully compatible with additive prototyping interventions.

It can be hypothesized the use of powder bed deposition technology to prototype volumes made of reconstructed stone, whose chemical-physical composition shall be as close as possible to the pre-existing one that composes the facade of the cathedral. The recognisability of new insertions from existing element could be managed by digitally modifying the level of detail of the architectural component to be 3D printed. This methodology could also be applied on buildings made of bricks hybridising the two possible printing technologies, that means extruding the mortar and then superimposing, through powder bed deposition, consecutive layers of *cocciopesto* (that can be obtained by grinding desegregated bricks longer usable) to produce a reconstructed brick.

A possible scenario, to be intended as a schematic visualisation of the process, can be examined in the following image (see Fig. 8), that is a representative example of 3D printing possibilities.

Fig. 8. Simulation of an on-site rapid prototyping intervention of the Novi of Modena's clock tower, in the situation after the first earthquake shock of 2012. It collapsed as a result of a subsequent shock (photo by prof. Pietromaria Davoli and elaboration by Sara Codarin).

5.3 Occurrence of Calamities and Cataclysms

Last example, chosen to be brought in this discussion, is the group of Medieval Monuments in Kosovo. In 2006, the property was inscribed within the *List of World Heritage in Danger* due to several difficulties in its management and conservation stemming from the political instability of the region in which it is located. The reasons given by the UNESCO Committee for this decision are:

- lack of legal status of the property;
- lack of legislative protection of buffer zones;
- lack of implementation of the Management Plan and of active management;

– difficulties to monitor the property due to political instability, post-conflict situation (visits under the Kosovo Stabilisation Force/United Nations Interim Administration Mission in Kosovo escort and lack of guards and security);
– Unsatisfactory state of conservation and maintenance of the property.

The site needs, first of all, short-term measures such as the immediate put in place of appropriate guarding/security arrangements and the preparation of a report on the conditions of the wall paintings and the status of conservation of the works (for example the lead roof of the nave of the Ljevisawa Virgin Church needs an urgent intervention). Then, long-term corrective measures are required, following UNESCO guidelines:

1. ensure the adequate long-term administrative, regulatory protection and management of the property;
2. put in place strong protective regimes for the buffer zones;
3. adequately delineate the boundaries;
4. prepare detailed state of conservation reports as a basis for adapted monitoring, preventative conservation measures, and specific conservation projects to reverse decline;
5. ensure appropriate and timely implementation of the Management Plan.

In this case, the survey procedures are facilitated by the fact that the site is accessible and the monuments are still in an acceptable state. Restoration interventions could include the substitution of deteriorated parts, especially of the envelopes, subjected to the action of time, the weather conditions and the lack of appropriate maintenance. The recovery project would be conservative, with no visible reconstructions that could change the figurative image of the property.

6   Conclusions

The presented case studies have been chosen to enlighten different scenarios in which 3D printing can be applied in substitution or in support of traditional methodologies, intended for the substitution of damaged elements, the integration of building gaps and volumes on the grounds of previously collapsed structures. This, to highlight the historical stratifications present in the architectural system.

Palmyra's archaeological excavations, for instance, due to the fact that original pieces are too deteriorated, does not allow anastylosis interventions. The components needed to reconfigure the destroyed volumes can be 3D printed and then positioned (the additions of the present time have to be declared), in respect of: 1931 *Athens Charter*, 1972 *Italian Charter*, 1964 *Venice Charter*, 1972 *Italian Charter*, 2003 *ICOMOS Charter*.

The restoration of the Cathedral of Ferrara and the Medieval Monuments in Kosovo, which provides more targeted actions, can be performed through additive manufacturing as well, always respecting the principles of the discipline (see Table 1).

Table 1. Analysis of possible innovative restoration interventions on Cultural Heritage

Cultural Heritage example	Current risk typology	Typology of the building	Actual damage of the building	Proposed innovative intervention	Proposed innovative materials
Ancient Site of Palmyra	Ongoing armed conflicts and vandalism actions	Archaeological site of ancient remains of the Roman Empire	Destruction and loss of components and entire volumes	Reproduction of the work to communicate its importance	Possible use of materials that recall the original artifact
Cathedral of Ferrara	Natural disruptions (especially earthquakes)	Historical medieval worship building	Damages on the figurative elements of the facade	3D printing and substitution of the damaged components	Use of a stone-like material similar to the elements of the facade
Medieval Monuments in Kosovo	Lack of maintenance or measures for conservation	Group of historical medieval buildings	Damages due to general deteriorations over time	3D printing and substitution of damaged components	Use of a stone-like material or reconstructed bricks
Cultural Heritage example	Innovative design process	Innovative construction process	Morphology of the integrations	Figurative language of the intervention	Compliance with Charters requirements
Arch of Palmyra	Processing of the digital model and implementation phase	Use of an automated technology	3D printed monolithic element or plural components	Experimental replica to encourage innovtion	Experimental and cultural dissemination of a work
Cathedral of Ferrara	Processing of the digital model through a 3D printer	Powder bad deposition 3D printing	3D printed monolithic architectural components	Integration of elements with a similar cromia to the originals	1931 Athens Charter, 1972 Italian Charter, 1964 Venice
Medieval Monuments in Kosovo	Processing of the digital model through a 3D printer	Powder bad deposition 3D printing or extrusion	3D printed monolithic or plural architectural components	3D printing and substitution of the damaged components	Charter, 1972 Italian Charter, 2003 1COMOS Charter

If properly applied, 3D printing allows achieving the same formal outcome that would follow a traditional process, but according to a revised methodology.

In other words, we believe that the exposed, classified, applicable technologies guarantee the fulfilment of the requirements of the Charters of Restoration, which theoretically legitimise their use within the contemporary cultural framework.

References

1. Codarin, S., Calzolari, M., Davoli, P.: Innovative technologies for the recovery of the Architectural Heritage by 3D printing processes. In: Proceedings of the XXXIII International Conference "Scienza e Beni Culturali", pp. 669–680. Edizioni Arcadia Ricerche (2017)
2. Bock, T., Thomas, L.: Site Automation. Cambridge University Press, Cambridge (2016)
3. Gramazio, F., Kohler, M.: Digital Materiality in Architecture, 2nd edn. Lars Müller Publishers, Baden (2008)
4. Mirjan, A., Augugliaro, F., D'Andrea, R., Gramazio, F., Kohler, M.: Building a bridge with flying robots. In: Reinhardt, D., Saunders, R., Burry, J. (eds.) Robotic Fabrication in Architecture, Art and Design 2016, pp. 34–47. Springer, Cham (2016). https://doi.org/10.1007/978-3-319-26378-6_3

5. Stevens, J., Ralph, N.: Digital Vernacular: Architectural Principles, Tools, and Processes. Routledge, London (2015)
6. Gershenfeld, N.: How to make almost anything: the digital fabrication revolution. Foreign Aff. **91**(6), 43–57 (2012)
7. D-shape Homepage. https://d-shape.com/. Accessed 15 Sep 2017
8. Wasp Homepage. http://www.wasproject.it/. Accessed 15 Sep 2017
9. List of World Heritage in Danger. http://whc.unesco.org/en/danger/. Accessed 15 Sep 2017
10. Brandi, C.: Teoria del restauro. Ed. di storia e letteratura (1963)
11. Corbusier, L., Eardley, A.: The Athens Charter. Grossman Publishers, New York (1973)
12. Consiglio Superiore Belle Arti: Norme per il restauro dei monumenti. Carta Italiana del Restauro (1932)
13. Venice Charter. https://www.icomos.org/charters/venice_e.pdf. Accessed 15 Sep 2017
14. Ministero della Pubblica Istruzione: Carta italiana del restauro. Circolare n 117 del 6 aprile 1972 (1972)
15. Declaration of Amsterdam. http://www.icomos.org/en/charters-and-texts/179-articles-en-francais/ressources/charters-and-standards/169-the-declaration-of-amsterdam. Accessed 15 Sep 2017
16. Washington Charter. https://www.icomos.org/charters/towns_e.pdf. Accessed 15 Sep 2017
17. Lausanne Charter. https://www.icomos.org/images/documents/Charters/arch_e.pdf. Accessed 15 Sep 2017
18. Cracow Charter. http://smartheritage.com/wp-content/uploads/2015/03/KRAKOV-CHARTER-2000.pdf. Accessed 15 Sep 2017
19. ICOMOS Charter. https://www.icomos.org/charters/structures_e.pdf. Accessed 15 Sep 2017
20. Bock, T., Linner, T.: Robot Oriented Design. Cambridge University Press, Cambridge (2015)
21. Lipson, H., Kurman, M.: Fabricated: The new world of 3D printing. John Wiley & Sons, Hoboken (2013)
22. Codarin, S.: Metodologie innovative nei processi di costruzione tra genius loci e globalizzazione. L'Ufficio Tecnico., pp. 8–16. Maggioli Editore, January–February 2016
23. Lacy, P., Rutqvist, J.: Waste to Wealth: The Circular Economy Advantage. Springer, Cham (2016)
24. Wolfs, R.J.M., Salet, T.A.M., Hendriks, B.: 3D printing of sustainable concrete structures. In: Proceedings of the International Association for Shell and Spatial Structures (IASS) Symposium 2015, Amsterdam, 17–20 August, pp. 1–8 (2015)
25. Rindfleisch, A., O'Hern, M., Sachdev, V.: The digital revolution, 3D printing, and innovation as data. J. Prod. Innov. Manag. **34**(5), 681–690 (2017)
26. Bock, T., Linner, T.: Robotic Industrialization. Cambridge University Press, Cambridge (2015)
27. Brandi, C.: Il trattamento delle lacune e la Gestalt Psychologie. In: Studies in Western Art. Problems of the 19th and 20th Centuries. Iv. Acts of the 20th International Congress of the History of Art, New York, pp. 146–151, 7–12 September 1961
28. Beorkrem, C.: Material Strategies in Digital Fabrication. Routledge, New York (2013)
29. Codarin, S.: Processi innovativi di conservazione e recupero del patrimonio culturale. L'Ufficio Tecnico, pp. 10–19. Maggioli Editore, July–August 2016
30. Institute of Digital Archaeology website. http://digitalarchaeology.org.uk/. Accessed 15 Sep 2017

Virtual Reality Annotator: A Tool to Annotate Dancers in a Virtual Environment

Claudia Ribeiro$^{(\boxtimes)}$, Rafael Kuffner, and Carla Fernandes

Universidade NOVA de Lisboa, Faculdade de Ciências Sociais e Humanas,
BlackBox Project, Lisbon, Portugal
claudia.ribeiro@fcsh.unl.pt

Abstract. In this paper we describe the Virtual Reality Annotator, a
visualization tool that allows users to dynamically annotate dancers in a
virtual reality environment. The current annotation types supported are
sketches, speech-to-text, and highlighting. Each type of annotation can
be applied to a bone or a set of bones of the skeleton data or a set of
points of the point-cloud data. Using a wireless mouse, users can interact
with the 3D objects of the virtual reality space, specifically a 3D menu
that allows to choose the type of annotation and desired color as well
as the skeleton and point cloud data. Examples of usage of this system
using data from expert dancers are presented and discussed as well as
suggestions for future work.

Keywords: Virtual reality · Annotations · Contemporary dance
Visualization · Interaction

1 Introduction

After Merce Cunningham has pioneered the use of the LifeForms software in the
late 1980s, choreographer William Forsythe was probably one of the strongest
enthusiast of the idea of exploring the huge potentiality of computation and
design to enhance the transmission, learning and creative processes of contemporary dance works. His first project connecting contemporary dance to digital media technology was developed in the 1990s in a CD-ROM (which has
quickly become rather emblematic until today) with the title "Improvisation
Technologies", and it clearly established a trendy basis for the use of computational design to communicate ideas behind dance composition. This project
was the inspiration for several other contemporary choreographers and dancers

Electronic supplementary material The online version of this chapter (https://
doi.org/10.1007/978-3-319-75826-8_21) contains supplementary material, which is
available to authorized users.

© Springer International Publishing AG, part of Springer Nature 2018
M. Ioannides (Ed.): ITN-DCH 2017, LNCS 10605, pp. 257–266, 2018.
https://doi.org/10.1007/978-3-319-75826-8_21

(a.o. Wayne MacGregor, Emio Greco PC (DS/DM Project)[1], Siobhan Davies (RePlay archive)[2], Rui Horta (TKB project)[3] and João Fiadeiro (BlackBox project)[4] towards the documentation and "archiving" of dance compositional methodologies, on the one hand, and towards the progress of more innovative Arts and Science studies leading to a fresher vision over the importance of deeply analyzing intangible and ephemeral art forms such as contemporary dance.

Performing arts such as dance were traditionally taught either by example or by following conventional scores on paper. In the specific field of contemporary dance, with different body movements emerging and the impossibility of creating a controlled vocabulary of movements in order to compose a score, watching videos of previous performances or of rehearsals is often the most effective way to learn a specific choreography. A common video, though, is not sufficient to communicate what is envisioned by the choreographer [9].

Video annotation systems have been used in this field to shorten the knowledge gap between choreographers and dancers, especially in the transmission process of very detailed bodily information. Nevertheless, current video annotators support a limited set of 2D annotation types, such as text, audio, marks, hyperlinks, and pen annotations. Some of them offer animation functionalities, which are only applied to classical choreographies, including ballet, for which numerous notation systems already exist, allowing to represent a wide spectrum of movement complexes [14]. This is not the case for contemporary dance, where movements are unpredictable and can change with every execution, either during rehearsals or live performances.

Previous works [16] have further developed this field by capturing dance performances in 3D using depth cameras, and extending the 2D annotations to this space. By doing so, new types of contextualized annotations are introduced, where information can be attached to individual performers and accompanying them during the time where the annotation is visible. However, annotating in a 2D environment and transposing the data to 3D presents several limitations. The mapping between views is not a straightforward task, and the 2D input during annotation limits the possibilities for other type of annotations that can make use of 3D annotations.

To overcome the limitations of transposing 2D annotations to a 3D environment, we have developed the Virtual Annotator that allows users to annotate specific body parts and movement sequences in a three-dimensional virtual reality space. The system was implemented in Unity3D[5] integrated with the Oculus Rift V2 development kit, and the interaction with the point cloud and skeleton data is provided by a wireless mouse.

---

[1] http://www.ickamsterdam.com/en/academy/education/ick/double-skin-double-mind-the-method-20.
[2] http://www.siobhandaviesreplay.com/.
[3] http://tkb.fcsh.unl.pt/user/rui-horta.
[4] http://blackbox.fcsh.unl.pt/joao-fiadeiro.html.
[5] https://unity3d.com.

Section 2 describes background work related to video annotators and their uses in the context of dance. Section 3 presents the Virtual Reality Annotator where is described data capture and visualization, the software architecture and interaction. Section 4 describes and discusses the obtained results. We finalize with conclusions and future work (Sect. 5).

2 Related Work

Several video annotation systems have been proposed to shorten the knowledge gap between the choreographer and dancers. The "Creation-Tool" [3] (labelled as DancePro in the framework of the recently concluded EuropeanaSpace project), the "Choreographer's notebook" prototype [18], Dance Designer, ReEnact, Danceforms, and more recently Motion Bank's Piecemaker2GO, are relevant examples, all of them serving quite specific purposes. DancePro is to our knowledge the most efficient video annotator to assist choreographers directly while rehearsing in situ, as it allows taking annotations over the captured videos in real-time.

Both non-specific systems [11,23] and specific ones [6,7,10,14,20] have been used with varying features or limitations. Dance targeted software will typically allow a choreographer to choose from a series of poses to create scores and visualize it in different manners, which can be limitative in the expressiveness of the movements.

The sketch based system from Moghaddam et al. [14] allows the user to compose a digital choreography by individually sketching each individual dance pose, which overcomes the previous limitation. These sketches are used to estimate poses that will be applied to a 3D avatar. However, this system does not include annotations or scoring as the other dance-specific software.

These systems have either the limitation of having a single viewpoint where one annotates, or a limited subset of movements to be used, or lack of expressiveness. Previous research has tackled this problem [16] by extending a 2D annotator to a 3D environment. This was performed by translating the 2D annotations on a video to a reconstructed point cloud in the 3D environment. However, the expressiveness of the 3D annotations was compromised by the translation process, since users do not directly annotate in the 3D environment.

Wearable technology and motion tracking have developed to the point where Virtual Reality (VR) and Augmented Reality (AR) are usable in a dance context with minimal disruption to its traditional practice. The article from Gould [8] discusses "AR art and performance", and how the mixture with technology creates a different type of art, putting the *body at the heart of its becoming*. The displayed content can now depend heavily on the perspective, gestures, and positions of the body of the one whos visualizing the work. One given example is the "Eyebeam" project where a dancer is partnered with an AR avatar which can only be seen through a device. A similar goal is shared by the WhoLoDance [4], which already uses head mounted display technology (HMD).

Both approaches show the importance of embodied systems and presence [17] in the context of dance. This has been used as a different approach for teaching dance. Kyan et al. [12] developed a system to train ballet poses in a cave environment, similarly to previous work from Chan et al. [5]. However, by not displaying the virtual world through an HMD, the sense of presence and body ownership is considerably lower.

Annotating through an HMD has been mainly targeted at AR scenarios, where real world problems can be observed and tagged for later inspection. The survey paper from [22] reviews these types of annotations in great depth. Virtual reality has not been thoroughly used for video annotation, due to the fact that free-viewpoint videos and point cloud based data that register real world events still not being commonplace. Different techniques have been proposed to annotate static point clouds in an non immersive scenario [2,21], but have limitations when translating them to HMD, where one cannot resort to using hand-held devices with an auxiliary screen, or other peripherals such as keyboard for input. Static inspection [1] and annotation of point clouds [13] has been done using VR, with a focus on architectural problems and rich environments. Using the advantages of embodied experiences in dance to annotate captured point cloud videos through a HMD is a problem that has yet to be addressed.

3 Virtual Reality Annotator

3.1 Data Capture and Point Cloud Visualization

A wide-baseline setup was used in the present study to capture point cloud and skeleton data, where each view was captured by a Kinect sensor. Kinect sensors positioned triangularly about two meters apart to optimize the capturing of point cloud and skeleton data and at the same time allowing dancers enough space to dance.

Regarding data synchronization, a network-based synchronization program was developed allowing triggering the capture remotely and simultaneously on each computer. The calibration of extrinsic and intrinsic parameters was performed using OpenCV and manual inputs from the developers since the process was performed in a controlled scenario.

Point clouds are generated using depth information, and all the streams were integrated in a single point cloud based on the calibration data (position and rotation) of each viewpoint. The amount of data produced capturing at 30 fps supports brief stretches of each performance to be viewed. We used Unity3D as a platform for rendering the recorded datasets, where the user could freely navigate the camera around the performance scene.

3.2 Architecture

The Virtual Reality Annotator is a network-based application (see Fig. 1) that integrates several software modules that support tracking, creating and managing annotations, point cloud and skeleton visualization and finally an interaction module that processes user inputs.

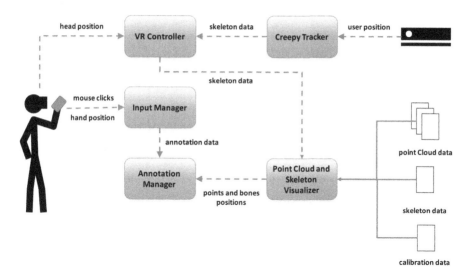

Fig. 1. Virtual Reality Annotator modular architect diagram

Users have an abstract body representation created by the skeleton provided by the "Creepy Tracker" module [19], since their real body is covered by the HMD. This system works by combining skeleton information from various Kinect cameras, allowing users to move freely in the capture space. Skeleton data is received by the application through the network, with users identifying themselves at the startup of the application by raising their hand.

The annotation manager module is an aggregated class containing a set of modules responsible for storing and managing annotation types in the Virtual Reality environment. Each annotation class has an associated mono behavior responsible for processing user input and managing the 3D objects related to the annotation. In this manner extending the current software with new annotation types is straightforward and involves minimal changes to the code.

The position where the annotation should be created in the virtual world is provided by the VR Controller module, which receives and processes the skeleton data given by the Creepy Tracker and the head orientation given by the Oculus Rift. This data is also used to update the user skeleton data in the VR environment.

The Input Manager receives the mouse clicks (see Fig. 2) and hand position. Based on this data, it toggles the mono behavior of the annotation type that is currently active. Moreover, it is responsible for visualizing and hiding the 3D menu and drawing the contextual heads-up display attached to the users' hand.

To interact with the menu, a raycast is drawn starting from the users' hand position and, when a collision is detected, the appropriate method is executed enabling or disabling the appropriate menu option. The 3D menu has five options: highlight points, speech-to-text, 3D drawing, change color, and delete (see Fig. 2).

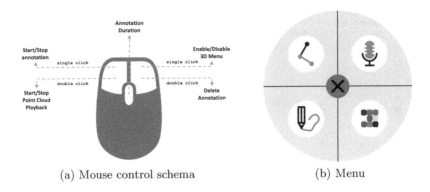

(a) Mouse control schema   (b) Menu

Fig. 2. 2 Figures side by side

3.3   User Interaction Paradigm

Interaction with the system is performed by free navigation in the environment, and mostly based on the position of the users' dominant hand. Figure 2(a) displays the input commands of the wireless mouse. Menu interaction is performed by right clicking to open a menu in the looking direction, and selection of the current function by pointing and left clicking.

Color selection (Fig. 4b) is performed by pointing at the desired color on a RGB spectrum and left clicking. Annotations are created by holding the left mouse button and performing the desired action. For 3D drawing (Fig. 3a) the hand position is used as a virtual brush. For cloud highlighting (Fig. 3b) the same metaphor is used, except the user chooses paints the desired points instead of a general area. Finally, text annotations are created at the users' hand location.

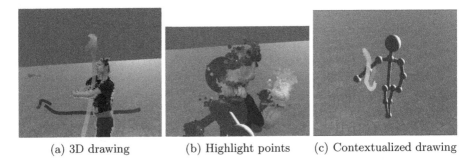

(a) 3D drawing   (b) Highlight points   (c) Contextualized drawing

Fig. 3. Implemented annotations/functions in our system

The duration of an annotation can be adjusted by placing the dominant hand near the center of the annotation, clicking and scrolling the mouse wheel until the desired duration is reached. This is then confirmed via a second wheel click. An annotation can be deleted by a double right-click near the desired annotation.

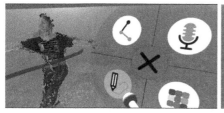

(a) Menu Selection

(b) Color picker

Fig. 4. Examples of interaction

4   Results and Discussion

The implemented system allows users to visualize and annotate temporal point-cloud data that can be associated with skeletal information. This is particularly important in the case of highlighting 3D points of a time-sequenced point cloud.

Given that there is no temporal relation between 3D points in different frames, we associate the annotations to the skeleton joints, which are updated every frame and passed to the shader that will affect the points in the vicinity of that joint. This is optional for 3D drawing and text annotations.

Some uses for this are to attach a text annotation, like a name of the person, to follow a certain subject in the video, or to create a note related to a series of actions. The same applies to drawing, which might be related to a certain body part, or simply markings on the floor. If annotations are created closer than a certain threshold to a specific skeleton joint in the frame, they are associated to that body part.

This is one of the advantages of the proposed system over previous attempts, where we are able to have both static and dynamic annotations, contextual or not, and affecting unstructured data (point cloud). Moreover, such 3D contextual annotations are only possible in the immersive VR environment, due to the inexistent depth component in more traditional inputs.

As opposed to more complex input solutions, our system has the advantage of using known metaphors for users (painting with your hand, pointing at something you want). Also, such an embodied solution allows users to more accurately perceive and interact with space such as it is perceived in a dance studio. Allowing one to freely navigate around the data overcomes the stated limitations of video-based teaching approaches [9].

The described system has been applied to both documenting and archiving dance choreographers' work [15] in the context of contemporary dance.

Instead of adding annotations targeted at teaching, scholars could highlight characteristic movements or tendencies of a certain choreographer. This is a crucial application for enhancing digital cultural heritage archives, where common videos combined with text-based descriptions are not able to efficiently represent certain temporal and spatial aspects embedded in an immediate context of the documented works. An added benefit of this type of annotated data is that it can be used to develop comparative studies on different genres, styles, or periods of time in the work of choreographers and dancers.

Some of our current limitations are shared by other VR-based systems. Some users may experience motion sickness in prolonged interactions with the system, due to the fact that the markerless tracking solution applied is subject to some noise and delay as mentioned in [19]. Also, the tracked space by current VR systems is limited, which is a problem if the captured area is larger than the VR tracked space, in that it restricts the users possibility to reach the position where they want to annotate. For a more detailed view of the interaction, please see the video attached to this publication.

5   Conclusion and Future Work

In this paper we described the Virtual Reality Annotator, which is a software tool that allows a user to visualize and annotate dynamically point cloud and skeleton data. Currently, is supports three types of annotations, namely highlight points, speech-to-text and 3D Drawing. Our tool supports dynamic annotations which is an improvement on previous existing systems.

One future development in the area of digital dance teaching is allowing students to overlay themselves with annotated data, which could also be visualized as a mirror. A scoring mechanism could be defined and used by instructors to help perfecting certain captured movements. Specific types of annotations for this matter would be created, so an instructor could create a virtual class that a student user could follow. Finally, using the perceived advantages of embodied VR applications in the context of dance, novel applications can be developed in the same direction to support other aspects of this domain, such as digital composing, drafting a dance piece, or editing existing data to better express an idea or concept underlying a specific movement.

Acknowledgements. This work was supported by the European Research Council under the project "BlackBox: A collaborative platform to document performance composition: from conceptual structures in the backstage to customizable visualizations in the front-end" (Grant agreement n. 336200).

References

1. Addison, A.C., Gaiani, M.: Virtualized architectural heritage: new tools and techniques. IEEE MultiMedia **7**(2), 26–31 (2000)
2. Bacim, F., Nabiyouni, M., Bowman, D.A.: Slice-n-swipe: a free-hand gesture user interface for 3D point cloud annotation. In: 2014 IEEE Symposium on 3D User Interfaces (3DUI), pp. 185–186. IEEE (2014)
3. Cabral, D., Valente, J.G., Aragão, U., Fernandes, C., Correia, N.: Evaluation of a multimodal video annotator for contemporary dance. In: Proceedings of the International Working Conference on Advanced Visual Interfaces, AVI 2012, pp. 572–579. ACM, New York (2012)

4. Camurri, A., El Raheb, K., Even-Zohar, O., Ioannidis, Y., Markatzi, A., Matos, J.-M., Morley-Fletcher, E., Palacio, P., Romero, M., Sarti, A., Di Pietro, S., Viro, V., Whatley, S.: WhoLoDancE: towards a methodology for selecting motion capture data across different dance learning practice. In: Proceedings of the 3rd International Symposium on Movement and Computing, MOCO 2016, pp. 43:1–43:2. ACM, New York (2016)
5. Chan, J.C.P., Leung, H., Tang, J.K.T., Komura, T.: A virtual reality dance training system using motion capture technology. IEEE Trans. Learn. Technol. 4(2), 187–195 (2011)
6. ChoreoPro. Dance designer (2014). https://www.choreopro.com
7. Credo Interactive. Danceforms (2014). http://charactermotion.com/products/danceforms/
8. Gould, A.S.: Invisible visualities: augmented reality art and the contemporary media ecology. Convergence 20(1), 25–32 (2014)
9. Guest, A.H.: Dance Notation: The Process of Recording Movement on Paper. Dance Horizons, New York (1984)
10. James, S., Fonseca, M.J., Collomosse, J.: ReEnact: sketch based choreographic design from archival dance footage. In: Proceedings of International Conference on Multimedia Retrieval, ICMR 2014, pp. 313:313–313:320. ACM, New York (2014)
11. Kipp, M.: ANVIL: the video annotation research tool. In: Handbook of Corpus Phonology. Oxford University Press, Oxford (2010)
12. Kyan, M., Sun, G., Li, H., Zhong, L., Muneesawang, P., Dong, N., Elder, B., Guan, L.: An approach to ballet dance training through MS kinect and visualization in a cave virtual reality environment. ACM Trans. Intell. Syst. Technol. (TIST) 6(2), 23 (2015)
13. Lubos, P., Beimler, R., Lammers, M., Steinicke, F.: Touching the cloud: bimanual annotation of immersive point clouds. In: 2014 IEEE Symposium on 3D User Interfaces (3DUI), pp. 191–192, March 2014
14. Moghaddam, E.R., Sadeghi, J., Samavati, F.F.: Sketch-based dance choreography. In: 2014 International Conference on Cyberworlds (CW), pp. 253–260, October 2014
15. Ribeiro, C., dos Anjos, R.K., Fernandes, C.: Capturing and documenting creative processes in contemporary dance. In: Proceedings of the 4th International Conference on Movement Computing, MOCO 2017, pp. 7:1–7:7. ACM, New York (2017)
16. Ribeiro, C., Kuffner, R., Fernandes, C., Pereira, J.: 3D annotation in contemporary dance: enhancing the creation-tool video annotator. In: Proceedings of the 3rd International Symposium on Movement and Computing, MOCO 2016, pp. 41:1–41:4. ACM, New York (2016)
17. Sanchez-Vives, M.V., Slater, M.: From presence to consciousness through virtual reality. Nat. Rev. Neurosci. 6(4), 332–339 (2005)
18. Singh, V., Latulipe, C., Carroll, E., Lottridge, D.: The choreographer's notebook: a video annotation system for dancers and choreographers. In: Proceedings of the 8th ACM Conference on Creativity and Cognition, C&C 2011, pp. 197–206. ACM, New York (2011)
19. Sousa, M., Mendes, D., Dos Anjos, R.K., Medeiros, D., Ferreira, A., Raposo, A., Pereira, J.M., Jorge, J.: Creepy tracker toolkit for context-aware interfaces. In: Proceedings of the 2017 ACM on Interactive Surfaces and Spaces, ISS 2017. ACM, New York (2017)
20. Umino, B., Soga, A., Hirayama, M.: Feasibility study for contemporary dance e-learning: an interactive creation support system using 3D motion data. In: 2014 International Conference on Cyberworlds (CW), pp. 71–76. IEEE (2014)

21. Veit, M., Capobianco, A.: Go'then'tag: a 3-D point cloud annotation technique. In: 2014 IEEE Symposium on 3D User Interfaces (3DUI), pp. 193–194. IEEE (2014)
22. Wither, J., DiVerdi, S., Höllerer, T.: Annotation in outdoor augmented reality. Comput. Graph. **33**(6), 679–689 (2009)
23. Wittenburg, P., Brugman, H., Russel, A., Klassmann, A., Sloetjes, H.: ELAN: a professional framework for multimodality research. In: Proceedings of LREC, vol. 2006, p. 5 (2006)

Rapid Reconstruction and Simulation of Real Characters in Mixed Reality Environments

Margarita Papaefthymiou[1,2](✉), Marios Evangelos Kanakis[1,2],
Efstratios Geronikolakis[1,2], Argyrios Nochos[3], Paul Zikas[2,3],
and George Papagiannakis[1,2,3]

[1] Institute of Computer Science, Foundation for Research and Technology Hellas,
100 N. Plastira Street, 70013 Heraklion, Greece
margarita@csd.uoc.gr
[2] Computer Science Department, University of Crete, Voutes Campus,
70013 Heraklion, Greece
[3] ovidVR, 100 N. Plastira Street, 70013 Heraklion, Greece

Abstract. This paper presents a comparison of latest software and hardware methods for rapid reconstruction of real humans using as an input RGB or RGB-D images, and base on this comparison is introduced the pipeline that produces high realistic reconstructions in a reasonable amount of time, suitable for real-time Virtual Reality (VR), Augmented Reality (AR) as well as Holographic Mixed Reality (HMR). In this work, we also present and compare usage of latest VR and AR Head Mounted displays (HDMs), which are Microsoft Hololens, Oculus Rift and mobile AR. Specifically, we compare the immersion experience, interaction system, field of view and level of presence that each of these technologies provide. We demonstrate our results at Asinou church, a UNESCO Cultural Heritage monument located in Cyprus. Our reconstructed virtual narrator is the real priest of Asinou church which gives a virtual tour in the church. This interactive virtual narrator supports a range of different capabilities like performing gestures, speech and lip synchronization.

1 Introduction

Virtual characters play a fundamental role for attaining high level of believability in Mixed-reality environments and they are the key-element for transferring knowledge and presenting scenarios in different Cultural Heritage applications. In this work, we populate our Mixed-reality applications with Virtual narrators which play a vital role in the presentation of Cultural Heritage by giving instructions to the users and transfer knowledge about the history of the Cultural Heritage monument. We strongly believe that Augmented Reality (AR) and Virtual Reality (VR) environments are a powerful and attractive medium for transferring knowledge to the users, for Cultural Heritage monuments through immersive and interactive experiences.

© Springer International Publishing AG, part of Springer Nature 2018
M. Ioannides (Ed.): ITN-DCH 2017, LNCS 10605, pp. 267–276, 2018.
https://doi.org/10.1007/978-3-319-75826-8_22

Such Virtual narrators are reconstructed out of real humans and have the ability for verbal as well as nonverbal communication skills. In this work, we compare latest 3D reconstruction methodologies of realistic Virtual characters by capturing real human geometry from photographs. This topic of research remains open since there are no straightforward methods of accurate and automatic reconstruction of high resolution virtual characters from real humans without significant human processing of the gathered data. We present and compare such latest software and hardware methodologies based on RGB or RGB-D images and we propose the best method or the combination of methods that produce the best and more realistic reconstructions suitable for real-time VR, AR as well as HMR. Our interactive reconstructed virtual narrators support a wide range of different behaviors like performing gestures, speech and lip synchronization.

In this work, we also present and compare the usage of latest Virtual Reality and Augmented Reality Head Mounted displays and related devices. These include Microsoft Hololens [1], Oculus Rift [6] and mobile AR [7]. Each one of these technologies provides different immersion experience, interaction system, field of view and different level of presence. We demonstrate our results at the Asinou Church, a Cultural Heritage monument protected by UNESCO, which is located in Cyprus. In this application we employ our reconstructed virtual narrator to provide a tour to the end-user about historical information concerning the history and critical events took place at the monument and particularly important information regarding the unique frescos of the church.

2   Related Work

Vacchetti et al. [12] presented an Augmented Reality system for real-time camera tracking which runs on a portable PC. The camera tracking system was integrated to the VHD++ character simulation framework, which was used for training and planning in industrial environments. The algorithm during the training stage, creates offline frames and detects the interest points using Harris detector and is able to retrieve the camera's displacement on real-time base on the offline frames. When the camera position is far away from the offline keyframes, the algorithm creates a reference frame online for more stable camera tracking. Also, the interest points do not depend on light conditions, which allows a more stable tracking. Papagiannakis et al. [9] presented an AR real-time storytelling scenario in the site of ancient Pompeii running on a HMD setup that can be used from the visitors of the ancient site for a trip to the past. For the character simulation was used the VHD++, for adding to the characters facial animation, speech, body animation with skinning, cloth simulation and human behaviors. The real-time markerless camera tracking was achieved with the use of a camera tracker. Also, Papaefthymiou et al. [7,8] presented a fast and robust pipeline for populating mobile AR scenes with life-size, animated, geometrically and photometrically accurately registered virtual characters into any environment in less than a minute using only modern smartphones or tablets and then revive the same augmentation from the same spot, in under a few seconds.

Arnold et al. [3] presented tools for populating Cultural Heritage environments with interactive virtual characters. These are VHD++ and UEA Scene Assembly Toolkit which are used to create 3D interactive real time virtual heritage simulations for the ancient city of Pompeii and the town of Wolfenbuttel. VHD++ framework is designed in an object orientated way using C++ and Python as a scripting language. VHD++ is suitable for the development of interactive audio-visual VR/AR environments, which integrates many virtual character simulation technologies. On the other hand, UEA provides capabilities for the creation of the 3D environment and includes the Avatar Research Platform (ARP) toolkit responsible for the design and the animations of the virtual humans, which supports many capabilities like procedural animation and facial morph creation. Also, Kateros et al. [6] presented a comparison of different s/w methodologies for real-time VR simulations of digital heritage sites by the development of immersive and gamified mini VR games for the Palace of Knossos archaeological site. They presented a pipeline for creating the 3D content of the games using different software and tested it by employing the Oculus Rift HMD DK-1 and DK-2 devices using two different 3D game simulation frameworks Unity3D game engine and the glGA framework.

Many methods and algorithms exist for data acquisition and reconstruction for Cultural Heritage (CH). Georgopoulos [4] presented existing data acquisition methods based on photogrammetry and Structure from Motion (SfM) techniques, for the Geometric Documentation of Cultural Heritage. The data acquisition methods are categorized to passive and active methods. Active methods comprise of devices that emit radiation, like scanners. Example kind of scanners are the Terrestrial Laser Scanners and the Structured Light Scanners. Also, Range Cameras or alternatively, time-of-flight (TOF) cameras considered to be an active acquisition method. Passive methods include sensors and methods which capture data base on the radiation emitted from the data. Example methods are Geodetic Data Acquisition and Image-Based Data Acquisition. In the paper above, example documentation results were presented, which are: four Byzantine churches of Troodos Mountains in Cyprus and two ancient vessels of Athens archaeological museum. An example of a 3D reconstruction of a Cultural Heritage (CH) monument was presented by Verbiest et al. [13]. Specifically, Verbiest et al. [13] presented the reconstruction process of the Priscilla catacombs in Rome, achieved with a SfM-Based 3D reconstruction technique. The reconstruction system which consists of seven cameras and multiple light sources, was placed on a mobile robot which autonomously navigated through the catacombs to capture the images. The reconstruction method was able to deal with illumination changes by analyzing the reflectance characteristics of the surface.

3   Methods for the 3D Reconstruction of the Virtual Narrator

In this section, we compare different software and hardware methods for reconstructing virtual characters suitable for AR, VR and Holographic MR.

These methods are Agisoft PhotoScan software, Occipital Structure Sensor (Fig. 4) and Fast Avatar Capture that utilizes the capabilities of Kinect v1 sensor [11]. Firstly, we tested all the methods on a subject and then base on our findings we reconstructed the virtual priest of Asinou church.

3.1 Agisoft PhotoScan Software

Agisoft PhotoScan is a software that uses photogrammetry techniques and computer vision methods for reconstructing 3D objects given as input a set of photographs. Agisoft PhotoScan software can produce high quality 3D mesh concerning the geometry and the texture of the virtual character. The resolution of the texture depends on the resolution of the input images. PhotoScan is the slowest method for reconstructing a mesh compared to the Occipital Structure Sensor and Fast Avatar Capture, so we decided to use it for reconstructing only the face. Moreover, we selected this method because the face is the part of the human that we would like to give more focus and maintain the details.

We gave to the software as an input a set of 120 photographs. We took photographs around the face from 3 different heights in order to cover the whole surface of the face. On the first one we were focusing on the lower part of the face, on the second one on the middle part and the third one on the upper part. Figure 1 shows the position and the rotation of the photographs captured around the face, that were given as an input to Agisoft Photoscan software. Firstly, we align the photographs and then build the dense cloud (Fig. 2 (left)). We build the cloud with medium resolution because if are generated large number of points, the shape of the 3D model is not so smooth. Then, we had to manually clear the cloud using the delete tool of Photoscan in order to remove the point data of other objects in the environment, and leave only the points of the face, to achieve faster 3D mesh reconstruction. Then we build the 3D mesh and the texture of the avatar (Fig. 2 (right)).

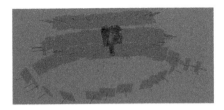

Fig. 1. The position and the rotation of the photographs captured around the face that were given as an input to Agisoft Photoscan software

Fig. 2. The dense cloud data (left) and the 3D mesh (right) produced from the photographs taken around the face, using the Agisoft Photoscan software

3.2   Fast Avatar Capture Application

The second software that we have tested was Fast Avatar Capture desktop application [11]. Fast Avatar Capture is not suitable for face reconstruction because it produces low resolution texture. This occurs because Fast Avatar Capture utilizes Kinect v1 for the reconstruction and captures images with resolution 640×480. The software captures the subject from 4 different viewing angles and each capture lasts approximately 15 s. For each capture, the subject rotates 90° around himself and his posture must be as stable as possible to achieve higher quality 3D model. Figure 3 shows the system used for the avatar creation. The Kinect was placed one meter distance from the subject that was stand on the base that we constructed for rotating the human during the capture process in order to be as stable as possible. After the scanning process, the software requires approximately two minutes for reconstructing the character.

Fig. 3. The system used for reconstructing the subject with Fast Avatar Capture software (left) and the character produced by Fast Avatar Capture software

3.3   Occipital Structure Sensor

The third reconstruction method that we have tested is Occipital Structure Sensor, illustrated on Fig. 4. We achieved the reconstruction via the "Scanner" application running on iPad Air 2 which requires the Occipital Structure Sensor to scan the objects. Structure Sensor provides rapid reconstruction of the object and the "Scanner" application produces and illustrates the 3D mesh while scanning, as a result the user can stop the scanning only when he achieves high quality 3D mesh. On Fig. 5 is shown the 3D mesh captured with Occipital Structure Sensor.

3.4   Comparison of Reconstruction Methods

Fast Avatar Capture and Occipital Structure Sensor are suitable for reconstructing the body and Agisoft Photoscan software is suitable for reconstructing the

Fig. 4. The Occipital structure sensor used to reconstruct the virtual priest of Asinou church

Fig. 5. Our subject (left) and the priest of Asinou Church (right) reconstructed by the Occipital Structure Sensor

face because it produces detailed geometry and high resolution texture without noise. We have decided to use Occipital Structure Sensor to reconstruct the priest of Asinou Church, because it is easier to use compared to Fast Avatar Capture. While capturing with Fast Avatar Capture the subject must rotate, as a result the posture is quite difficult to be exactly the same to all captures, thus the reconstruction in some cases is not possible. On the other hand, with the Occipital Structure Sensor the subject is stable, so it is more potential to produce higher quality reconstruction. Moreover, Fast Avatar Capture captures images from only 4 different points of view from a certain distance in contrast to Structure Sensor that the user can capture data from any point of view and from any distance around the subject. This allows producing high quality textures and more accurate geometry.

3.5   Virtual Priest Reconstruction

Base on our results, we decided to use the Occipital Structure Sensor to reconstruct the priest of Asinou church. On Fig. 5 is shown the 3D mesh captured with Structure Sensor. The 3D mesh produced needed further improvement in order to have the desirable result. We have improved the body and the face of the virtual narrator using 3ds Max modeling software. To avoid a lot of manual work, one alternative option is to reconstruct the face of the priest using the Agisoft Photoscan software (Fig. 6).

Rigging and Animations. For the rigging and skinning of the virtual narrator we have used Mixamo online platform [2]. Mixamo provides auto-rigging and a wide range of animations. The total joints of the skeleton is 65 joints. We have selected animations that perform basic gestures and movements that are physical to be performed during talking. For the animations' part was deemed necessary to create a number of blend shapes (morph targets) that will be performed during speech and lip synchronization process. In total, we created 13 blend shapes using Maya 3D modeling software which some of them are illustrated on Fig. 7.

Fig. 6. Digitization of the priest of Asinou church using Structure Sensor

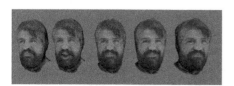

Fig. 7. Some of the Blend shapes created on the face of the virtual character that are used for lip synchronization.

Fig. 8. The HDR light probe of the interior of Asinou church used to illuminate our virtual narrator.

Illumination of the Virtual Narrator Using Conformal Geometric Algebra (CGA). For the illumination of the virtual narrator we have employed the algorithm [7] for shading on real-time under distant diffuse illumination represented by irradiance maps. We have captured the HDR light probe in the interior of Asinou church which is illustrated on Fig. 8. The main novelty of the algorithm employed, is that the Precomputed Radiance Transfer algorithm [10] is extended by representing Spherical Harmonics (SH) with CGA [5] and rotate the light coefficients using CGA entities. SH are orthogonal basis functions that are defined on the sphere's surface and they are used in Computer Graphics for approximating the incident light of irradiance maps and rendering diffuse surfaces. Using this CGA illumination algorithm, we achieve higher performance of light coefficients rotation since SH rotations are represented by CGA rotors (4 numbers) as opposed to 9×9 sparse matrices that are usually employed and high quality and accurate results.

4   Virtual Tour in Asinou Church in Mixed Reality

4.1   Comparison of VR and AR Technologies

In this section, we compare the usage of latest VR and AR Head Mounted displays (HDMs) and related devices, which are Microsoft Hololens, Oculus Rift and mobile AR. Specifically, we compare the immersion experience, the interaction system, the field of view and the level of presence that each technology provides.

In mobile AR we have used the MetaioSDK for the camera tracking. We have used the toolbox application to create the 3d map file which includes the features of the scene, then pass this file to our application bundle and the MetaioSDK is able to compute the view matrix in order to place our virtual narrator on a stable position in the real environment. The field of view depends on the device's camera and it's partially immersive since it combines virtual and real world. The interaction system in mobile AR is the Graphical User Interface (GUI). Through the buttons of the GUI the user is able to transform the virtual narrator and start the virtual tour in the church. Figure 9 shows the reconstructed priest in the church from two different points of view in mobile AR.

Fig. 9. Our digitized priest giving a virtual tour in Asinou church in Mobile AR

In Microsoft Hololens the user interacts with the virtual narrator through gestures and voice commands. Via specific words the user can select the type of transformation (translation, rotation, scale) that would like to apply to the virtual narrator. After selecting the type of transformation via voice commands the user performs the manipulate gesture to apply the selected transformation to the holographic priest. Microsoft Hololens provides full body tracking and it is partially immersive since in combines virtual and real world. One drawback of Microsoft Hololens that affects the user experience is the narrow field of view (Fig. 10).

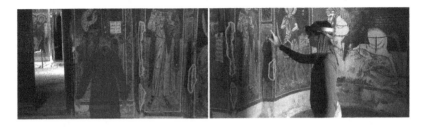

Fig. 10. Our digitized priest giving a virtual tour in Asinou church in Microsoft Hololens

Oculus Rift provides fully immersive virtual environment since the user does not have any access in the real world. Oculus rift provides rotational and positional tracking but in contrast to Microsoft Hololens and mobile AR the movements are restricted to a more limited space in front of the sensors. The user interacts with the virtual environment using the touch controllers. Through Oculus Rift the user is able to navigate in the exterior and interior part of the Asinou church as shown on Fig. 11.

Fig. 11. The virtual tour in Asinou church running on Oculus Rift

5   Conclusions

In this paper, we have presented and compared different hardware and software methods for reconstructing virtual characters out of real humans, suitable for real-time Virtual Reality (VR), Augmented Reality (AR) as well as Holographic Mixed Reality (MR) and proposed the best method for reconstructing virtual characters. Moreover, we compared and presented the usage of different Mixed-Reality technologies which are Oculus Rift, Microsoft Hololens and mobile AR. We have demonstrated our results at Asinou church, by creating a virtual tour in the church in Mixed-reality environments. The tour in the church is provided by the reconstructed virtual priest. By employing our reconstructed interactive virtual priest in our Mixed-Reality environments we have achieved a very interesting virtual tour that attracts the user attention and further provokes the interest of the users for learning historical information about the church.

Acknowledgments. The research leading to these results was partially funded by the European Union People Programme (FP7-PEOPLE-2013-ITN) under grant agreement 608013 and was partially funded by the Virtual Multimodal Museum (ViMM), a Coordination and Support Action (CSA), funded under the EU Horizon 2020 programme (CULT-COOP-8-2016).

References

1. Microsoft Hololens. www.microsoft.com/hololens. Accessed 12 May 2017
2. Mixamo. www.mixamo.com. Accessed 12 May 2017
3. Arnold, D., Day, A., Glauert, J., Haegler, S., Jennings, V., Kevelham, B., Laycock, R., Magnenat-Thalmann, N., Maïm, J., Maupu, D., Papagiannakis, G., Thalmann, D., Yersin, B., Rodriguez-Echavarria, K.: Tools for populating cultural heritage environments with interactive virtual humans. In: Open Digital Cultural Heritage Systems, EPOCH Final Event 2008, February 2008
4. Georgopoulos, A.: Data acquisition for the geometric documentation of cultural heritage. In: Ioannides, M., Magnenat-Thalmann, N., Papagiannakis, G. (eds.) Mixed Reality and Gamification for Cultural Heritage, pp. 29–73. Springer, Cham (2017). https://doi.org/10.1007/978-3-319-49607-8_2
5. Hildenbrand, D.: Foundations of Geometric Algebra Computing, vol. 8. Springer, Heidelberg (2013). https://doi.org/10.1007/978-3-642-31794-1
6. Kateros, S., Georgiou, S., Papaefthymiou, M., Papagiannakis, G., Tsioumas, M.: A comparison of gamified, immersive VR curation methods for enhanced presence and human-computer interaction in digital humanities. Int. J. Heritage Digital Era **4**(2), 221–233 (2015). Also presented in The 1st International Workshop on ICT for the Preservation and Transmission of Intangible Cultural Heritage, EUROMED2014
7. Papaefthymiou, M., Feng, A., Shapiro, A., Papagiannakis, G.: A fast and robust pipeline for populating mobile AR scenes with gamified virtual characters. In: SIGGRAPH Asia 2015 Mobile Graphics and Interactive Applications, SA 2015, pp. 22:1–22:8. ACM, New York (2015)
8. Papaefthymiou, M., Kateros, S., Georgiou, S., Lydatakis, N., Zikas, P., Bachlitzanakis, V., Papagiannakis, G.: Gamified AR/VR character rendering and animation-enabling technologies. In: Ioannides, M., Magnenat-Thalmann, N., Papagiannakis, G. (eds.) Mixed Reality and Gamification for Cultural Heritage. Springer, Cham (2017). https://doi.org/10.1007/978-3-319-49607-8_13
9. Papagiannakis, G., Schertenleib, S., O'Kennedy, B., Arevalo-Poizat, M., Magnenat-Thalmann, N., Stoddart, A., Thalmann, D.: Mixing virtual and real scenes in the site of ancient pompeii: research articles. Comput. Animat. Virtual Worlds **16**(1), 11–24 (2005)
10. Ramamoorthi, R., Hanrahan, P.: An efficient representation for irradiance environment maps. In: Proceedings of the 28th Annual Conference on Computer Graphics and Interactive Techniques, SIGGRAPH 2001, pp. 497–500. ACM, New York (2001)
11. Shapiro, A., Feng, A., Wang, R., Li, H., Bolas, M., Medioni, G., Suma, E.: Rapid avatar capture and simulation using commodity depth sensors. Comput. Anim. Virtual Worlds **25**(3–4), 201–211 (2014)
12. Vacchetti, L., Lepetit, V., Ponder, M., Papagiannakis, G., Fua, P., Thalmann, D., Thalmann, N.M.: A stable real-time AR framework for training and planning in industrial environments. In: Ong, S.K., Nee, A.Y.C. (eds.) Virtual and Augmented Reality Applications in Manufacturing, pp. 129–145. Springer, London (2004). https://doi.org/10.1007/978-1-4471-3873-0_8
13. Verbiest, F., Proesmans, M., Van Gool, L.: Autonomous mapping of the Priscilla Catacombs. In: Ioannides, M., Magnenat-Thalmann, N., Papagiannakis, G. (eds.) Mixed Reality and Gamification for Cultural Heritage, pp. 75–98. Springer, Cham (2017). https://doi.org/10.1007/978-3-319-49607-8_3

3D Pose Estimation Oriented to the Initialization of an Augmented Reality System Applied to Cultural Heritage

Ricardo M. Rodriguez[1], Rafael Aguilar[1], Santiago Uceda[2],
and Benjamín Castañeda[1(✉)]

[1] Department of Engineering, Pontificia Universidad Católica del Perú, Lima 32, Peru
{m.rodriguezo,raguilar}@pucp.pe, castaneda.b@pucp.edu.pe
[2] Huacas del Sol y de la Luna Archaeological Project, Universidad de Trujillo, Trujillo, Peru
santiago_uceda@hotmail.com

Abstract. Augmented reality (AR) applied to cultural heritage intends to improve the learning experience in archaeological sites, not only for visitants but also for researchers. 3D Pose estimation is a common problem in applications for AR, object recognition, 3D modeling, among others. AR systems use different methods to estimate the camera pose: edge detection and key-point detection among others. The choice of the method to be used depends on the features of the scenario to be detected. In this work, a comparison study of the main 3D model-based pose estimation methods is performed. In addition, we present the implementation and validation of a pose estimation algorithm, oriented to the initialization of an AR system applied to "Huaca de la Luna", an adobe brick pyramid built by the Moche civilization in the northern Peru. The proposed algorithm presents two phases, a training phase, where 3D key-points are extracted from a reference image, and a detection phase, where the initialization process is performed by comparing 2D/3D points correspondence using a PnP algorithm. We have compared four variations of the 3D pose estimation algorithm using different methods: SIFT and SURF descriptors for key-point description and EPnP and REPPnP algorithms for PnP pose estimation. Results show a translation error of 1.54 cm, with a mean processing time of 2.78 s, a maximum re-projection error of 1.5 pixels and a successful estimation rate of 100% in scenarios with normal and high light conditions.

Keywords: Augmented reality · Virtual reality · Pose estimation · Digital culture
Photogrammetry

1 Introduction

1.1 Problem Statement

Augmented reality (AR) is a technology that has gained popularity in the cultural heritage field [1]. AR systems project virtual objects in real scenarios enhancing the learning experience. Likewise, this tool can also be used as an alternative to physical reconstruction, allowing the preservation of the originality of monuments.

© Springer International Publishing AG, part of Springer Nature 2018
M. Ioannides (Ed.): ITN-DCH 2017, LNCS 10605, pp. 277–288, 2018.
https://doi.org/10.1007/978-3-319-75826-8_23

Implementation of AR systems presents several challenges to create the illusion of coexistence between the virtual object and the real scenario. The virtual object must be positioned correctly and the projection done in real time. To locate the virtual object in the right position, the extrinsic parameters of the camera capturing the scene must be computed. This is known as the camera pose estimation problem. It consists in the computation of the rotation and translation parameters of a camera in a known coordinate system, given an image captured by that camera, its intrinsic parameters and the 3D model of the object or scene. In Fig. 1, a representation of the extrinsic parameters computation is shown. Figure 1(b) shows an input image, captured from a real scenario. In Fig. 1(c) is shown this real scenario combined with a virtual coordinate system. The pose estimation problem consists in computation of the extrinsic parameters given this coordinate system. For this case, a key-point based method was used to estimate the pose, using a known reference image.

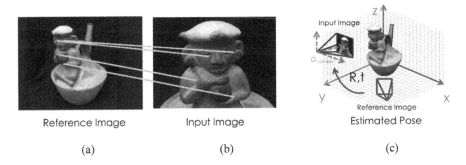

Reference Image	Input Image	Estimated Pose
(a)	(b)	(c)

Fig. 1. Camera pose estimation problem: Computation of the extrinsic parameters of a camera in a known coordinate system, given an image, its intrinsic parameters, and the 3D model of the object.

Different methods can solve the pose estimation problem, as we detail in Sect. 3, the choice of one of these depends on the properties of the target scenario.

AR systems can be divided in three phases: (1) an initialization phase, where no prior information of pose is given, (2) a tracking phase, where recursive information of the previous frame is used to estimate the pose of the virtual object, (3) and the augmentation phase, where the virtual object is rendered in the projection.

In this paper, we focus on the initialization phase of the AR system, using optical sensors. The main contributions are: (1) A detailed framework of a 3D pose estimation algorithm for AR initialization. (2) The evaluation of different configurations of the algorithm which can be used as a reference by other AR researchers. (3) The validation of the proposed algorithm in the Huaca de La Luna scenario.

This paper is organized as follows. Section 2 describes the case of study during this research. Section 3 details the requirements for the implementation of the pose estimation algorithm, alternatives of solution and the proposed design. Section 4 explains the methods and experiments developed in this work and the metrics for evaluation. Section 5 discusses the results obtained in each experiment. The conclusions and future work are shown in Sect. 6.

2 Case of Study: Archeological Complex "Huaca de La Luna"

In this section, the history and architecture of the archeologic monument "Huaca de La Luna" is described briefly. In addition, details of the target scenario used in our tests are provided.

2.1 Site Description

Located in the northern coast of Peru, the archeological complex "Huaca de La Luna" is a religious adobe monument built during the pre-Columbian age from 100 A.D. to 650 A.D. by the Moche civilization [2]. This complex has been recovered by archeological excavations since 1991.

Huaca de La Luna lies on the lower slopes of "Cerro Blanco" mountain, as can be seen in Fig. 2(a). Three main platforms and four squares form this monument. The platform I is known as the Main Platform and it is located between platform II and the Ceremonial Square.

(a)   (b)

Fig. 2. Huaca de la Luna: (a) View of Huaca de la Luna excavations on the lower slopes of Cerro Blanco. (b) Solid model of Huaca de la Luna, figure taken from [4].

Several works for the study of preservation of the structural health has been performed by researchers [3], these studies include the reconstruction of complex 3D models [4], damage identification, among others [5, 6].

Despite the pass of the years, the iconographic designs are well preserved represented on relief and mural paintings. However, there exist areas with severe damages due to attacks during the Spaniard conquest. Virtual in situ reconstructions can be possible using AR applications.

2.2 Target Scenario: Corner Enclosure

The "corner enclosure" is a structure located in the main façade of platform I (see Fig. 2(b)). In this area, religious rituals were performed during the ancient years. This area was selected to test the performance of our algorithm since it is suitable for displaying the religious ceremonies of the Moche civilization from the iconographic designs.

The access of visitors is limited until a position suitable for an AR application using handheld devices (see Fig. 3(a)). This area offers the view of well-preserved iconographic textured designs as can be seen in Fig. 3(b).

(a)   (b)

Fig. 3. Corner enclosure. (a) Two visitors can be seen in a position where AR can be used - image taken from [7]. (b) Textured view of the corner enclosure section.

3   Algorithm Design

In this section, we introduce the requirements of the implementation of the pose estimation algorithm, given the target scenario. Subsequently, we present a survey of the pose estimation algorithms alternatives and finally, we detail the selected algorithm.

3.1   Application Requirements

The requirements of the system to implement the initialization phase of the AR system are:

- Low rotation and translation error (absolute translation error < 5 cm; absolute rotation error < 30° or 0.52 rads).
- High successful estimation rate (Successful estimation rate > 90%).
- Fast computation processing (Processing time < 3 s).

3.2   Pose Estimation Survey

We found many alternatives to solve the pose estimation problem. Available methods can be classified in two types: marker based and markerless methods.

Marker based methods are well known for being high accurate and robust. These methods use artificial patterns placed along the scenario as target references to estimate the pose of the objects. These patterns can be retro-reflective fiducials or planar fiducials.

On the other hand, markerless based methods use natural features of the scenario as a reference, like key-points or edges. These methods can be classified in image based and model based methods, the use of one of these approaches depend on the complexity of the scenario geometry.

In Table 1, we present a review of the mentioned methods, detailing when they are suitable to be used and their level of accuracy. More details of these methods can be found in [8, 9].

Table 1. Analysis of methods for pose estimation. Table adaptation from [8, 9].

Method based on:	Description
Retro-reflective fiducials, infrared cameras [10]	This method presents a high accuracy and pose estimation errors are very rare. It is suitable when the scenario allows to locate fiducials. The cost of retro-reflective fiducials is expensive
Planar fiducials [11]	Synthetic planar fiducials are positioned along in the scenario, visible to the camera. This method is accurate, however estimation errors can occur when fiducials are hidden
2D interest points [12]	This markerless based method use the 2D key-points of the scenario to estimate the pose. It is suitable when the scenario presents texture images, but errors can occur for scenarios with complex geometry
3D Models/3D interest points [13]	This method is a 3D model based method. It is suitable for textured complex geometry scenarios
3D Models/Views – Edge based [9]	3D Model/Edge based methods are suitable for textureless scenarios with a complex geometry. The detection using this method is limited to a restricted range of view

3.3   Selected Algorithm

Although marker based methods present high accuracy and robustness, they are limited by the visualization of the fiducials. If marker occlusion occurs, the pose estimation fails. Likewise, markers placed along the environment can hide important regions of the scenario and since these patterns are calibrated, markers must be static. In our case of study, 3D model markerless based methods are the best option since the geometry of the scenario is not planar. Given the texture of the scenario, the 3D interest points based method was selected as the algorithm for initialization.

The proposed algorithm presents two phases: training and detection (see Fig. 4). During the first phase, a 3D model is reconstructed using photogrammetry and one of the images used in this reconstruction is selected as a reference image. Key-points are detected from this image and the correspondent 3D points are computed based on the known depth image. This data is stored in memory to be used in the next phase.

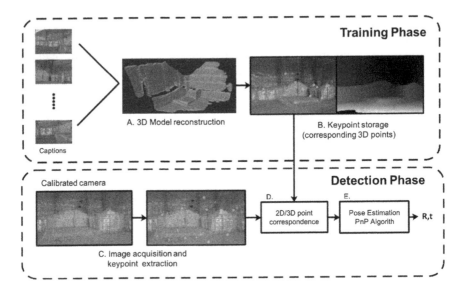

Fig. 4. Block diagram of the algorithm proposed. This design presents two phases: A training phase and a detection phase. During the first phase, the 3D model reconstruction is performed (A) and key-point descriptors are stored with their 3D correspondence (B). These descriptors are compared to the descriptors obtained during the detection phase (C) and a 2D/3D correspondence is obtained (D). Finally, a PnP pose estimation algorithm (E) is used to detect the rotation and translation parameters.

During the second phase, the initialization process is performed. Here, an image is acquired and decimated for fast processing. Then, key-point features are detected. These features are compared against the stored data and a 2D/3D correspondence is estimated. Finally, a Perspective n-Point (PnP) pose estimation algorithm is used to detect the rotation matrix and translation vector.

Based on this framework, four variations of the algorithm can be evaluated. SIFT [14] and SURF [15] descriptors can be used for key-point description and EPnP [16] and REPPnP [17] algorithms can be used for PnP pose estimation. The REPPnP algorithm unlike EPnP, computes outlier detection and pose estimation simultaneously. In the case of the EPnP based variations, a RANSAC algorithm [18] was implemented for outlier detection.

These four variations are named as follows: SIFT/REPPnP, SIFT/EPnP, SURF/REPPnP and SURF/EPnP.

4   Evaluation Method

Two experiments are proposed to test the implemented algorithm. The first experiment was performed using synthetic data and the second experiment was performed using real images.

4.1   Experiment 1: Using Synthetic Data

A 3D model of the corner enclosure was reconstructed using 40 images captured by a Canon EOS REBEL T3 camera. From this model, we captured 51 different synthetic views (resolution of 1280×720 px.) using the software Blender (Blender Foundation, Amsterdam), by creating virtual cameras located at 14 m from the target object, as it can be seen in Fig. 5(a). One of these synthetic views and its correspondent depth image was selected for the training phase and the other 50 images were evaluated during the detection phase.

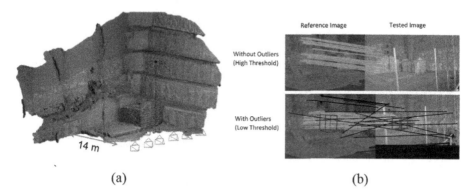

(a)   (b)

Fig. 5. Experiment 1. (a) Synthetic views captured using Blender software. (b) Representation of the variation in the threshold for features matching.

We compare the robustness of the methods using different thresholds for the keypoint matching, as it can be seen in Fig. 5(b). The metrics evaluated in this experiment were translation and rotation errors, processing time and re-projection error.

From the virtual camera poses, the true camera translation $\mathbf{t}_{true}$ and rotation $\mathbf{R}_{true}$ are used to compute the translation error by $e_{trans} = \|\mathbf{t} - \mathbf{t}_{true}\|$ and the rotation error by $e_{rot} = \|$Rodrigues$(\mathbf{R})$ − Rodrigues$(\mathbf{R}_{true})\|$.

Re-projection error computes the distance between a projected estimated point and a projected reference point. Eleven points of the virtual object are defined and the re-projection error is computed in pixel units, as shown in Fig. 6. Then, the median error for each point is obtained and the maximum value is evaluated from each method.

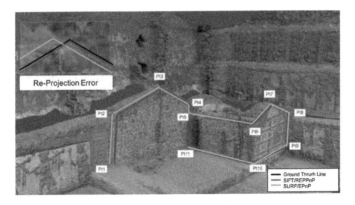

Fig. 6. Representation of the re-projection error: Eleven 3D points are defined in the virtual object. Re-projection error computes the distance between the estimated projected points and the reference projected points.

4.2   Experiment 2: Using Real Images

In this experiment, pose estimation was evaluated visually under different lighting conditions. This scenario is affected by illumination changes. The purpose of this experiment is to validate the robustness of the algorithm during the visiting time.

A set of 100 images was capture during the morning from different poses, simulating an AR user behavior. At that time, no shadows were presented. In the same way, during the afternoon, a set of 50 images were captured.

The validation of each estimation is performed using the projection of the same eleven points described above for the re-projection error (see Fig. 6). The joint of these points simulates an application of RA, if lines are misaligned, it is considered as an incorrect estimation.

5   Results

All the tests were performed using Matlab R2015b, and a MacBook Pro i7, 2.5 GHz.

5.1   Results from Experiment 1

To compare the obtained results, we show the graphs of the metrics in Fig. 7. We observe that the SIFT/EPnP method presents the lowest median translation error and rotation error: 1.62 cm and 0.22 radians with outliers, and 1.54 cm and 0.19 radians without outliers. On the other hand, we can see that the SURF/REPPnP presents the highest error. In terms of pixels, the lowest re-projection error is equivalent to 1.29 px with presence of outliers and 1.46 px without outliers.

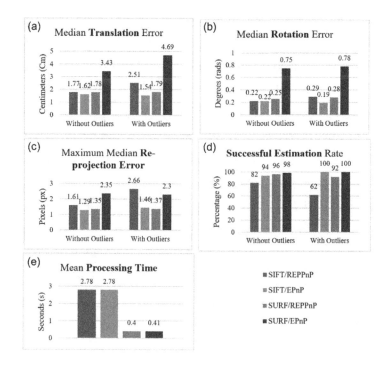

Fig. 7. Graphics of the results from experiment 1. Evaluated metrics: (a) Median translation error, (b) median rotation error, (c) maximum median re-projection error, (d) successful estimation rate and (e) mean processing time. (a), (b) and (c) show the best performance for the SIFT/EPnP method. In (d) we can observe a higher successful estimation rate for EPnP based methods. In (e) we observe a faster processing time for SURF based methods.

The results of successful estimation rate show a better performance for the configurations that include the EPnP algorithm. SIFT/EPnP and SURF/EPnP present a 100% in presence of outliers. Finally, we evaluate the processing time. As it was expected, SIFT based configurations are approximately seven times slower compared to SURF based methods, with 2.78 s of mean processing time.

5.2   Results from Experiment 2

From the results presented above, we notice that the most remarkable configurations are SIFT/EPnP and SURF/EPnP because of their high accuracy and high successful rate estimation. These two configurations were validated using real images at different lighting conditions. In Fig. 8(a) and (c), results of the pose estimation at regular lighting conditions are shown, in the same way Fig. 8(b) and (d) show the estimated pose at high lightning conditions.

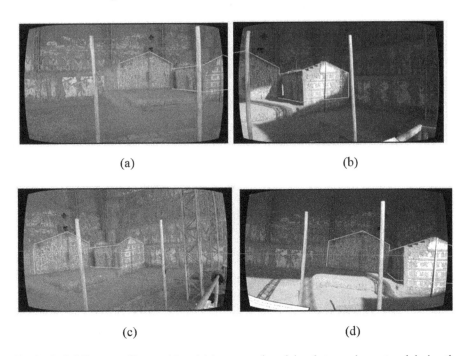

(a)   (b)

(c)   (d)

Fig. 8. Reliability tests. Figures (a) and (c) are samples of the photographs captured during the morning; on the other hand, figures (b) and (d) were captured during the afternoon. The green lines simulate an application of RA, if they are misaligned, we determined it as an incorrect estimation. (Color figure online)

From results showed in Table 2, we notice that the best performance is done by the SIFT/EPnP with a 100% of successful estimation rate.

Table 2. Results of experiment 2. Successful pose estimation rate at different lightning conditions.

Method	Lightning condition	Successful pose estimation rate
SURF/EPnP	Regular lightning conditions	79.24%
	High lightning conditions	60%
SIFT/EPnP	Regular lightning conditions	100%
	High lightning conditions	100%

5.3   Discussion of Results

In Table 3, a qualitative summary of the obtained results is presented. As it was seen before, the best results were obtained using the SIFT/EPnP configuration. This method presents the lowest translation and rotation error and the higher successful estimation rate. Despite this configuration present a higher processing time compared to SURF/REPPnP, 2.7 s for processing, this is an adequate time for an AR initialization phase.

Table 3. Summary of the obtained results. SIFT/EPnP configuration presents the most remarkable results.

Criteria	SIFT/REPPnP	SIFT/EPnP	SURF/REPPnP	SURF/EPnP
Translation and rotation error	Very low	Very low	Very low	Low
Successful estimation rate	Very low	Very high	Low	Very high
Processing time	High	High	Very low	Very low
Re-projection error	Low	Very low	Very low	Low
Successful rate varying lightning conditions		Very high		Low

6 Conclusions

We have demonstrated that this algorithm is suitable for the initialization of augmented reality applications, just by using one reference image in the training phase. This initialization process will be used to estimate the pose of the camera every determined period to obtain an accurate rendering process.

The translation error obtained was 1.54 cm, with a mean processing time of 2.775 s, a maximum re-projection error of 1.5 pixels and a successful estimation rate of 100% in scenarios with normal and high light conditions.

As future work, we will consider the use of GPU based algorithms for key-point extraction and description to reduce the processing time. At the same way, we will develop the complete augmented reality system, using more sensors as accelerometers and gyroscopes. 3D based methods are well adapted for cultural heritage scenarios.

Acknowledgments. We thank CIENCIACTIVA for funding the development of the research "Monitoreo remoto de la salud estructural de edificaciones emblemáticas de adobe: Integración de conocimiento y tecnología para un diagnóstico estructural adecuado" (Project ID 222-2015 FONDECYT). The authors want to dedicate this article in memory of Dr. Santiago Uceda who devoted his life to the study of Peruvian and specially Moche heritage.

References

1. Papagiannakis, G., Singh, G., Magnenat-Thalmann, N.: A survey of mobile and wireless technologies for augmented reality systems. Comput. Animat. Virtual Worlds **19**, 3–22 (2008)
2. Uceda, S.: Investigations at Huaca de la Luna, Moche Valley: an example of Moche religious architecture. Stud. Hist. Art **63**, 46–67 (2001)
3. Chácara, C., Zvietcovich, F., Briceño, C., Marques, R., Perucchio, R., Castañeda, B., Uceda, S., Morales, R., Aguilar, R.: On-site investigation and numerical analysis for structural assessment of the archaeological complex of Huaca de la Luna. In: Proceedings of the 9th International Conference on Structural Analysis of Historical Constructions (2014)

4. Zvietcovich, F., Castaneda, B., Perucchio, R.: 3D solid model updating of complex ancient monumental structures based on local geometrical meshes. Digit. Appl. Archaeol. Cult. Herit. **2**, 12–27 (2015)

5. Zavala, G., López, S., Ebinger, C., Pando, M., Lambert, C., Morales, R., Uceda, S., Perucchio, R., Castañeda, B., Aguilar, R.: Preliminary geophysical survey for assessing the geotechnical conditions and geohazards at Huaca de la Luna, Perú. In: AGU Fall Meeting Abstracts (2014)

6. Aguilar, R., Zavala, G., Castañeda, B., Lopez, S., Retamozo, S., Montesinos, M., Pando, M., Dong, Y., Perucchio, R.: Structural damage assessment of Huaca de la Luna, Perú: preliminary results from ongoing multidisciplinary study. In: Structural Analysis of Historical Constructions: Anamnesis, Diagnosis, Therapy, Controls: Proceedings of the 10th International Conference on Structural Analysis of Historical Constructions (SAHC), Leuven, Belgium, 13–15 September 2016, p. 465. CRC Press (2016)

7. Official site, Huacas del Sol y de la Luna. http://www.huacasdemoche.pe/index.php?menuid=5&submenuid=38&articuloid=87&subarticuloid=. Accessed 20 Aug 2017

8. Lepetit, V., Fua, P.: Monocular model-based 3D tracking of rigid objects: a survey. Found. Trends® Comput. Graph. Vis. **1**, 1–89 (2005)

9. Lima, J.P., Simões, F., Figueiredo, L., Kelner, J.: Model based markerless 3D tracking applied to augmented reality. J. 3D Interact. Syst. **1** (2010)

10. VICON. https://www.vicon.com/. Accessed 20 Aug 2017

11. ARToolkit. http://www.hitl.washington.edu/artoolkit/. Accessed 20 Aug 2017

12. Simon, G., Fitzgibbon, A.W., Zisserman, A.: Markerless tracking using planar structures in the scene. In: Proceedings of the IEEE and ACM International Symposium on Augmented Reality, 2000 (ISAR 2000), pp. 120–128. IEEE (2000)

13. Vacchetti, L., Lepetit, V., Fua, P.: Stable real-time 3D tracking using online and offline information. IEEE Trans. Pattern Anal. Mach. Intell. **26**, 1385–1391 (2004)

14. Lowe, D.G.: Distinctive image features from scale-invariant keypoints. Int. J. Comput. Vis. **60**, 91–110 (2004)

15. Bay, H., Ess, A., Tuytelaars, T., Van Gool, L.: Speeded-up robust features (SURF). Comput. Vis. Image Underst. **110**, 346–359 (2008)

16. Lepetit, V., Moreno-Noguer, F., Fua, P.: EPnP: an accurate O(n) solution to the PnP problem. Int. J. Comput. Vision **81**, 155–166 (2009)

17. Ferraz, L., Binefa, X., Moreno-Noguer, F.: Very fast solution to the PnP problem with algebraic outlier rejection. In: Proceedings of the IEEE Conference on Computer Vision and Pattern Recognition, pp. 501–508 (2014)

18. Fischler, M.A., Bolles, R.C.: Random sample consensus: a paradigm for model fitting with applications to image analysis and automated cartography. Commun. ACM **24**, 381–395 (1981)

Exploring Cultural Heritage Using Virtual Reality

Laurent Debailleux[1](✉) ⓘ, Geoffrey Hismans[1](✉), and Natacha Duroisin[2,3(✉)] ⓘ

[1] Faculty of Engineering, University of Mons, Mons, Belgium
{laurent.debailleux,geoffrey.hismans}@umons.ac.be
[2] Department of Methodology and Training, University of Mons, Mons, Belgium
natacha.duroisin@umons.ac.be
[3] Charles de Gaulle University – Lille III (PSITEC), Villeneuve d'Ascq, France

Abstract. Virtual modelling featuring realistic, constructed environments has progressed significantly over the last decade and is largely used for scientific, educational and recreational purposes. Helped by gaming industry advances, 3D engines are continuously pushing the technological frontiers by providing more and more realistic environments, which allows increased interactions with users. In this context, a head-mounted display, such as Oculus Rift, facilitates interactivity allowing more realism in an immersive experience.

This paper presents an innovative use of Oculus Rift, without any other connected device, in order to allow virtual mobility without constrained navigation. It also meant that visual item selection or information requests in a 3D scene could be done using a virtual pointer. This innovation brings an added value to the existing virtual reality experience by making it possible to streamline the interaction between the user and the model while valuing the intuitiveness and spontaneity of actions. The system might therefore be easy to handle even for a non 3D expert user.

The main square of the city of Mons (Belgium), European Capital of Culture in 2015, was chosen as a case study to put the project into practice. The historical centre of the city has many architectural heritage buildings from the gothic and classical periods which constitute an ideal heritage site to work on. The virtual model was built with Rhino software and later imported into the Unity 3D real time engine to perform the animations and enable the 3D environment to interact with the Oculus Rift.

The project proposes a virtual tour of the historical town centre where each building is described through audio storytelling. Each audio description informs the user about the cultural heritage value of the building under scope. The gaming experience has been tested by a group of children aged between 9 and 12. Although free to take a virtual walk around the main square, each user has to follow audio instructions and listen to indications in order to make the visit in a particular order. The assessment of the virtual tour through the learning outcome of the users is evaluated and discussed in this paper.

Keywords: Virtual reality · Virtual heritage · Oculus Rift · 3D visualisation
Spatial cognition · Learning space · Information and communication technology
Cognitive psychology

© Springer International Publishing AG, part of Springer Nature 2018
M. Ioannides (Ed.): ITN-DCH 2017, LNCS 10605, pp. 289–303, 2018.
https://doi.org/10.1007/978-3-319-75826-8_24

1   Introduction

Using virtual environments as a space simulator has shown its effectiveness and potential in gaining various spatial and informational knowledge and in analysing the cognitive and behavioral skills of people.

The advances in the IT field allow today to navigate in virtual environments without behavioural interfaces (i.e. joystick). This research study shows an example of a device that can be used to discover an environment without motor interfaces.

This research study assesses three different aspects. First, the authors study the efficiency of the software from the learning outcomes of the cultural heritage of the city. Then, spatial knowledge after navigating across the city is evaluated by recognition of landmarks and construction of mental maps. Finally, the perceptions of the users after the virtual tour are considered.

In a first part, the authors define spatial cognition and present a specific model (L-R-S) for understanding how a person develops a representation of his environment. The role of virtual reality for spatial cognition studies is also discussed in this section. In a second part, the authors present the software used to build a realistic 3D model of the city centre of Mons. The technical solutions for navigating and selecting interactive information buttons about different buildings in the main square are detailed as well. In a third part (the experimental plan), the results and conclusion of the research study are presented.

This research study is an original contribution combining works in architecture, computer science and spatial cognition- a specific field of Cognitive Psychology.

2   Research Aims

The first part of the research study is dedicated to a technical approach in which the virtual experience is made more intuitive by using a unique virtual helmet to move and interact with a realistic 3D model. In this context, the effectiveness and possible benefit of these new functionalities are assessed. The second phase of the project consists in evaluating the spatial representation of the virtual built environment through the mental map depiction of users. The third phase explores the possible use of virtual reality as a tool for learning in a built context that embodies significant cultural heritage values.

3   Spatial Cognition and Virtual Reality

3.1   Spatial Cognition: A Concept at the Crossroads of Disciplines

Defined by Neisser [1] as the act of knowing, acquisition, organisation and use of knowledge, cognition is a complex process that relies on the interaction of sensorimotor structures and neurological systems of a person. Without being exhaustive, the few definitions presented define the term "spatial cognition" and account for the variety of its meanings. As Peruch and Corazzini [2] point out, "the study of spatial cognition has its origins [...] in psychology, [...] in the geography of perception, urbanism and architecture". In the field of architecture, Lynch's work [3] entitled "The image of the city" is an unavoidable reference. In his writing, the author clearly demonstrates that the mental images that individuals make of a city differ from their own experiences. He has proposed a categorization of mental images based on the notions of markers (point elements), paths and boundaries (linear elements allowing to connect the point elements and delimiting an area), and nodes (junction elements between the channels). Lynch (ibid.) has inspired all spatial cognition researchers (geographers, cognitivists and neuro-cognitivists) in the field of spatial cognition for the analysis and understanding of the mental images of a given space.

According to Hart and Moore [4], spatial cognition "is the knowledge and internal or cognitive representation of the structure, entities, and relations of space; [...] the internalized reflection and reconstruction of space in thought." Spatial cognition is therefore described here as a spatial representation of the environment, its content and the organization of spatial knowledge necessary for the handling and processing of spatial information. In other words, spatial cognition can be viewed as a process by which somebody perceives, stores, recalls, edits, and communicates spatial images. Barowsky and Freksa [5] insist that the mobilised environments may be of a different nature and describe spatial cognition as «acquisition, organisation, utilisation, and revision of knowledge about spatial environments be it real or abstract, human or machine». In addition, Freksa [6] states that spatial cognition also refers to "the ways in which humans, animals or machines think of space, how they act and interact in space, how they can exploit spatio-temporal structures through computational processes". From the point of view of research, space is therefore no longer just an object that one learns (at school in particular) and that someone uses on a daily basis, but is also a means to apprehend and understand the cognitive processes involved in various activities. It is in this sense that spatial cognition has been and is still considered by researchers in the cognitive sciences in particular. Whether research is carried out on animals (rodents, dogs ...) or on humans (with or without pathologies), one of the main objectives pursued by research in cognitive psychology is to understand how ospatial information is organised in memory to be reused later in similar or new situations. This is why there is an interest in "representations (...) and in the processing of information that allows us to talk about the reconstruction of reality" [7]. Indeed, to understand the way in which an individual apprehends a given space, two major solutions are open to the researcher. On the one hand, it can be based on data derived from neurophysiology (see Bohbot and Duroisin work's for more information); on the other hand, it can resort to the observable behaviour of an individual (i.e. the external representations that it produces according to its own internal representations).

3.2   L-R-S Model

The spatial knowledge taxonomy was developed by Thorndyke and Hayes-Roth [8]. More commonly known as L-R-S, this taxonomy defines three types of interrelated knowledge that are essential to any complete mental representation of a given environment. The first type is "landmark knowledge" (L). While Vinson [9] indicates that any object that provides direction information may be a landmark, other authors point out that points of reference are objects perceived and recognised by an individual given their specific characteristics (forms, structures and/or socio-cultural meanings) and their visibility. For Lynch [3], the landmark is an external physical object that acts as a reference point. This author indicates that the peculiarity and the personal meaning of an object are two complementary reasons which make it a point of reference.

In general, a landmark can be considered as an object which, due to its intrinsic qualities and taking into account the extrinsic characteristics defined by a given observer, makes it possible to be differentiated from the environment in which it is located and to serve as a point of reference.

Landmarks can have a directional function, constitute decision-making aids (where to turn), or have a marker function (the presence of such a marker indicates that I am in an exact place). The landmarks are considered as anchor points from which the individual is able to locate objects more precisely or to develop a more complete mental map, a part of its environment. The landmark knowledge is considered as declarative knowledge and Darken et al. [10] insist on its static nature. Points of reference are identified and recognised by someone as existing objects or places, but the latter cannot move from one object or place to another because of the ignorance of the paths that separate each point of the landmarks. To get from one place to another, people must acquire a second type of knowledge: route knowledge.

As Bovy and Stern [11] point out, the most universal way of learning about space is to travel through it.

This type of knowledge involves learning sequences of landmarks, segments of angles and actions performed while navigating through an environment. Knowledge of the route (R) can be defined as a form of procedural knowledge. This type of knowledge is acquired through personal experience in a given environment, with reference to an egocentric framework, and depends on visual memorisation. It is by navigating the environment that individuals perceive and record the stimuli encountered, such as landmarks, location of landmarks, relationships between landmarks, etc.

Using the allocentric (or exocentric) frame of reference, the third type of knowledge is that of the survey (S). The coding of spatial information in an allocentric repository is carried out with respect to an external arbitrary repository. This type of coding makes it possible to evaluate the distances and to judge the relative relations between two objects external to the individual. The calculation of distances and angles takes place independently of the position of the individual. Thus, it is not necessary to carry out the updating of the positions of the objects during each actual or simulated displacement of the individual. The position of the objects and the distances separating the objects composing a given environment therefore define the knowledge of the survey.

3.3   Using Virtual Reality to Evaluate Spatial Knowledge

Based on engineering (graphical computer science, real-time computation, software engineering, robotics …), virtual reality allows the presentation of selected stimuli in a defined context. For instance, virtual reality makes it possible to create environments (a city, for example) that are more or less enriched by stimuli of various forms (buildings, vehicles, pedestrians).

Building on the field of human sciences, the use of virtual reality makes it possible to explore a person's behavioural, cognitive and motor dimensions simultaneously. From a technical point of view, virtual reality can be defined as a "scientific and technical domain exploiting computing and behavioural interfaces in order to simulate in a virtual world the behaviour of 3D entities" [12]. Designed to perform specific actions in a given space, virtual environments require the use of human-computer interaction (HCI). In virtual reality, HCI is a determining element assured by different interfaces based on the use of the sensory and motor channels. In this perspective, Fuchs and Moreau [13] discuss two types of behavioural interfaces: sensory interfaces and motor interfaces. Klinger et al. [14] point out that the individual who perceives stimuli from his senses through the sensory interfaces acts on the virtual environment through actions he carries out via motor interfaces. The actions performed by the individual are then transmitted to the computer, which, in response, modifies the environment. The interfaces aim at particular sensory modalities and it is the quality and the degree of sensorial coverage offered to the user that reinforce (or do not reinforce) the immersive character of the device. In order to guarantee fluidity and a real interaction between the man and the computing device, it is important that the reaction times of the machine are similar to the updating time of the corresponding real environment.

Questions about spatial learning, spatial sense, orientation, and the like are not recent. However, since the advent of new technologies such as virtual reality, spatial cognition research has multiplied [15, 16]. While it is not possible to exert precise control over all the variables of a real environment, or even to carry out all the operations necessary to answer the questions related to a particular spatial skill, this has become achievable through virtual reality. The use of virtual reality also allows activities to be carried out in safe conditions.

The use of virtual reality thus makes it possible to replicate a study on a large number of subjects without introducing bias into the results. In addition, virtual reality captures, in real time, the activity and the performance of the individual according to behavioural, cognitive, motor and/or physiological components. The majority of the actions performed by the subject can be quantified simultaneously, precisely and naturally, without the subject being aware of it. Virtual environments thus appear to be useful assessment tools for studying behaviour and cognition in the field of space learning [17, 18].

4 Virtual Reality Implementation Tools

4.1 Virtual Environment

As stated by Champion [19], virtual heritage may be viewed as an attempt to convey not just the appearance but also the meaning and significance of cultural artefacts. Therefore, virtual reconstructions should not be achieved without following guidelines. In this respect, the London Charter states that virtual reconstruction is justified and recommended when it is the most adequate means to communicate, learn or document as long as enough information is available. Indeed, in the field of cultural heritage, virtual models used for education and learning purpose should not be confused with video games which are mostly appropriate for recreation. The border between these approaches is more and more tenuous as the gaming industry also provides innovative developments and tools able to develop learning skills through edutainment, which is entertainment that is designed to be educational.

Rhino 3D software was used as a surface modeller to build up a realistic 3D model. Detailed 3D models are composed of millions of polygons and high resolution images, making it very difficult for common computers to process them. Therefore, technical issues, such as editing time, can limit real-time displacement in a virtual environment due to the management of large polygonal datasets. As a result, virtual environments are usually modelled in low poly with a loss of quality with regard to the details, although the rendering may remain visually realistic. For the purpose of the research study, a cadastral map and ortho-photos of the building's facades were used for the virtual reconstruction of the main square. This information is considered sufficient to build a realistic 3D model since an exact survey with a higher level of detail would not increase the realism of the virtual environment (Fig. 1).

Fig. 1. Example of facade modelled with Rhino 3D and textured with picture

4.2 Virtual Head Set and Interactivity

Emerging technologies in the field of Virtual Reality are opening new opportunities which improve heritage education [20]. Within the specific context of this research study, interactivity with the virtual environment is brought off by the use of the Oculus Rift [21] which is a virtual reality head-mounted display, developed by Oculus VR initially in order to make the gaming experience more immersive, as it duplicates the movements of the user's head within the virtual reality environment.

Past research has been dedicated to interactivity within a virtual cultural heritage environment [22–24]. Recently, Fernández-Palacios et al. [25] combined a head-mounted display with a Kinect (depth sensor for user interaction) thereby enabling the user to explore the complexity of an archaeological site, and to get access to informative content. From an educational point of view, historical metadata linked to the model constitute added value for an interactive and immersive learning experience.

For the purposes of this project, the Oculus Rift is used as a unique device to view and interact with the 3D model. Available since 2012, this virtual helmet has two Oled screens with a resolution of 1080×1200 pixels allowing a vision at 110 degrees in real time. Although its first function is a 3D viewer, it also enables movements with controllers within a 3D scene by means of a gyroscope with built-in accelerometer and an infrared camera. Based on the current possibilities offered by the Oculus, the research study presents a new development for moving, changing direction and operating the selection of interactive zones.

The interaction between the user, his head set and the virtual environment is carried out by importing the 3D model into Unity software. This game engine is widely used in the video game industry and allows the animation of 3D virtual environments in real time using C # Sharps or Unity scripts.

In the frame of the research, a software application developed in Unity generates a virtual pointer centred in the 3D view. The pointer allows movements and interactions by the user within the virtual model. As such, it substitutes the traditional control devices as no joystick or hand movements are required. The pointer is represented by a red dot on the user's screen and refers to a coordinate system (x, y, z) within the virtual environment. A downward head movement between 20 and 30° of the user is interpreted as a forward moving action which can be combined with head tilts to turn left or right. The pointer also allows the selection of interactive buttons located above the buildings. A selection is operated when the pointer overlays one of these spots for sufficient time in order to reveal historical documents such as photographs and prints. Head movement to left or right is also used to scroll through the image library.

The discovery of the virtual cultural heritage environment is constructed around story telling by means of audio descriptions which give information about particular buildings. For the purpose of the study, the virtual tour is set in such a way that the user has to follow audio instructions to reach a subsequent destination. The soundtrack starts when the user is sufficiently close to his destination, in front of the indicated building.

4.3   Case Study

The city of Mons (Belgium), a historical centre and European Capital of Culture in 2015, was chosen as a case study to put the project into practice. In particular, the main square of the city is a tourist attraction with many architectural heritage buildings which give a magnificent architectural panorama from the 15th century to the present day. The city is also famous for the legendary battle between St George and the Dragon which takes place in the main square on Trinity Sunday.

A total of 10 buildings surrounding the main square have been selected for the project. Among them, the gothic town hall is probably the most impressive. Topped by a Baroque bell tower, the construction was unfinished as an upper storey had initially been planned. Near the main entrance, the statue of a little monkey is the mascot of the city. It is believed that stroking his head with your left hand will bring you a year of happiness. Along with the great theatre (inaugurated in 1843), the Hotel of the Crown is one of the neoclassical buildings on the square with the distinction of having hosted Mozart during one of his travel around Europe. The building called "blanc levrier" belongs to the gothic period and features beautiful carved stones. Some astonishing buildings no longer exist, but thanks to historical documentation, a number of them can be virtually reconstructed. One of these buildings has been studied as part of this project and added to the virtual tour. Built in 1589, it was used as a Slaughter House and occupied the greater part of one side of the main square until it was destroyed in 1842 (Fig. 2).

Fig. 2. Original drawing of an old building belonging to the main square (slaughter house); the 3D reconstruction and the current building.

5   Experimentation

5.1   Methodology

The virtual model was evaluated with 19 children aged between 9 and 12. The purpose of the test was threefold, namely to evaluate first, the efficiency of the software based on the learning outcomes of the cultural heritage of the city; second, the spatial knowledge after navigating across the city, and third the perceptions of the user after the virtual tour.

The main square of the historical city of Mons and its related 3D model was used for the experiment (Figs. 3 and 4). The test was preceded by questioning all the children to gather information about their age, their ability to recognise colours, their sense of direction, and previous experience with games and virtual reality. It was noted that only four children had a previous experience with a virtual headset while all of them were familiar with computer gaming.

Fig. 3. 3D modelling of the main square of Mons city centre seen from the west.

Fig. 4. 3D modelling of the main square of Mons city centre seen from the south.

Each participant was asked to try a demo version first in order to familiarise himself with the use of the headset so as to navigate in a basic virtual environment and interact with objects. The great majority of them has already been to the main square although this is not a frequent occurrence. During the test itself, each child was invited to take a virtual tour around the main square of the city by following audio instructions which gave historical or architectural descriptions of remarkable buildings. At the end of each audio sequence, the user was asked to head for another location, helped by directions and/or a visual characteristic of the façade. A total of 10 buildings were listed along a predefined itinerary and no time limit was set for the test (Fig. 5).

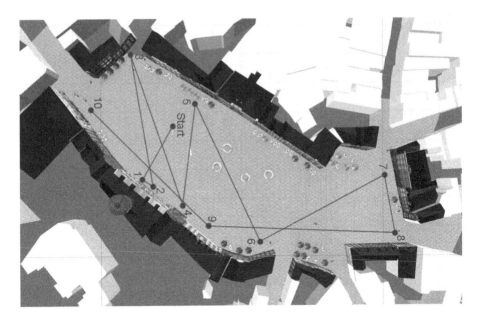

Fig. 5. Virtual tour around the main square of the city.

Immediately after the test, each participant was questioned about his mental perception of the environment and his opinion about the functionality and ease of operation of the virtual headset. The mental perception of the environment was evaluated in two steps. First, each user was asked to select the shape which corresponded the most to his mental representation of the main square from among six such shapes proposed (Fig. 6). The exact outline was then revealed to the candidate and used as a map to locate images of buildings presented to him subsequently, i.e. a total of 15 images including 4 intruders, 10 buildings belonging to the main square and a duplicate in black and white. He was then asked whether each image of a building belongs to the virtual tour, and if so, what was its name and its location on the map. Finally, could the child quote any information it heard about it.

Fig. 6. Alternative proposal for the presumed shape of the main square of the city.

5.2   Learning Outcomes

Two of the 19 participants were removed to establish the results of the test. One withdrew from the experiment very quickly because she was not well, and the other was clearly not serious and gave wrong answers on purpose. The recognition rate of the exact shape of the main square, basically constituted by the combination of two rectangles, is six of seventeen (35%). According to five children, the main square corresponds to a circular or hexagonal shape, while four were sure it was rectangular. Two children saw a more complex polygonal shape.

The perception of the built environment is shown in Fig. 7. For all the images, the recognition rate is up to 60% with a maximum of 100% for three buildings, namely the façade with stained glass windows, a neoclassical building surmounted by a crown and the sculpture of a monkey which is the mascot of the city. The town hall, which is the most impressive building of the main square, where the visit started, as well as the 3D model of a demolished neoclassical building received the least votes. The influence of the colour pattern on the pictures shown does not seem to be noticeable, as black and white or colour pictures of a same gothic building have a substantially similar rate of recognition. In addition, intruders were correctly identified with an average of three out of four facades.

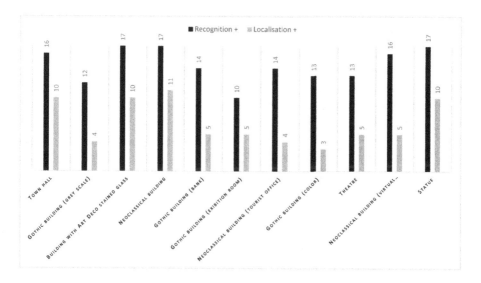

Fig. 7.   Evaluation of the built environment by the children.

The results concerning the accuracy of the building's location show much lower rates compared to recognition, ranging between three and eleven out of seventeen, i.e. 17% and 59% respectively. An indicated location is considered to be correct for the statistical results if it actually belongs to one of the six corners of the main square.

In addition, the results tend to indicate that there is a link between the recognition and location rates, indicating that mostly recognised buildings are also more correctly located. This might be explained by the fact that best recognised buildings have more characteristic features that were emphasised during the storytelling of the visit. Distinctive elements of a building such as a flag, a sign or its function also helped the children to retain a mental picture of the built environment. An image of a bank, in particular, used as an intruder, created confusion, although its architectural style was different.

The experiment was also intended to assess what the children learned from the virtual tour. All along the visit, historical or architectural audio descriptions presented as anecdotes were part of the storytelling. All this information was adapted for children, so elaborate depictions were avoided. Figure 8, illustrates the distribution rates of the anecdotes mentioned by the children for all the buildings. The results indicate that the statue and the neoclassical building are the most cited (24% and 23% respectively), followed by the main hall (18%) and the theatre (13.6%). It is interesting to note that the virtual reconstruction of a neoclassical building did not leave a mark on the children's memory (only 1.5%).

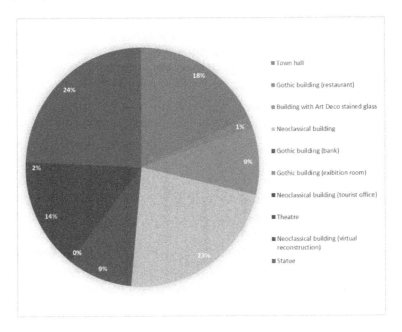

Fig. 8. Distribution rates of the anecdotes cited by children.

The difficulty of concentrating on the audio information rather than enjoying the game was also reported. However, all in all, it can be said that the virtual tour was effective in its ability to teach children, as more than 75% of the information concerned the most important buildings.

5.3   Perceptions and Functionality Test

More than 70% of the children found the virtual environment very realistic because of its level of detail that reproduces the reality of the main square environment. On this point, it was interesting to note the remaining habits of natural responses when the users interact with their arms to protect themselves from collisions with walls or urban furnishings or try to catch artefacts.

Almost 60% of the children had no difficulty using the virtual headset and its pointer to interact and navigate in the 3D environment while the rest of the group found it easy enough with sufficient practice.

The great majority of the users stood during the test. Almost half of them did not lose their balance, but the others could hardly stand at least during the first minutes, while two children had to sit down on a chair which they found more comfortable.

6   Conclusion

This research presents recent achievements in the field of virtual reality and cultural heritage learning. Oculus Rift is used as a unique device to interpret user's head movements, allowing real-time interactions with a realistic 3D model. In this context, the virtual model is considered as a support for information by means of a virtual tour with audio descriptions of the historical city center of Mons (Belgium). This virtual experience was assessed through the spatial representation of the virtual built environment and learning outcome of young users.

Results indicate that a 3D model of the main square constitutes a relevant support for exploring cultural heritage while its realism a user frendly interface reinforces the immersive experience. The use of Oculus Rift as a tool to operate visual selections and navigate within a virtual environment proved its effectiveness for the great majority of users. In addition, it was also reported that interacting with the environment by using head movements is very easy and natural while it also expands the feeling of reality.

The possible benefit of a virtual tour was also examined in the scope of spatial cognition and learning space. The spatial representation of the virtual built environment was evaluated through the mental map depiction of users and the recognition of landmarks. About the mental map, the results showed that few children succeed in determining the shape of the great square. This is due to the changement of spatial frame of reference. Indeed, the child has navigating on the main square using an egocentric frame of reference while the task required (recognition of the shape of the main square) presupposes an allocentric frame of reference. About the landmarks, the tests reveal that the great majority of children correctly identifies and localizes the historical buildings but also recognize intruders, although all of them present similar architectural characteristics compared to city buildings. In addition, it is interesting to note that children also withhold most tourist information given through audio descriptions. Although, it was also observerved that visual details concerning buildings and their architecture play an important role compared to historical facts. This may be explained by the young ages of the users. In addition, it was also reported that the virtual tour was so realistic and impressive that it may also disturb the user's concentration.

In view of these preliminary results, a virtual and realistic environment combined with virtual headset may provide an added value compared to traditional tourist web sites. Such a tool seems relevant to explore and learn about the cultural heritage values of sites. In addition, such innovation could allow people to remotely discover historical sites through virtual environments with a reinforced immersive experience. Future research will cover the assesment of the project with older people such as students with architectural and historical backgrounds. In addition such experience might be also evaluated with people with sensory-motor handicap in order to discuss possible benefit offered by the developments of this research.

References

1. Neisser, U.: Cognition and Reality: Principles and Implications of Cognitive Psychology. WH Freeman and Company, New York (1976)
2. Péruch, P., Corazzini, L.: Se déplacer et naviguer dans l'espace. In: Fuchs, P., Moreau, G., Berthoz, A., Vercher; J.-L. (eds.) Le traité de la réalité virtuelle, vol. 1, pp. 189–204. Les Presses des Mines de Paris, Paris (2006)
3. Lynch, K.: The Image of the City. MIT Press, Cambridge (1960)
4. Hart, T., Moore, G.: The development of spatial cognition: a review. In: Downs, R., Stea, D. (eds.) Image and Environment, pp. 246–288. Aldine Press, Chicago (1973)
5. Barkowsky, T., Freksa, C.: Transregional collaborative research center SFB/TR 8 spatial cognition: reasoning - action - interaction. In: Proceedings of EuroCogSci 2003, pp. 453–458. Lawrence Erlbaum, Mahwah (2003)
6. Freksa, C.: Spatial cognition an AI perspective. In: Proceedings of ECAI 2004. IOS Press, Amsterdam (2004)
7. Depeau, S.: De la représentation sociale à la cognition spatiale. Revue Travaux et Documents de l'UMR ESO 25, 7–17 (2006)
8. Thorndyke, P., Hayes-Roth, B.: Differences in spatial knowledge acquired from maps and navigation. Cogn. Psychol. 14, 560–589 (1982)
9. Vinson, N.: Design guidelines for landmarks to support navigation in virtual environments. In: Proceedings of CHI 1999 Conference, CHI, Pittsburgh (1999)
10. Darken, R., Allard, T., Achille, L.: Spatial orientation and wayfinding in large-scale virtual spaces. Presence Teleop. Virtual Environ. 8(6), 3–6 (1999)
11. Bovy, P., Stern, E.: Route Choice: Wayfinding in Transport Networks. Studies in Operational Regional Science. Springer, Dordrecht (1990). https://doi.org/10.1007/978-94-009-0633-4
12. Arnaldi, B., Fuchs, P., Guitton, P.: Les applications de la réalité virtuelle – Présentation des applications de la réalité. In: Fuchs, P. (ed.) le Traité de la réalité virtuelle, vol. 4, pp. 16–23. Presses de l'Ecole des Mines, Paris (2006)
13. Fuchs, P., Moreau, G.: Le traité de la réalité virtuelle. Presse de l'Ecole des Mines de Paris, Paris (2003)
14. Klinger, E., Marie, R.-M., Fuchs, P.: Réalité virtuelle et sciences cognitives Applications en psychiatrie et neuropsychologie. Cognito 3(2), 1–31 (2006)
15. Farran, E., Cranwell, M., Alvarez, J., Franklin, A.: Colour discrimination and categorisation in williams syndrome. Res. Dev. Disabil. 34, 3352–3360 (2013)
16. Wallet, G., Sauzéon, H., Larrue, F., N'Kaoua, B.: Virtual/real transfer in a large-scale environment: impact of active navigation as a function of the viewpoint displacement effect and recall tasks. In: Advances in Human-Computer Interaction, pp. 1–7 (2013)
17. Duroisin, N.: Quelle place pour les apprentissages spatiaux à l'école ? Etude expérimentale du développement des compétences spatiales des élèves âgés de 6 à 15 ans. Thèse de doctorat. Presses de l'Université de Mons, Belgique (2015)

18. Duroisin, N., Demeuse, M.: Impact of the spatial structuring of virtual towns on the navigation strategies of children aged 6 to 15 years old. PsychNol. J. **13**(1), 75–99 (2015)

19. Champion, E.: Entertaining the similarities and distinctions between serious games and virtual heritage projects. Entertain. Comput. **14**, 67–74 (2016). Nakatsu, R., Rauterberg, M. (eds.)

20. Mendoza, R., Baldiris, S., Fabregat, R.: Framework to heritage education using emerging technologies. In: Agresti, W., Aje, J.O., Baek, S., Bojanova, I., Bouthillier, F., Cantú Ortiz, F.J., Carswell, A., Casas, I., Darkazalli, G., Edmonds, E.A., Ghezzi, C., Khan, R., Koval, M., Levy, M., Lin, B., McCarthy, R.V. (eds.) International Conference on Virtual and Augmented Reality in Education (2015). Procedia Comput. Sci. **75**, 239–249. https://doi.org/10.1016/j.procs.2015.12.244

21. Goradia, I., Doshi, J., Kurup, L.: A review paper on Oculus Rift & Morpheus. Int. J. Curr. Eng. Technol. **4**(5) (2014). Mhatre, D. (eds.). https://scholar.google.com/scholar?q=Goradia%2C%20I.%2C%20Doshi%2C%20J.%2C%20Kurup%2C%20L.%3A%20A%20Review%20Paper%20on%20Oculus%20Rift%20%26%20Project%20Morpheus

22. Fernández-Palacios, B.J., Nex, F., Rizzi, A., Remondino, F.: ARCube-the augmented reality cube for archaeology. Archaeometry **57**(S1), 250–262 (2014). https://doi.org/10.1111/arcm.12120. Reiche, I., Walton, M., Artioli, G., Batt, C. (eds.)

23. Barceló, J.A.: Visualizing what might be. An introduction to virtual reality in archaeology visualizing archaeological data. In: Barcelo, J.A., Forte, M., Sanders, D. (eds.) Virtual Reality in Archaeology, pp. 9–36. Archeo Press, Oxford (2000)

24. Papagiannakis, G., Schertenleib, S., O'Kennedy, B., Arevalo-Poizat, M., Magnenat-Thalmann, N., Stoddart, A., Thalmann, D.: Mixing virtual and real scenes in the site of ancient Pompeii. Comput. Animat. Virtual Worlds **16**(1), 11–24 (2005). https://doi.org/10.1002/cav.53. Magnenat Thalmann, N., Thalmann, D. (eds.)

25. Fernández-Palacios, B.J., Morabito, D., Remondino, F.: Access to complex reality-based 3D models using virtual reality solutions. J. Cult. Herit. **23**, 40–48 (2017). https://doi.org/10.1016/j.culher.2016.09.003. Tomasin, P. (ed.)

3D Visualisation of a Woman's Folk Costume

Tanja Nuša Kočevar, Barbara Naglič, and Helena Gabrijelčič Tomc[(✉)]

Department of Textiles, Graphic Arts and Design, Faculty of Natural Sciences and Engineering,
University of Ljubljana, Ljubljana, Slovenia
helena.gabrijelcic@ntf.uni-lj.si

Abstract. This paper presents the 3D-modelling process and visualisation of a woman's folk costume from the Gorenjska region. In order to create a realistic 3D visualisation of the clothing, a real dress was modelled and a thorough examination of all the patterns was conducted. The 3D visualisation was completed using Blender, which is an open source software program for 3D computer graphics.

All parts of the costume were modelled on a virtual female body, and the complexity of the garment's pattern required the 3D modelling process to be very precise. In order to render the costume realistically, a very accurate texturing process was required, which follows the modelling process. The computer generated materials were cotton, linen, wool and brocade. Our goal was to present real materials that showed some signs of deterioration. Therefore, photographs and scans were taken for the purpose of digitalising the real textures.

The cloth used for the shirt *(rokavci)*, is a cotton fabric in plain weave that is visibly porous. In order to create a realistic 3D visualisation of this kind of fabric, it is vital that image data is taken for the pores and that the porous structure is extracted precisely from the raw photograph. We therefore researched and established the workflow for porous texture preparation and for creation of an alpha map. The results revealed the importance of lighting when the photograph was taken for the quality of the image data. It was also established that the optimal method for preparing the alpha map for visualising the analysed woven fabric was by manually defining the histogram threshold.

Keywords: 3D visualisation · 3D modelling · Gorenjska folk costume
Image analysis · Alpha map · Woven fabric porosity

1 Introduction

Cultural heritage is one of the most important ways for a nation, region or country to express its identity in terms of its origin, history and culture. A very broad concept, it includes tangible and intangible phenomena such as food, drink, architecture, interiors and clothes, on the one hand, but also tradition, music, rituals, customs, poetry, tales and dancing on the other. Textiles and clothes are very representative of the nation and society concerned, as they express the social status of a group and individuals and represent the characteristic of a region and local environment. The preservation and representation of cultural heritage is crucial due to its direct and subliminal impact on

© Springer International Publishing AG, part of Springer Nature 2018
M. Ioannides (Ed.): ITN-DCH 2017, LNCS 10605, pp. 304–323, 2018.
https://doi.org/10.1007/978-3-319-75826-8_25

modern humans, which through the help of cultural heritage can help us better understand all the layers of life, including habits, behavioural patterns and ethical and moral directions. This is why it is vital for national, regional and local stability that a respectful and positive relationship with cultural heritage is maintained; however, this tends to present difficulties owing to the strong influences associated with globalisation and our tendency as a species to constantly introduce novelty and change in our lives. Nevertheless, the intertwining of tradition and modernity can also work well and result in better lifestyle guidelines for a society.

Slovenian folklore groups present Slovene culture and its origins through dance, song, music and the telling of tales, all of which are accompanied by the appropriate costumes (costumography). Although, some of the most well-known Slovene folklore groups focus on more modern approaches to delivering folk tradition [1, 2] (excessive artistic interference can also cause a deviation from the primary mission of the tradition), many experts insist on adhering to traditional activities to develop and maintain society's awareness of the main goal of the folklore groups – to preserve and disseminate knowledge about folk tradition. Here, note should be made that folklore groups are not alone when it comes to piquing interest, especially the curiosity of young people; museums, galleries and educational organisations also have a key role to play. The development and establishment of 3D technologies in this area changed the way cultural heritage was documented, interpreted and presented, resulting in more possibilities and new-media based applications that were more successful. In addition to 3D scanning and 3D printing, 3D computer graphics and computer-generated visualisations are optimal for implementations in interactive media and targeting users for the purpose of creating an excellent user experience [3].

1.1 Folk Costume, Attire

The term 'folk costume' (used in folklore groups) defines the replica and reproduction of original clothes, so called attires, and usually dates back to the 19th or early 20th centuries. These costumes are mostly produced by using photographs, texts or images that are representative of the clothing culture of a defined period from the past. Since the 19th century, many museums and personal collections have preserved various pieces of folk costumes and also whole sets of attires [4] which, through the functionality and aesthetics of the clothes themselves, represent a specific region, location, province or nation. However, the general term 'folk costume' is not sufficiently defined where there is a need for analysis, study and reproduction. Other meaning adjectives used to provide detail for the costumes would be: arts and crafts, working, country, etc. [5].

In the past, some significant factors were crucial for the development and production of costumes; one example would be the historic circumstances that played an important role in the accessibility of the defined materials in the Slovene region. The accessibility of the materials defined (more expensive and prestigious) and their implementation in clothes was an indicator of that person's social class.

In the 18th century, three types of folk costume emerged (which was not an independent country at that time): these were Alpine, Pannonian and Mediterranean, all of which are presented in Fig. 1 next to the treemap chart of Slovene folk costumes [6].

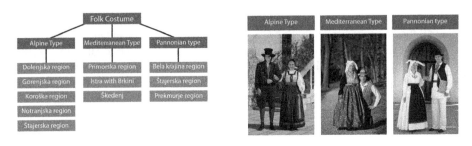

Fig. 1. Treemap and presentation of the three main types of folk costumes (with their subtypes) in the Slovene region [6, 8]

There were no major differences between the three folk costumes. Moreover, each type also incorporated variations according to the gender, age, purpose, social class and affluence of the wearer. Furthermore, the variations between the costumes in different regions and even different towns also included differences in the cloth's appearance and details [7].

1.2 National Costume

The national costume emerged in the 1860s and started to be worn by the towns' residents in order to express a sense of belonging to the nation. It developed at the same time as national public reading rooms started springing up in those towns. Although the costume's primary characteristics were taken from the original Alpine costume, its accessories reflected the bourgeois influences over local and regional traditions. The clothes of different classes started to become more standardised, which became clear during various meetings and celebrations. The country's citizens were loath to neglect their traditional costumes, which were also considered to express nationality. Regardless of the context of its occurrence (in the sense that this costume is a non-authentic representation), the influence and meaning of the national costume of the Slovene region persists, particularly for special occasions, with individuals choosing to dress in national costume for the purpose of expressing their belonging to the nation. Moreover, this type of costume is still subject to gradual aesthetic and constructional changes [5, 8].

Nevertheless, it is clear that the national costume does not represent the authentic clothing worn by the local country people in the 19th century (Fig. 2).

Fig. 2.   Slovene national costume [8]

1.3   Women's Alpine Folk Costume from the Region of Rateče

The women's Alpine folk costume features more components. The main part is a dress from woollen skirt and the upper part, bra made from brocade. The bra is sewed with a cotton or velvet band, while the lower part of the skirt is decorated with silk ribbon. The representative part of the dress is also a linen, cotton or, more rarely, silk apron [8].

The extremely draped and voluminous form of the women's traditional dress from the region of Rateče town is particularly distinctive, since it also features a connecting joint or sorts and a decorative belt (in different materials) with a bow.

In Slovene dialect, a shirt with voluminous sleeves is referred to as *rokavci*. *Rokavci* are made from white cotton fabric and plain weave and peep out from under the dress. They are embroidered and decorated with blue coloured shoulder decorations, called also *pirkelci* (a typical decoration on shirt sleeves and always coloured blue) presented in Fig. 3.

Fig. 3. *Pirkelci* – blue shoulder decorations on women's *rokavci* shirts [8] (Color figure online)

1.3.1 Underwear

Under the dress, there are one or more under skirts that were also voluminous, starched and hemmed with laces. These underskirts are referred to in dialect as *untre* and, although coloured on occasion, were usually white. The length and volume of the dress were indicative of social standing and affluence; therefore the poorer girls and woman sewed and used what are known as *golj'fivce* (best translated as "cheating" underskirts), which were shorter and less abundant underskirts that required less material but still gave the impression of a wider and luxurious skirt and lower-part of the dress.

In the Alpine region, the socks worn were normally red, while the leather ankle boots featured a low, thick and dark coloured heel. In some cases, leather boots were worn

 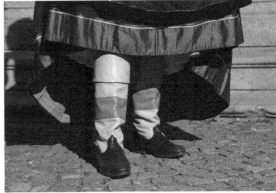

Fig. 4. Underskirt of Alpine women folk costume from Rateče and replica of the boots from the first half of the 19th century [8] (Color figure online)

instead of shoes (presented in Fig. 4). For the female folk costumes from the region of Rateče, the socks were white with a typical bump structure with a red garter in the upper part.

1.3.2   Hair-Cut and Headpieces

The difference between married and unmarried women was also expressed through hairstyles and headpieces. Unmarried woman wore long plaits with interlaced colourful strips that rested on the back. The plaits were usually tied together with red and black strips. When the women reached a certain age, they were required to wear a headpiece, i.e. a headscarf called a *zavijačka* (Fig. 5), which is a wide wrapping band with a black velvet textile structure in the forehead part that is referred to as the *čelnik*.

Fig. 5. Bonnet (left) and tightened headpiece above the *zavijačka* for the winter season (right) [8] (Color figure online)

Married women were not allowed to have untightened plaits; their plaits had to be fastened beside their head. The plaits were modelled in buns, wreaths, figures-of-eight and were wrapped through brass rings. In some cases, bonnets were also used [5, 7].

1.4   3D Technologies in the Preservation and the Presentation of Textile Cultural Heritage

The presentations of cultural heritage pose many challenges to researchers, as they need to be not only accurate in terms of documenting the facts about the object of interest but also attractive, interactive and engaging regarding the user experience. Due to the high levels of saturation we experience with visual messages in our everyday lives, users are becoming increasingly critical in their choices about what they want to see and interact with. When it comes to the documentation, interpretation and presentation of cultural heritage, this requirement was satisfied through the introduction of 3D technologies that are better at fulfilling all the requirements of the professional field; however, the users still present several challenges that can be categorised as follows [3]: 1. acquisition of virtual data, 2. geometric description, 3. organisation of data and metadata; 4. presentation and display of 3D cultural heritage objects; 5. implementation of interactivity; 6. supporting professionals in accessing data for research and study and 7. the interchangeability of the data from virtual to physical, i.e. the reconstruction of digitally acquired 3D cultural heritage objects with 3D printing technologies.

3D technologies have been applied in cultural heritage with increasing frequency, usually for the purpose of archiving data, providing support for conservation-restoration interventions, support for object reconstructions, cultural heritage management, the creation of virtual collections and museums and for interpretations of heritage in the form of scale models, visualisations and 3D printing models intended for education, promotion and popularisation [9, 10]. In Fig. 6, the workflow is presented for the acquisition and 3D interpretation of Snežnik castle, located in the southwest part of the Lož Valle in the municipality of Loška Dolina (Slovenia) that was implemented as part of the project titled Student Innovative Projects for Social Benefit 2016–2018 (financially supported by the Public Scholarship, Development, Disability and Maintenance Fund of the Republic of Slovenia) in the region of Loška Dolina (Slovenia). The castle dates back to the 13th century and was reconstructed in the second half of the 19th century, so that the interior parts date from this period. The castle features a defensive wall, a placement in natural rock, castle estates, various meadows, a tree-lined lane of chestnut and linden trees and two artificial lakes.

3D technologies are also pivotal for the documentation, virtual preservation and interpretation of textile cultural heritage since it is rare for ancient cloth and textiles to be observed on a live human body. Owing to the specific visual, textural, compositional and dynamic properties of textile and cloth, the cultural heritage of these objects demands special attention and expertise. Sometimes the textile objects are exhibited on mannequins, but are usually preserved in archives, where they are inaccessible to visitors and other interested observers. Every time the cloth or textile is exposed to light, humidity and user interaction, it can be irreversibly damaged. With the support of 3D technologies, the quality and the realism of the representations of textile cultural heritage can remain reliable [11], especially when the computer aided modelling, animations and simulations are equipped with the tools and principles for a more immersive user experience.

The acquisition of the geometric data can be performed using 3D scanning techniques on small (smaller heritage artefacts as coins, clothes, statues, etc.) and large (for instance buildings) scales, which are especially suitable for archiving textile cultural heritage, the preparation of virtual collections and museums and for supporting conservation-restoration interventions. Regarding the cloth simulation, 3D scanning is usually used for 3D body model acquisition and further (also real-time) animations and visualisations of cultural heritage [12, 13]; however the exact laser techniques are also suitable

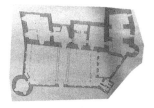

1) photography, maps, 2D sketches -   2) conceptual scale model

3a) import in software for 3D computer graphic   3b) import in CAD system – 3D modelling - mesh corrections

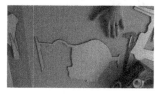

4) preparation for 3D visualisation   5) preparation for scale model

Fig. 6. The workflow for the acquisition and 3D interpretation of Snežnik castle (with the permission of the authors: Aja Knific Košir, Luka Dakskobler and Eva Razložnik)

for documenting the relief, texture and structure of complex materials such as fabric, leather, wood and their accurate and realistic reconstruction [14, 15].

Cloth and textile visualisations are made possible using the 3D reconstructions and 3D models of the object. Here, computer aided design and modelling tools and techniques have a well-established role for helping with the appearance of cloth for close proximity observations and an accurate visualisation of the level of the fibres [16] but also visualisations including colour, relief, specular and alpha maps [17].

With the implementation of interactivity, the presentation and display of textile cultural heritage objects are equipped with new paradigms for user immersion and experience. Here, researchers and developers are experimenting with the accuracy of realism achieved in real-time visualisations [18], solutions of virtual and augmented reality [19–22], motion capture [23] and 3D printing [24].

In the Slovene region, the level of knowledge about the textile cultural heritage, its preservation and restoration and the understanding of its importance is not satisfactory [25]. That is the challenge for Slovene researchers, who only in years have realised that the implementation of 3D technologies could be a great way to heighten public awareness. There are concerns about the fact that most people from Slovenia do not draw a distinction between the national costume and the folk one (especially due to the popularity of 'Oberkrainer' music, in which the participants are usually dressed in national costume), which causes confusion about "what folk culture is" and "what folk cloth tradition is". These serve as encouragements for professionals who are attempting to establish strong links between the use of 3D technologies and textile cultural heritage. The purpose of the research was the study and analysis of the ethnology of the Alpine folk costume and its 3D reproduction. The focus was on the optimal implementation of the sewing patterns of the costume in 3D virtual space and their modelling with a high definition polygonal mesh, including dynamic simulations of cloth draping for optimal visualisation of the forms and volumes of the folk costume. We were also interested in an accurate reproduction of the textures and colour effects from the 19th century. Special attention was also directed to faithfully reproducing the porous shirt material, which is a representative upper part of folk costume with evident structural deformations and deterioration. For this purpose, the experiment included an analysis of the influence of illumination (type and number of lights) during the acquisition of the textures of the shirt and the methodology for preparing alpha maps for a reproduction of cloth porosity.

2   Experimental Part

2.1   Modelling of Woman Alpine Folk Costume

In general, cloth geometry and physical-mechanical parameters are modelled as a dynamic object, i.e. a 3D polygon model that interacts with internal and external forces. The results of this methods focus on the virtual reinterpretation of the real constructional and mechanical parameters of cloth (stretch, shear, bending) and a simulation of the dynamic behavior of a cloth [26].

In Blender, the computer program that was used for the 3D modelling, a cloth is any mesh that has been assigned the modifier "Cloth" and has been designated as such. The Blender physics engine considers the vertices of a mesh that are set as cloth as if they were connected to a network of springs that could extend and contract, depending on the parameters defined. These parameters are material structure, spring damping, material bending and others that influence the simulation and creation of various qualities of a material, such as leather, silk, rubber, denim and others.

All the parts of the costume were modelled on a virtual female body. The complexity of the garment's pattern required the 3D program to model it very precisely. For accurate modelling, sketches and sewing patterns of the costume were used (presented in Fig. 7). Some details were especially challenging to construct, such as highly pleated parts on the upper piece of the costume – shirt (*rokavci*), draping and layering of skirts and also the modelling of the special head pieces.

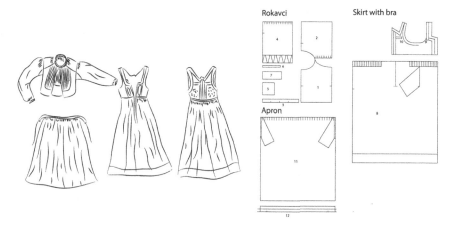

Fig. 7. Drawing of the folk costume from the Gorenjska region and sewing pattern of *rokavci*, skirt, bra and apron

2.1.1 Modelling of Skirts

All skirts such as underskirt, skirt and *golj'fivc* were modelled using a 3D primitive cylinder. The waists of the models were redesigned and the lower parts of skirts were let out. In Fig. 8 shows the wireframe view of the underskirt before the cloth simulation process was performed. The cloth simulation process for the underskirt was performed using the "Denim" material setting, while the real cloth of *untra* is a rather stiff and starchy cotton or linen fabric. The result is presented in Fig. 8.

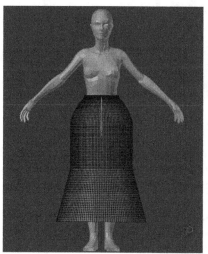

Fig. 8. Wireframe view of the model of underskirt before the simulation, underskirt *untra* after cloth simulation

It is also sometimes necessary to correct a simulated cloth model, as in the case with the *golj'fivc* skirt shown in Fig. 9. The upper skirt was simulated as "Cotton", while the real material is much softer. The skirt appears wider, while the underskirt and *golj'fivc* are hidden underneath.

Fig. 9. Correction of the *golj'fivc* model and upper skirt after cloth simulation

The upper parts of the costume, such as the *rokavci* shirt and the bra, were challenging to model, especially the small creases in the *rokavci*. This process is shown in Fig. 10.

Fig. 10. The *rokavci* modelling process

The bra is a part of the costume that is worn over the *rokavci* shirt. It was modelled using a part of a model of a woman's body and redesigned. The cloth simulation process was not performed on that part because the cloth of the garment is very stiff and should fit the body tightly. The modelled bra is shown in Fig. 11.

Some accessories were also modelled, such as high socks, shoes, a *zavijačka* head piece and a belt with a bow, what is presented in Fig. 12. The socks and shoes were modelled using a model of a woman's body. The *zavijačka* was also a challenge to design and was modelled using a 3D primitive sphere.

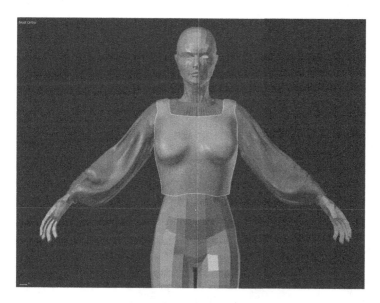

Fig. 11. Modelled bra

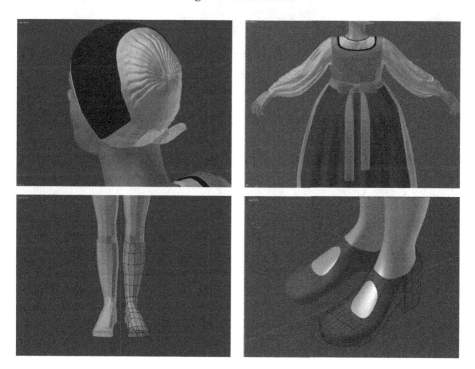

Fig. 12. *Zavijačka*, belt with a bow, high socks and shoes [25]

The next step on the path towards creating a faithful visualisation of the costume was the 3D-texturing process. All the visible parts of the costume and their 3D models were textured. Photographs and scans were used to capture realistic and accurate images of the materials for this purpose. The textures were captured using a Nikon D5200 photo camera with a 18–105 mm lens, 1:3, 5-5, 6G ED VR at 105 mm and a scanner. The colours and repeat patterns were edited precisely using the Adobe Photoshop 2D graphic program.

The UV-mapping process was used to allocate textures to the models and some adjustments were needed in order to align the images to the meshes correctly. It was necessary to pay close attention to the direction and position of the patterns in cases where the material patterns were very distinctive, such as the apron, the upper part of the costume (e.g. the bra), the silk ribbon on the lower part of the skirt and the belt (Fig. 13).

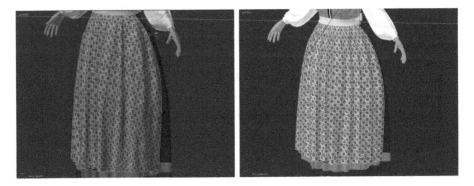

Fig. 13. Texturised apron before adjustment of the pattern, on the left, and after, on the right [25]

3   Results and Discussion

Blender's engine Cycles render was used for final visualisation of the costume in designed environment. Figure 14 presents the computer generated costume (left) and a photograph of the real costume (right) and Fig. 15 presents the upper part of the visualisations (left) and photographs (right).

Fig. 14. Picture of 3D computer generated costume on the left and photography of the real costume on the right [25]

Fig. 15. Computer generated visualisations (left) and a photograph (right) of upper part of the costume [25]

3.1   3D Visualisation of the Cloth's Details

When visualising a cloth from a short distance, more precise details should be shown correctly. Using the Blender 3D program, various maps can be randomly composed, reorganized and modified in order to achieve the optimal visual result, a realistic texture. The maps that are commonly used in the visualisation of textiles are a diffuse map, which presents the basic colour of a texture; a bump map and a displacement map which simulate the relief of textiles; a normal map - which information influences the angle of the object's normals; a specular map defines the surface areas of higher reflectivity and an alpha map which presents the porosity of texture [27].

In the case of the folk costume from Gorenjska region, the cloth that is used for the shirt *(rokavci),* is a cotton fabric in plain weave and is visibly porous. When the pores between the threads in a fabric are open sufficiently enough they reveal a material that lies underneath. It is therefore necessary that the visual character of the porous materials is visualised precisely while it influences the overall appearance of a rendered object. The size and shape of the pores between the warp and weft threads of the *rokavci* are also very uneven, while the garment is deteriorated and has visible irregularities. In order to create a realistic 3D visualisation of deteriorated cloth, it is vital that a very large sample surface is used as the basis for recording the data. As a method for the visualisation of uneven structures and the deformation of cloth that are time-dependent, it is certainly the most appropriate.

In our research, we analysed and established nature of the workflow for porous texture preparation for creation of alpha maps [28–31].

Visual information was gathered by photographing the back side of the *rokavci*. The cotton fabric is woven in plain weave with density of warp that is 20 threads/cm and weft, 15 threads/cm and Z twist of warp and weft threads.

The image acquisition was performed in a photo studio at the Department of Textiles, Graphic Arts and Design (Faculty of Natural Sciences and Engineering, University of Ljubljana). For the photographing Nikon camera was used (105 mm). For determining the optimal lighting conditions for photographing, the fabric was photographed at 7 different lighting schemes, where combinations of diffuse lighting from left and right direction and direct lightning was used in settings and combinations (of diffuse and direct lights) [25]: sample 1. right and left diffuse; sample 2. right diffuse; sample 3. left diffuse; sample 4. right diffuse and direct; sample 5. left diffuse and direct; sample 6. right and left diffuse and direct and sample 7. direct light.

The light characteristics were: power 1000 W, type IFF Q 1250, manufacturer OSRAM. Diffuse illumination was obtained using the light diffuser Softbox. The samples of dimensions 1500×1500 px were extracted from the middle parts of the original .raw images and converted into the lossless format .tif. Images were converted into grayscale mode. and histograms were created with an application for image analysis Image J to obtain corresponding information for an alpha map definition. For the purpose of further image analysis, image areas of interest were defined using the method of image segmentation, the threshold, where a grayscale image was transformed into a binary.

Using the ImageJ application, we tested three various thresholding methods for image processing in order to obtain the optimal alpha map - an image of a porous structure for 3D visualisation. Those methods were: thresholding with algorithm Yen [32, 33], the method for defining the local minimum between histogram peaks and the method with the manual (visual) definition of the threshold. In Fig. 16, visualisation of fabric samples that were photographed with diffuse or with direct light are presented. Alpha maps of them were defined using the aforementioned of histogram thresholding methods. In Fig. 17 comparison of number of pores, average pore size and area covered by pores of woven fabric samples differently illuminated and analysed with three different methods of histogram thresholding.

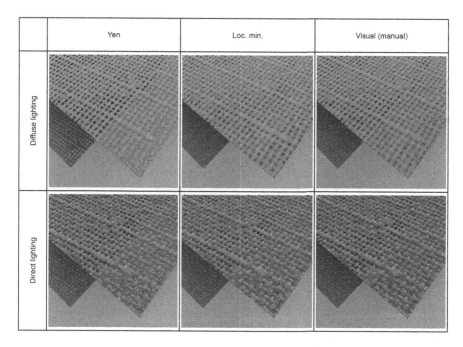

Fig. 16. Visualisation of fabric samples that were photographed with diffuse or with direct light and thresholding techniques: Yen, Local minimum and visual (manual)

Figure 17 shows that the average size of the pores and the area covered by them are greatest when a threshold is set with a Yen algorithm and smallest when set with a local minimum.

When thresholding images using the Local Minimum Method, the results for the average size of the pores and the area covered by them reveal a trend of smaller average pore sizes and smaller areas covered with pores at samples 1 to 4 illuminated with mainly diffuse lights during the image acquisition, and higher at samples 5 to 7, illuminated with only direct light (sample 7) or in combination with diffuse lights (samples 5 and 6).

When preparing porosity maps for the visualisation of woven fabrics, special attention should also be devoted to the formation of connected and closed pores in the map for porosity. The connected pores are treated as erroneous, since this phenomenon cannot exist in real fabric, whereas closed pores can also occur in real fabric. These connected and closed pores are presented in Fig. 18.

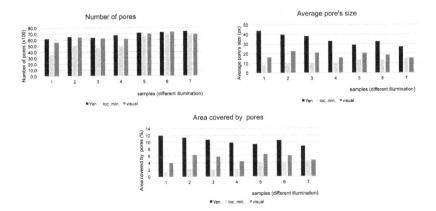

Fig. 17. Comparison of number of pores (a), average pore size (b) and area covered by pores (c) of woven fabric samples differently illuminated and analysed with three different methods of histogram thresholding [34]

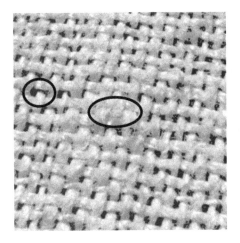

Fig. 18. Connected pores in a small circle and closed pores in a bigger circle on a 3D visualisation of a woven cloth

A conclusion established during our research as that Visual (manual) thresholding is the most appropriate method of the three analysed, while there are no connected pores on porosity maps and the number of closed pores is smaller than when a local minimum or Yen are used as thresholding methods.

4   Conclusions

The presented paper is a research contribution to Slovenia's textile cultural heritage and the presentation how the 3D computer graphic, cloth simulations and realistic static computer generated imagery can be applied in the presentation and display of 3D cultural heritage objects. The analysis presents the rich Slovene clothing tradition of a defined region and draws attention to the importance of a detailed study of the cloth cultural heritage (through a focus on details, materials, sewing patterns and aesthetics) in order to reproduce a plausible and photorealistic 3D visual reproduction. Since the results were not intended to be used in interactive presentations, focus was instead devoted to the texture and structural details and the virtual reconstruction of the appearance of the porous structure of the *rokavci* shirt. In this part, the importance of various factors in the workflow of the alpha map preparation method for 3D visualisation of woven fabric porosity was demonstrated. During an image (texture) acquisition of an uneven and deteriorated shirt structure, the area of a fabric that was photographed had to be sufficiently large to gather all the important visual data for correct visualisation (material, its pattern, unevenness and other features that can be consequences of wearing). The direction and type of the illumination also influenced the results. The conclusion was also reached that direct lighting is more appropriate than diffuse for correct visualisation since it shows more contrast, which in turn enhances the relief and specularity of the material.

It was also proved that Visual (manual) method for thresholding images to obtain porosity map is the most appropriate method among the three analysed methods while there were no connected pores on the porosity maps and the number of closed pores is very small.

Acknowledgment. Some of the methodologies and practices presented in the contribution were partly financed by the project titled Student Innovative Projects for Social Benefit by Public Scholarship, Development, Disability and Maintenance Fund of the Republic of Slovenia, Ministry of Education, Science and Sport (Republic of Slovenia) and European Social Fund. The authors of this contribution would like to thank the supporters of this project and all the dedicated participants involved (the Ars Viva institute and the students in the project).

References

1. Katalena band Homepage. http://www.katalena.net/. Accessed 12 Sept 2017
2. Brina band Homepage. http://www.brina-slovenia.net/. Accessed 12 Sept 2017
3. Ioannides, M., Quak, E.: 3D Research Challenges in Cultural Heritage: A Roadmap in Digital Heritage Preservation. Springer, Heidelberg (2014). https://doi.org/10.1007/978-3-662-44630-0. 142 p.
4. Kunaver, D.: Ljudske noše od pomladi do pomladi – Folk Costumes from Spring to Spring, Self-Publishing, Ljubljana, 144 p. (1997)
5. Makarovič, M.: Slovenska ljudska noša – Slovene folk costume, Založba Centralnega zavoda za napredek gospodinjstva s sodelovanjem Slovenskega etnografskega muzeja, Ljubljana, 110 p. (1971)
6. Hervardi Homepage: Narodne noše – Folk Costume. http://www.hervardi.com/ narodne_nose.php. Accessed 12 Sept 2017
7. Bogataj, J.: Ljudska umetnost in obrti v Sloveniji – Slovene Arts and Crafts in Slovenia. Domus, Ljubljana, 260 p. (1993)
8. Ozara, AFS. Bilten AFS Ozara. Kranj: AFS Ozara Kranj, 31 p. (2012)

9. Stylianidis, E., Remondino, F.: 3D Recording, Documentation and Management of Cultural Heritage, 1st edn. Whittles Publishing, 388 p. (2016)
10. Ozebek, K.: 3D vizualizacija antičnega Rima – 3D Visulisation of Antique Rome. Diploma thesis, Ljubljana, 41 p. (2013)
11. Martin, K., Ko, H.-S.: Virtual historic costume across cultures and disciplines. In: Sablatnig, R., Kampel, M., Lettner, M. (eds.) 15th International Conference on Virtual Systems and Multimedia, VSSM 2009, IEEE, Vienna (2009). https://doi.org/10.1109/vsmm.2009.21
12. Magnenat Thalmann, N., Foni, A.E., Cadi-Yazli, N.: Real-time animation of ancient Roman sites. In: Lee Y.T., Shamsuddin, S.M., Gutierrez, D., Suaib, N.M. (eds.) GRAPHITE 2006 Proceedings of the 4th International Conference on Computer Graphics and Interactive Techniques in Australasia and Southeast Asia, pp. 19–30, ACM New York, Kuala Lumpur (2006). https://doi.org/10.1145/1174429.1174432
13. Sénécal, S., Cadi, N., Arévalo, M., Magnenat-Thalmann, N.: Modelling life through time: cultural heritage case studies. In: Ioannides, M., Magnenat-Thalmann, N., Papagiannakis, G. (eds.) Mixed Reality and Gamification for Cultural Heritage, pp. 395–419. Springer, Cham (2017). https://doi.org/10.1007/978-3-319-49607-8_16
14. Müller, G., Bendels, H.G., Klein, R.: Rapid synchronous acquisition of geometry and appearance of cultural heritage artefacts. In: Mudge, M., Ryan, N., Scopigno, R. (eds.) The 6th International Symposium on Virtual Reality, Archaeology and Cultural Heritage, pp. 13–20. VAST, Eurographics Association, Pisa (2005). https://doi.org/10.2312/vast/vast05/013-020
15. Gabrijelčič Tomc, H., Pivar, M., Kočevar, T.N.: Deffinition of the workflow for 3D computer aided reconstruction of a lace. In: Simončič, B., Tomšič, B., Gorjanc, M. (eds.) Proceedings of 16th World Textile Conference AUTEX 2016, Ljubljana, Slovenia, 8 p. (2016)
16. Kočevar, T.N., Gabrijelčič Tomc, H.: Modelling and visualisation of the optical properties of cloth. In: Cvetković, D. (ed.) Computer simulation, Computer and Information Science, Computer Science and Engineering, pp. 45–65. InTech, Rijeka (2017). https://doi.org/10.5772/67736
17. Zhao, S., Jakob, W., Marschner, S., Bala, K.: Building volumetric appearance models of fabric using micro CT imaging. ACM Trans. Graph. (TOG) – Proc. ACM SIGGRAPH 2011 **30**(4), 98–105 (2011). Article no. 44
18. de Heras Ciechomski, P., Schertenleib, S., Maïm, J., Maupu, D., Thalmann, D.: Real-time Shader rendering for crowds in virtual heritage. In: Mudge, M., Ryan, N., Scopigno, R. (eds.) The 6th International Symposium on Virtual Reality, Archaeology and Cultural Heritage, pp. 91–98. VAST, Eurographics Association, Pisa (2005). https://doi.org/10.2312/vast/vast05/091-098
19. Magnenat-Thalmann, N., Papagiannakis, G.: Virtual Worlds and Augmented Reality in Cultural Heritage Applications, MIRALab, University of Geneva, Geneva, Switzerland. http://citeseerx.ist.psu.edu/viewdoc/download;jsessionid=7A0D2BC1D22E2617 C97FD251702DB3D5?doi=10.1.1.106.9743&rep=rep1&type=pdf. Accessed 9 Sept 2017
20. Koutsonanos, D., Moustakas, K., Tzovaras, D., Strintzis, M.G.: Interactive cloth editing and simulation in virtual reality applications for theater professionals. In: Chrysanthou, Y., Cain, K., Silberman, N., Niccolucci, F. (eds.) The 5th International Symposium on Virtual Reality, Archaeology and Cultural Heritage, pp. 37–46. VAST, Eurographics Association, Oudenaarde (2004). https://doi.org/10.2312/vast/vast04/037-046
21. Papagiannakis, G., Foni, A., Magnenat-Thalmann, N.: Real-Tine Recreated Ceremonies in VR Restituted Cultural Heritage Sites. https://www.researchgate.net/publication/228424503_Real-time_recreated_ceremonies_in_VR_restituted_cultural_heritage_sites. Accessed 9 Sept 2017

22. Vidmar, G.: 3D digitalizacija in vizualizacija situle z Vač. Notorious solutions (2011). http://mfc2.notorious-solutions.com/PrispevekGVidmar_mar2012.pdf. Accessed 7 Sept 2017

23. Strand, E.A., Lindgren, S., Larsson, C.: Capturing our cultural intangible textile heritage, MoCap and Craft technology. In: Ioannides, M., Fink, E., Moropoulou, A., Hagedorn-Saupe, M., Fresa, A., Liestøl, G., Rajcic, V., Grussenmeyer, P. (eds.) EuroMed 2016. LNCS, vol. 10059, pp. 10–15. Springer, Cham (2016). https://doi.org/10.1007/978-3-319-48974-2_2

24. Angheluță, L.M., Rădvan, R.: 3D digitalisation of an antique decorative textile artifact using photogrammetry. Rom. Rep. Phys. **69**(801), 1–10 (2017). http://www.rrp.infim.ro/IP/AN801.pdf. Accessed 9 Sept 2017

25. Naglič, B.: 3D modeliranje in vizualizacija ženske gorenjske ljudske noše - 3D modeling and visualisation of women's folk costume originating from gorenjska region. Diploma thesis, Ljubljana (2014)

26. Magnor, M., Grau, A., Sorkine-Hornung, O., Theobalt, C.: Digital Representations of the Real World, pp. 225–238. CRC Press, Taylor and Francis Group, Boca Raton (2015)

27. Dorsey, J., Rushmeier, H., Sillion, X.F.: Digital Modeling of Material Appearance, 1st edn., pp. 147–150. Morgan Kaufmann/Elsevier, Burlington (2008). https://doi.org/10.1016/b978-0-12-221181-2.x5001-0

28. Havlová, M.: Model of vertical porosity occurring in woven fabrics and its effect on air permeability. Fibres Text. East. Eur. **22**(4, 106), 58–63 (2014)

29. Kang, T.J., Choi, S.H., Kim, S.M., Oh, K.W.: Automatic structure analysis and objective evaluation of woven fabric using image analysis. Text. Res. J. **71**(3), 261–270 (2001). https://doi.org/10.1177/004051750107100312

30. Cardamone, J.M., Damert, W.C., Phillips, J.C., Marmer, W.N.: Digital image analysis for fabric assessment. Text. Res. J. **72**(10), 906–916 (2002). https://doi.org/10.1177/004051750207201009

31. Tàpias, M., Ralló, M., Escofet, J., Algaba, I., Riva, A.: Objective measure of woven fabric's cover factor by image processing. Text. Res. J. **80**(1), 35–44 (2010). https://doi.org/10.1177/0040517509104471

32. Yen, J.-C., Chang, F.-J., Chang, S.: A new criterion for automatic multilevel thresholding. IEEE Trans. Image Process. **4**(3), 370–378 (1995). https://doi.org/10.1109/83.366472

33. Sezgin, M., Sankur, B.: Survey over image thresholding techniques and quantitative performance evaluation. J. Electron. Imaging **13**(1), 146–165 (2004). https://doi.org/10.1117/1.1631315

34. Kočevar, T.N., Gabrijelčič Tomc, H.: 3D vizualizacija poroznosti tkanin = 3D visualisation of woven fabric porosity. Tekstilec **59**(1), 28–40 (2016). https://doi.org/10.14502/tekstilec2016.59.28-40

The VR Kiosk

Using Virtual Reality to Disseminate the Rehabilitation Project of the Canadian Parliament Buildings

K. Graham[1,2(✉)], S. Fai[1,2], A. Dhanda[1], L. Smith[1], K. Tousant[1,2], E. Wang[1], and A. Weigert[1]

[1] Carleton Immersive Media Studio, Carleton University, Ottawa, Canada
kgraham@cims.carleton.ca
[2] Azrieli School of Architecture and Urbanism, Carleton University, Ottawa, Canada

Abstract. Since 2013, the Carleton Immersive Media Studio (CIMS) has partnered with the Canadian government to document the West Block, East Block, and Centre Block of the Parliamentary Precinct. Using laser scanning, photogrammetry, and photography, an accurate recording of the current condition is created and translated into a building information model (BIM). This data will aid in the planning and management of a multi-year rehabilitation project that will close the Centre Block building. CIMS saw a need to take the existing content generated from the documentation work and BIM and find a way to disseminate it to the general public through digitally assisted storytelling, thus creating the project: The VR Kiosk. Beginning in May 2017, an installation containing five Virtual Reality (VR) stations was located in front of the Capital Information Kiosk, also known as the visitor's centre, where tourists go before touring the Parliament buildings. Five short experiences were available that show, through 360-degree videos, aspects of the Centre Block building and rehabilitation project that are not accessible during the physical tour. Careful selection of the equipment, interface, and style of experience was made to ensure a smooth and quick event for the thousands of expected tourists who ranged in age, mobility, and technological knowledge. The content of The VR Kiosk leveraged existing gathered data from the documentation and BIM conducted by CIMS, through this new application, revisions to existing protocols improved the transition from data acquisition, building information model and digitally assisted storytelling through virtual reality.

Keywords: Virtual reality · Building information model · Digital heritage
Point cloud · Digital storytelling · Dissemination

1 Introduction

In 2017, Canada celebrated its 150th birthday, with Ottawa, the capital city, being the centre of many additional events, exhibits, and celebrations. An increase in tourism was expected with national and international visitors flocking to the city to experience the added attractions. The centre point of an average tourist's trip to Ottawa is the Parliament

© Springer International Publishing AG, part of Springer Nature 2018
M. Ioannides (Ed.): ITN-DCH 2017, LNCS 10605, pp. 324–336, 2018.
https://doi.org/10.1007/978-3-319-75826-8_26

Hill Historic Site and its iconic buildings in the Gothic Revival style. Centre Block, the main building in the complex, is open for free public tours where visitors are shown the House of Commons chamber, the Senate chamber, the Library of Parliament, and lastly allowed to freely visit the Peace Tower, the 92-m centrepiece and observation deck facing the public grounds of Parliament Hill.

Unknown to most visitors, the Centre Block will be closing in 2018 to undergo a multi-year rehabilitation project. For more than a decade, all Parliamentary activities will be moved from their home and relocated into other buildings in the parliamentary precinct. Public Services and Procurement Canada (PSPC), a department of the Canadian government, hired Carleton Immersive Media Studio (CIMS) to help document and model the Centre Block, the West Block, the exterior of the East Block, and the Parliament Hill grounds in preparation of the rehabilitation project. The purpose was to create an historical record of the iconic buildings and to aid in the pending design and construction. During the decade-long closure, tours will no longer be available, changing how the tourism industry operates within the city.

PSPC saw an opportunity, with the added events for Canada's 150th birthday, to highlight the rehabilitation project of the Parliamentary Precinct that will close the Centre Block. CIMS was asked to help create a virtual reality experience that would use its extensive documentation and modelling material and transform it into a virtual storytelling experience to showcase the buildings of Parliament Hill and upcoming rehabilitation.

The resulting project was the VR Kiosk at the Capital Information Kiosk, also known as the visitor's centre, across the street from Parliament Hill. The kiosk contained five virtual reality experiences that combined 360-degree photography, point cloud data, building information models (BIMs), and archival drawings to tell short, passive stories that focus on unseen parts of the buildings, the rehabilitation project, the historical transformation of the site, and the process of documentation.

2   Documentation and Modelling of the Centre Block of Canada's Parliament

2.1   The Centre Block Rehabilitation Project

The Parliament Hill National Historic Site – comprised of the Library of Parliament, the Centre Block, the West Block, the East Block, and the Parliamentary grounds – was constructed starting in 1859. It quickly became a symbol of Canadian democracy and was admired architecturally for its exemplary Gothic Revival style. In 1916, a fire destroyed the original Centre Block. The building was reconstructed using a new design by Jean Omer Marchand and John A. Pearson. Construction was completed in 1927. The new Centre Block benefited from using the new technology of structural steel to allow for a taller and more delicate building than its predecessor. The new Centre Block stands six stories high with a ninety-two metre tower known as the Peace Tower as its centrepiece.

A rehabilitation project began on Parliament Hill in 2011 to improve building services and functionality. The purpose of the rehabilitation is to restore and modernize the

Parliament buildings, preserve their architectural heritage character, upgrade safety and services to meet current standards, and improve functionality to meet the needs of the present day. Restoration is currently underway in the West Block with the Centre Block scheduled to be closed for rehabilitation in 2018 and East Block to follow shortly after.

In preparation of the closure of the Centre Block where many parliamentary activities take place, new temporary accommodations are being constructed. The House of Commons will move to the West Block courtyard, which is being enclosed with a new glass roof. The Senate of Canada is relocating to the Government Conference Centre, a nearby former railway station built in 1912. Tours will no longer be available at the Centre Block, meaning that for a decade tourists and school children will not be able to experience the main feature of an average visit to Canada's Capital.

2.2   Documentation of the Building

In 2015, on behalf of the Parliamentary Precinct Branch (PPB) of PSPC, CIMS worked with Heritage Conservation Services (HCS), another division of PSPC, to document the grounds and buildings of the Parliament Hill National Historic Site in preparation for the rehabilitation. Documentation was completed using a combination of terrestrial laser scanning and photogrammetry (Fig. 1). More than 2000 scans and over 3 TB of data were captured.

Fig. 1.   Combined laser scan of Centre Block

To add colour to the points of the point clouds created with the laser scanners, 360-degree photography was completed at each scan station. After the laser scan was complete, the scanner was removed from the tripod and replaced with a Nodal Ninja – a special attachment that allows for manual rotation of a DSLR camera with a fisheye lens. A total of six photos were taken at 60-degree intervals and one photo was taken pointing up at the sky. The seven photographs were stitched together and used to add high quality colour, superior to the scanner's on-board camera, to the point cloud.

2.3   Building Information Model of Centre Block

The data acquired through laser scanning and photogrammetry, in addition to historic construction drawings and photographs from Library and Archives Canada, was used by CIMS to create a highly detailed Building Information Model (BIM) of the Centre Block in Autodesk Revit. The purpose of the documentation and model was to support the extensive rehabilitation, assist in the design and construction management of the project, and act as an historical record of the iconic heritage building.

The BIM of the Centre Block is modelled at a high level of detail and information. The decision for both the imbedded information and graphical accuracy to be of a high caliber was made with the intended purposes of the model in mind. To aid with the future rehabilitation project and building management, the accuracy of imbedded information, including materiality, source material, and structural information, is highly important. To act as a historic record as well as potentially be used for visualization purposes, the model requires a high graphical standard. The BIM therefore acts as both a visualization and construction management and design tool without minimizing either criteria.

3   The VR Kiosk

3.1   What to Do with All This Content

In late 2016, CIMS and PSPC began discussions on how the documentation and BIM could be used as a method of outreach to the public. The celebrations for Canada's 150th birthday were a perfect opportunity to create a product using the existing material that would have significant public exposure. The decision was made to create a walk-up virtual reality (VR) counter where visitors could experience the Parliament buildings and the rehabilitation project through a VR headset. The point cloud and photogrammetric data, the 360-degree photographs created through the documentation process, the historic photographs compiled from Library and Archives Canada, and the BIM produced by CIMS would be used to tell the stories of the unseen spaces of Parliament, introduce aspects of the rehabilitation project, show the process of documentation and modelling, and glimpse the past of Parliament Hill. The kiosk would be located outside the Capital Information Kiosk where tourists receive their free tour tickets of the Centre Block.

3.2   Final Design

The VR Kiosk (Fig. 2) was designed and fabricated by Dymech Engineering Inc. using a refurbished shipping container measuring 2.43 by 6.06 m. The shipping container opened to reveal a counter facing the plaza at 90 Wellington Street to allow for people to walk up to one of five VR stations – four in the front and one on the short side. The operators, located inside the container, could access all equipment from the interior of the space while the visitor was not able to interfere with the equipment. The interior of the kiosk was set up to have computer monitors mounted above the counter opening and computers stored below. The VR headsets and sensor bars were placed on the counter and tethered with security cables to prevent theft.

Fig. 2. VR kiosk at 90 Wellington

The kiosk was designed to be fully wheelchair accessible and to allow a large number of visitors to pass through. For further accommodation, the VR station on the short side was designed for easy maneuvering of a wheelchair.

3.3   The 5 VR Experiences

The VR experiences were each designed to be approximately two minutes long to provide a quick passive virtual experience to supplement the physical tour. The first four experiences were released for the opening date of the VR Kiosk on May 17, 2017 while the fifth experience, *From Yesterday to Today: Discover the Hill,* was released in early July 2017. Each story is a standalone experience that uses audible narration to guide the viewer through the graphically edited scenes. The stories are:

- **Digitization of Parliament:** The first story (Fig. 3) to be developed focuses on the process of documentation and modelling and discusses possible purposes for the work. The viewer stands in the Senate Chamber as the space gradually appears and comes into focus as a point cloud. The narration introduces and defines the concepts of laser scanning. The space transforms into solid lines as the narrator explains the translation of points into a BIM using Autodesk Revit. The surfaces of the walls, ceiling, and floors disappear to reveal the structure while the narration notes how the steel beams are modelled from historic structural drawings from the 1916 to 1927 construction, that are held by Library and Archives Canada. The experience ends by discussing how the data will be used for the rehabilitation project that will close Centre Block in 2018, causing the relocation of parliamentary activities.

Fig. 3. Scene from Digitization of Parliament

- **Peace Tower: Unveiled:** The Peace Tower, the iconic symbol of Parliament Hill, is the focus of the second VR story (Fig. 4). The experience begins in the Memorial Chamber at the base of the Peace Tower, a space dedicated to the Canadians who died in service during the First World War. The scene transitions to a distant view of the point cloud of the Peace Tower. The sound of an elevator door is heard and a small elevator travels up the Peace Tower to the next stop – the large bells of the carillon. The narration introduces the bells as the oldest and finest in North America, including 53 bells weighing in a range from 4.5 to 10,090 kg. The scene transitions for a second time with the elevator bringing the viewer to the inside of the clock face. Here, the viewer is told that the clock was given to Canada by the United Kingdom to celebrate the 60th anniversary of the Canadian Confederation. The scene transitions for one last time with the elevator and sound of steps on stairs bringing the viewer up to the highest point of the Peace Tower – the Flag Master's Loft. A tiny space covered in the graffiti of hundreds of names, it is located directly below the

Fig. 4. Scene from the Peace Tower: unveiled

flag that is changed daily. The viewer is informed they are in a space visited by very few and the narrator encourages them to look for the names of those they might recognize.

- **Relocation of the Senate:** The third story (Fig. 5) informs the viewer of the upcoming rehabilitation project and how it will affect the Senate of Canada. The scene begins in the Senate Foyer of the Centre Block and highlights the architectural features of the space before transitioning into the Senate Chamber. A point cloud aids in showing the transition from the current space to the lobby of the Government Conference Centre (GCC) where the viewer learns of the impending closure that requires the Senate to move to a new home. The scene ends with the GCC juxtaposed with the laser scan of the current Senate Chamber.

Fig. 5. Scene from relocation of the Senate

- **Relocation of the House of Commons:** The fourth story (Fig. 6) is similar to the Relocation of the Senate experience. The scene begins in the foyer of the House of Commons, where the architectural features are highlighted, and transitions into the Chamber. The narration informs the viewer of the activities that occur in the space and points out the key architectural features. The scene transitions to reveal the point cloud of the West Block courtyard that will be the new home of the House of

Fig. 6. Scene from relocation of the House of Commons

Commons during the rehabilitation project. While the narration describes the impending closure and work, the scene changes to a panoramic photo of the West Block courtyard overlaid with the point cloud of the current House of Commons Chamber.

- **From Yesterday to Today: Discover the Hill:** The fifth experience (Fig. 7) was developed and released halfway through the inaugural run of the VR Kiosk. This experience continues the narration styles previously tested while experimenting with additional effects such as greater animations, different transitions, and ambient noise. The story focuses on the history of the Parliament Hill Historic Site beginning in 1826 with the opening scene of the former Barrack Hill located on the site of the future Parliament Buildings. Historic drawings of the elevation of the original Centre Block, West Block, and East Block appear while the viewer is informed that Queen Victoria selected Ottawa to be the capital city for the new Dominion of Canada in 1857. The drawings fall to the ground and reveal the historic buildings. The scene fades to black and the narration becomes solemn. The original Centre Block appears as a silhouette lit up against a depiction of the fire of 1916 that destroyed the building. The scene brightens as the new Centre Block is built before the viewer's eyes. The last transition takes the viewer to the current Parliament Hill while the narration discusses the rehabilitation project and how contemporary documentation techniques, such as laser scanning, photogrammetry, building information modelling, and digitally assisted fabrication are aiding in the rehabilitation process.

Fig. 7. Scene from yesterday to today: Discover the Hill

3.4   The Equipment and Software Used

During the development of the VR Kiosk, many options for equipment were tested, including mobile VR and other head mounted display (HMD) options. The final equipment chosen, based on a balance of quality and price, were Oculus Rift headsets and Alienware Aurora desktop computers. Steam's Virtual Desktop was used as the software for playing the videos due to its ease of use by the operator.

- **VR Headset Option - Oculus Rift:** The Oculus Rift provided the correct balance of quality and cost. Mobile VR, the initial concept, proved to have too many disadvantages for the intended kiosk model. Battery life, overheating fears, quality of video output, and risk of theft were great concerns. Other HMD options, such as Playstation

VR and HTC Vive, had inadequate applications for playing high quality 360-degree video or were too costly. The Oculus Rift, a popular mid-range HMD, met all requirements for the VR Kiosk and was therefore chosen as the most suitable option.

- **Hardware Option - Alienware Computers:** The Alienware Aurora desktop computer was used in the VR Kiosk since it was an affordable option that met the Oculus Rift system requirements. It contains a AMD Radeon Rx 480 with 8 GB GDDR5 video card, an Intel Core i5-7400 Processor, 16 GB DDR4 at 2400 MHz of memory, and uses Windows 10 operation system. Liquid cooling was chosen as an upgrade to help reduce overheating as a result of constant use during Canada's hot summer days.

- **Software Option - Virtual Desktop:** Oculus Rift has ample 360-degree video playing applications available with varied controls and video quality. The criteria for an appropriate application was one that could play the videos at a high quality and allow all operation to be in the hands of the operator – not the visitor. The majority of applications are intended for use by an individual who wants to control the program while wearing the VR headset. Virtual Desktop provides an alternative to the standard 360-degree video players by mirroring the monitor display onto the headset. All controls occur through the keyboard and mouse keys. The operator simply opens Virtual Desktop and chooses the desired video in a dialogue box. One disadvantage with Virtual Desktop was that once the video begins playing, there is a delay before the dialogue boxes disappear to show only the video. For this reason, each 360-degree video experience was built with a two-second delay before starting. An additional concern was if the mouse or keyboard were activated during the video playing, the dialogue box would reappear. Luckily, with sufficient training, the kiosk operators were able to prevent this from occurring.

3.5 VR Kiosk Reception

The VR Kiosk was in operation at the Capital Information Kiosk from May 17 to September 4, 2017. It was well received with 31499 total views of the experiences. Due to its popularity, discussions have begun on the future of the kiosk during the fall and winter of 2017 and subsequent summer seasons.

4   VR Content and Processing

The VR experiences were created using a variety of content that CIMS has previously produced and gathered in addition to newly acquired material. All content was not VR or 360-degree video specific, but was adapted to fit the new medium and create an immersive environment. Processing of material was completed using a variety of software not unique to virtual reality or 360-degree video.

4.1   Source Materials

Source materials, described below, included panoramas, point clouds, BIM, archived photographs and drawings, narration, background music, and sound effects:

- **Panoramas:** The initial intention was to use the panorama photographs acquired through the laser scanning process mentioned earlier. However, the panoramas from site documentation did not meet the requirements for the VR experiences. For a 360-degree experience, it is important for the format of the photos to be RAW to allow for greater post processing, unlike the jpg format captured during documentation. Additionally, for a VR experience a photo must be taken pointing straight down to capture the floor; this is not required during site documentation to colour the point cloud. Due to these conflicts, all new panoramas had to be captured.

To increase the quality of the new panoramas, new protocols were introduced to ensure high precision. Twelve photos at 30-degree intervals were taken to increase overlap for stitching photos together. In addition to the one photo taken pointed up, three photos were taken pointed down – two with the tripod with the camera in two locations to position the tripod legs differently and one with the tripod removed. This allowed for the tripod to be easily removed in post processing.

The fisheye photos, in RAW format, were batch edited using Adobe Bridge CC and Photoshop Image Processing tool. The edited photos were stitched together using PTGui to create an equirectangular panorama, also known as a spherical map. For easier post-processing, the equirectangular panorama was converted into a cubic map consisting of six tiles using the program KRPano. The new cubic map was brought into Adobe Photoshop for further editing if required, such as removing unwanted objects or people. The cubic map was converted back into an equirectangular panorama, ready to be inserted into the final composition.

Panoramas were used in all VR experiences, generally as the background image. In *The Peace Tower: Unveiled* the panoramas are the predominant component showing the visitor spaces not accessible to the public. Comparatively, in *From Yesterday to Today: Discover the Hill* panorama photographs were used minimally. The panorama of the grounds of the original Parliament Buildings was created by layering a panorama capturing a foggy day in 2016, with additional imagery.

- **Point Cloud Data:** The point clouds used in the VR experiences were edited and unified in Autodesk Recap 360 and converted into a single RCP file which was exported into Autodesk 3ds Max. To allow for points to be animated, various modifiers were applied to the point cloud, such as point size fade-in fade-out. An animation was structured and rendered frame by frame using V-Ray, a 3ds Max plugin. V-ray exports each frame in RGB, Alpha, Normal Maps, and X-Depth channels, which were used to manipulate the composition in Adobe After Effects.

Point cloud data was used in all VR experiences, but was highlighted in *Digitization of Parliament* (Fig. 8). In this experience the point clouds were manipulated to gradually come into focus and acquire colour, illustrating the process of documentation. In other experiences, such as *The Relocation of the Senate,* the point cloud was layered on top of the panorama to show a transformation of the space.

- **Building Information Model:** The BIM created using Autodesk Revit was reduced in size prior to processing by deleting all unwanted elements. Next, within Revit it was exported as an FBX file to allow for importing into Autodesk 3ds Max. Texture was applied to the surfaces and, similar to the point cloud, an animation was created and exported as single frames with multiple channels using the plug-in V-ray. The scene was brought into Adobe After Effects for final composition editing.

Fig. 8. Pointcloud and BIM in Digitization of Parliament

The BIM was used mainly in the *Digitization of Parliament* (Fig. 8) where multiple layers of the model are shown, including the structure. In *The Peace Tower: Unveiled* the BIM is overlaid with the point cloud as a navigation tool to travel up the tower.

- **Archived Photographs and Drawings:** The Library and Archives Canada (LAC) has a vast catalogue of historic photographs and drawings including design and construction drawings of the original Parliament buildings and high-quality photographs of the grounds, neighbouring buildings, fire of 1916, and construction sequence of the new Centre Block. The use of archival photographs and historical drawings was reserved for the fifth experience, *From Yesterday to Today: Discover the Hill.* Using Adobe Photoshop, historic buildings, landscape elements, and people were inserted into an edited, present-day panorama to create a 360-degree scene from the early 1900's. The photograph of the fire was carefully overlaid to create a solemn scene that focused on the Centre Block. The historical drawings of the elevations of the original Parliament buildings (Fig. 9) were used as a scene change. They were animated in Autodesk 3ds Max to appear and fall to the ground from the weight of gravity. The use of archival photographs and historical drawings gives viewers of the fifth experience the feeling of traveling through time. The seamless stitching and editing of the photos to be incorporated into the 360-degree images is very effective in giving a strong sense of presence within the scene.

Fig. 9. Historical drawings from LAC in from yesterday to today: Discover the Hill

Audio: Each experience is narrated in English and French – the two official languages of Canada. The scripts were written by CIMS and edited by PSPC, the Library of Parliament, The House of Commons, and The Senate of Canada. To keep the experiences short, each scene was limited to approximately 50 words. In addition to the narration, background music and sounds were used and obtained from royalty-free internet sources or personal recordings. Using a Zoom H4n portable handheld recorder with an attached Audio-technica AT804 omni directional microphone, different noises such as elevator and footstep sounds were recorded. All audio editing was conducted using Adobe Audition.

4.2   Compiling the 360-Degree Experiences

All video editing was conducted using Adobe After Effects CS. The 360-degree scene was edited in an equirectangular format using traditional effects such as motion graphics. Once the visual effects were as desired, the composition was imported into Adobe Premiere Pro CC where audio was added. The video was then exported into a panorama format, a new feature in the Premiere Pro CC release.

5   Conclusion

The inaugural run of the VR Kiosk was from May 17 to September 4, 2017 and was well received from the thousands that visited. During its first week of operations more than 2000 visitors tried on the VR headsets and were transported to one of five VR experiences. The strength of the VR Kiosk content was its reuse of material created for the purpose of the rehabilitation project. Most of the content was derived from data already acquired and created through CIMS' involvement in documentation and modelling for the Parliament buildings. By using existing content, the virtual reality experiences benefitted from extensive work already completed. Additionally, data such as point cloud and building information models not usually disseminated to the public was given a public venue to showcase the tools of heritage documentation. Through changes to existing protocols for documentation, such as the location of the scanner for laser scanning and the procedure for taking panorama photos, subsequent VR experiences will benefit from an even greater use of existing material.

Reference

Government of Canada. Following the Rehabilitation of the Parliamentary Buildings (2017). https://www.tpsgc-pwgsc.gc.ca/citeparlementaire-parliamentaryprecinct/rehabilitation/index-eng.html

Technologies of Non Linear Storytelling for the Management of Cultural Heritage in the Digital City: The Case of Thessaloniki

Ofilia I. Psomadaki[(✉)], Charalampos A. Dimoulas,
George M. Kalliris, and Gregory Paschalidis

Aristotle University of Thessaloniki, 54124 Thessaloniki, Greece
opheliapsomadaki@windowslive.com,
{babis,gkal,paschagr}@jour.auth.gr

Abstract. Technology is currently promoting unprecedented changes in urban areas, which are often labeled as smart city developments. This paper presents the main findings of the PhD thesis entitled "Technologies of Non Linear Storytelling for the Management of Cultural Heritage in the Digital City: The Case of Thessaloniki". This thesis focuses on the dedicated digital storytelling strategies that promote active audience engagement in urban cultural heritage. A collaborative model is proposed and analyzed (in multiple perspectives), aiming at providing an integrated approach to cultural heritage documentation, management and dissemination. The model has been built for the Digital City of Thessaloniki (in Greece), a big city, rich in Cultural Heritage, but with rather poor heritage management mechanisms. The research focuses on practices that promote Cultural Heritage in the Digital City and the prospects for improvement, examining theoretical and practical aspects of engaging people for the collection and interpretation of digital Cultural Heritage (places, artifacts, etc.). The outcome of this research is the development of a new model that fuels audience engagement and collaboration of cultural organizations. A pilot implementation strategy has been employed taking into consideration different perspectives of four different target groups that included art lovers, artists, representatives of cultural institutions and art journalists. A related survey was carefully designed and executed, seeking for formative qualitative and quantitative evaluation prior and after the development of the model. The proposed model brings forward novel technological and methodological guidelines regarding audience engagement, which could be successfully deployed in cities with similar cultural, geographical, and technological features.

Keywords: Collaborative heritage management · Mediated cultural experience
Non-linear storytelling · Arts participation · Audience engagement
Crowdsourcing

© Springer International Publishing AG, part of Springer Nature 2018
M. Ioannides (Ed.): ITN-DCH 2017, LNCS 10605, pp. 337–349, 2018.
https://doi.org/10.1007/978-3-319-75826-8_27

1   Introduction

Technology is currently promoting unprecedented changes in urban areas, which are often labeled as smart city developments. This paper presents the main findings of the PhD thesis entitled *"Technologies of Non Linear Storytelling for the Management of Cultural Heritage in the Digital City: The Case of Thessaloniki"*. This thesis focuses on the dedicated digital storytelling strategies that promote active audience engagement in urban cultural heritage.

A collaborative model is proposed and analysed in multiple perspectives), aiming to provide in integrated approach to cultural heritage documentation, management and dissemination. The model has been built for the Digital City of Thessaloniki (in Greece), a big city, rich in Cultural Heritage, but with rather poor heritage management mechanisms. The research focuses on practices that promote Cultural Heritage in the Digital City and the prospects for improvement, examining theoretical and practical aspects of engaging people for the collection and interpretation of digital Cultural Heritage (places, artifacts, etc.).

The outcome of this research is the development of a new model that fuels audience engagement and collaboration of cultural organizations. A pilot implementation strategy has been employed taking into consideration different perspectives of four different target groups that included art lovers, artists, representatives of cultural institutions and art journalists. A related survey was carefully designed and executed, seeking for formative qualitative and quantitative evaluation prior and after the development of the model. The proposed model brings forward novel technological and methodological guidelines regarding audience engagement, which could be successfully deployed in cities with similar cultural, geographical, and technological features.

2   Introduction to Media and Storytelling in Relation to Cultural Heritage

In the last years digital storytelling is a digital practice that gives individuals the ability to make small, audio-visual stories about any topic of interest. However, in practice it is much more than a simple use of digital technology as it is in fact a powerful personal means of expression through which anyone's point of view can be heard and can be viewed. Digital storytelling is defined as the combination of traditional oral storytelling with modern tools (Web 2.0 and beyond) [1]. Today, Information and Communication Technologies (ICT) is widely used in the view of the Heritage project. Huge volume websites, virtual/e-museums and Cultural Heritage (CH) institutions, cultural archived documents, provide relevant information and content management and distribution services [2, 3].

The first "cultural" questions of the research which are related to the theory of the media focus on the models of communication that have been used over time as cultural communication practices and also if these models are used in modern society. In the case of a positive outcome, another question that comes out is where these models are being used.

The second important issue of such a research, is related to the impact of new technologies on the experience of meaning in the new emerging world, according to the perception of "mediation". Communication that is based on nonlinear technologies can have far-reaching consequences on how we know the world and how we perceive our position within it. Another question that should be answered is whether the models of communication that are based on nonlinear technologies can be used in storytelling that is related to cultural heritage. Hence, it is very important to make a comparison between the first media age, in which linear technologies have been used and the second media age, in which nonlinear technologies are being used.

2.1 First Media Age

In the first media age the phenomenon which was observed was the lack of feedback in communication procedures. Interaction between the communicators and the receivers of the message was incomplete to nil. That was happening because the media that the communicators were using, didn't offer any opportunities to receivers to develop their point of view related with the message of communication (Fig. 1). There are many models of communication that are based on this fact and were used in the past, not only for daily practices, but also in cultural domain. The representative models are: *Lasswell's model* [4–7], *DeFleur model of Mass Communication* (based on *Shannon – Weaver's mathematical model*) [8, 9] and *model of Katz and Lazarsfeld* [10–15]. It is observed that these models have common characteristics in communication with a few variations. Such similarity is that the communicator sends a message through a channel to a receiver. The message effects in the receiver so as to make an action. Such practices are still being used in cultural domain (i.e. when stakeholders inform people about new exhibitions of art, etc.).

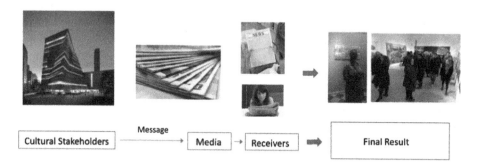

Fig. 1. First media age – limited interactions – no feedback.

But in the last years, where the Science of Museology sets up, the receivers' feedback is considered as a very important fact. Hence new models of communication that are based on nonlinear technologies take place in cultural domain.

2.2   Second Media Age

What is mostly encountered in the second media age is the change of the last stage of communication. Communication was a linear procedure without interaction, until the use of new technologies. The models that represent a new era in communication are based on interaction between the communicator and the receiver. Receiver doesn't have a pathetic role in communication, but instead offers feedback, that is very important for further evaluation and analysis (Fig. 2). Such models of communication that are based on interaction are: *Circular model of Osgood and Schramm* [16] and *Spiral model of Dance* [17, 18].

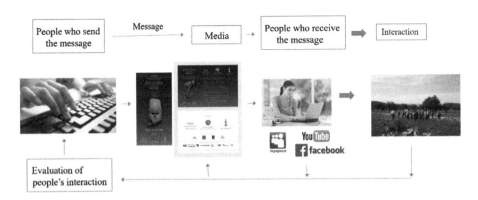

Fig. 2. Second media age – the power of feedback.

These models are being used not only in business administration theory and practice, but also in cultural domain. The feedback that stakeholders of cultural institutions get from their visitors during an exhibition help them to create and to produce content that is based on business criteria. Nowadays, this phenomenon is significant for the regular function and development of cultural institutions, museums and art galleries. Moreover, the results of such practices strengthen the museum education [19–26].

2.3   Non Linear Technologies

In the last fifteen years, the development of digital technology and the evolution of the Internet have made several symbolic goods more accessible to the public via digitization and file sharing, thus transforming the ways and costs of production [27]. Undoubtedly, ICT are broadly used for digitizing, archiving, documenting and making available digital content of CH. Related web-sites, e-museums, virtual and augmented reality applications are very common in heritage projects, aiming at offering rich media experience, even to the distant attendants (e-visitors). However, the diversity of the CH expressions and the associated digital content (i.e. manuscripts, paintings, sculptures, photos, etc.) and the involvement of many different cultural bodies and organizations create certain difficulties that are related to large-scale heterogeneity [28–30]. The problem appears to be more intense in the case of urban CH in contemporary cities, especially when there is lack of an integrated heritage management strategy supported by central CH digitization and documentation repositories. On the other hand, this creates a great opportunity for cultural organizations and individuals to collaborate towards integrated CH collection and interpretation, thus promoting more sophisticated documentation, management and dissemination ways through digital storytelling with active audience engagement.

Audience engagement is considered very important, both in terms of active participation into the non-linear storytelling interactions, as well as through the contribution of CH content (crowdsourcing). Technology can accelerate CH management, overcoming various difficulties that are related to geographical limitations, as well as to the absence of centralized CH management mechanisms for the physical cultural places and artifacts. In particular, digital storytelling and audience engagement is pursued through non-linear interaction and content contribution, as supplement to CH management deficiencies.

3 Promotion and Management of Cultural Heritage: The Case of Thessaloniki

The urban centers are marks of an historical and architectural heritage that should be protected and safeguarded [29]. The main idea and the motivation behind this thesis, is the promotion of CH particularities of Thessaloniki with respect to CH policies and strategy planning. The center of Thessaloniki is the region where most creative and cultural enterprises of the county can be clustered (theaters, galleries, museums, libraries etc.), while in the prefecture suburbs there were created mainly rallied leisure businesses (cinemas, bar). In particular, Thessaloniki can be considered as a pole of creative economy, due to its specific characteristics. Most of the cultural facilities and monuments are mainly concentrated in the town center (Roman and Byzantine character).

The case of Thessaloniki is the most suitable for a collaborative CH management model to be build, relying not only on active audience engagement (enhanced interaction, crowdsourcing, etc.), but also on the interdisciplinary collaboration between various cultural institutions and individuals. This is due to its cultural wealth (40 museums, 15 art galleries, 3 art spaces etc.) and its active citizens' participation on contests related to digital technology. In the same time a centralized (digital) CH management mechanism is missing. Summing up, Thessaloniki can be viewed as a characteristic digital-city case, where CH management prototype services can be modelled and integrated. These prototype services can be considered as a representative example of policy and strategy planning for other cities in Greece and world-wide [30].

4   Introduction to Media and Research

4.1   Research Questions

As has already been mentioned the main aim of the research was to develop a new model that fuels audience engagement and collaboration of cultural organisations. For that reason, a survey was carefully designed and executed, seeking for formative qualitative and quantitative evaluation prior and after the development of the associated high-fidelity prototypes for a cultural pilot website named Smart Project. The research questions were focused on specific issues related with culture and audience engagement. Specifically, the first question was focused on the relationship that art lovers, stakeholders of cultural institutions (museums, art galleries and other art spaces), journalists and artists have with the nonlinear technologies. Another issue that was important so as to create the website was the audience's media preference. This question is important for making better decisions of what the audience expects from a cultural website which is specialized in fine arts. The proposed answers were the web, television, radio, or cultural mobile applications. Moreover, it was very informative to ask their opinion about how should a cultural website related to fine arts be, so as to be a significant tool of communication. The results of the answers had considerable value for the design of the pilot website. This question focused on their preference in having interaction between them and getting opportunities to take the role of a cultural journalist. The last research question was related to the degree of their efficiency with nonlinear technologies.

4.2   The Sample of the Research

The sample of the survey included: (a) Art lovers who are citizens of Thessaloniki and are visiting 8 to 10 exhibitions of art per year (visitors of Thessaloniki weren't included in the sample because they are visiting art exhibitions more rarely, about 2 per year), (b) Artists who have exhibited their works in museums and galleries of the city in the last five years, (c) Representatives of cultural institutions, art galleries and art spaces and (d) Journalists who are related with cultural content in the last five years. Their selection was targeted. They were approached during art exhibition openings in the last four years in Thessaloniki's cultural institutions. 198 participants represent the survey's sample of art lovers who are interested about contemporary art and Thessaloniki's CH. 100 participants were females and 98 males. 20% are students at Universities and Technological Institutions of Thessaloniki, 21% are civil servants, 29% are private employees, 28% are self-employed and 2% are pensioners. The last group of art lovers is quite low because the ages ranges between 18 to 65 years old.

52 artists who have exhibited their work in the last five years represent the sample of artists in this survey (Fig. 3). This sample consists of 20 painters (a satisfying percentage considering that the official association of painters of Thessaloniki and Northern Greece consists of 144 painters from 2007), 10 photographers from the 58 who are official members of the two notorious unions and photography schools in Thessaloniki (*Stereosis* and *F14 photographers' commune*), 7 sculptors and engravers

(from the 36 sculptors and engravers, who exhibited their work in the last four years) and 15 artists of mixed media. The amount of artists using mixed media can't be accurately calculated because these artists usually represent different domains of art including this technique. Due to the fact that about 3 significant contemporary art exhibitions per year had taken place in the last four years the amount of artists using mixed media, is estimated between 80 to 100.

52 artists is the total amount in the Research sample who represent stakeholders of cultural institutions. 25 of them are stakeholders of Thessaloniki's private and public museums (Thessaloniki has 40 museums as already mentioned), 17 stakeholders out of the 15 art galleries of Thessaloniki's art galleries and 3 art multi-spaces and also 6 owners and 4 managers of restaurants and bars that also host art spaces.

The journalists who participate in this research represent a satisfying percentage of the journalists of cultural content. 6 journalists of television broadcast, 7 journalists of radio broadcast, 8 journalists of cultural websites and 5 journalists of newspapers deservedly complement this sample. It is important to mention that the promotion of cultural issues in journalism in Greece is quite insufficient, and that is the reason why the representatives in this sample aren't many.

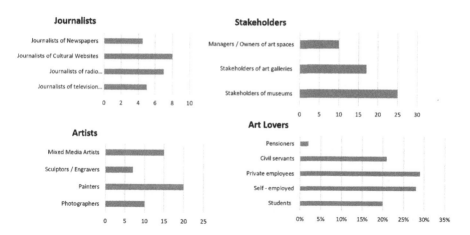

Fig. 3. The sample of the research.

4.3   The Results of the Research

The outcomes of the first research question showed that art lovers and stakeholders of cultural institutions have better relationship with nonlinear technologies. There is a concern about the relationship that journalists have with nonlinear technologies. Despite the fact that nowadays nonlinear technologies are familiar to a great amount of people and are considered important for a more interactive journalism, the result concerning journalists is not the expected (Fig. 4).

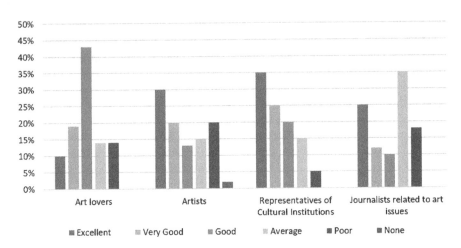

Fig. 4. Which is the sample's relationship with the non linear technologies?

The media that these four samples prefer to get informed about art issues is the same. Their first choice are websites. In a second degree, television, radio and mobile cultural applications follow the samples' preferences. Only artists prefer newspapers in a bigger amount than the others (Fig. 5).

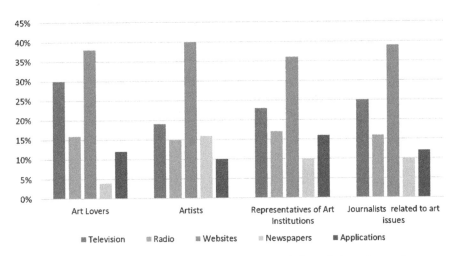

Fig. 5. Which media do they prefer so as to get informed about fine arts?

The main research aim of the analysis (prior to the design phase) focused on the degree of interactivity that the provided services should offer. The answers pointed out the needs for (a) easy navigation, (b) reliability/validity of the provided information,

(c) inclusion of personal comments and opinion articles of art representatives, (d) use of timely and up-to-date content and (e) active participation of art lovers, engaging them to establish asynchronous communications and interactive dialogues with each other. Figure 6 presents the corresponding results for the various categories of the involved participants.

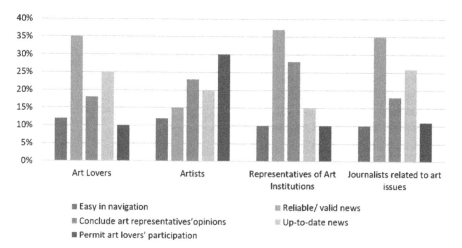

Fig. 6. How should be a cultural website so as to be a significant tool of communication for them?

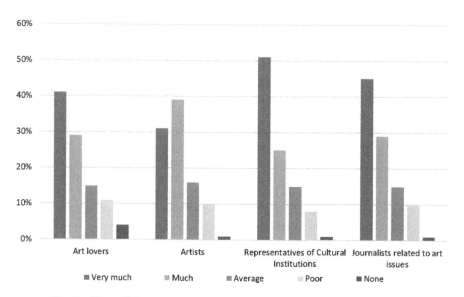

Fig. 7. How efficient are non linear technologies for the research's sample?

As it can be seen in the provided graph, while different priorities were expressed by the involved groups, there is a certain need pointed out from all the participants regarding the validity of the provided information. Equally important is considered (by nearly all groups) that the provided news should be up-to-date, while significant differences appear regarding the remaining questions. This outcome verifies the need for intelligent services that will accommodate the appearance and the content of the pages with respect to the users' personalized preferences. For instance, the sample of artists and representatives of art institutions consider that the proposed web services should mostly facilitate interactive dialogues between the users. On the other hand, journalists and art lovers prefer mostly up-to-date news and not their participation on art issues. The results of this research were very useful for the design and implementation processes that followed. It is important to mention that all the samples consider nonlinear technologies efficient enough in the domain of CH (Fig. 7). Specifically, the results of the conducted research confirms that a digital storytelling mechanism is necessary for the promotion of urban CH of Thessaloniki.

5 A Model Proposal for Thessaloniki's Cultural Heritage Based on Non Linear Storytelling

5.1 Model Design and Creation of a Pilot Website

The above attributes have been incorporated in the proposed model. Following the user-centric design principles, audience is placed at the centre of interest, both for attending (browsing) the associated CH storytelling and for more active engagement, through content contribution, commenting and tagging services (content and meta-data crowdsourcing). Hence, cultural content can be in the form of multimedia (text, images, audio, video, interactive applications, etc.), while related tags and semantic meta-data associate these media assets with time, location and context-aware labels. With the support of art incubators and technology experts (i.e. dedicated personnel of Creative Enterprises, Governmental bodies and Universities) this urban CH content is properly documented and organised in cloud repositories. The recommended architecture interconnects all the involved parties, providing networked access to the archived CH media and interaction mechanisms between them, thus integrating all the wanted services (content creation - distribution, legislative actions, provision of a healthy financial environment, continuous training and supporting activities, etc.). Hence, active audience engagement is propelled, while, multidisciplinary knowledge acquisition and know-how management practices are developed at the same time.

As already implied, parts of the proposed model have been already deployed in the design of the *SmArt Project* web portal. A fast prototyping pilot implementation strategy has been employed, taking into consideration different perspectives of the four different target groups that are listed above. A related survey was carefully designed and executed, seeking for formative qualitative and quantitative evaluation prior and after the development of the associated high-fidelity prototypes. Specifically, the investigations focused on the verification of the wanted attributes/services that were extracted by the preceding analysis, as well as in a preliminary evaluation of the usability attributes (based on the implemented high-fidelity interactive prototypes).

5.2 Evaluation of the Pilot Website

Moreover, quantitative assessment was conducted in the implemented prototypes for evaluating their usability, based on the heuristic analysis metrics suggested by Nielsen [31]. In particular, it proved that the implemented pilots satisfy the "Five-E" criteria (Effectiveness, Efficiency, Engagement, Error tolerance, Ease of learning), showing that the designed user interfaces (UIs) and the associated navigation structure offer easy learning, with effective and efficient browsing and interaction mechanisms. Moreover, users' engagement is considered to be adequately satisfactory (from all the categories) with the error tolerance to be in low levels. The associated evaluation results are presented (Fig. 8), making a proof of concept of the proposed model.

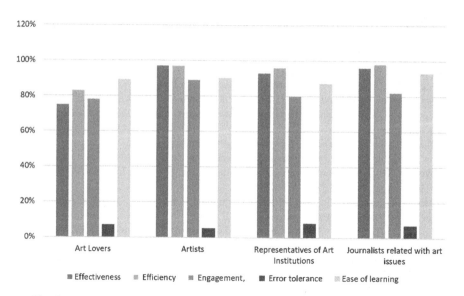

Fig. 8. Quantitative evaluation based on the heuristic usability analysis of Nielsen.

6   Conclusions

Thessaloniki has many perspectives as long as citizens will be actively involved in the documentation, dissemination and management of the significant cultural heritage wealth. The pilot website named "Smart Project" focuses on active audience engagement mechanisms, aiming at propelling crowdsourcing of CH artifacts and generally the involvement of citizens in the creation and management of new art repositories and (digital) incubators. Preliminary results regarding the materialisation and the evaluation of the proposed model are very positive and encouraging, making a proof of concept of the whole idea. Apparently, the proposed model can be easily adapted and accommodated to other cities with similar cultural, geographical, and technological attributes. A future aim is to offer this pilot website to many more students of School of Journalism and Mass Communications so as to get a significant touch with the new proposed cultural model. Another effort that will take place in the future will be the creation of a cultural application based on the pilot website's services. This application will include not only Thessaloniki's citizens but also its visitors, so as to create new tourism strategies for the city related to art issues.

Acknowledgements. This work was supported by the State Scholarships Foundation (IKY) program and NATIONAL BANK OF GREECE acad. year 2014–2015 under the Scholarship program for postgraduate second cycle studies (PhD) in Greece, which Ofilia Psomadaki received as a PhD Student.

References

1. Lombardo, V., Damiano, R.: Mobile digital interactive storytelling. New Rev. Hypermed. Multimed. **18**(1–2), 3–9 (2012)
2. Meyer, E., Grussenmeyer, P., Perrin, J.P., Durand, A., Drap, P.: A web information system for the management and the dissemination of CH data. J. CH **8**(4), 396–411 (2007)
3. Economou, M.: Museum: warehouse or live organisation? museological reflections and questios. In: Kritiki (eds.), pp. 32–33 (2003)
4. Katz, E.: Mass communications research and the study of popular culture: an editorial note on a possible future for this journal. Departmental Papers, pp. 1–6 (1959)
5. Wenxiu, P.: Analysis of new media communication based on Lasswell's "5W" model. J. Educ. Soc. Res. **5**(3), 245–250 (2015)
6. Makweil, D., Vidal, S.: Contemporary communication models for the research of mass media. In: Kastanioti (eds.), pp. 39–41 (2001)
7. Lasswell, H.D. (ed.): The Structure and Function of Communication in Society: The Communication Ideas. Harper and Brothers, New York (1948)
8. DeFleur, M.L. (ed.): Theories of Mass Communication. David McKay, New York (1996)
9. Makweil, D.: Contemporary communication models for the research of mass media. In: Kastanioti (eds.), pp. 44–45, 94–99 (1996)
10. Fragkoulis, T., Livieratos, K.: The media message- The explosion of mass media communication. Translated by Lykiardopoulou, A. (eds.), Alexandreia (1990)
11. A.I.D. Metaxas, Political Communication. Sakkoulas (eds.), pp. 41–121 (1976)
12. Serafetinidou, M.: Sociology of mass media. Gutenberg (eds.) (1987)
13. Sundar, S.S., Limperos, A.M.: Uses and Grats 2.0: new gratifications for new media. J. Broadcast. Electron. Med. **57**(4), 504–525 (2013)
14. Katz, E., Lazarsfeld, P.F.: Personal Influence. Free Press (eds.) (1955)
15. Lazarfeld, P.F., Berelson, B., Gaudet, H. (eds.): The People's Choice. Columbia University Press, Chicago (1944)
16. Schramm, W. (ed.): How Communication Works: The Process and Effects of Mass Communication. University of Illinois Press, Urbana (1954)
17. Dance, F.E.X.: A Helical Model of Communication, Human Communication Theory. Holt, Rinehart and Winston (eds.) (1967)

18. Ruggiero, T.E.: Uses and gratifications theory in the 21st century. Mass Commun. Soc. **3**(1), 3–37 (2000)
19. Communication models and design communication activities of the cultural institution "Aegina". http://dinachatzina.blogspot.gr/2013/12/blog-post_8035.html
20. Pearce, S.M. (ed.): Museum Objects and Collections: A Cultural Study, pp. 1–2. Leicester University Press, Leicester (1992)
21. Edward, P.A. (ed.): Museums in Motion: An Introduction to the History and Function of Museums. American Association for State and Local History, p. 9. Rowman, Altamira (1979)
22. Pearce, S.M. (ed.): On Collecting: An Investigation into Collecting in the European Tradition. Routlege, New York (1995)
23. Bounia, A.: The collector's voice: critical readings in the practice of collecting. Anc. Voices **1**(73), 41–50 (2000)
24. Greenhill, E.H.: Thoughts on museum education and communication in the postmodern age. Archeol. Arts **1**(72), 47–49 (1999)
25. Hein, G. (ed.): Learning in the Museum, pp. 155–179. Routledge, New York (1998)
26. Avdikos, B.: The cultural and creative industries in Greece. Spotlight (eds.), p. 120 (2014)
27. Dimoulas, C.A., Kalliris, G.M., Chatzara, E.G., Tsipas, N.K., Papanikolaou, G.V.: Audiovisual production, restoration-archiving and content management methods to preserve local tradition and folkloric heritage. J. Cult. Herit. **15**(3), 234–241 (2014)
28. Sylaiou, S., Liarokapis, F., Kotsakis, K., Patias, P.: Virtual museums, a survey and some issues for consideration. J. Cult. Herit. **10**(4), 520–528 (2009)
29. Hauttekeete, L., Evens, T., De Moor, K., Schuurman, D., Mannens, E., Van de Walle, R.: Archives in motion: Concrete steps towards the digital disclosure of audiovisual content. J. Cult. Herit. **12**(4), 459–465 (2011)
30. Psomadaki, O., Pashalidis, G., Tsarchopoulos, P.: Urban Interventions, narratives and new technologies. Presented at the 1st Thessaloniki's Science Festival, 17 May 2015
31. Nielsen, J. (ed.): Usability Engineering. Academic Press, Boston (1993)

Minimal Functionality for Digital Scholarly Editions

Federico Caria(✉) ⓘ and Brigitte Mathiak ⓘ

Cologne Univeristy, Albertus-Magnus-Platz, 50923 Cologne, Germany
caria@inventati.org

Abstract. In this paper, we are analysing the quality of use of digital scholarly editions (DSEs), via usability testing. We do a competitor analyses in which a small sample of target users is gathered in a usability lab, asked to answer research questions via different research tools, and finally to rate the experience. In our first study, we compared three DSEs and found that not all the editions are ideal in their usability and that efficiency is valued more than content. In a second study, we pitched three different media: a printed book, a digitized edition (or PDF) and a digital edition of Nietzsche *Also Sprach Zarathustra*. We found that users preferred using the PDF edition due to its higher accessibility, portability, and annotation features. This paper introduces our user research and hypothesizes on the benefit and feasibility of developing DSE with a user requirement document.

Keywords: Usability · Human-computer interaction · Human factors

1 Introduction

1.1 Use of DSEs Below Expectation

Digital Scholarly Editions have been around for a while and yet it seems that scholars are not using them as much as we would expect considering their richness in data and content. Studying Porter's surveys [22, 23], we learn that while digital tools are on the rise in the scholarly community, the use of DSEs stays at a very low level. Porter compares the two surveys she conducted in 2003 and 2016, showing that the use of journals and facsimiles in digital format has gone up considerably in the ten years between the user studies. Yet, this digitization trend does not seem to still over to DSEs, instead PDF versions of print editions seem to be increasingly used by scholars and now have a "market share" comparable to the print edition, while the DSE remains in low use.

1.2 Hypothesis

Porter does not explain the reason why this happens. It can easily be argued that DSEs are potentially better from many perspectives, but they are not necessarily better from the point of view of the user. Our hypothesis is that DSEs are more difficult to use and less responsive to the needs of the end-user, so users go for the other options available,

© Springer International Publishing AG, part of Springer Nature 2018
M. Ioannides (Ed.): ITN-DCH 2017, LNCS 10605, pp. 350–363, 2018.
https://doi.org/10.1007/978-3-319-75826-8_28

PDFs or print editions. This would help explaining Porter's findings, in that the low usability of DSEs penalizes user engagement at different levels.

User engagement is, generally speaking, dependent on a research goal and composed of diverse and interconnected parameters, which can be measured using different methods. However, we assume that scholars tend towards the medium that makes them most efficient. Thereby any problems from usability that lower efficiency will deter users from choosing DSEs over more efficient media.

1.3   Preliminary Work

From our previous findings [5], we know that users believe DSEs can be useful to their research, but might value usability more than expected, probably more than what designers – and even users – expect. Three DSE testers overwhelmingly preferred the most efficient and effective system,[1] despite the fact that it did not offer the content requirements that users *believed* they needed. Poor quality of use penalizes the use of DSEs even among those who approach them with positive expectations.

2   Minimal Functionality

2.1   A Practical Solution

The ideal way to ensure high usability is certainly to define a user group and to integrate it into the development process through structured user testing. But for those who do not have the resources and the expertise to do so, we strive to compile a list of the functionality that makes e-Books so attractive, and to take this as a set of minimal functionalities that should be implemented. From here, the idea of identifying a minimal functionality arises as a way to explore the benefits of conceptualizing a DSE that puts humans at the centre of the modelling phase.[2]

2.2   Impact

Most DSEs are developed in research projects with only one or at most two technical experts in the project team. This can be a barrier to applying more sophisticated usability methods, considering that not only the expertise is missing, it is also unknown how much applying them would cost. To give a better overview on what kind of functionalities are strongly advised to implement, we try to identify the functionality a DSE might have in order to maximize the use of editions, and also may serve as the groundwork for a hypothetical publishing system for those who cannot or are not interested in implementing a prototype from scratch.

---

[1] The only one that went through structured testing.
[2] This is unconventional, given that the majority of DSEs are currently document-centric; however user-centricity is an opportunity to rethink DSEs as a process.

3 Literature

3.1 Background

Past user studies (on print and digital) were primary sources of information.
We reviewed user studies conducted on digital humanities resources [31–33], digital tools for historians [14], and digital editions [17, 22, 23, 28, 30], most of which provided us with mainly quantitative insight. Despite the fact that the challenges that animate the digital librarian might significantly differ from those faced by users of DSEs, we have gained much insight by surveying user studies conducted on print and digital libraries [12, 15].

A further path of investigation was opened by Unsworth [29], and the literature regarding the concept of primitives of the scholarly research [21] together with research on the information-seeking and research behavior of scientists in the humanities [1, 4, 7] and elsewhere [2, 13].

We moved from Drucker's humanities approach to interface theory to adapt evaluation methods [26], in particular usability [19] in its extended version [3], to assess the quality of use of DSEs as knowledge tools.

Other authors have contributed to shape our approach, due to their previous engagement with the topic or the particular depth of their perspective. Among these are Ruecker [27], Cooper [8], Drucker [11], McCarty [18].

Four fundamental sources were behind the second user study. We moved from the results of our first user study [5] and Porter's surveys [22, 23]. Rimmer [24] provided us with a previous example of transversal analysis on the quality of research on print and digital and results. Finally, D'Iorio [10] editor of the DSE selected for the experiment, was key to understand the concept underlying the DSE to be tested.

3.2 Quality of Use

Bevan provides the framework to "extend" usability from easiness to usefulness, measured as the extent to which a product can be used by specified users to achieve specified goals in a specified context of use. We used Bevan's definition of usability as "quality of use" measured as effectiveness, efficiency and satisfaction. *Effectiveness* is the completeness and accuracy with which users achieve specified goals [3].

Efficiency can be described as the speed (with accuracy) with which users can complete the tasks for which they use the product. It is defined as the total resources expended in a task by ISO 9241 [16]. *Satisfaction* is the comfort and acceptability of the work system for its users and other people affected by its use.

An extended usability puts the usefulness of the website in the foreground, where context, particular users, tasks and environments are all important variables of the assessment (Fig. 1).

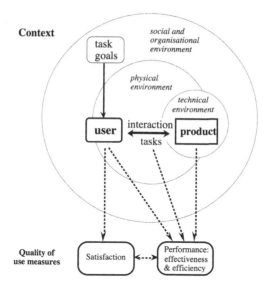

Fig. 1. Quality of use, by Nigel Bevan [3]

4 Design of the Experiment

4.1 Strategy

We hypothesized a scenario in which a DSE is an element within a media ecology, together with various competitor media, all of which offer functionalities that users may more or less prefer to take advantage of, given certain goals and tasks. Previous literature tells us that media may instead be complementary, depending on the task at hand, users both kinds of media. We simulate the research of a user in a library, or in a university laboratory, who interacts with a variety of media simultaneously to assist his queries in a given area of research. We ask the users to perform a task, and then to rate the media they used in a questionnaire and focus group discussion.

4.2 Design

We compare a print edition, a digitized edition and a DSE all covering Nietzsche's "Also Sprach Zarathustra." Our sample group consists of 14 M.A. and Ph.D. students for whom we set out a number of tasks. First, they were asked to fill out a survey with questions taken from Porter's survey for comparison, then they were asked to explore the media via open tasks, and finally to convey their experience in a focus group discussion. The tasks were timed, and the final debriefing was audio recorded for later analysis. The experimental setting consisted of a usability lab, personal computers, print books, an audio recorder to capture the final debriefing, paper, pen, and a camera.

4.3 Media

The text selected was Also Sprach Zarathustra by Frederick Nietzsche, which was presented to the testers in three different versions:

1. The print edition of Nietzsche *Also Sprach Zarathustra*, ed. by Colli and Montinari, consisting of two volumes, one for texts and one for apparatus [6].
2. A PDF-like digitized edition of *Also Sprach Zarathustra*, ed. by Colli and Montinari.
3. nietzschesource.org, edited by Paolo D'Iorio [9].

4.4 Testers

Our testers ranged from 20 to 30 years old and were all enrolled in a philosophy program, the majority in the second year of their MA, and four of them working on their Ph.D. Their computer skills were medium-high to high, as judged from their self-evaluations on a scale from 1 to 7 (Table 1).

Table 1. Demographic

ID	Department	Level	Web skills
P1	Philosophy	Ph.D.	7
P2	Philosophy	Graduate	3
P3	Philosophy	Graduate	6
P4	Philosophy	Graduate	5
P5	Philosophy	Ph.D.	6
P6	Philosophy	Ph.D.	5
P7	Philosophy	Graduate	6
P8	Philosophy	Graduate	5
P9	Philosophy	Graduate	7
P10	Philosophy	Graduate	6
P11	Philosophy	Graduate	6
P12	Philosophy	Graduate	4
P13	Philosophy	Graduate	4

4.5 Tasks

Tasks were essentially interpretative and required testers to identify recurring themes in different primary and secondary resources, and to interpret changes from apparatus to text via commentaries. Each participant received two such tasks to direct them in exploring the editions.

5   Findings

5.1   Research Habits from Survey

We reused Porter's survey with the aim of discovering, if her results applied to philosophers, and to clarify the difference between digital and digitized editions. The figures below show that our small sample is a faithful representation of the larger survey. In particular, the majority of testers answered that electronic journals and digitized editions are amongst the tools most used in the last three months (Fig. 2).

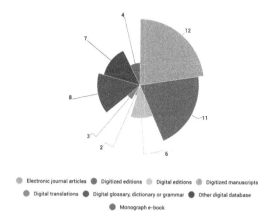

Fig. 2. Most used digital resources in the last three months.

5.2   Most Used Printed Resources

As for print media, journal articles, print editions, monographs, and glossaries/dictionaries are amongst the most used sources of information for our testers (Fig. 3).

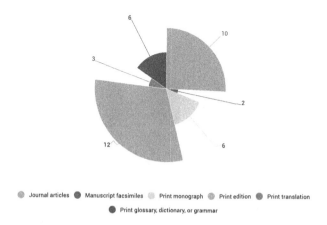

Fig. 3. Most used print resources in the last three months.

The graph below shows how testers access some of the most used resources (Fig. 4).

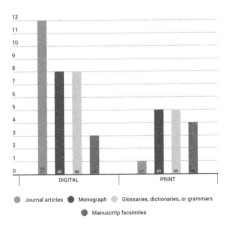

Fig. 4. Access of digital vs. print resources

5.3 Quality of Use of the Media from Questionnaire

Participants were asked to fill in a short satisfaction questionnaire for each medium after completing the tasks. The questionnaire only asked to rate efficiency, effectiveness and satisfaction of the different media, and was focused on the need to capture participants' immediate felt experience right after performing the tasks. The main results of the study are that (a) the PDF/digitized edition had the greatest satisfaction and (b) efficiency among users (Fig. 5).

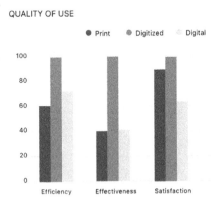

Fig. 5. Quality of use broken down by media.

5.4 Focus Group Discussion/Qualitative Findings

The final discussion was recorded, transcribed, translated and coded in atlas.ti with the open coding method. We identified functions, and then coded positive and negative criticism. The core functions discussed by our testers were retrieval, annotation, compatibility, and portability.

Our participants said they preferred the pdfs/digitized edition to nietzschesource.org, not only because of its higher availability and compatibility with different software, but also because of the inherent usability of having a "search function," "clearer navigation," "ability to annotate," and "familiarity with the interface." Participants generally welcomed nietzschesource.org, despite the fact that the majority of them "would still choose to work on a PDF/digitized edition." The PDF/digitized edition is the best choice "for long term work," "it can be always read," "easily annotated" ("or imported in a software that can smartly store and manage annotations"). "It is always available once on the laptop (or phone)."

5.5 PDF/Digitized Edition

It was unanimously perceived as the best tool for efficiency in information retrieval.

"The PDF/digitized edition was giving me my results instantly"; "PDF was faster to work with and finding the right sentence"; "one doesn't have to search your way through the page";

PDF/digitized editions offer annotation functions to individuals who are used to strongly relying on it.

"I annotate all the time," "annotate very much" or "so much that sometimes it does not even fit into PDF/digitized edition," said one ironically.

In addition, PDF/digitized editions are compatible with different software:

"the PDF/digitized edition is able to work with other programs like Zotero where you can save notes or quotations"; "you can import PDF/digitized edition documents into a program and comment them, also you've got all the comments collected then." "PDF/digitized edition is always me on my laptop or phone and it doesn't make my eyes tired at all."

It is finally portable, and readable.

"PDF/digitized edition is always me on my laptop or phone and it doesn't make my eyes tired at all."

5.6 nietzschesource.org

All our testers demonstrated awareness of the usefulness of a thematic collection, where "one gets a good overall, unlike the PDF." On the whole, as it was in our first study, the DSE nietzschesource.org got some quite positive comments due "to being good for certain tasks," which testers tend to connect with the ability to mine a larger corpus.

However, a good 70% of participants found the structure of nietzschesource.org "unclear" or "inconsistent" or "irritating," "not clearly arranged enough."

A significant number of testers complained about problems with the search function:

"It did not return expected results"; "I didn't find it."

The lack of annotation was perceived as a weakness of the DSE.

"While in a PDF/digitized edition you can add comments to the text, nietzschesource.org is missing this function."

Other comments raised questions about the benefit opening pop-ups, compared to having various PDFs opened on the desktop (Fig. 6).

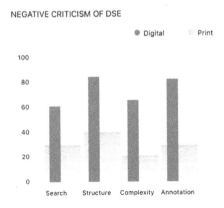

Fig. 6. Negative criticism of DSE.

5.7   The Print Edition

We dedicate a separate paragraph to the print edition, whose role in the experiment was to simulate a likely research setting. Apart from one participant, who said he worked exclusively with digital resources, participants overwhelmingly expressed their preference for print to read and dig into longer texts for close reading:

> "to gain deeper understanding I get books"; "to read the whole text"; "for longer research processes I prefer using print books." "If I need to go more deeply into research I like books better"; "In case I must read the whole text, I chose the book"; "For longer research and getting to know the whole story it's the book."

The print book is perceived as more comfortable to read:
> "more comfortable for the eyes"; "it does not distract you so much";

Books are also perceived as more efficient learning tools, which is somehow connected to annotation by hand. The theme of "haptic feeling" is deeply connected to learning. The haptic is associated with "understanding and learning" complex content, confirming the widely accepted idea that digital note-taking has shallower cognitive affordances [20].

6   Discussion

6.1   General Observations

Testers are relatively aware of the details of their information environment and its affordances, whose perception draws on several parameters, like supply and demand, but also efficiency [5], where one tool is seen as better in certain stages of the research, for particular tasks, or for certain goals. Furthermore, the testers perceived that each of the media had its own specific virtue, defined in the framework various stages of their research strategies (the book for getting to know the whole story, the PDF to search keywords, etc.).

6.2 Digitized Versus Digital

The testers found that PDF is the best solution to meet the demand for a greater range of information [33], for being highly accessible, portable, offering retrieval functions, and for annotation. This calls for some consideration. According to Sahle's theory, PDF is purely print, or something that a DSE should ideally try to take distance from. Nonetheless, given the success of PDF (and also eBooks[3] at this point), everything apart from the *page paradigm* seems negative for the DSE. One could even say that the more a DSE approximates a bi-dimensional metaphor, the more it is going to be a success[4].

6.3 Annotation

These current findings are about a DSE that is missing functionalities, which users seem to positively value in PDF/digitized editions. This may seem trivial, but it is what tends to happen when software is built without getting to know who the users are and what they want. All testers are aware of the intrinsic quality of nietzschesource.org, and they agree on the usefulness of thematic resources, yet if the system behaviour fails in meeting expectations, they look for alternatives. As a result, PDF is simply better. We know nietzschesource.org offers several significant benefits compared to print editions and PDFs. It has a more accurate text and access to primary and secondary materials, which are relatively hard to find otherwise. We also know that D'Iorio [10] has carefully developed a system to meet the conditions of possibility for scholarship, like *quoting* (which in his opinion is the first requirement to meet). Unfortunately, he ends up not taking into account functions like annotation, which do not relate to the content of the DSE, but to the way users report that they prefer processing information.

Interestingly, our findings substantiate Unsworth's intuition [29]. A look at the history of the book suggests that annotation may well be considered a key activity at least since the codex format replaces the scroll. This passage is exemplary of how constraints of physical media are inextricably linked to higher mental processes. At the cognitive level, the simple fact of being able to free one hand (reading the scroll implies that the support is hold with two hands) and gripping the pen with the other while reading (silently) can be considered at the base of modern science. Not at least, annotation boosts retention [Mueller], and an opportunity to feed back the engine or the system.

---

[3] Look at the success of the PDF and e-book, which all point towards the document paradigm having a lower cost. It shows that Nielson [1998] was wrong about e-books, dismissing them as being slower than a print book, unresponsive, etc. The delay in the success of the e-book might be due to those factors, though.

[4] There is no reason to believe that they are aware of or sensitive to the new epistemological perspective that multi-dimensionality gives.

6.4 Minimal Functionality

The concept of threshold, for which a DSE offering less than a PDF is not worthwhile using, arises from a simple competitor analysis [5], the result of which also gives potential solutions to bring DSEs to the next level of usefulness. There are functions that users expect to have, due to having them in real life. These are largely due to research behaviour and habits optimized in relation to physical constraints, like reading and writing on paper.

Understanding the nature of these relations, based on the methodology of the user, the research, and also the implications on higher mental processes, is the way to arrive at crafting the best quality of use for a DSE. We limit ourselves to hypothesize some requirements that we have defined as minimal, in the sense that they are oriented toward maintaining an acceptable level of effectiveness and efficiency for DSEs, over a certain threshold of usability where a DSE can be more useful than a digital edition in terms of functionality and use.

Implementing this minimal functionality will not make the edition absolutely superior—one can see for now that our criteria are based upon being only slightly better than digitized editions—but more useful than other media given certain circumstances and tasks at hand. Again, the idea of a general framework for DSEs seems obvious. It would require an implementation of this minimal functionality only once, and in so doing dramatically assist a great number of editors and students who could not implement this by themselves.

6.5 Use Requirements Document (URD)

Minimal functionality can be specified in the form of a user requirement document that provides guidance on system behavior without going into technical implementation details. This is a common technique in software engineering. This should include

- Search over all the content
- Comparison between different version (preferably on one screen)
- Annotation for personal use

These can be among the first priority requirements for DSE in a hypothetical prototype, to be further refined via use cases. Other high priority requirements should concern

- Responsiveness of the DSE or suitable management of loading times
- Export functions for PDF and .txt
- Navigation based on user needs

These user requirements are *free of implementation*, which means any creator of DSEs is free to use (or reuse) technology that is suitable to a given project. Most of the suitable technologies should be able to support the requirements with only a low cost in time and effort. In does not hinder the experts, who feel the necessity to customize, however, as Unsworth already noted, the minimal functionality can be seen as a goal to collectively pursue, with or without government funding - because right now, even these very basic scholarly activities are very poorly supported [29]. As regards the diversity of approaches across disciplines and cultures, international testing could help validate the applicability of the document to other media ecologies.

References

1. Barrett, A.: The information-seeking habits of graduate student researchers in the humanities. J. Acad. Librariansh. **31**(4), 324–331 (2005)
2. Belkin, N.: Interaction with texts: information retrieval as information seeking behavior. In: Knorz, G., Krause, J., Womser-Hacker, C. (eds.) Information Retrieval 1993: Von der Modellierung zur Anwendung, Regensburg, vol. 12, pp. 55–66. Schriften zur Informationswissenschaft (1993)
3. Bevan, N.: Measuring usability as quality of use. Softw. Qual. J. **4**, 115 (1995)
4. Buchanan, G., Cunningham, S.J., Blandford, A., Rimmer, J., Warwick, C.: Information seeking by humanities scholars. In: Rauber, A., Christodoulakis, S., Tjoa, A.M. (eds.) ECDL 2005. LNCS, vol. 3652, pp. 218–229. Springer, Heidelberg (2005). https://doi.org/10.1007/11551362_20
5. Caria, F., Mathiak, B.: Hybrid focus group for the evaluation of digital scholarly editions of literary authors, digital scholarly editions as interfaces. In: International Symposium. Austrian Centre for Digital Humanities at the University of Graz (2016)
6. Colli, G., Montinari, M.: Also sprach Zarathustra: I-IV. Sämtliche Werke: Kritische Studienausgabe in 15 Bänden, Friedrich Nietzsche, vol. 4. Deutscher Taschenbuch Verlag (1999)
7. Chu, C.: Literary critics at work and their information needs: a research-phases model. Libr. Inf. Sci. Res. **21**(2), 247–273 (1999). https://libres.uncg.edu/ir/uncg/f/C_Chu_Literary_1999.pdf. Accessed 03 Oct 2017
8. Cooper, A., et al.: About Face 3. The Essential of Interaction Design. Wiley Publishing Inc., Indianapolis (2007)
9. D'Iorio, P.: http://www.nietzschesource.org. Accessed 05 Oct 2017
10. D'Iorio, P.: On the scholarly use of the internet. A conceptual model. In: Bozzi, A. (ed.) Digital Texts, Translations, Lexicons in a Multi-modular Web Application: The Method and Samples, pp. 1–25. Olschki, Firenze (2015)
11. Drucker, J.: Humanities approaches to interface theory. Cult. Mach. **12**, 1–20 (2011). https://www.culturemachine.net/index.php/cm/article/viewArticle/434. Accessed 03 Oct 2017
12. Duff, W.M., Johnson, C.: Accidentally found on purpose: information-seeking behavior of historians in archives. Libr. Q. **72**(4), 472–496 (2002)
13. Ellis, D.: A comparison of the information seeking patterns of researchers in the physical and social sciences. J. Doc. **49**(4), 356–369 (2003)
14. Gibbs, F., Owens, T.: Building better digital humanities tools: toward broader audiences and user-centered designs. Digit. Hum. Q. **6**, 2 (2012). http://www.digitalhumanities.org/dhq/vol/6/2/000136/000136.html. Accessed 03 Oct 2017
15. Leblanc, E.: Thinking about users and their interfaces: the case of fonte Gaia bib. In: International Symposium, Lecture at Digital Scholarly Editions as Interface. Austrian Centre for Digital Humanities, University of Graz (2016). https://static.uni-graz.at/fileadmin/gewi-zentren/Informationsmodellierung/PDF/dse-interfaces_BoA21092016.pdf. Accessed 03 Oct 2017
16. ISO 9421, Ergonomic requirements for office work with visual displays (VDTs). https://www.iso.org/standard/64840.html. Accessed 05 Oct 2017

17. Kelly, A.: Tablet computers for the dissemination of digital scholarly editions. Manuscritica **28**, 123–140 (2015). http://revistas.fflch.usp.br/manuscritica/article/view/2430/2141. Accessed 03 Oct 2017

18. McCarthy, J., Wright, P.: Technology as Experience. MIT Press, Cambridge (2007)

19. Nielsen, J.: Guerrilla HCI: using discount usability engineering to penetrate the intimidation barrier (1994). http://www.nngroup.com/articles/guerrilla-hci/. Accessed 03 Oct 2017

20. Mueller, P., Oppenheimer, D.: The pen is mightier than the keyboard. Psychol. Sci. **6**(25), 1159–1168 (2014)

21. Palmer, C.L., Teffeau, L.C., Pirmann, C.M.: Scholarly information practices in the online environment: themes from the literature and implications for library service development, for OCLC research. OCLC Online Computer Library Center, Inc., Dublin (2009). http://www.oclc.org/content/dam/research/publications/library/2009/2009-02.pdf. Accessed 03 Oct 2017

22. Porter, D.: Medievalists and the scholarly digital edition. Scholarly Editing, vol. 34 (2013), http://scholarlyediting.org/2013/essays/essay.porter.html. Accessed 03 Oct 2017

23. Porter, D.: What is an Edition anyway? A critical examination of Digital Editions since 2002. In: Keynote Lecture. International Symposium on Digital Scholarly Editions as Interfaces. Austrian Centre for Digital Humanities at the University of Graz (2016). https://static.uni-graz.at/fileadmin/gewi-zentren/Informationsmodellierung/PDF/dse-interfaces_BoA21092016.pdf. Accessed 03 Oct 2017

24. Rimmer, J., Warwick, C., Bladnford, A., Gow, J., Buchanan, G.: An examination of the physical and digital qualities of humanities research. Inf. Process. Manag. **44**(3), 1374–1392 (2008). http://citeseerx.ist.psu.edu/viewdoc/download?doi=10.1.1.462.4222&rep=rep1&type=pdf. Accessed 03 Oct 2017

25. Sahle, P.: Digitale Editionsformen. Zum Umgang mit der Überlieferung unter den Bedingungen des Medienwandels. Teil 1: Textbegriffe und Recodierung. Ph.D. thesis, Universität zu Köln (2013)

26. Stanton, N., Hedge, A., Brookhuis, K., Salas, E., Hendrick, H.: Handbook of Human Factors and Ergonomics Methods. CRC Press, Boca Raton (2005)

27. Ruecker, S., Radzikowska, M., Sinclair, S.: Visual Interface Design for Digital Cultural Heritage. A Guide to Rich Prospect Browsing. Routledge, New York (2011)

28. Santos, T.: LdoD archive: user experience and identity design processes. Digital Literary Studies, Coimbra (2015). https://www.researchgate.net/publication/280621302_LdoD_Archive_User_Experience_and_Identity_Design_Processes. Accessed 03 Oct 2017

29. Unsworth, J.: Scholarly primitives: what methods do humanities researchers have in common, and how might our tools reflect this? In: Part of a symposium on "Humanities Computing: Formal Methods, Experimental Practice" Sponsored by King's College, London (2000). http://www.people.virginia.edu/~jmu2m/Kings.5-00/primitives.html. Accessed 03 Oct 2017

30. Visconti, A.: Songs of innocence and of experience: amateur users and digital texts. Dissertation, School of Information, University of Michigan (2010). http://deepblue.lib.umich.edu/handle/2027.42/71380. Accessed 03 Oct 2017

31. Warwick, C., Terras, M., Huntington, P., Pappa, N., Galina, I.: The LAIRAH project: log analysis of digital resources in the arts and humanities. Final Report to the Arts and Humanities Research Council, Arts and Humanities Research Council (2006). http://www.ucl.ac.uk/infostudies/claire-warwick/publications/LAIRAHreport.pdf. Accessed 03 Oct 2017

32. Warwick, C., Terras, M., Huntington, P., Pappa, N.: If you build it will they come? The LAIRAH study: quantifying the use of online resources in the arts and humanities through statistical analysis of user log data. Lit. Linguist. Comput. **23**(1), 85–102 (2008)
33. Warwick, C., Terras, M., Nyhan, J.: Digital Humanities in Practice. Facet Publishing, London (2012)

Digital Preservation: How to Be Trustworthy

Lina Bountouri[1(✉)], Patrick Gratz[2], and Fulgencio Sanmartin[1]

[1] Publications Office of the European Union, Luxembourg, Luxembourg
{Vasiliki.BOUNTOURI,fulgencio.sanmartin}@publications.europa.eu
[2] infeurope, Luxembourg, Luxembourg
pgratz78@googlemail.com

Abstract. The Publications Office of the European Union has started a project for the long-term preservation of its digital publications to a new digital archival repository that contains legislative collections (such as the *Official Journal of the European Union*, treaties, international agreements, etc.), non-legislative collections (such as general and scientific publications), master data (such as descriptive, technical and provenance metadata specifications) and other data (such as datasets and websites). With the aim of safeguarding EU digital publications without any alteration during their life cycle, we have decided to follow standards ISO 14721:2012 (Open Archival Information System) to define the model of our digital preservation system and ISO 16363:2012 to verify the trustworthiness of the digital archival repository. In this context, we will deal with the following issue: how can we be sure that a digital object is the same as when it was created and has not been altered during its life cycle, both before and after its ingestion to the repository? In other words, how can our digital archival repository be trusted? The basic actions of the Publications Office towards this direction are: (a) to define a digital preservation plan; (b) to define and preserve representation information (master data and other specifications); (c) to define the designated community and its monitor; (d) to define and implement digital preservation strategies such as fixity, maintaining a read-only archive, keeping two copies in different physical data centres, etc.; (e) to define and implement provenance metadata; and (f) to have a technology watch of formats, standards and digital preservation strategies.

Keywords: Digital preservation · OAIS · Provenance · Authenticity · PREMIS

1 Introduction

One of the main problems that cultural heritage institutions, publishers and other organisations have to cope with is the efficient management of the digital resources they manage and/or produce in order to ensure their long-term digital preservation. Nowadays, a growing number of resources is digitised and/or digitally produced. How can archivists and information professionals ensure future access and long-term preservation to these resources, especially when software and hardware obsolescence have a direct effect on their management?

© European Union 2018
M. Ioannides (Ed.): ITN-DCH 2017, LNCS 10605, pp. 364–374, 2018.
https://doi.org/10.1007/978-3-319-75826-8_29

In order to tackle this issue, various institutions have recently started dealing with digital preservation/digital archiving. In line with [1], digital preservation is 'the series of managed activities necessary to ensure continued access to digital materials for as long as necessary', despite the problems that may occur because of any media failure or technological change. These activities both refer to the preservation of digitally born and to digitised resources.

It is of vital importance to separate the preservation of resources through digitisation and digital preservation, given that they are two distinct tasks. In the former, practitioners implement preservation strategies that hope to achieve the physical protection of analogue resources; while in digital preservation, practitioners try to ensure the continued access and usability of digital resources [2]. As a consequence, digital preservation issues differ from those that arise in the 'traditional' preservation field. This is mainly due to the subject of preservation, which in the first case is a digital resource while in the second case it is an analogue resource [3]. However, both processes may share some central ideas such as copying with the protection and long-term access to the resources, and both can be in danger, regardless of their analogue or digital substance.

The big question remains: how can information managers and archivists ensure future access to digital resources, especially when software and hardware obsolescence are having a direct impact on their management? In this paper we will present the main actions taken by the Publications Office of the European Union (OP) [4] towards the development of a trustworthy digital archival repository with the purpose of preserving its valuable digital publications over the long term. With this in mind, we will analyse the steps as well as the standards followed (such as the Open Archival Information System (OAIS) [5]) in order to create a trustworthy digital archival repository.

This paper is structured as follows: Sect. 2 presents the OP's mandate for digital preservation and the implementation of its project for the creation of a trustworthy long-term digital archival repository; Sect. 3 presents all the action taken by the OP in order to support the long-term digital preservation goal as well as the future plans towards this direction; and Sect. 4 presents the lessons learnt from this effort and the future goals of the OP.

2 Digital Preservation in the Publications Office of the European Union

The OP has the legal mandate to manage and provide a long-term digital preservation service. The legal basis is defined by the following official documents:

- Decision 2009/496/EC on the organisation and operation of the OP, where it is stated that the part of the mandate of the OP is to preserve 'the publications of the European Communities and the European Union' [6]; and
- Council Regulation (EU) No 216/2013, which defines that with regard to the authentic electronic version of the *Official Journal of the European Union*, that the OP is responsible for 'preserving and archiving the electronic files and handling them in line with future technological developments' [7].

The OP has recently launched a project to migrate its existing archived digital publications to a new digital archival repository in order to allow their long-term digital preservation. This repository contains legislative collections (such as the Official Journal, treaties, international agreements, etc.), non-legislative collections (such as general and scientific publications), master data (such as descriptive, technical and provenance metadata specifications) and other data (such as datasets or websites). These publications are significant, in particular the authentic Official Journal, which has had legal value in its digital format since 2013 [7]. In this context, all efforts are targeted to safeguard these publications in the long term while preserving their integrity and authenticity.

3   Standards Compliance and Digital Preservation Policy

Based on the analysis of the bibliography and related projects in the digital preservation field, we have concluded that there are no perfect solutions or risk-free options. With the aim of safeguarding EU digital publications without any alteration during their life cycle, we have decided to follow the current internationally accepted standards: ISO 14721:2012 (OAIS) [5] to define the model of our digital preservation system and ISO 16363:2012 [8] to verify the trustworthiness of the digital archival repository.

The OAIS reference model is a conceptual framework for an archival system dedicated to preserve and maintain long-term access to digital information for a designated community, which is an identified group of users who should be able to understand the preserved information [9]. The OAIS helps archival and non-archival institutions become familiarised with the preservation procedures by providing the fundamental concepts for preservation and its related definitions. The objective is to avoid any confusion on the used digital preservation terminology. As a conceptual framework, the OAIS does not provide guidelines on policy issues, such as the standard metadata schema to use or the preservation strategy to implement. Nonetheless, it clearly states that 'representation information', including all kinds of information needed to interpret a data object (i.e. metadata schemas, Knowledge Organisation Systems (KOS), ontologies, documentation, style and format guidelines, etc.), should also be preserved so as to make the objects in the archival repository self-explanatory and self-contained. The OAIS can also be implemented and act as a solid basis for the certification of a digital archival repository, but it was not written to act as an audit or certification manual for archival repositories. For this purpose, the International Organisation for Standardisation has published the ISO 16363 reference standard, which provides analytical guidance for auditing an archival repository. The OP is in the process of implementing the OAIS in the interest of obtaining the ISO 16363 certification for its archival repository.

In this context, we will deal with the following issue: how can we be sure that a digital object is the same as when it was created and has not been altered during its life cycle, both before and after its ingestion to a digital archival repository? In other words, how can our digital archival repository be trusted? Both ISO 14721:2012 and ISO 16363:2012 emphasise the importance of the documentation, evidence and preservation of the semantics so as to achieve the aforementioned purposes. The more evidence is provided for the preserved digital objects, the less the risk is of losing their integrity and authenticity.

With a view to support its digital preservation commitment, the OP has chosen a long-term digital archival repository, implemented mostly in Europe, which is called the Repository of Authentic Digital Records (RODA) [10]. RODA is a digital archival repository developed in Portugal in cooperation with the Portuguese national archive. This digital archival repository is open source and freely available to download. It is built on Fedora and can support the existing XML metadata schemas, such as the Encoded Archival Description (EAD) [11], the Metadata Encoding and Transmission Standard (METS) [12] and the Preservation Metadata: Implementation Strategies (PREMIS) [13]. In terms of preservation actions, the repository supports normalisation in ingest and other actions such as format conversion and checksum verification.

Apart from the implementation of the new software, the OP had to define related policies and take the following additional actions:

- definition of a digital preservation plan (DPP);
- definition and preservation of all possible representation information (master data and other specifications, such as XML syntax specifications);
- definition of the designated community of the long-term digital archival repository and its monitor;
- definition and implementation of fixity policies;
- definition and implementation of provenance metadata;
- technology watch of formats, standards and digital preservation strategies (i.e. migration, emulation and proactive digital preservation).

3.1 Digital Preservation Plan

The DPP [14] is the set of documented strategies for preserving the collections of an archival repository and is a prerequisite for its trustworthiness. The OP's DPP is a key instrument to describe and share how the OP fulfils its obligations in the domain of long-term digital preservation. It defines and documents the vision and strategy of the long-term digital preservation service that the OP is managing on behalf of the EU institutions. This policy document is an official commitment of the OP for the provision of this service and is in the process of receiving the official approval of the EU institutions, after having already been internally approved.

The DPP defines the legal basis on which the OP is based in order to provide the digital preservation service as well as all the important definitions that will make the implementation of the digital preservation policy accurate and complete. For example, it defines what an EU digital publication is: all information in digital format produced by the EU institutions, bodies or agencies, either directly or on their behalf by third parties, and made available to the public. Moreover, the DPP defines the vision, the mission, the strategy and the scope of the digital preservation service. Though the OP's long-term digital preservation service should aim to cover all EU digital publications, the current scope of this DPP is narrower: it will cover all EU publications whose custody has been transmitted by the EU institutions to the OP to be preserved.

Defining the preservation policy is one of the most significant parts of the digital preservation life cycle. It is not only the important directives and guidelines that this document provides in order to cope with technological and organisational issues; it also helps to build the 'preservation culture' inside an organisation by defining its commitment towards a specific digital preservation policy [3]. In [15], the author reports that in order to build a strong foundation for a DPP, the documentation of policies, procedures and standards is one of the most important steps in the digital preservation process.

3.2 Designated Community

According to the OAIS [5], a designated community is 'an identified group of potential consumers who should be able to understand a particular set of information.' Defining the designated community for each set of information that has to be preserved is significant, since this will also indicate the content of the knowledge base and of the representation information that are needed in order for the designated community to be able to interpret the data. An analysis of them will be presented in Sect. 3.3.

In the context of the OP's long-term digital archival repository, the designated community was defined based on the collection preserved, given that each collection has its own characteristics. In reference to this, there are different designated communities, one for each preserved collection. For example, for our legislative collection (*Official Journal of the European Union*, EU and national case-law and pre-legislative documents), the designated community consists of professionals linked to law (such as lawyers, academics of this discipline and re-users), EU and national public authorities, and EU professionals that may use the legislative collections as part of their work.

3.3 Representation Information

One of the main goals of OAIS implementers is 'to preserve information for a designated community' [5]. In order for a designated community to be able to understand the preserved information, a long-term digital archival repository also has to preserve and/ or refer to representation information of the preserved information.

Representation information is the information that maps a data object (which is metadata and content) into more meaningful concepts. It is expressed in many ways, depending on the content and context of each preserved information set. For example, the representation information of an EAD metadata record can be, among others, the EAD XML schema onto which the generation of the EAD metadata record was based, the XML schema specifications onto which the EAD XML schema was based, or the KOS and the authorities from which values inside the EAD metadata record have been taken, etc. Representation information must enable or allow the recreation of the significant properties of the original object, meaning that the information should be able to recreate a copy of the original object [16].

Understanding what representation information is and managing/storing it at the same time can be a painful task, with many parameters to take into account. It can be very helpful to have a knowledge base, which is 'a set of information, incorporated by a person or a system that allows that person or system to understand the received information' [17]. In the OP there is a knowledge base that is also a collection in our digital archival repository, called master data, which helps the interpretation of the archived content and its respective metadata. Some of our master data are the following.

- Controlled vocabularies, such as authority tables for countries, corporate bodies, legislative procedures, types of decisions, etc. These vocabularies are used both within the OP and within the EU institutions and agencies. The complete list can be found online and reused on the Metadata Registry website [18]. Therefore, every set of preserved information must be related to these tables in order to be understandable.
- Ontologies, such as the Common Data Model [19], which is implemented in the digital dissemination repository of the OP for encoding and validating descriptive metadata.
- Grammars and schemas, which are the schemas or document type definitions used in the OP to encode the content of documents (such as Formex for the Official Journal and case-law) [20], and the METS profile of the OP used to wrap metadata and content during ingestion of data to the digital dissemination repository and to the digital archival repository of the OP.

Master data mostly provide information to interpret the metadata. Nevertheless, this is not enough to interpret it as well as the digital content stored in our long-term digital archival repository. Some of the extra representation information that is needed is the following.

- Encoding languages specifications, such as the XML schema 1.0, the simple KOS (SKOS) specification, the Resource Description Framework Schema (RDFS) specification, etc. (instead we provide a link to it in the namespace definitions of each XML, SKOS or RDF file).
- Language dictionaries for the 24 languages of the European Union.
- The specifications of the PREMIS metadata schema [13], which is used to encode provenance and preservation metadata (instead we provide a link to it in the namespace definitions of each PREMIS file).
- Documentation, which can explain the various identifiers, structures and policies implemented such as the European Legislation Identifier [21] and the DPP.

Moreover, we refer to a format registry, such as PRONOM for having a stable reference for the formats stored in the digital archival repository. The incorporation of additional representation information as the one mentioned is in the future goals of the long-term digital archival repository.

3.4 Fixity Policies

According to the PREMIS Data Dictionary [22], fixity is a property of a digital object that indicates it has not changed between two points in time. Fixity checks have many uses and they must always be encoded as part of the provenance/preservation metadata since it can help to prove the authenticity and integrity of a digital object over time. Fixity is often related to checksums of different algorithms, as it is associated with bit-level integrity, though not exclusively: think of a workflow of files moving through many temporary buffer folders; calculating the checksum for each step can delay the whole system, especially if it is real-time or big data ingestion. For these cases, other fixity methods could be acceptable, like file size, name or count. Checksums can be calculated at the beginning (reception) and at the end (archival) of systems.

In case a fixity check fails, the next step is to verify the other existing copies of a digital object. If the copy is satisfactory, it will substitute the incorrect object, and the long-term digital archival repository will register this event/action as well. If the copy is not satisfactory, then the digital object or part of it might be irrecoverable. If several (two or any other threshold defined) copies in the same physical support fail, then one option is to substitute the latter completely.

As part of our fixity policy, different fixities can be applied depending on the granularity of the digital objects collection, i.e. not only at the file level. There could also be fixity checks of a collection, controlling whether a particular file or even sub-collection (based on the language or the format of the collection) might go missing, but this only works for closed, well-defined collections. At the OP, we can think of a checksum of an Official Journal issue, including all its languages and formats. Granularity at different levels leads to another discussion: what to do in the case of updates on the digital objects? Depending on what is being modified (metadata or anonymisation of a page, for example), fixity to higher levels shall be recalculated.

Fixity also involves knowing the physical support in which the data are stored, and defining policies accordingly. It is well known that optical supports start to lose properties after 5 years, and most fail after 10 years. Magnetic supports keep data with electric power, which loses strength as time passes. Refreshing data (i.e. reading and rewriting the same bits) for magnetic supports and transferring for optical supports are the kind of periodical policies that should be taken into account. How often these actions will take place depends on many variables: the importance of the collection, when the content is extracted or if it will be migrated, and the financial means provided. A risk assessment will provide the answer to this question.

3.5 Provenance Metadata

In order to provide all the semantic information that is needed to support the digital preservation process, lately various models, standards and metadata schemas have been created and evolved. Digital preservation is an integral part of all the stages of resources management. Semantic information assigned to digitised/digitally born resources must be supplied, providing information on its content, structure, rights and technical characteristics. Providing explanations on the technical procedure of digitisation and digital creation will facilitate specialists involved with the digital preservation process to be aware of all the necessary information regarding the content, structure, rights and technical characteristics of the digital resource to be preserved [3].

One of the most significant parts of the semantic information needed to document the life cycle of a digital resource is the provenance metadata. Provenance metadata encode the custody of a digital object, in other words all the events that may have produced a change of any type during its life cycle [3]. As stated in [23], a provenance event is where 'any event producing a change of the object has to be described and documented at every stage in the life cycle to have, at any time, a sort of authenticity card for any object in the repository: the crucial point is to clearly state that the identity of an object resides not only in its internal structure and content but also—and maybe mostly—in its complex system of relationships, so that a change of the object refers not only to a change of the bits of the object but also to something around it and that anyway contributes to its identity, i.e. to its authenticity.' Moreover, according to the OAIS standard [5], provenance metadata can support the authenticity of a digital object.

A long-term digital archival repository is responsible for generating provenance metadata starting from the ingestion of the digital object to the repository; however, provenance metadata can be provided in earlier stages of the life cycle of the digital object, such as by its producer and in different information systems than the long-term digital archival repository. It is advisable that the documentation of provenance metadata starts at the early stage of the creation of a digital object and that these metadata are also implemented inside the production systems and not only inside long-term digital archival repositories. Preservation metadata are a prerequisite for ensuring the authenticity and integrity of a digital object, and they encode the preservation actions taken on a digital object. Preservation actions are specific activities that are parts of preservation strategies, such as digitisation, integrity checks of digital objects, and policies such as migration and emulation. As previously mentioned, digital resources, similarly to the actions taken on analogue resources, have to be treated as a fragile object on which preservation rules and actions should apply.

In the OP, the implementation of provenance metadata is planned so that it starts in the early stages of a digital object's life cycle. In detail, before its archiving in the long-term digital archival repository, a digital object passes through two additional information systems. The first system deals with the reception of metadata and digital content. During the reception workflow, the OP receives digital objects and metadata, while at the same time takes action on both of them, such as generating new formats of a digital object and transforming the metadata to richer structures. The second system oversees their storage and dissemination. In this system, different actions are taking place in parallel on the digital content and its respective metadata, such as modifications and deletions, etc. In this context, provenance metadata will be attributed during the reception and storage workflows so as to encode all the actions aforementioned. It is important to note that in the long-term digital archival repository, all provenance and preservation metadata are already encoded based on the PREMIS Data Dictionary [22]. The following is an indicative example with all the events encoded during ingestion:

- ingest start: the ingest process has started;
- unpacking: extraction of objects from package in the Submission Information Package (SIP) format;
- well-formedness check: checked that the received SIP is well formed and complete and that no unexpected files were included;
- well-formedness check: checked whether the descriptive metadata are included in the SIP and if these metadata are valid according to the established policy;
- message digest calculation: creation of base PREMIS objects with file original name and file fixity information (SHA-256);

- format identification: identification of the object's file formats and versions using Siegfried;
- authorisation check: user permissions have been checked to ensure that they have sufficient authorisation to store the Archival Information Package (AIP) under the desired node of the classification scheme;
- accession: addition of the package to the inventory—after this point, the responsibility for the digital content's preservation is passed on to the repository;
- ingest end: the ingestion process has ended;
- replication: the replication of AIPs, its events and agents to RODA.

3.6 Technology Watch

The requirements of digital preservation and the action towards its long-term implementation involve continuous updating. This is due to the fact the technological obsolescence occurs so drastically: formats are updated to newer versions, software can be continuously updated and conformance may be in question. With the aim of being continuously updated on the new trends and evolutions on the digital preservation field, the OP team responsible for long-term preservation is focusing on the following resources and actions:

- participations to scientific conferences, scientific committees of the related discipline and seminars (such as the International Conference on Digital Preservation and the PREMIS Working Group for events);
- consultancy contract;
- list of events, news, etc.

4 Conclusion

Useful outcomes have been delivered during the long-term archiving projects of the OP. One of the most significant conclusions is that even if an information system for digital preservation/archiving is highly sophisticated and reliable, it always needs to be accompanied by an accurate and well-defined digital preservation policy. Moreover, implementers have to take into account the international standards of the field, which must be correctly implemented during the whole process of digital preservation. In addition, traditional archival theories and values, such as preserving 'the custody of the archive', are also implemented in the digital preservation field, in which they have equal importance.

Regarding the encoding of provenance metadata, it is important to note that there is no perfect solution: there is not one model or schema that covers all the documentation that is needed for preservation descriptive information. The OAIS provides the outline that must be followed when developing a long-term digital archival repository as well as guidelines on what kind of semantic information is needed for long-term preservation [3]. PREMIS focuses on encoding the preservation actions taking place before and during the ingestion of a digital object into an archival repository, while others, such as PROV-O and OPM, are instead focusing on encoding the provenance history.

Combining different schemas and models for encoding the most possible provenance information could be an adequate solution for ensuring the authenticity and integrity of a digital object.

References

1. Digital Preservation Coalition: Preservation management of digital materials: the handbook. Digital Preservation Coalition, October 2008. http://www.dpconline.org/docs/digital-preservation-handbook/299-digital-preservation-handbook/file. Accessed 04 Sept 2017
2. Deegan, M., Tanner, S.: Digital Preservation. Facet Publishing, London (2006). ISBN 9781856044851
3. Bountouri, L.: Archives in the Digital Age: Standards, Policies and Tools. Chandos Publishing, Cambridge (2017). ISBN 9781843347774
4. The Publications Office of the European Union: The Publications Office of the European Union, 11 September 2017. https://publications.europa.eu/en/home. Accessed 08 Sept 2017
5. International Organization for Standardization: ISO 14721, 2012: space data and information transfer systems, open archival information system (OAIS), reference model. International Organization for Standardization (2012). https://www.iso.org/standard/57284.html. Accessed 28 Mar 2017
6. European Union: Decision of the organisation and operation of the Publications Office of the European Union. Official Journal of the European Union — Series L, vol. 168, pp. 41–47, 30 June 2009
7. Council of the European Union: Council Regulation (EU) No. 216/2013 of 7 March 2013 on the electronic publication of the Official Journal of the European Union. Official Journal of the European Union — Series L, vol. 69, 13 March 2013
8. ISO: ISO 16363, 2012: space data and information transfer systems, audit and certification of trustworthy digital repositories (2012). https://www.iso.org/standard/56510.html. Accessed 27 Mar 2017
9. The OCLC/RLG Working Group on Preservation Metadata: Preservation metadata and the OAIS information model: a metadata framework to support the preservation of digital objects, June 2002. http://www.oclc.org/content/dam/research/activities/pmwg/pm_framework.pdf. Accessed 27 Mar 2017
10. RODA: Welcome to RODA: an open-source digital repository designed for preservation, 08 September 2017. https://demo.roda-community.org. Accessed 09 Sept 2017
11. The Library of Congress: Encoded archival description: official site, 31 July 2017. https://www.loc.gov/ead/. Accessed 08 Sept 2017
12. The Library of Congress: Metadata encoding and transmission standard, 18 August 2017. http://www.loc.gov/standards/mets/. Accessed 08 Sept 2017
13. PREMIS Editorial Committee: PREMIS data dictionary for preservation metadata, 31 August 2017. http://www.loc.gov/standards/premis/. Accessed 08 Sept 2017
14. The Publications Office of the European Union: Digital Preservation Plan (2017)
15. McGovern, N.Y.: A digital decade: where have we been and where are we going in digital preservation? RLG DigiNews (2006)
16. OAIS 7: Representation Information. Alans notes and thoughts on digital preservation, 24 January 2008. https://alanake.wordpress.com/2008/01/24/oais-7-representation-information/. Accessed 08 Sept 2017

17. Rusbridge, C.: Representation Information: what is it and why is it important? 06 July 2007. http://www.dcc.ac.uk/news/representation-information-what-it-and-why-it-important. Accessed 08 Sept 2017

18. The Publications Office of the European Union: Metadata Registry (MDR) (2017). http://publications.europa.eu/mdr/index.html. Accessed 08 Sept 2017

19. The Publications Office of the European Union: Common Data Model (CDM), 21 July 2017. Accessed 08 Sept 2017

20. The Publications Office of the European Union: Formex: formalized exchange of electronic publications (n.d.). http://formex.publications.europa.eu/. Accessed 08 Sept 2017

21. The Publications Office of the European Union: ELI technical specifications, 21 September 2016. http://publications.europa.eu/mdr/eli/index.html. Accessed 08 Sept 2017

22. PREMIS Editorial Committee: PREMIS data dictionary for preservation metadata, November 2015. http://www.loc.gov/standards/premis/v3/premis-3-0-final.pdf. Accessed 08 Sept 2017

23. Factor, M., et al.: Authenticity and provenance in long term digital preservation: modeling and implementation in preservation aware storage. In: Proceedings of the First Workshop in Theory and Practice of Provenance (2009)

Author Index

Printed in the United States
By Bookmasters